'We know crime is primarily a group activity, ye[t] research models too often focus on criminal beha[vior of] individuals. In this fascinating study, Beth Weaver [recounts his]tories of not just individuals, but an entire street "gang" that went straight. It is one of the most creative research designs I have seen in the past decade, and the stories that emerge are simply riveting.'

Shadd Maruna, *Dean, School of Criminal Justice, Rutgers University Newark, USA*

'This is an outstanding book. Through a blend of sophisticated theory and grounded analysis, Beth Weaver brings to life the complex journeys of six men as they attempt to extricate themselves (and each other) from multiple cycles of imprisonment and release. The in-depth and lucid accounts of how co-offenders might become co-desisters will surely stand as a unique and lasting contribution to the field of criminology and penology. *Offending and Desistance* offers, in short, an array of theoretical and practical challenges for anyone concerned with offender rehabilitation and reintegration.'

Mark Halsey, *Professor of Criminology, Centre for Crime Policy and Research, Flinders University, Australia*

'This book offers an innovative perspective on the process of desisting from crime, and is a must-read for scholars and practitioners interested in the underlying mechanisms associated with continuity and change in criminal behavior. Weaver focuses on members of a particular friendship group as they change their lives and relationships to one another, develop new concerns and social ties, and to varying degrees move away from earlier patterns of criminal involvement. Her analyses develop an elegant relational theory of desistance – one that moves beyond simple notions of network influence (i.e. the role of "bad companions," or "good wives") on one hand or atomistic views of the change process on the other.'

Peggy C. Giordano, *Distinguished Professor of Sociology, Department of Sociology, Bowling Green State University, USA*

'This important and intriguing book is (strangely) the first to engage seriously with giving up crime as a shared social process, rather than as an individual one. Although, like all brilliant intellectual advances, this may sound obvious, that's only because we all should have thought of it before. Beth Weaver does a remarkable job of advancing our understanding of desistance, both through painstaking empirical work and through genuinely innovative theoretical work. Everyone interested in rehabilitation and desistance must read and re-read this text – it is destined to become a classic.'

Fergus McNeill, *Professor of Criminology and Social Work, University of Glasgow, UK*

Offending and Desistance

In *Offending and Desistance*, Beth Weaver examines the role of a co-offending peer group in shaping and influencing offending and desistance, focusing on three phases of their criminal careers: onset, persistence and desistance. While there is consensus across the body of desistance research that social relations have a role to play in variously constraining, enabling and sustaining desistance, no desistance studies have adequately analysed the dynamics or properties of social relations, or their relationship to individuals and social structures. This book aims to reset this balance.

By examining the social relations and life stories of six Scottish men (in their forties), Weaver reveals the central role of friendship groups, intimate relationships and families of formation, employment and religious communities. She shows how, for different individuals, these relations triggered reflexive evaluation of their priorities, behaviours and lifestyles, but with differing results.

Weaver's re-examination of the relationships between structure, agency, identity and reflexivity in the desistance process ultimately illuminates new directions for research, policy and practice. This book is essential reading for academics and students engaged in the study of criminology and criminal justice, delinquency, probation and criminal law.

Beth Weaver is a Senior Lecturer in the Department of Social Work and Social Policy, University of Strathclyde. She is actively engaged in a number of research networks, research projects and knowledge exchange activities with specific interests in desistance, user involvement and co-production and the use of through-the-prison-gate social cooperative structures of employment. All of Beth's research has an applied focus on penal reform.

International Series on Desistance and Rehabilitation

The *International Series on Desistance and Rehabilitation* aims to provide a forum for critical debate and discussion surrounding the topics of why people stop offending and how they can be more effectively reintegrated into the communities and societies from which they came. The books published in the series will be international in outlook, but tightly focused on the unique, specific contexts and processes associated with desistance, rehabilitation and reform. Each book in the series will stand as an attempt to advance knowledge or theorising about the topics at hand, rather than being merely an extended report of a specific research project. As such, it is anticipated that some of the books included in the series will be primarily theoretical, whilst others will be more tightly focused on the sorts of initiatives which could be employed to encourage desistance. It is not our intention that books published in the series be limited to the contemporary period, as good studies of desistance, rehabilitation and reform undertaken by historians of crime are also welcome. In terms of authorship, we would welcome excellent PhD work, as well as contributions from more established academics and research teams. Most books are expected to be monographs, but edited collections are also encouraged.

General Editor

Stephen Farrall, University of Sheffield

Editorial Board

Ros Burnett, University of Oxford
Thomas LeBel, University of Wisconsin-Milwaukee, USA
Mark Halsey, Flinders University, Australia
Fergus McNeill, Glasgow University
Shadd Maruna, Queens University Belfast
Gwen Robinson, Sheffield University
Barry Godfrey, University of Liverpool

1 **The Dynamics of Desistance**
Charting pathways through change
Deidre Healy

2 **Criminal Behaviour in Context**
Space, place and desistance from crime
Nick Flynn

3 **Cultures of Desistance**
   Rehabilitation, reintegration and ethnic minorities
   Adam Calverley

4 **Offender Rehabilitation and Therapeutic Communities**
   Enabling change the TC way
   Alisa Stevens

5 **Desistance Transitions and the Impact of Probation**
   Sam King

6 **Black Men, Invisibility and Desistance from Crime**
   Towards a critical race theory of desistance
   Martin Glynn

7 **White-Collar Offenders and Desistance from Crime**
   Future selves and the constancy of change
   Ben Hunter

8 **Offending and Desistance**
   The importance of social relations
   Beth Weaver

Offending and Desistance
The importance of social relations

Beth Weaver

LONDON AND NEW YORK

First published 2016
by Routledge
2 Park Square, Milton Park, Abingdon, Oxfordshire OX14 4RN

and by Routledge
711 Third Avenue, New York, NY 10017

First issued in paperback 2017

Routledge is an imprint of the Taylor & Francis Group, an informa business

© 2016 Beth Weaver

The right of Beth Weaver to be identified as author of this work has been asserted by her in accordance with sections 77 and 78 of the Copyright, Designs and Patents Act 1988.

All rights reserved. No part of this book may be reprinted or reproduced or utilised in any form or by any electronic, mechanical, or other means, now known or hereafter invented, including photocopying and recording, or in any information storage or retrieval system, without permission in writing from the publishers.

British Library Cataloguing in Publication Data
A catalogue record for this book is available from the British Library

Library of Congress Cataloging-in-Publication Data
Weaver, Beth.
  Offending and desistance: the importance of social relations / Beth Weaver. — First Edition.
    pages cm — (International series on desistance and rehabilitation; 8)
  Includes bibliographical references.
  1. Criminals—Rehabilitation. 2. Crime. 3. Interpersonal relations. 4. Peer pressure. I. Title.
  HV9275.W415 2015
  364.3—dc23
  2015003275

ISBN 13: 978-1-138-06261-0 (pbk)
ISBN 13: 978-1-138-79972-1 (hbk)

Typeset in Times New Roman
by Apex CoVantage, LLC

To Allan Weaver

Contents

List of figures	xv
List of tables	xvii
Acknowledgements	xix
Glossary	xxi
Foreword	xxiii

1 Introduction   1
  Empirical and theoretical context 1
  Aims of the book 2
  Overview of the book 3
  Note 5
  References 5

2 A critical review of desistance research   7
  Introduction 7
  Definitions of desistance 8
  Theories of desistance 9
  Individual and agentic theories of desistance 10
  Social and structural theories 13
  Interactionist theories 22
  Situational theories 27
  Supporting desistance through supervision 28
  Discussion 32
  Notes 34
  References 36

3 Critical realism and relational sociology: a conceptual framework for theorising desistance   47
  Introduction 47
  The morphogenetic approach and the internal conversation 49

Deconstructing Archer's internal conversation 51
Donati's relational sociology: an overview 54
Donati's relational theory of reflexivity 58
Conceptual schema for study 59
Notes 63
References 63

4 The dynamics of co-offending: from formation to fragmentation   66
Introduction 66
Overview of the sample 67
Overview of context/conditioning structures 68
The relational context of offending 71
From fragmentation to reformation 94
Conclusion 97
Notes 99
References 99

5 Work, family and transitional masculinities: Seth's story   104
Biographical overview 104
Experience of punishment 105
Roles, reflexivity, relationality and desistance 110
The meanings and outcomes of work 117
Conclusion 123
Notes 125
References 125

6 Fighting, football and fatherhood: Harry's story   131
Biographical overview 131
Roles, reflexivity, relationality and desistance 132
The meanings and outcomes of work 138
Conclusion 141
Notes 143
References 143

7 From delinquency to desistance and back again? Jed's story   146
Biographical overview 146
Roles, reflexivity, relationality and desistance 147
The meanings and outcomes of work 155
Conclusion 158
Notes 159
References 160

8 Being, becoming and belonging – from gangs to God: Jay's story 162
Biographical overview 162
Religiosity, reflexivity, relationality and desistance 163
The meanings and outcomes of work 173
Conclusion 175
Notes 177
References 177

9 Reflexivity, relationality, religiosity and recognition: Evan's story 180
Biographical overview 180
Religiosity, reflexivity, relationality and desistance 181
The meanings and outcomes of work 190
Conclusion 192
Notes 193
References 194

10 An imprisoned life: Andy's story 196
Biographical overview 196
Experiencing punishment 197
Conclusion 206
Notes 207
References 208

11 The dynamics of desistance 212
Brief collective biographical overview 214
Roles, religiosity, reflexivity, relationality and desistance 215
The meanings and outcomes of work 229
Conclusion 234
Notes 234
References 235

12 Conclusion 238
Introduction 238
Desistance through the lens of a peer group 238
The significance of social relations 241
Implications of findings 245
Conclusion 254
Notes 254
References 255

Annex: research methods 259
   Research purpose and participants *259*
   A brief résumé of the life-story method in criminology
      and desistance *259*
   Research design *261*
   The sample *262*
   Transcribing data *264*
   Analytical considerations *264*
   Analysis *264*
   Conclusion *266*
   Notes *267*
   References *267*

Index 269

Figures

3.1	The basic morphogenetic sequence	50
3.2	The morphogenetic sequence applied to the internal conversation	52
3.3	Overview of investigative framework	60
3.4	The morphogenetic sequence applied to the internal conversation (individual contributions)	60
3.5	The morphogenetic sequence applied to social relations (relational contributions)	62
4.1	Overview of investigative framework	68
5.1	Overview of investigative framework	124
6.1	Overview of investigative framework	142
7.1	Overview of investigative framework	159
8.1	Overview of investigative framework	176
9.1	Overview of investigative framework	193
10.1	Overview of investigative framework	207
11.1	Overview of investigative framework	213
11.2	The morphogenetic sequence applied to the internal conversation (individual contributions)	213
11.3	The morphogenetic sequence applied to social relations (relational contributions)	213

Tables

2.1	Probation practice in four paradigms	8
11.1	Overview of offending trajectories	214

Acknowledgements

Special thanks go to John Wiley and Sons, Routledge and *Scottish Justice Matters* for their permission to reproduce previously published materials in this book. Thanks also to the American Sociological Association and SAGE for their kind permission to reproduce previously published materials in this book.

Glossary

cannae can't
couldnae couldn't
daftie idiot
didnae didn't
fae from / for
got a doing assaulted
Hogmanay New Year's Eve
housebreaking burglary
pegged labelled
maw mother
nae no / not
polis police
tag label
tan break into
wasnae wasn't
weans children
wouldnae wouldn't

Foreword

The *International Series on Desistance and Rehabilitation* aims to provide a forum for critical debate and discussion surrounding the topics of why people stop offending and how they can be more effectively reintegrated into the communities and societies from which they came. The books published in the series will be international in outlook, but tightly focused on the unique, specific contexts and processes associated with desistance, rehabilitation and reform. Each book in the series will stand as an attempt to advance knowledge or theorising about the topics at hand, rather than being merely an extended report of a specific research project. As such, it is anticipated that some of the books included in the series will be primarily theoretical, whilst others will be more tightly focused on the sorts of initiatives which could be employed to encourage desistance. It is not our intention that books published in the series be limited to the contemporary period, as good studies of desistance, rehabilitation and reform undertaken by historians of crime are also welcome. In terms of authorship, we would welcome excellent PhD work, as well as contributions from more established academics and research teams. Most books are expected to be monographs, but edited collections are also encouraged.

Whilst there have been several recent very good studies of desistance from crime (many of them published with in this series, I ought to note), Beth Weaver's excellent study pushes both the methodological and the theoretical approaches for exploring why people stop offending in a new direction. True, whilst several researchers have employed case study approaches to explore the individual dynamics of desistance, drawing on autobiographies, life histories or repeated interviews with those once caught up in offending, Beth establishes what, I believe, is a useful and innovative approach. Many individuals who offend do so in the company of others, and whilst Mark Warr very usefully studied the role of gangs in offending and desistance several years ago, few have explored in depth the ways and processes by which groups of people desist in association with one another – in some cases via their disassociation from one another. Via a series of interviews with the members of one (loosely defined) former gang, Beth is able to chart the ways in one group of six individuals who regularly 'hang out' together, becoming involved in fights and various other forms of offending, started to desist. Research with active and former offenders is full of ethical dilemmas, but Beth was able to successfully navigate such intricacies in order to bring us a fascinating and rich account of the lived realities of desistance from and within a 'gang'. The result is a truly enlightening study which makes considerable contributions to both the study of desistance and the study of the formation and dissolution of gangs.

Stephen Farrall
February 2015
Sheffield

1 Introduction

Empirical and theoretical context

Criminological interest in desistance developed in the 1970s and 1980s (for example Cusson and Pinsonneault, 1986; Meisenhelder, 1977, 1982; Rand, 1987; Shover, 1983) and became a significant area of enquiry in criminal career research in the 1990s (for example Graham and Bowling, 1995; Maruna, 1997; Sampson and Laub, 1993). Since this time, desistance research has moved beyond identifying who desists, and when, to propose a range of theories that seek to account for and explain desistance as a process (for example Bottoms and Shapland, 2011; Giordano, Cernkovich and Rudolph, 2002; Farrall et al., 2011; Laub and Sampson, 2003; Maruna, 2001).

In elaborating the process of desistance, researchers and theorists generally conceptualise the desistance process as an interaction between, or integration of, agentic and structural factors. These accounts of the desistance process place differing emphases on the role of individuals and their social contexts. Throughout the literature, desistance is represented as the outcome of an individual seeking to alter their socio-structural situation and context, and in so doing acquiring new behaviours and new pro-social roles, or vice versa, variously resulting in associated shifts in the individual's personal and social identity (see for example Barry, 2010; Bottoms et al., 2004; Farrall, 2002; Farrall, Bottoms and Shapland, 2010; Giordano et al., 2002; Maruna and Farrall, 2004; Uggen, Manza and Behrens, 2004). Within these divergent explanations, while there is a more or less implicit or explicit recognition of the individual as a reflexive subject, limited attention has been given to what processes of reflexivity actually entail (notable recent exceptions include Farrall et al., 2010; King, 2014; Vaughan, 2007). Such theories are therefore restricted in their capacity to reveal *how* individuals' reasoning and actions are variously enabled or constrained by the relational, cultural and structural contexts within which they are embedded. While many principally agentic theories of the change process elaborate the early stages of desistance, they do not explain what triggers the resultant cognitive transformation or why one social relation at one time rather than another exerts this effect (see for example Giordano et al., 2002). Neither can they explain why people stay in particular relationships or jobs when the meanings and dynamics of these social relations change over time (Vaughan, 2007). While, then, agentically weighted theories are limited in their capacities to explain what triggers reflexivity, structural theories similarly fail to illuminate *how* social structures shape decisions, ignoring or under-analysing how the individual perceives and responds to such influences (see for example Laub and Sampson, 2003).

While there is some consensus across desistance research that social relations, such as friendship groups, marriage, parenthood, employment and religious communities have a role to play in variously constraining, enabling and sustaining desistance, few desistance studies have adequately analysed the dynamics or properties of social relations, or their relationship to individuals and social structures. Moreover, while there is increasing consensus that the desistance process is an outcome of the interplay between the agent and their structural context, the methodological focus is generally on individuals rather than groups even though the collective context within which much offending takes place is well established (see for example Akers, 1998; Cloward and Ohlin, 1960; Sutherland, 1947; Warr, 2002). While there has been considerable attention to 'gangs' (Aldridge, Medina and Ralphs, 2007, Bannister and Fraser, 2008; Deuchar, 2009; Fraser, 2010, Klein, Weerman and Thornberry, 2006; Pyrooz, Decker and Webb, 2010; Pyrooz, Sweeten and Piquero, 2012), there has been scant research revealing the experiences of people who co-offend and on their subsequent processes of desistance. This methodological focus on the individual precludes an analysis of the role of the group, as a social relation in and of itself, in shaping and affecting offending and desistance, and thus of how individual, relational, cultural and social contexts influence onset, persistence and desistance. There is therefore a significant gap in criminological understanding of the impact that friendship groups (among other social relations) can exert on criminal careers – both empirically and theoretically.

Aims of the book

This book aims to address this gap in our knowledge and understanding by exploring the role of a co-offending peer group in shaping and influencing offending and desistance. It presents group and individual level analyses into the life stories of six Scottish men (in their forties) who were part of a gang called 'the Del'. It examines three phases of their criminal careers: onset, persistence and desistance. In so doing, it reveals the relational dynamics of co-offending and desistance through an exploration of the relationships between these men and the wider social relations in which they individually and collectively participated over the life course.

In taking social relations as a central unit of analysis, rather than solely the individual agent and/or social structure, this book explores the relative contributions of individual actions, social relations and social systems to the process of desistance. The aim is to gain a greater understanding of the dynamics of offending and desistance as it occurs between co-offending peers. This book does not, however, intend to be construed as a study of gangs, gang behaviour, identities or processes of extrication from gang membership. Nevertheless studies of gangs can offer a useful context for understanding the relational dynamics of groups of people who co-offend and processes of extrication, and where relevant, this is drawn on and discussed in Chapter 4.[1] Rather, this book specifically aims to identify the individual, relational and structural contributions to the desistance process as they occur within and between individuals and, as part of that, to reveal the role of social relations in accounting for desistance over time. In so doing, this book reveals the central role of friendship groups, intimate relationships and families of formation, employment and religious communities. It shows how, for different individuals, these social relations triggered reflexive evaluation of their priorities, behaviours and lifestyles but with differing results. However, despite these differences, the common theme is that desistance from crime was a means of realising and maintaining the men's individual and relational concerns, with which continued offending became (sometimes incrementally) incompatible. It is hoped that by re-examining the relationships between structure, agency, identity and reflexivity in the desistance process, this book can inform how these understandings can and should translate into policy and practice.

Overview of the book

This chapter has introduced the context within which the rationale for the study emerged. Chapter 2 critically analyses the international body of research on desistance. The chapter explores the various definitions of desistance in the research literature, prior to presenting an overview of theoretical explanations of desistance and the empirical studies that inform these explanations. This literature is categorised under three broad headings that echo the classificatory distinctions drawn by Maruna (1997) and Barry (2010): namely, individual and agentic; social and structural; and interactionist – adding a new category, situational. In particular, the analysis presented in this chapter considers how contemporary understandings of desistance conceptualise the relationships between structure, agency, reflexivity and identity in the desistance process. The chapter concludes with a review of the limited research that examines the role of professional practice in supporting desistance.

Building on the review of research in Chapter 2, Chapter 3 progresses an alternative conceptual framework for theorising desistance. It draws heavily on the complementary approaches of Archer's Critical Realist Morphogenetic Approach and Donati's Relational Sociology. This framework gives proper weight to individual actions, social relations and social systems where actions, systems and relations are provided with inner characteristics and influences which are particular to them. In so doing, I propose that this framework represents an alternative conceptual framework through which to empirically analyse and theorise desistance, one which can overcome the limitations of existing approaches outlined above.

The data analysis is presented in eight data chapters (Chapters 4–11). Chapter 4 presents a group level analysis of their shared lives and in so doing discusses the formation of the group, the onset and maintenance of their offending and the nature and dynamics of the group while situating their lived experiences within their shared historical, cultural and structural contexts. It pursues a discussion on the nature of friendship and reveals both the nature and form of the group as a social relation and the relational rules which structure and characterise the (changing) nature and form of their interactive dynamics and collective action. It reveals the heterogeneity of individual experiences of the group and how the group variously influenced individuals' behaviour. The chapter concludes by describing the situational nature of the 'fragmentation of the Del' and the divergent outcomes for individuals. In so doing it foreshadows the role of the splinter or 'revised group' in mutually supporting the early phases of each other's desistance. This chapter thus reveals the story of 'the Del' from formation to fragmentation and serves as a foundation to the individual analyses presented in Chapters 5–10.

Chapters 5–10 present an analysis of the individual life stories of the six men on whom this study is based. These chapters examine individuals' lives beyond the fragmentation of the Del, analysing events and experiences subsequent to the group experience to provide a nuanced analysis of the individual, relational and structural contributions to the desistance process. Each individual story commences with a brief biographical overview of the individual and an explanation of how each individual structures their life story after the fragmentation of the group. The content of each story progresses chronologically, but each story is structured in accordance with the identified superordinate themes emerging from both individual and cross case analysis, in accordance with the methodological approach of the study. While superordinate themes recur across individual stories, reflecting both broad thematic categories and higher order concepts (as discussed in the Annex), some subordinate themes within this vary to reflect the individual experiences they incorporate and, thus, unique idiosyncratic instances.

Chapter 11 provides a summary of the recurrent elements of the change process, manifesting across these individuals' stories presented in Chapters 5–10 through the lens of the investigative framework advanced in Chapter 2. In essence, this chapter reveals that the kind of social relations that are most causally influential in the desistance process are characterised by a manner of relating to each other which manifests as solidarity and subsidiarity, or in other words – a sense of 'we-ness'. Subsidiarity is a way to support another person in such a manner that it allows and assists the other to do what they need to do for themselves to realise their goals or aspirations. Subsidiarity cannot work without solidarity (which means sharing a common responsibility through reciprocity which implies *inter*dependence). These principles consign mutual responsibilities on each person for supporting change and in taking responsibility for personal change.

Chapter 12 summarizes the learning from this study and elaborates the implications for policy and practice by exploring how these insights can inform the kinds of professional relationships, policies and practices that can generate, support and sustain the kinds of relational networks that reside at the heart of the desistance process. The Annex details the methods through which this study was conducted and locates the study as an exemplar of the qualitative, life story method applied to desistance research. In addition to describing the methods used in operationalising this research, ethical considerations, the fieldwork process and approach to data analysis are also elaborated.

Note

1 Current research on desistance or extrication from gangs is limited in terms of providing insights into processes of desistance over time; such studies are principally concerned with revealing processes of extrication from gang membership, affiliations and associated behaviours. By emphasising the collective nature of offending and the individual nature of extrication, such studies primarily focus on severance or continuance of ties to the gang. In general, the literature does not pursue questions surrounding individual persistence in crime beyond the gang, nor processes of desistance beyond gang membership (see for example Bannister et al., 2010; Decker and Lauritsen, 2002; Pyrooz et al., 2012; Vigil, 1988).

References

Akers, R.L. (1998) *Social Learning and Social Structure: A General Theory of Crime and Deviance*. Boston, MA: Northeastern University Press.

Aldridge, J., Medina, J., and Ralphs, R. (2007) *Youth Gangs in an English City: Social Exclusion, Drugs and Violence*. Full Research Report ESRC End of Award Report, RES-000-23-0615. Swindon: ESRC.

Bannister, J., and Fraser, A. (2008) Youth Gang Identification: Learning and Social Development in Restricted Geographies. *Scottish Journal of Criminal Justice Studies* 14, pp.96–114.

Bannister, J., Pickering, J., Batchelor, S., Burman, M., Kintrea, K., and McVie, S. (2010) *Troublesome Youth Groups, Gangs and Knife Carrying in Scotland*. Edinburgh: Scottish Government.

Barry, M. (2010) Youth Offending and Youth Transitions: The Power of Capital in Influencing Change. *Critical Criminology* 15(2), pp.185–198.

Bottoms, A.E., and Shapland, J. (2011) Steps Towards Desistance Among Male Young Adult Recidivists, in Farrall, S., Hough, M., Maruna, S., and Sparks, R. (eds.) *Escape Routes: Contemporary Perspectives on Life After Punishment*. London: Routledge, pp.43–80.

Bottoms, A.E., Shapland, J., Costello, A., Holmes, D., and Mair, G. (2004) Towards Desistance: Theoretical Underpinnings for an Empirical Study. *Howard Journal of Criminal Justice* 43(4), pp.368–389.

Cloward, R., and Ohlin, L. (1960) *Delinquency and Opportunity: A Theory of Delinquent Gangs*. Chicago, IL: Free Press.

Cusson, M., and Pinsonneault, P. (1986) The Decision to Give Up Crime, in Cornish, D.B., and Clarke, R.V. (eds.) *The Reasoning Criminal: Rational Choice Perspectives in Offending*. New York, NY: Springer-Verlag, pp.72–82.

Decker, S.H., and Lauritsen, J. (2002) Leaving the gangs, in Huff, C.R. (ed.) *Gangs in America* (3rd ed.). Thousand Oaks, CA: Sage, pp.51–67.

Deuchar, R. (2009) Urban Youth Cultures and the Re-building of Social Capital: Illustrations from a Pilot Study in Glasgow. *Scottish Youth Issues Journal* 1, pp.7–22.

Farrall, S. (2002) *Rethinking What Works with Offenders: Probation, Social Context and Desistance from Crime*. Cullompton: Willan.

Farrall, S., Bottoms, A.E., and Shapland, J. (2010) Social Structures and Desistance from Crime. *European Journal of Criminology* 7(6), pp.546–570.

Farrall, S., Sharpe, G., Hunter, B., and Calverley, A. (2011) Theorizing Structural and Individual-Level Processes in Desistance and Persistence: Outlining an Integrated Perspective. *Australian and New Zealand Journal of Criminology* 44(2), pp.218–234.

Fraser, A. (2010) *Growing Through Gangs: Young People, Identity and Social Change in Glasgow*. Unpublished PhD dissertation.

Giordano, P.C., Cernkovich, S.A., and Rudolph, J.L. (2002) Gender, Crime and Desistance: Toward a Theory of Cognitive Transformation. *American Journal of Sociology* 107, pp.990–1064.

Graham, J., and Bowling, B. (1995). *Young People and Crime*. Home Office Research Study No. 145. London: HMSO.

King, S. (2014) *Desistance Transitions and the Impact of Probation*. Abingdon: Routledge.

Klein, M.W., Weerman, F.M., and Thornberry, T.P. (2006) Street Gang Violence in Europe. *European Journal of Criminology* 3(4), pp.413–437.

Laub, J.H., and Sampson, R.J. (2003) *Shared Beginnings, Divergent Lives*. Cambridge, MA: Harvard University Press.

Maruna, S. (1997) Going Straight: Desistance from Crime and Life Narratives of Reform, in Lieblich, A., and Josselson, R. (eds.) *The Narrative Study of Lives*, Vol. 5. Thousand Oaks, CA: Sage, pp.59–93.

Maruna, S. (2001) *Making Good: How Ex-Convicts Reform and Rebuild Their Lives*. Washington, DC: American Psychological Association Books.

Maruna, S., and Farrall, S. (2004) Desistance from Crime: A Theoretical Reformulation. *Kolner Zeitschrift für Soziologie und Sozialpsychologie* 43, pp.171–194.

Meisenhelder, T. (1977) An Exploratory Study of Exiting from Criminal Careers. *Criminology* 15, pp.319–334.

Meisenhelder, T. (1982) Becoming Normal: Certification as a Stage in Exiting from Crime. *Deviant Behavior: An Interdisciplinary Journal* 3, pp.137–153.

Pyrooz, D.C., Decker, S.H., and Webb, V.J. (2010) The Ties that Bind: Desistance from Gangs. *Crime and Delinquency*. doi:10.1177/0011128710372191

Pyrooz, D.C., Sweeten, G., and Piquero, A.R. (2012) Embeddedness, Continuity and Change in Gang Membership and Gang. *Journal of Research in Crime and Delinquency*. doi:10.1177/0022427811434830

Rand, A. (1987) Transitional Life Events and Desistance From Delinquency and Crime, in Wolfgang, M.E., Thornberry, T.P., and Figurelio, R.M. (eds.) *From Boy to Man, From Delinquency to Crime*. Chicago, IL: University of Chicago Press, pp.134–162.

Sampson, R.J., and Laub, J.H. (1993) *Crime in the Making: Pathways and Turning Points Through Life*. London: Harvard University Press.

Shover, N. (1983) The Later Stages of Ordinary Property Offender Careers. *Social Problems* 31(2), pp.208–218.

Sutherland, E.H. (1947) *The Principles of Criminology* (4th ed.). Chicago, IL: J.B. Lippincott.

Uggen, C., Manza, J., and Behrens, A. (2004). Less Than the Average Citizen: Stigma, Role Transition and the Civic Reintegration of Convicted Felons, in Maruna, S., and Immarigeon, R. (eds.) *After Crime and Punishment: Pathways to Offender Reintegration*. Cullompton: Willan, pp.258–290.

Vaughan, B. (2007) The Internal Narrative of Desistance. *British Journal of Criminology* 47(3), pp.390–404.

Vigil, J.D. (1988) *Barrio Gangs: Street Life and Identity in Southern California*. Austin: University of Texas Press.

Warr, M. (2002) *Companions in Crime: The Social Aspects of Criminal Conduct*. Cambridge: Cambridge University Press.

2 A critical review of desistance research[1]

Introduction

In 2003, McNeill argued that the implications of the evolving body of research on desistance necessitated a major shift in probation practice. This meant a departure from contemporary practices underpinned mainly by cognitive behavioural psychology focused on changing individual mindsets, to practices attending to the relational and social contexts within and through which desistance occurs. In developing a vision of what a desistance informed paradigm might entail, McNeill (2006) observed that a fundamental problem with preceding probation paradigms[2] (the non-treatment paradigm, the revised paradigm and the 'what works' paradigm) (see Table 2.1) is that they focused on how *practice* (whether 'treatment', 'help' or 'programmes') should be constructed rather than conceptualising how *change* should be understood.

The argument that McNeill (2006) advanced was:

> that desistance is the process that work with offenders exists to promote and support;[3] that approaches to intervention should be embedded in understandings of desistance; and that it is important to explore the connections between structure, agency, reflexivity and identity in the desistance processes.
>
> (p.55)

More than a decade since McNeill's original argument for a paradigm shift, how the interaction between structure and agency in the process of desistance should be conceived and how such a paradigm shift might be realised in practice remain inadequately understood. While some academics have recognised that desistance and a conceptualisation of the individual entails reflexivity, precisely what reflexivity entails and how this contributes to identity formation has been under theorised (although see Farrall, Bottoms and Shapland, 2010; King, 2014; Vaughan, 2007).

This chapter discusses current knowledge about desistance through a critical review of findings on studies of desistance and the ensuing implications for penal practice. The chapter proceeds by addressing the various definitions of desistance in the research literature, prior to presenting an overview of theoretical

Table 2.1 Probation practice in four paradigms (McNeill 2006:56)

The non-treatment paradigm	The revised paradigm	A 'what works' paradigm	A desistance paradigm
Treatment becomes help	Help consistent with a commitment to the reduction of harm	Intervention required to reduce re-offending and protect the public	Help in navigating towards desistance to reduce harm and make good to offenders and victims
Diagnosis becomes shared assessment	Explicit dialogue and negotiation offering opportunities for consensual change	'Professional' assessment of risk and need governed by structured assessment instruments	Explicit dialogue and negotiation assessing risks, needs, strengths and resources and offering opportunities to make good
Client's dependent need as the basis for action becomes collaboratively defined task as the basis for action	Collaboratively defined task relevant to criminogenic needs and potentially effective in meeting them	Compulsory engagement in structured programmes and case management processes as required elements of legal orders imposed irrespective of consent	Collaboratively defined tasks which tackle risks, needs and obstacles to desistance by using and developing the offender's human and social capital

explanations of desistance and the empirical studies that inform these explanations. In particular, the analysis presented in this chapter considers, where applicable, how contemporary understandings of desistance conceptualise the relationships between structure, agency, reflexivity and identity in the desistance process. This chapter concludes with a review of the research that examines the role of professional practice in supporting desistance.

Definitions of desistance

Debates surrounding definitions of desistance reflect the diversity of theoretical conceptualisations of desistance and the inherent difficulties in measuring desistance for empirical purposes. While the term itself implies abstinence from offending, criminologists have expanded on this to include consideration of the process by which people come to cease and sustain cessation of offending behaviour (see for example Bushway et al., 2001; Laub and Sampson, 2001; Maruna, 2001).

Shover (1996 p.121) defines desistance as 'the voluntary termination of serious criminal participation', suggesting that the presence of minor incidences of offending does not necessarily mean that someone is not desisting. Evidently, this is rather vague for the purposes of identification and measurement but what it does suggest, however, is that desistance is not only a process but that participation in low level offending, perhaps as part of that, is not uncommon. Most empirical measures of desistance emphasise the state of non-offending rather than the process of desistance, typically identifying individuals who evidence a significant lull or crime-free gap in the course of a criminal career, essentially redefining desistance as temporary non-offending,[4] due to the practical challenges of verifying permanent cessation of offending (see for example Bottoms et al., 2004[5]). Indeed, as Maruna and Farrall (2004) argue, permanent cessation can only be established posthumously (see also Maruna, 2001). Bushway et al. (2001) argue that a focus on the final state of non-offending neglects to address the process by which individuals arrive there. Alternatively, they propose that desistance should be construed as the study of change in criminality (defined as propensity to offend), which they suggest is implicit in qualitative accounts of desistance.[6]

The process of desistance has been likened to a zig-zag path (Glaser, 1964, cited in Maruna, 2001) and to a drifting in and out of offending (Matza, 1964), and these oscillations between conformity and criminality have been recognised in both empirical studies and theoretical accounts of desistance.[7] The process of desistance has been further conceptualised as encompassing distinguishable phases. Uggen and Kruttschnitt (1998) suggest that desistance has two implicit components: a change from offending to non-offending; and the arrival at a permanent state of non-offending. As previously highlighted, although this notion of permanency is problematic, the notion of graduated or distinguishable phases in the process of desistance is not without its precedents or antecedents (see for example Fagan, 1989;[8] Loeber and LeBlanc, 1990;[9] Weitekamp and Kerner, 1994[10]). Laub and Sampson (2001 p.11) differentiate between 'termination' (the outcome, 'the time at which criminal activity stops' [ibid p. 11]), and 'desistance' ('the causal process that supports the termination of offending' [ibid p. 11]). Maruna and Farrall (2004) criticise this definition as conflating the causes of desistance with desistance itself, alternatively proposing a dichotomous definition, analogous with Lemert's (1951) conception of primary and secondary deviance.[11] They propose that there are two distinguishable phases in the desistance process: primary and secondary desistance.[12] Primary desistance refers to any lull or crime free gap in the course of a criminal career (see Maruna and Farrall, 2004 for discussions of measurement). Secondary desistance is defined by the authors as the movement from the behaviour of non-offending to the adoption of a non-offending role or identity (Maruna and Farrall, 2004). This definition would not require that the process be terminal (ibid), rather, the study of desistance, which they argue should concentrate on secondary desistance, is thus construed as the 'study of continuity rather than change' (Maruna, 2001 p.27).

Theories of desistance

Significant criminological interest in desistance developed in the 1970s and 1980s (for example Cusson and Pinsonneault, 1986; Meisenhelder, 1977, 1982; Rand, 1987; Shover, 1983) and became a major area of enquiry in criminal career research in the 1990s (for example Graham and Bowling, 1995; Maruna, 1997; Sampson and Laub, 1993). Since this time, desistance research has moved beyond identifying who desists, and when, to propose a range of theories that seek to account for and explain desistance as a process (for example Bottoms and Shapland, 2011; Giordano, Cernkovich and Rudolph, 2002; Farrall et al., 2011; Laub and Sampson, 2003; Maruna, 2001).

The theories and studies reviewed in this chapter are by no means exhaustive of the literature on desistance; rather the following review is intended to be illustrative of the wider body of work on desistance. Whilst there are commonalities across theories of desistance, for the purpose of classification the theories of desistance are presented under four broad headings. The first three echo the classificatory distinctions drawn by Maruna (1997) and Barry (2007): namely, individual and agentic; social and structural; and interactionist. The fourth, situational, reflects Bottoms' (2014) more recent assertion that the spatial and situational aspects of desistance deserve attention in their own right. 'Individual and agentic' theories are based on the established links between age and certain criminal behaviours, locating explanations of desistance within age and maturational reform theories (or 'ontogenic theories'); agentic explanations of desistance informed by rational choice theories are also subsumed under this category. 'Social and structural' theories include social bonds and social control (or 'sociogenic') theories which, generally, advance an association between desistance and circumstances 'external' to the individual (although these include the individual's reaction to, and interaction with, those circumstances). Such theories emphasise the significance of ties to family, employment or educational programmes which are considered to create a stake in conformity. 'Interactionist' theories include those which attend, to varying degrees, to the interaction between individual agency and social structures in their accounts of desistance. Interactionist theories broadly emphasise the significance of subjective changes in the person's sense of self and identity, and as part of that, their aspirations, in response to their (changing) social contexts. More recently, Bottoms (2014) has added a fourth classification: 'situational desistance'. Bottoms points out that various aspects of our social environments and of our situated 'routine activities' also influence our behaviour.

Individual and agentic theories of desistance

Criminal careers research suggests that people begin offending in early adolescence, that rates of offending peak in late adolescence or young adulthood and that most people stop offending before reaching 30 or 40 years of age, thus construing offending primarily as an age-related phenomenon (see for example Blumstein and Cohen, 1987; Farrington, 1986, 1997). The aggregate age-crime curve (which is calculated by dividing the total number of arrests of individuals of a given age by the total population size of the specific age) indicates a sharp increase in the arrest rate in the early teen years; a peak age of arrest in the late teen or early adult years (dependent on crime type); and a decrease in the rate of arrest over the remaining age distribution. Evidence of the age-crime relationship can be found in studies that analyse quantitative data relating crime rates to aggregates of various sizes. These studies consistently report that overall the age distribution of any population is inversely related to its crime rate (see for example Cohen and Land, 1987; Hirschi and Gottfredson, 1983; Steffensmeier and Harer, 1987; Steffensmeier et al., 1989).

The relationship between age and crime is the fundamental cause of what has been termed the 'Great Debate' in criminology (Vold, Bernard and Snipes, 1998 p.285). This debate hinges on whether the analysis of *individual-level* data evidences the same relationship between age and crime as the analysis of *aggregate* data. Two main factions formed within this debate; one represented by Hirschi and Gottfredson (1983; Gottfredson and Hirschi, 1986, 1988, 1990) and the other by Blumstein and others (Blumstein and Cohen, 1979, 1987; Blumstein et al., 1986; Blumstein, Cohen and Farrington 1988; Farrington, 1983, 1986). Hirschi and Gottfredson (1983) argue that crime is universally inversely related to age at both the individual and aggregate levels of analysis i.e. the relationship between age and crime is considered to be invariant; all people, everywhere, within any historical period tend to commit less crime as they age regardless of both offence type and individual criminal propensity.

Blumstein and others, however, argue that this does not pertain at the individual level of analysis among active offenders. Rather, they contend that Gottfredson and Hirschi confuse changes in participation and incidence rates with changes in the frequency of individual offending among active offenders. A change in either participation or incidence rates affects the empirical shape of the curve. Put simply, as long as offenders are still active they may continue to commit crimes at a relatively constant rate independent of their age; thus changes in aggregate crime rates are likely to reflect changes in prevalence (see Farrington, 1986, 1997).

'Ontogenic' or 'maturational reform' theories all conclude that over time and with age, young people tend to naturally 'grow out of crime' (Rutherford, 1992 quoted in Newburn 2002 p.541). One of the largest longitudinal studies of crime and desistance was undertaken by Sheldon and Eleanor Glueck in the 1930s (Glueck and Glueck, 1940[13]). In their theory of 'maturational reform', the Gluecks (1940, 1974) argued that physical and mental changes, rather than environmental or social changes, explained behavioural transformations and, thus, desistance was both normative and expected, with exceptions being explained by a lack of maturity.

Maturational reform is an influential theory of desistance in criminology. Wilson and Herrnstein (1985) argue that none of the possible correlates of age, such as employment, peers or family circumstances, explain crime and criminality quite as well as the variable of age. Similarly, Gottfredson and Hirschi (1990) suggest, in a variation of the Gluecks approach, that '[s]pontaneous desistance is just that, change in behaviour that cannot be explained and change that occurs regardless of what else happens' (p.136, quoted in Laub and Sampson 2001 p.40). They attribute decreases in offending over time to biological changes which slow down the individual and which reduce the motivation and capacity to re-offend (see similarly Gove, 1985). From this perspective, criminal behaviour is impervious to life-course events or any social, situational or institutional influences. However, Maruna (1997, 2001) has highlighted, in reference to male crime, that although testosterone levels decrease with age, they do so less rapidly than the sharply peaking age-crime curve and that while physical strength tends to peak at age 30, the age-crime curve decreases from the late teens.

Bushway et al. (2001) argue that the identification of desistance as a process rather than as an end-point problematises the idea of age as a causal explanation of desistance, particularly from a developmental perspective. As Maruna (1997 p. 3) put it, 'age indexes a range of different variables, including biological changes, social and normative transitions, and life experiences, and in itself is not an explanation for change'. Rather, a focus on ageing and maturation as a universal or natural phenomenon fails to account for differences in individuals' pathways to desistance. Critically, it divorces the individual from the context within which these developmental changes occur by eliding the role of relational, cultural, social or structural processes. Moreover, such theories neglect to consider the role of cognition, reflexivity or agency in the process of change, and they inadequately account for the development of such internal processes.[14] As such, ontogenic theories are limited in their capacity to explain why or how this change occurs (Maruna, 1997). Explanations as to how and why this change occurs can perhaps be better located within what have been broadly classified in this chapter as 'social and structural', 'interactionist' and 'situational' theories of desistance.

Rational choice theories

Some theories that place explanatory weight on the individual's agentic role in desistance draw on concepts of rational choice (Clarke and Cornish, 1985; Cornish and Clarke, 1986). Such theories suggest that an individual's decisions to desist are motivated by the pursuit of an alternative future that does not involve offending (see for example Paternoster, 1989; Paternoster and Bushway, 2009; Paternoster and Pogarsky, 2009; Piliavin et al., 1986; Soyer, 2014), perhaps as a consequence of exposure to an aversive experience (Haggard, Gumpert and Grann, 2001) or, for example, in response to an accumulation of unfavourable experiences (Cusson and Pinsonneault, 1986). The essence of the rational choice framework of desistance is that the decision to desist from offending is based on a conscious reappraisal of the costs and benefits of crime (see Clarke and Cornish, 1985; Cornish and Clarke, 1986). From this perspective, individuals are conceptualised as 'reasoning decision-makers' (Cornish and Clarke, 1986 p.13). Nonetheless, rational choice theorists recognise that this decision is not made in isolation in as much as it is informed by individuals' experience of, and involvement in, wider social institutions and processes. Critically, however, these authors neglect to elaborate how such processes might exert a constraint on either offenders' decision-making or their capacities to realise these intentions.

Paternoster and Bushway (2009) developed an 'identity theory of criminal desistance' which, by their own admission, is a principally cognitive and individualistic model of the desistance process. They suggest that people make a conscious decision to change based on increasing dissatisfaction with their life, characterised as a 'crystallization of discontent' (p.1121) which becomes conceptually linked by the person to an anticipated future, and weighed up against a self as a future non-offender. This recalculation induces motivation to change. In a departure from social and structural theories (discussed below) they view any movement towards 'social institutions' such as marriage or employment, for example, as coming *after* the process of (identity) change has been initiated. The authors reason that, after a decision to desist has been made, the desister engages in a deliberate and intentional realignment of their social network towards more pro-social others: 'We think that ... social relationships ... are not accessed until after offenders *first decide to change* and then actually begin to change their sense of who they are' (Paternoster and Bushway, 2009 p.1106). However, in focusing on changes in network composition, and in polarizing social relations into either pro-social or anti-social others, the authors neglect to attend to the implications of changes in (existing) network dynamics and social relationships and their role in triggering, enabling and sustaining desistance.

In the last few years, a number of other researchers have also engaged in the important task of deconstructing and refining concepts of agency and its role in the process of desistance (see for example Healy, 2013, 2014; King, 2014; Shapland and Bottoms, 2011). Given these authors' more explicit recognition of, or attention to, the interaction between agency and structure, I have located a brief summary of their work under 'interactionist theories' in this chapter. Generally, however, rational choice perspectives usefully depart from the determinism often implied by accounts of desistance which primarily focus on 'structural influences' such as employment and marriage (discussed below) and which attribute a more peripheral role to individual agency. However, few accounts of the role of agency in the desistance process elaborate either what the process of reflexivity entails or how this process of reflexivity contributes to identity formation and change (notable recent exceptions include Dufour, Brassard and Martel, 2013; King, 2014). In so doing, many such theories fail to consider how individuals' reasoning and actions are variously enabled or constrained by the relational, cultural and social contexts within which these processes are embedded.

Social and structural theories

Social learning theories/differential association

Social learning frameworks, which offer explanations for both involvement in and desistance from offending, suggest that factors associated with onset of offending correlate with those that account for desistance. Factors associated with desistance include, for example, differential association with non-criminal peers and significant others (such as a partner or spouse), less exposure to or opportunities to model or imitate criminal behaviour, the development of attitudes favourable to conformity, and differential reinforcement discouraging continued involvement in offending. The most important of these factors for desistance is, according to

Warr (1998), disassociation or weakened ties to peer relations as a consequence of the transition to marriage. He contends that involvement in an intimate relationship reduces the amount of time spent with peers although he does not elaborate on how or why this occurs. Rather, his explanation coheres around the outcomes, suggesting that when an individual disassociates from their peer network they may lose both the motivation and the means of committing certain types of criminal behaviour.[15] However, Laub and Sampson (2001) suggest that in the absence of a mechanism explaining desistance from crime in Warr's analysis, alternative explanations for the observed relationship between marriage and desistance could account for this phenomenon. They suggest that possible explanations of the marriage effect could include changes in routine activities and, thus, opportunities for crime. They propose that spouses may, for example, encourage their partners to spend more time in the family home and, perhaps alongside new pro-social associates, exert informal social control.

Informal social control theories

Social control theorists suggest that informal ties to 'institutions of social control', such as family, education or employment, particularly in early adulthood, explain changes in criminality during the life course (Laub and Sampson, 2003). Therefore, unlike maturational or developmental theories, such theories suggest that the experiences that lead to desistance are not necessarily universal and they can often, to an extent, be under the control of the individual, in terms of obtaining employment or getting married for example (Laub and Sampson, 2001). The theorist most closely identified with control theory is Hirschi (1969) who identified four aspects of social bonds: attachment (emotional connection to others); commitment (investment in relationships and conformity); involvement (participation in legitimate activities) and belief (acceptance of the rule of law). However, current formulations of control theory can be attributed to the framework developed by Matza (1964). Matza's (1964) notion of a 'drift' centred on attachment, or otherwise, to social bonds; he suggested that most young people engaged in offending are caught somewhere in between the social bonds of adulthood and peer subcultures without a deep attachment to either, and that where adult roles become available, young people are likely to desist from crime (see also Trasler, 1979). In this vein, there is substantial research confirming that desistance from crime is correlated with completing education, acquisition of employment and investment in familial and personal relationships particularly in terms of the social control exerted by these factors (see for example Gibbens, 1984; Glueck and Glueck, 1940; Graham and Bowling, 1995; Leibrich, 1993; Meisenhelder, 1977; Rand, 1987; Sampson and Laub, 1993; Shover, 1985; West, 1982). Correspondingly, those who lack such attachments or bonds may be more likely to persist in offending because they have the least to lose, for example from the imposition of social sanctions.

Social control theorists (Hirschi, 1969; Laub and Sampson, 1993) argue that offending reflects weak social bonds and that desistance is enabled where bonds or ties to mainstream institutions (such as a spouse or a career[16]) are developed or reinforced. Laub, Nagin and Sampson (1998) emphasise the 'independent' and 'exogenous' impact of these bonds. They argue that these triggering events can occur, at least in part, by 'chance' (ibid p.225) or by 'default' (Sampson and Laub, 2004), rather than simply as an outcome of an individual's rational decision-making or personal preferences. More generally, they take the position that employment and marriage confer obligations and expectations on the individual that generate informal controls through a network of social bonds, regardless of prior individual differences in criminal propensity. Laub and Sampson (2001), however, building on their earlier work (Sampson and Laub, 1993), present a theory of crime that more explicitly recognizes the interaction between personal choice, situational context and social control, manifesting within and between different environmental contexts such as the family, work and the military.

There is a wealth of research that suggests that key life events such as marriage, parenthood or employment are likely to be correlated with, although not necessarily causal of, desistance (although see Sampson, Laub and Wimer (2006), discussed below). To date, explanations of this phenomenon are conflicting and contingent.

Marriage

Marriage has variously been associated with changes in adult crime (Glueck and Glueck, 1940), and reductions in alcohol and drug use (Knight, Osborn and West, 1977; West, 1982). Cusson and Pinsonneault (1986) argued that what was important in terms of facilitating desistance, was not marriage in and of itself, but the quality of the relationship and the criminality, or otherwise, of the chosen partner (see also Osborn and West, 1979; Ouimet and LeBlanc, 1996; Rutter, 1996; Shavit and Rattner, 1988; Simons et al., 2002; West, 1982). This would suggest that the partner's pro-social attributes, or otherwise, rather than any characteristic of the relationship are more significant in effect.

The various correlations between marriage and desistance are often explained in reference to a variety of criminological theories and, in particular, life course (Farrington, 1999; Loeber and Le Blanc, 1990), rational choice (Cusson and Pinsonneault 1986), social control (Laub and Sampson, 2003; Sampson and Laub, 1993; Sampson and Laub, 2005) and social learning theories (Warr, 1998). Control theorists suggest that these transitions are the effects of interpersonal ties and integration into or social bonds to mainstream, normative institutions (Laub and Sampson, 2003; Nagin and Paternoster, 1994) which 're-order short-term situational inducements to crime and, over time, re-direct long-term commitments to conformity' (Sampson and Laub, 2001 p.51). At the same time these connections can limit criminal involvement by reducing opportunities for crime or access to offending peers (Osgood and Lee, 1993; Warr, 1998) or by exerting informal social control over the individual in the form of 'obligations and constraints' (Sampson and Laub 1993 p.141). These are the most frequently cited explanations for the correlation between marriage and desistance. Other explanations suggest that such life-course transitions can enhance self-control, such that the desister chooses to avoid offending, based on a cost-benefit analysis of short-term gains against long-term consequences (Forrest and Hay, 2011), or that intimate relationships can provoke shifts in attitudes, values and identities which render offending incompatible with these changes in the self, suggestive of a more agentic dynamic than social control theories generally imply (Giordano, Cernkovich and Rudolph, 2002; Giordano, Schroeder and Cernkovich, 2007).

More recently, however, Sampson et al. (2006 p.467) have identified various mechanisms to explain the effect of marriage on desistance. They suggest that the influence of the marital relationship can be attributed to the interplay between the creation of 'interdependent systems of obligation, mutual support and restraint that impose significant costs for translating criminal propensities into action'; changes in daily routine activities and patterns of association; informal social control – which they conceptualise as a process of supervision, monitoring and direction, and as a symbol of respectability (Giordano et al., 2002). In other words, marriage can be seen as a part of a developmental process, characterized by deliberate responsibility taking which is generally associated with transitions to adulthood. Sampson et al. (2006) suggest that marriage is not only correlated with desistance, but has a causal effect, although, as the authors acknowledge, the historical context of their research is relevant here, in terms of cultural and normative expectations surrounding the nature of marital relationships, and the degree to which marriage per se exacts this effect, rather than, or compared to, cohabitation, for example.

The socio-historical and cultural contexts of research samples have come under increased scrutiny as a lens through which to understand the impact of normative, transitional or developmental life-course events on desistance (see for example Bersani, Laub and Nieuwbeerta, 2009; Giordano et al., 2002; King, Massoglia and Macmillan, 2007; Lyngstad and Skardhamar, 2011; Monsbakken, Lyngstad and Skardhamar, 2012b; Savolainen, 2009; Shanahan, 2000), reflecting increasing recognition of the distinct socio-economic changes that have occurred in frequencies and patterns of marriage, marriage stability and in normative expectations surrounding marriage and co-habitation. Despite these changes, Bersani et al. (2009 p.20) found that 'the influence of marriage on the desistance process is strongest in the most contemporary context' in part as a consequence of pre-marital cohabitation and later marriages, which, they infer, engender increased marital stability, quality and investment in the relationship. Lyngstad and Skardhamar's (2011) quantitative study of Norwegian males similarly revealed a gradual and substantial decrease in offending in the five years prior to marriage, although they observed that marriage was followed by a small but non-trivial increase after the formalisation of the relationship through marriage. They suggest that desistance does not emerge as a consequence of the event of getting married; the emotional attachment and any behavioural changes this gives rise to occur in the years preceding marriage, particularly in a contemporary context where cohabitation and longer pre-marital relationships are the norm. In contrast to Sampson et al (2006), Lyngstad and Skardhamar (2011) argue that it is possible to treat marriage as an *outcome* of, rather than a causal factor in, desistance (see similarly Kiernan, 2004; Monsbakken et al., 2012b; Savolainen, 2009).

There is some evidence to suggest that the impact of marriage on criminality is less evident for women (Giordano et al., 2002; King, Massoglia and Macmillan, 2007; Kreager, Matsueda and Erosheva, 2010) which may be attributable to important gendered differences in experiences of the marital relationship, reflecting their disparate gender roles within the marriage. Monsbakken et al. (2012b) alternatively hypothesise that the different gendered social control effects of marriage on desistance might reflect the normatively-informed controls stemming from women's friendship and family networks throughout the life course; when seen through this lens, they argue that for women, marriage heralds no new mechanisms of social control and therefore engenders less change promotive effects. On the other hand, as Sampson et al. (2006) suggest, these apparent differences might equally reflect the gendered nature of criminal involvement, in so far as men are statistically more likely to marry a pro-social partner than women. Equally, any decrease in women's criminality may be further attributable to the influence of parenthood, which, as the following subsection elaborates, has a greater and more immediate impact on women's lifestyles (Bersani et al., 2009; Giordano et al., 2002; Graham and Bowling, 1995; Uggen and Kruttschnitt, 1998).

Building on the foregoing analysis, at the very least, this would suggest that the impact of marriage on offending is both gendered and changeable within and across different cultural contexts and between different socio-historical eras, as much as it is contingent on the variances within a given relationship, over the life course. However, while the quantitative studies referred to here can provide overview of *what* happens in most cases most of the time, in terms of elaborating on the effects they document, the extent to which they can shed light on the mechanisms and mechanics of the underlying process is constrained.

Parenthood

The effects of parenthood remain a comparatively under-researched dynamic of desistance. While there is some evidence to suggest that parenthood can encourage extrication from gangs (Fleisher and Krienert, 2004; Moloney et al., 2009; Moore and Hagedorn, 1999) and contribute to desistance (see for example Edin and Kefalas, 2005; Kreager et al., 2010; Monsbakken Lyngstad and Skardhamar, 2012a; Savolainen, 2009), other studies suggest that becoming a parent has a negligible effect on offending trajectories (Blokland and Nieuwbeerta, 2005; Giordano et al., 2002; Giordano et al., 2011; Laub and Sampson, 2003; Rand 1987; Sampson and Laub, 1993; Warr, 1998) or, in the face of financial pressures for example, can even exacerbate offending (Wakefield and Uggen, 2008 cited in Savolainen, 2009). It is likely that a coalescence of factors will affect the dynamic experience of parenthood (see for example Arendell, 2000; Hauari and Hollingworth, 2009; Marsiglio and Pleck, 2004) and influence its significance and impact including age, gender, maturity, one's experience of being parented, the status, nature and dynamics of the relational context within which a given form of parenting occurs, and individual personal, cultural and socio-economic contexts that variously constrain and enable the realisation of this social role and identity consistent with one's internalised values and beliefs. Perhaps as a consequence of this level of individual variation, numerous explanations as to *how* parenthood contributes to desistance have been proposed and, in the main, they echo those mechanisms associated with explanations for the marriage effect discussed above (Kreager et al., 2010; Monsbakken, Lyngstand and Skardhamar, 2012a). In addition, however, Moloney et al. (2009) found that fatherhood motivated change in triggering subjective and affective modifications which led to changes in outlook, priorities and future orientation. However, the authors also identified that for these shifts to ultimately translate into behavioural change, then changes in the amount of time spent on the streets and an ability to provide for oneself or one's family needed to occur.

Bersani et al. (2009) suggest that parenthood is more highly correlated with female than male desistance because the impact on one's lifestyle of becoming a mother, not only practically, but also in terms of social expectations surrounding 'good mothering' and the assumption of maternal responsibilities is more immediate and consequentially direct in terms of reducing opportunities to offend through changes in routine activities and association with others who offend (see similarly Keizer, Dykstra and Poortman, 2010) and in relation to the perceived impacts of, for example, imprisonment on their children (see also Edin and Kefalas, 2005; Graham and Bowling, 1995; Kreager et al., 2010; Monsbakken et al., 2012a; Uggen and Kruttschnitt, 1998).

Recognising that some of the social or behavioural effects of parenthood might be attributable to the degree of involvement in parenting, various research studies have revealed conflicting evidence when controlling for the status or context of the parents' relationship – for example whether cohabitating, married or separated – and the timing of pregnancy, birth and behavioural changes (see for example Farrington and West, 1995; Giordano et al., 2011; Monsbakken et al., 2012a). In general, quantitative research rarely seems to concur with the positive relationships that qualitative research identifies between parenthood and desistance (see for example Edin and Kafalas, 2005; Fleisher and Krienert, 2004; Giordano et al., 2002; Laub and Sampson, 2003; although see Kreager et al., 2010 as an exception). It might be suggested that these divergences relate to different research objectives. Quantitative research tends to focus on the degree to which intimate relationships or parenthood are causative of or conditional on desistance, in terms of the relative sequencing of relational investments and involvement in offending (or otherwise). In contrast, qualitative analyses tend to focus on revealing the relative contribution of the identified change agent to the outcomes, be it the role of the partner, for example, as change agent (as in social control theories), or the role of the individual as change agent (as in more agentic or cognitive theories of desistance).

Employment

Cromwell, Olson and D'Aunn (1991 p.83) argued that 'desistance [is] associated with the disintegration of the adolescent peer group and with employment and the ability to earn money legitimately' (see also Wright and Cullen, 2004). Conversely, other authors have observed that employment also provides opportunities for offending (Hirschi,1969; Sviridoff and Thompson, 1983; West and Farrington, 1977). Nevertheless, whilst employment may reduce the likelihood of re-offending, a lack of employment does not necessarily correlate with an increase in offending. Indeed, as Maruna (1997) observed, the connection between unemployment and crime is not sustained when applied to women, who have historically been disadvantaged in terms of employment, but remain marginally represented in crime statistics. Age has also been cited as a factor in determining the impact of employment on criminality (Hagan and McCarthy, 1997); Uggen (2000), in an analysis of data from a national work experiment in the US, found that those aged 27 or older were more likely to desist when provided with employment. Uggen inferred from this that the meaning attached to employment and participation in crime may change as individuals age, indicating a subjective component to desistance. Similarly problematising a social control interpretation of the role of employment in influencing behavioural change is Skardhamar and Savolainen's (2012) recent quantitative research on the timing of behavioural change and participation in employment, which identified that employment emerged *after* individuals had ceased offending. Rather than triggering desistance, Skardhamar and Savolainen suggest that participation in employment emerges as a consequence of desistance.

In this vein, while employment has been generally associated with desistance (for a review of this literature see Owens, 2009; Skardhamar and Savolainen, 2012), it is also increasingly acknowledged that employment in and of itself does not produce or trigger desistance; rather it is the meaning and outcomes of either the nature and/or quality of the work or participation in employment and how these influence an individual's self-concept and social identity and how these interact with a person's priorities, goals and relational concerns that can explain this relationship (Owens 2009; Savolainen 2009; Weaver, 2012). Farrall (2005) similarly suggests that work, and as part of that, association with a new social group, can be a mechanism for rebuilding who one is and forging who one will become. As Owens states, the impact of work goes beyond the effects of obtaining an income or even the injection of a daily or weekly routine; 'employment is part of the idea of what is acceptable' (Owens 2009 p.50) and communicates in itself that one has a place in the world and a role to play – be it in society or even in one's own family – as a reliable partner and provider or a good parent for example. Indeed, the interaction between employment and investment in significant intimate relations and/or parenthood (which for some people works to encourage and enable change) has been generally observed (see for example Bianchi, Casper and King, 2005 cited in Bersani et al., 2009; Edin, Nelson and Paranal, 2001; Laub and Sampson, 2001; Owens, 2009; Rhodes, 2008; Savolainen, 2009). Employment can provide the economic resources, for example, that facilitate both marriage and family formation (Lichter, LeClere and McLaughlin, 1991 in King et al., 2007) and the realisation of the assumed social role as provider (Bersani et al., 2009). Similarly, providing for one's family, (which remains a central aspect of fathering, of identity as a father and, in turn, contributes to feelings of self-worth (Pleck,

2004)), can be a powerful motivator to obtain and sustain employment (Edin et al., 2001; Edin and Kefalas, 2005; Savolainen, 2009). However, the absence of employment can generate financial pressures on young families who may resort to offending to resolve (Shannon and Abrams, 2007; Moloney et al., 2009; Wakefield and Uggen, 2008 in Savolainen, 2009) just as participation in employment can itself herald new pressures and challenges which can undermine its potential to bring about change (Weaver, 2012).

Religion/spirituality[17]

While religiosity is not among the 'social institutions' that generally attract empirical attention, there is an increasing interest in revealing the mechanisms through which religiosity and affiliations to religious communities might enable change. As with analyses of the role of marriage, parenthood and employment, the role of religious beliefs and practices in deterring crime has produced varying results and generated varying explanations across a wide number of studies (for an overview see Baier and Wright, 2001). Topalli, Brezina and Bernhard (2012 p.1), for example, found that their 'hardcore street offenders' referenced their religious beliefs to justify past and current participation in serious offending to counteract 'the deterrent effect that existential and transcendental consequences of anticipated, current, or previous criminal activity typically have' (Topalli et al., 2012 p.14) – an antidote to, perhaps, or defence against the 'feared self' (Paternoster and Bushway, 2009 p.1103). In this sense, religion can also provide motivation and support for deviant action, crime and violence particularly in extreme forms (Miller, 2006). Although until recently (see for example Armstrong, n.d.; Giordano et al., 2007; Maruna, Wilson and Curran, 2006; Schroeder and Frana, 2009) religion and spirituality have not been central units of analysis in desistance studies, it has nonetheless emerged as a salient factor for some people in initiating, enabling and sustaining change, and, in that, constraining or restraining offending (see for example Calverley, 2013; Maruna, 2001).

Marranci's (2009) anthropological research within prisons and Muslim communities in the UK illustrates how, for a number of interrelated reasons, Muslims often rediscover Islam within prison (see also Marranci, 2007). Amongst those reasons is the desire to repent and to make good, presenting an opportunity for change as they 'reconsider their life and link their experience of prison not to human punishment but to an opportunity granted by Allah to change their life' (Marranci, 2007 p.8).[18] Marranci (2006) elucidates a theory of identity as encompassing two functions – it allows human beings to make sense of their autobiographical self and it allows them to express that self through symbols which communicate feelings that could not otherwise be externally communicated (see also Marranci, 2007). Marranci (2007 p.8) differentiates between Islam as 'an act of identity' and Islam 'as an act of faith'. He argues that Muslims in prison often see Islam more as an act of identity than of faith. Nonetheless, drawing on the findings of Calverley (2013) (discussed below), it might be inferred that the rediscovery of Islam has the potential to assist Muslim offenders to reconnect with their religious identities, traditions and culture so as to support their efforts to change.[19]

Calverley's (2013) study of the desistance pathways of 33 men of Indian, Bangladeshi and Black and Dual Heritage resident in London found that the (re)discovery of Islamic faith was a significant feature of desistance for Bangladeshi participants (n=6/11). Embracing Islam provided opportunities for the establishment of an alternative non-offending identity, but which was contiguous with their past selves, and thus represented a discovery or return to their 'true self' (see relatedly Armstrong, n.d.; Maruna, 2001; Maruna et al., 2006). Moreover, Calverley suggested that the narrative and teachings of Islam provided a moral compass, and a resource for emotion coping (see also Giordano et al., 2007[20] and Schroeder and Frana, 2009 on Christianity[21]). While religious *faith* was not a significant feature of Indian participants' narratives, participation in religious events and ceremonies was construed as an opportunity for Indian desisters to prove the sincerity of their efforts to desist. Participation in religious practices and institutions had a performative function, and association with an alternative community provided not only an important source of social recognition but also enabled the relinquishment of former friendship groups.[22] Similarly, Giordano et al. (2007) found that desisters' new found commitment to Christianity enabled the development of different forms of social capital in terms of the consolidation or reparation of existing relationships, particularly where such relationships reinforced or affirmed their religious commitments, and the development of new relationships and social networks through affiliation to religious institutions or faith groups (see also Chu (2007) in relation to desistance from drug use).

In contrast to studies which emphasise the significance of internalized faith to processes of change (see for example Giordano et al., 2002; Giordano et al., 2007; Schroeder and Frana, 2009), Lim and Putnam (2010) suggest that private and subjective dimensions of religiosity are not significantly related to subjective well-being and life satisfaction. They propose that the positive association between religiosity and life satisfaction resides in the social relationships forged within religious institutions, generating a strong sense of religious belonging, which, through processes of mutual identification, reinforces religious identities. They concluded that for life satisfaction 'praying together seems to be better than either bowling together or praying alone' (Lim and Putnam, 2010 p.927). Of particular relevance here is their suggestion that the effects cannot be reduced to network size or strength of ties, but to the specific context in which these networks are forged and identities shared, and which endows these friendships with particular significance. However, the availability of these specific supports inherent in religious communities depends to an extent on the willingness of faith based communities and institutions to offer support to desisters, and on offender's receptivity to and experiences of engaging with them (for a nuanced analysis of this dynamic, see Armstrong, n.d.).

Taken together, these studies emphasise the significance of internalized faith to processes of change, which can be reinforced through participation in religious practices and communities. Conversely, however, participation in religious observances or externalized faith is, in isolation, insufficient to sustaining change over time (Armstrong, n.d.), although, where involvement with a community of believers generates a strong sense of religious belonging, and, through processes of mutual identification, reinforces cultural and religious identities, this can enhance subjective wellbeing and life satisfaction (Lim and Putnam, 2010). However, with notable exceptions (i.e. Armstrong, n.d.), it remains that the extent to which the content of faith or 'the nature of the religion adopted, as opposed to religiosity per se, alters or modifies in some way the trajectory associated with desistance [is] yet [to be] fully considered' (Calverley 2013 p.102).

This section has reviewed the evidence base surrounding the relationships between desistance and the principle 'institutions of social control' which are generally construed in the literature as 'structures'. What this analysis has revealed is not only the contingent and conditional interaction between these social relations but divergences in results and conclusions as to their effects depending on the methodology deployed and the theoretical explanations progressed. Moreover, while social and structural theories variously recognise and explain the role of social institutions in the desistance process, they fail to illuminate how social structures or institutions shape decisions, under-analysing how the individual perceives and responds to such influences.

Interactionist theories

The preceding analysis has illustrated that desistance cannot be readily reduced to the influence of either internal or external factors. Indeed, an increasing number of desistance theories conceptualise the desistance process as an interaction between, or integration of, agentic and structural factors which are developed from the perspectives of the offenders themselves, drawing on the subjective perceptions of their lived experiences and the narrative accounts of their individual desistance processes. In these 'interactionist' theories, desistance essentially occurs as the outcome of an individual seeking to alter their socio-structural context, and in so doing acquiring new behaviours and new pro-social roles, or vice versa, variously resulting in associated shifts in the individual's personal and social identity (see for example Barry, 2007; Bottoms et al., 2004; Dufour et al., 2013; Farrall, 2002; Farrall, Bottoms and Shapland, 2010; Giordano et al., 2002; Healy, 2013; Maruna and Farrall 2004; Uggen, Manza and Behrens, 2004). Thus, such accounts of the desistance process place differing emphases on the role of individuals and their social contexts; that difference exemplifies in a desistance focused context, a familiar sociological tension generally known as the 'structure-agency' debate (Bottoms et al., 2004), which concerns the relative primacy of, or interplay between, structure or agency with regard to human behaviour, on which social theories some desistance theorists explicitly draw.[23]

In *Making Good* Maruna (2001) demonstrated the important role that narratives play in structuring offenders' and ex-offenders' understanding of themselves and their relationships in an exploration of the subjective dimensions of change. He used content analysis to identify different 'mindsets' exhibited by 20 career criminals (people who thought they would persist with crime) and 30 desisters (those who expressed a desire to change and had desisted from offending for approximately 2–3 years) who shared similar criminogenic traits and backgrounds and who lived in similarly criminogenic environments. Maruna found that a 'condemnation script' emerged from the persisters in contrast to the 'redemption script' that emerged from the desisters. Both the persisters and the desisters articulated a level of fatalism in their accounts of the development of their criminal careers; however, Maruna interpreted the minimisation of responsibility implied by this fatalism as evidence of their fundamentally normative values and aspirations and of their need to believe in their inherent integrity. Furthermore, in their accounts of achieving change there is evidence that people have to 'discover' agency in order to resist the structural pressures that are favourable to the commission of crime. This is not an entirely individualistic process, however; Maruna observed that people benefited from the supports of significant others in recognising and reinforcing the identity transformations that ensue. In particular, he identified that involvement in 'generative activities' (which make a contribution to the well-being of others) plays a part in testifying to the desister that an alternative agentic identity is being or has been forged. In this vein, McNeill (2006) suggested that Maruna's (2001) narrative analysis revealed (at least implicitly) the mediating role of reflexivity between agency and structure.

Farrall and Bowling (1999) draw on life-course perspectives (namely, Sampson and Laub, 1993) and structuration theory, introduced by Giddens (1984) and adapted to criminology by Bottoms and Wiles (1992), to propose a developmental theory of desistance, in an attempt to disentangle the role of internal versus external changes enabling and sustaining desistance. The life-course perspective aims to combine, in ways compatible with Gidden's theory of structuration, personal histories and experiences within a structural setting: 'structural influences which are beyond the control, or perhaps even awareness, of individual respondents' (Farrall and Bowling, 1999 p.258). Farrall and Bowling (1999 p.261), following a review of studies dichotomising structural or agentic influences on desistance, argue that the process of desistance is 'one that is produced through an *interplay* between individual choices, and a range of wider social forces, institutional and societal practices which are beyond the control of the individual' (emphasis in original). Using the concepts of 'duality of structure', power, social identities and position practices, Farrall and Bowling contend that power differentials within individuals over the life course will influence the 'timing and pace' of desistance (ibid p.265). In two case studies drawn from a wider qualitative sample, they illustrate the influences of significant others and events in individual decisions to stop offending.

Desistance theorists have also sought to identify which changes at the level of personal cognition (see for example Giordano et al., 2002) or self-identity and self-concept (Burnett, 1992; Graham and Bowling, 1995; Maruna 1997; Shover, 1996) might precede or coincide with changes in social bonds (LeBel et al., 2008). In contrast to control theories, cognitive or agentic explanations suggest that role transitions occur 'subsequent to the emergence of a cognitive openness to change that spurs interest in both marriage and reform' (Siennick and Osborn, 2008 p.169–70) (see relatedly Paternoster and Bushway, 2009). Using the data set from the Oxford Recidivism Study (Burnett, 1992), LeBel et al. (2008) attempted to disentangle the interaction between such 'subjective/agency' factors and 'social/environmental' factors. They found that subjective states measured before release had a direct effect on recidivism as well as indirect effects through their impact on social circumstances experienced post release. LeBel et al. (2008) reasoned that 'subjective changes may precede life-changing structural events and, to that extent, individuals can act as agents of their own change' (ibid p.155).

Cognitive/agentic theories suggest that 'turning point'[24] events may have a different impact depending on the actor's level of motivation, on readiness to reform, and on their interpretation or assignation of meaning to the events. Giordano et al. (2002), for example, develop a symbolic interactionist[25] perspective on desistance, as a counterpoint to Sampson and Laub's (1993) theory of informal social control, to propose a four-part theory of cognitive transformation. Giordano et al. (2002 p.1000) argue that the desistance process involves the following stages:

1. '. . . a shift in the actor's basic openness to change';
2. '. . . one's exposure to a particular hook or set of hooks for change' (ibid p.1000) and 'one's attitude toward [it]' (ibid p.1001).
3. The envisioning and fashioning of 'an appealing and conventional "replacement self"' (ibid p.1001);
4. '. . . a transformation in the way the actor views the deviant behaviour or lifestyle itself' (ibid p.1002).

Giordano et al. (2002) argue that agency is most significant where, in reference to various external opportunities, the objective odds of desisting are evenly balanced. Where this balance is offset other factors appear to be of greater importance. Not dissimilarly, Rumgay (2004 p.408) considered that an individual has to recognise new social roles as an opportunity to change their identity which 'marks the beginning of active attempts at personal change'. She suggests that these roles provide a 'skeleton script' giving the individual behavioural cues as to how to proceed as a changed person. However, while Giordano et al.'s (2002) theory, and indeed, many principally agentic theories of the change process, can elaborate the early stages of desistance, they cannot explain what triggers this cognitive transformation, or why one institution at one time rather than another exerts this effect, or why people remain in marriages or in jobs during challenging times when their investment in these social relations has diminished (Vaughan, 2007).

Bottoms and Shapland's (2011) (see also Farrall et al., 2010) analysis of their prospective, longitudinal, mixed method study of early desistance among young adult recidivists construes agency as occupying a central role in the desistance process. Drawing on Mouzelis (2008), they situate agency in interaction with individual dispositions (as a result of personal, social and criminal history) and socio-structural dimensions (see similarly Farrall et al., 2011[26]). Bottoms and Shapland's analysis has led them to progress an interactive model of the early stages of desistance but, due to their prospective study design, they are not yet able to comment how desistance is sustained. They suggest that desistance is influenced by individuals' dispositions and by their changing social capital (which may trigger desistance), which can present as an opportunity for change. They suggest that despite taking action towards desistance, failure to maintain these changes in the face of obstacles, temptations or provocations may lead to relapse, although not necessarily back to the individual's starting point. They therefore emphasise the need for reinforcing factors – perhaps emerging from within the individual or their (changing) social relationships. While, then, they recognize that histories, habits and social opportunities influence this process, individual agency is given a prominent role in negotiating a new way of living, breaking habits with the support of significant others, in influencing their changing social contexts.

King (2014) draws on Emirbayer and Mische (1998) to explore the dynamics of agency in the early stages of desistance based on the accounts of 20 people subject to probation supervision. Notably, he reveals the processes which led towards a decision to attempt to desist; the intended strategies that individuals considered in order to sustain desistance; and the anticipated obstacles that individuals believed they would encounter and how they intended to overcome these. King reasons that during the transitional phases, individuals may begin to construct strategies for future action triggered by their perceived need for change and/or as an outcome of their reflection on their personal and social circumstances. In a departure from preceding research into the early phases of desistance (i.e. Healy, 2012), King's research revealed that the nature of agency in the transition to desistance is active and mutable; people adjust their goals and their strategies for realising these goals in the light of incoming information and may, in turn, adjust their preferences accordingly. This reordering of preferences is, then, the result of a reappraisal of goals in accordance with their assessment of the possibilities and potentials that inhere in their social contexts. King therefore observes that individuals' priorities change in accordance with the availability (or otherwise) of certain roles and resources, which produce different forms of agency and which result in difference forms of action. Agency is, in King's formulation, context dependent; agency is conditioned by an individual's social context which delimits the range of future possibilities available by variously enabling or constraining change. This marks a departure from Paternoster and Bushway (2009) in that in King's formulation, desistance emerges as an outcome of the interplay between structure and action, and, specifically, the individual's reflexive evaluation as to the extent to which he can realize his positive future self within the constraints and enablements that inhere in his social context. However, while King's analysis offers important insights into the relationships between agency, structure, identity, reflexivity and the desistance process, he is unable to explain what triggers this reflexive process in the first place.

Following an evaluative review of agency-centred theories of desistance, Healy (2013 p.7) proposes an integrated framework for conceptualizing agency which also 'elaborates on the mechanisms that operate at the intersection between structure and agency' utilising Côté's (1997) identity capital model. While Healy's discussion does much to advance insights into concepts and constructs of agency, its interconnections with structures and its application to studies of desistance, like many other integrated accounts, it retains a somewhat solitary view of the self. While social bonds and social roles are referred to as enablements or constraints in identity formation and change, in its somewhat instrumental, resource based formulation, the elision of the relational in Côté's identity capital thesis (and, therefore, Healy's (2013) application of this in a desistance context) is arguably a significant shortcoming, not least in its neglect to attend to how social relations motivate, enable or constrain decision-making and action and contribute to identity formation and change.

Uggen, Manza and Behrens (2004) emphasise both the role of age graded social bonds and roles and the social-psychological process underpinning various role transitions. In addition to employment and family, they stress the significance of 'civic reintegration'. Building on Maruna's (2001 p.7) contention that desistance is only possible when ex-offenders 'develop a coherent pro-social identity for themselves', and his recognition of the salience of involvement in 'generative activities' as critical to the desistance process, they specify the varieties of civic participation that contribute to such an identity and their associated subjective meanings to desisters. They proceed to show how a symbolic interactionist theory of role transition across socio-economic, familial and civic domains might explain identity shifts over the life course. In this study, they emphasise the reduced citizenship status and the enduring stigma experienced by offenders, resulting in 'the reduced *rights* and *capacities* of ex-offenders to attain full citizenship' (Uggen et al., 2004 p.260) which serve to undermine their commitment to conformity and create new obstacles to desistance and the assumption of pro-social roles. They further highlight that even where ex-offenders articulate a desire to assume such pro-social roles, they 'often lack the resources and social relationships necessary to establish role commitments and solidify new identities' (ibid p.284–5). These obstacles represent a significant problem because of the important role of societal reaction in supporting (or undermining) new self-conceptions and the reinforcement of pro-social identities.

The findings of this study resonate with Maruna and Farrall (2004), who propose a theoretical account of the desistance process centring on notions of self-determination and pro-social labeling. They discuss the role of societal reaction in supporting self-conceptions, derived from the experience of self as causal agent, and the reinforcement of pro-social identities and the significance of the development of human and social capital in fostering desistance (see also Farrall, 2002). Maruna and Farrall (2004) suggest that community supervision can be viewed as an attempt to improve the development of human capital in individuals, for example by referring them to employment training initiatives, or delivering programmes underpinned by cognitive psychology or pursuing harm reduction. However, the development of social capital, which may be fostered through employment opportunities for example, is more problematic, and subject to the influence of both meso- and macro-level circumstances, such as employment rates, which have been exacerbated by economic changes which have disproportionately affected already disadvantaged communities (see also Farrall et al., 2010, 2011).

Situational theories

The situational and spatial dynamics of desistance have barely featured in the criminal careers literature and yet, as Flynn (2010) observed, criminality is decidedly situational in terms of the influences that social structures and social relations, which inhere in the places that people inhabit, exert on various dimensions of their lives. Places, then, 'are important generators of actions and not merely venues in which actions are performed' (Bottoms and Wiles, 1992 cited by Farrall et al., 2014 p.160). In this vein, Bottoms (2014) reasons that people's behaviour can change when one or more features of their surrounding environment is altered, which might include for example changes in places of residence, the avoidance of criminogenic places and spaces and disassociation from peers who offend. Bottoms (2014) associates situational desistance with a particular form or manifestation of agency termed self-binding or diachronic self-control which is manifest in attempts to control potential future courses of action by consciously imposing certain constraints on one's movements and associations.

Farrall et al. (2014) explore how desistance impacts on individuals' everyday activities, including the spaces and places in which these occur. Echoing Bottoms, they reason that 'desistance is not just about no longer offending, it is also about adopting a different set of routines which take individuals to very different places from when they used to offend' (ibid p.160). Their analysis draws on geographies of time and space which explore the routine and rhythm of a day or week (or longer time period), and the spatial dimensions in which these routines occur, which, they recognise, are themselves shaped and influenced by wider social institutions. They found that desisters, unlike persisters, 'appeared to consciously create routines for themselves and others' (Farrall et al., 2014 p.173) not least in terms of family routines. While some persisters' lives were structured around family responsibilities, they observed a qualitative difference in levels of enthusiasm for, or 'emotional engagement' (ibid p.174) in, these routines reflecting levels of perceived voluntarism towards family roles and responsibilities. In terms of routines imposed by work, Farrall et al. (2014) found that 42 percent of desisters were in full or part time work compared to only 7 percent of persisters, which for the desisters injected structure and routine which was notably absent in the accounts of persisters. They also noted a difference in both the frequency and nature of the appointments people engaged in which contribute to the formation of routines and the nature of activities that structure people's lives and, as part of that, border their movements. Where desisters' appointments cohered around family or work related activities, persisters' appointments cohered around visits to probation officers or drug dealers and, again, they observed differences in perceived choice and willingness to accept these 'intrusions'. They observed, thus, that shifts in 'time space routines' (ibid p.164) reflect wider transformations in the spheres of family and work.

However, it is not just the place but the character of a place which is partly determined by its other inhabitants. 'The explanation given by the likes of Meisenhelder (1977) and Goffman (1963) is that the places where an individual lives out his or her life communicate some element of 'who' they are and 'what' they do' (Farrall et al., 2014 p.162). Farrall et al. observe that routines also inform both personal and social identities to the extent that they communicate that there is something different about who they are now which can also inform ideas about who they can become in the future. In this vein, the authors identified a shift in people's relationships to and the meaning associated with specific places in accordance with both processes of change (i.e. in terms of avoiding specific places or accessing new ones) and processes of maturation (i.e. characterized by a shift in preferences). Thus, there is an important relationship between selfhood and place and the way in which place becomes imbued with meaning and in turn, the way in which place infers something of the self; in both senses identity is shaped through the social interactions that inhere in place and space (Farrall et al., 2014; Flynn, 2010).

Farrall et al. (2014) conclude that the temporal and spatial dimensions of human activities 'reflects the interaction of one individual's priorities, the priorities and requirements of the institutions they are engaged with, and the *longue durée* influences of "historical" time' (Farrall et al., 2014 p.164). In particular, they suggest that the spatial dynamics of desistance can be understood as working on two levels. 'Moves *within* towns or cities appeared to be part of the story of desistance for non-drug-injecting desisters, and were associated with moves away from particular parts of the city where crime was common and in which they had a name and a reputation to defend' (ibid p.185). On the other hand, 'moves *between* towns or cities . . . were a feature of the narratives of reform for desisting drug users (and the opposite – that is locational stability and persistence – was observed too)' (ibid).

Supporting desistance through supervision

As this review makes clear, although there is an ever-increasing body of research investigating the phenomena of desistance, there has been much less research on the role of penal practitioners in supporting the process. One of the first studies to explore the relationship between probation supervision and desistance was Leibrich's (1993) qualitative study of probationers in New Zealand. The study was based on semi-structured interviews with a randomly selected sample of people who had been placed on probation in 1987 and who by 1990 had incurred no further criminal convictions. The findings of this study, based on 48 'desisting' male and female ex-probationers, presented varied perceptions on the efficacy or role of probation in supporting their desistance. Few people spontaneously cited probation as a factor in their desistance (ibid p.172) and only half of the sample considered probation to have been useful in this regard (ibid p.184). A revision of personal values, reassessing what is important, responding to new family commitments, desire for a better future and the development of self-respect were cited as the reasons for wishing to desist (Leibrich, 1993) as were fear of the continued consequences of offending and shame. Interestingly, 'shame' was the most commonly mentioned reason for going straight and the most commonly mentioned cost of offending (see also Leibrich, 1996). Three kinds of shame were evident: public humiliation, personal disgrace and private remorse. Private remorse was the most influential and was triggered by an individual offending their personal morality – coming to think that their offending was wrong. What Leibrich seems to be identifying here is a broadly reflexive process, although what this process entails is not elaborated. In addition, participants suggested that desistance was accomplished by tackling personal problems using interpersonal resources, accompanied by a sense of life management, which might be conceptually allied with the discovery of agency (see Maruna, 2001). In the context of probation interventions, the quality of the supervisory relationship was cited as pivotal in supporting the process of desistance. The characteristics which the desisters cited as crucial to the supervisory relationship reflected those which were identified by probation officers and included someone that they could get on with and respect; who treated them as individuals; was genuinely caring; was clear about what was expected of them and trusted them when required. Negative appraisals of the supervisory relationship were attributed to a sense of being merely 'processed' manifest in a lack of concern.

Rex's study (1999) sought to relate the literature on 'What Works?' (or evidence based interventions with offenders) (see for example McGuire, 1995) to why people desist from offending. The findings of this study indicated that most of the probationers considered probation to have assisted the process of their desistance from offending (Rex, 1999). This was attributed to the relational aspects of supervision and attempts to support a probationer to sustain a decision to stop offending, discussing past offending, addressing low levels of social ties and pro-social work. In this study, Rex (1999) explored the experiences of 60 probationers and additionally interviewed 21 probation officers. Probationers who attributed changes in their behaviour to probation supervision described it as active and participatory; they conveyed a sense of being engaged through negotiation in a partnership. Probationers' commitments to desist appeared to be generated by the personal and professional commitment shown by their probation officers whose reasonableness, fairness and encouragement seemed to engender a sense of personal loyalty, obligation and accountability. Probationers saw advice about their behaviour or underlying problems as evidence of concern, and were motivated by this interest. Rex found that as many as half of the probationers revealed feelings of personal loyalty and accountability towards their supervisors.

These findings are particularly pertinent to the current context of probation interventions, wherein the role of tools and programmes in the pursuit of 'effective' practice has to some extent marginalized more traditional concerns in social work with offenders surrounding the development of social capital (McNeill, 2006) which resides in the relationships through which participation and inclusion in society is facilitated (Farrall, 2004). In Rex's study, it seemed that probationers could recognize and appreciate efforts to improve their reasoning and decision-making skills, perhaps the most common focus of contemporary intervention programmes. However, attempts to exert influence had to be recognized as both credible and legitimate to be effective (Rex, 1999) which seemed to relate to the commitment and concern conveyed by the practitioner. Another feature of probationers' accounts of positive supervision was practitioners' efforts to reinforce pro-social behaviour (see Trotter 1999). Again, acceptance of such influence was generated by their ability to identify advice in this regard as evidence of concern for them as people (Rex, 1999). These findings lend support to the re-emergence of the significance of the practitioner-probationer relationships in enabling change in contemporary discussions of practice (see for example Burnett, 2004; Burnett and McNeill, 2005; Holt, 2000; Leibrich, 1993, 1994; McNeill et al., 2005; McNeill, 2006; McNeill and Weaver, 2010), and in enhancing compliance and promoting the legitimacy of interventions (Robinson and McNeill, 2008). Beyond the significance of processes and relationships, Rex's findings also relate to the content of probation interventions; her findings suggest that probationers valued guidance concerning their personal and social problems which she summarises as strengthening social ties.

As part of the 'Scottish Desistance Study', Barry (2007) asked young people for their perceptions about what helped them to reduce offending and their opinions on good practice. In relation to the former, addressing personal and social problems through the development of significant relationships with friends or family emerged as a central concern. Participants were particularly receptive to the interventions of practitioners who had taken the time to develop empathetic and constructive relationships with them. In particular, Barry's participants suggested that desistance supportive practices would include the provision of advice and guidance surrounding substance use; the provision of individualized interventions that recognize the realities of their lives; and assistance to access opportunities to make positive contributions to their community.

In looking toward the personal and social contexts of desistance, the most wide-scale longitudinal study of probation and desistance has been conducted by Farrall (2002; Farrall and Calverley, 2006; Farrall et al., 2014). In the first phase of this research programme, Farrall (2002) explored the progress, or otherwise, towards desistance achieved by a group of 199 probationers. Though over half of the sample evidenced progress towards desistance, he found that desistance could rarely be attributed to specific interventions by practitioners, although assistance in identifying employment opportunities and mending damaged familial relationships appeared particularly important. Yet it was in these areas that practitioners were found to be wary of intervening. The findings indicate that in terms of the identification and resolution of 'obstacles to desistance' only a minority of probationers and practitioners worked in partnership, with strategies to obstacle resolution pivoting around discussions of obstacles rather than more proactive and direct approaches. Successful resolution was perceived by both probationers and practitioners to be contingent on a range of factors often outside the control of either practitioner or probationer, and no specific method of probation intervention could be credited with successful obstacle resolution.

Rather, desistance seemed to relate more clearly to the probationers' motivations and to the social and personal contexts in which various obstacles to desistance were addressed. Changes in employment and family circumstances were related to positive changes in lifestyle and offending and were predominantly attributed to the efforts of probationers.

In 2002, then, the principle contribution of probation supervision to enabling desistance was indirect in terms of supporting probationers' self-initiated efforts to change. Since 2002, Farrall and colleagues (Farrall and Calverley, 2006; Farrall et al., 2014) have observed that these indirect benefits (i.e. instances of practical assistance or motivational and attitudinal shifts engendered by their interaction with probation officers) have been increasingly retrospectively recognized by those probationers as having a positive impact on them – in the longer term.[27] This suggests that probation supervision can 'sow the seeds of change ... but it may be some time before change actually occurs' (Farrall et al., 2014 p.123). Limitations to the impact of supervision include inadequate resources constraining probation officers' capacity to help, 'belligerent or obstructive' practitioners (ibid p.150) or the perceived inconsequence of such supervision where probationers viewed themselves as agents of their own change process.

Based on the findings of this study, Farrall (2002) advocates for interventions to be directed towards the community, and the social and personal contexts in which people are situated (see also McCulloch, 2005), utilizing, for example, the Capabilities Approach (Nussbaum, 2000; Sen, 1985, cited by Farrall et al., 2014). After all, 'social circumstances and relationships with others are *both* the object of the intervention *and* the medium through which ... change can be achieved' (Farrall, 2002 p.214). Necessarily this requires that interventions be focused not solely on the individual and his/her perceived deficits (McNeill, 2002). As Farrall (2002) observes, the problem with such interventions is that while they can build human capital, for example, in terms of enhanced cognitive skills or improved employability, they cannot generate social capital, which resides in the relationships through which participation and inclusion in society is facilitated (see also Farrall, 2004). Similarly, Shapland, Bottoms and Muir (2012), commenting on their Sheffield Desistance Study participants' perspectives of the criminal justice system, revealed that participants felt that work, relocation, disassociation from peers, and attachments to a partner or a family might enable change. However, like Farrall (2002), they learnt that practitioners were not attending to these desistance enabling factors in their interventions. Perhaps unsurprisingly then, only 9 percent of Shapland et al.'s (2012) participants felt that probation was helpful in enabling change; 45 percent did not consider probation to be helpful. They propose thus that probation might be more helpful in supporting change if workers engaged with practical issues of concern to participants.

The desistance-enabling features of current probation practice identified by King (2014) include enhancing a sense of agency by helping probationers to construct future strategies for change and equipping probationers with the necessary skills to support desistance. Relatedly, he identified that bureaucratic factors and procedural constraints impeded the progression of more proactive practices and affected the nature of the supervisory relationship. He found that the time constraints that bureaucratic and managerial pressures engendered limited the time that probation officers spent discussing the issues of relevance to probationers and the amount of practical assistance they provided. The result was a discrepancy between would-be-desisters' strategic planning for change and the kinds of discussions they might have about how these aspirations might be realised. As a consequence, King found that probationers moved from a projective form of agency, one that is future focused, to an iterational form, one that is retrospective wherein individuals draw on their past repertoires of thought and action to inform future activity in the absence of the kinds of individualised support that might help them find new ways of being and doing. While familial relations were central to some people, and places of residence important to others, all of his participants placed an unequivocal emphasis on the centrality of work to their strategies for reform, either as an objective in its own right or as a means of realising other objectives. Yet, as King's discussion of the barriers that his participants encountered acknowledges, this is an area in which many people with convictions experience discrimination and in which policy has focused almost exclusively on enhancing employability rather than addressing structural constraints and creating opportunities for employment.

McCulloch's (2005) study, based on twelve semi-structured interviews with probationers and their probation officers in Scotland, drew on probationer and practitioner perspectives to explore the attention given to probationers' social contexts in supporting desistance from crime. In contrast to Farrall (2002) she found that probationers and practitioners had little difficulty in reconciling the apparently polarised objectives of social support and offence-focused strategies, although, akin to Farrall (2002) and King (2014), she found that direct work in the area of employment was limited; that 'talking methods' were the most frequently cited approach to addressing social problems. Where obstacles to desistance were successfully resolved, participants attributed this both to probation intervention and the wider normative processes that occurred in the probationer's life. While, like Farrall (2002), she advocates an increased level of probation involvement in families and local communities, and a greater focus on integration, she does not elaborate on the kinds of practices through which this might be realized. Beyond suggesting that probation should 'direct its efforts towards developing the individual and community partnerships needed to enable probationers to achieve these goals themselves' (McCulloch, 2005 p.19), she does not elaborate how this might be realized, or how these relationships might be reconfigured.

Discussion

Desistance is arguably a central concern of the criminal justice system yet, as the preceding analysis has illustrated, much of the research on desistance has not been concerned directly with criminal justice interventions. Rather, as Maruna, Immarigeon and LeBel (2004 p.11) clarify, the desistance literature originally emerged from a 'critique of the professionally driven 'medical model' of corrections' and was concerned with the study of individuals who ceased offending without the assistance of criminal justice interventions. Indeed, the foregoing analysis seems to suggest that desistance occurs in spite of, or at least rarely because of, the interventions of the criminal justice system. Nevertheless, Maruna et al. (2004) argue that, in theory and in practice, desistance and rehabilitation do not need to be viewed as opposites; indeed 'desistance (self-change) and rehabilitation (change through intervention) might best be understood, for all practical purposes, as the same thing, or at least part of the same process' (ibid p.12). When behavioural change is understood as occurring through a combination of measures including self-initiated change, professional intervention, informal help, social support and social controls from informal social relationships, then the distinction between receiving professional intervention and not receiving any professional input becomes less important than understanding the actual experiences and processes to desistance (Farrall, 2002). In this sense, as McNeill (2003, 2006) argues, it is crucial then to understand not just 'what works' in terms of interventions but also *how and why* ex-offenders come to change their behaviours and, in turn, how professional interventions might effectively promote, support and assist these processes. To this end, Porporino (2010) commented that

> [t]he desistance paradigm suggests that we might be better off if we allowed offenders to guide us . . . listened to what they think might best fit their individual struggles out of crime, rather than continue to insist that our solutions are their salvation.
>
> (p.80)

Maruna and LeBel (2010 p.81) conclude that 'the desistance paradigm understands rehabilitation as a relational process best achieved in the context of relationship with others'. However, although the collective nature of much offending has been well documented (see for example Akers, 1998; Cloward and Ohlin, 1960; Sutherland, 1947; Warr, 2002) and while there has, more recently, been considerable attention to gangs (Aldrige, Medina and Ralphs, 2007; Bannister and Fraser, 2008; Deuchar, 2009; Klein, Weerman and Thornberry, 2006; Pyrooz, Decker and Webb, 2010; Pyrooz, Sweeten and Piquero, 2012) there has been scant research revealing the experiences of people who co-offend (a notable recent exception is Goldsmith and Halsey, 2013[28]), or on their subsequent processes of desistance. Indeed, the literature discussing the role of peers in relation to onset and persistence (see for example Farrington, 1992; Haynie, 2001, 2002; Warr, 1993, 2002) and desistance (see for example Calverley, 2013; Giordano, Cernkovich and Holland, 2003; Graham and Bowling, 1995; Massoglia and Uggen, 2010; Uggen and Kruttschnitt, 1998) rather polarises peers into 'anti-social' pressures or 'pro-social' influences, with each category representing different people or groups. Discussion principally surrounds the would-be-desister's decisive (Paternoster and Bushway, 2009, Paternoster and Pogarsky, 2009) or developmental (Giordano et al., 2003) disassociation from 'negative' influences and either re-connection with pro-social former associates or development of new pro-social relationships (see for example

Giordano et al., 2003; Knight and West, 1975) with further explanations principally deriving from social learning, differential association (Akers, 1973; Sutherland, 1947; Warr, 1993) or social control theories (see for example Sampson and Laub, 1993). These studies are usually refracted through the lens of the individual desister (see for example Warr, 1998; Cromwell et al., 1991) or more infrequently from the standpoint of the individual situated in a structural network of relations in a given context (see for example Haynie, 2001). There is, then, a limited understanding as to the ways in which the peer group, as a social relation, shapes and affects criminal behaviour and desistance, and how individual, relational, cultural and social contexts influence onset, persistence and desistance, and, thus on precursors, processes and consequences. There is, then, a significant gap in criminological understanding of the impact that a naturally forming group can exert on criminal careers – both empirically and theoretically.

Notes

1 Thanks to SAGE and to Professor Fergus McNeill for their kind permission to reproduce Professor McNeill's table 'Probation Practice in Four Paradigms', originally published in F. McNeill (2006), A Desistance Paradigm for Offender Management. *Criminology and Criminal Justice* 6(1), pp.37–60.
2 Probation paradigms generally delineate a set of practice ideals which historically include an outline of the form, nature or orientation of intervention; the method or approach applied to determine the type of intervention to be undertaken; and the basis or rationale for intervention. Since this time, McNeill (2012) has cautioned against a distractive focus on paradigmatic divisions and conflicts.
3 Maruna (2006a p.16) similarly argued that reintegration properly belongs to communities and to formerly incarcerated persons and that the role of the practitioner is to 'support, enhance and work with the organically occurring community processes of reconciliation and earned redemption'.
4 For an overview of operational definitions deployed in a range of empirical studies see Kazemian (2007).
5 Bottoms et al., (2004) present an argument for the study of desistance to include 'any significant lull or crime-free gap in the course of a criminal career' (p. 371).
6 See Bushway et al., 2001 for further discussions surrounding this conceptual distinction; see also Blumstein et al. (1986, 1988), Gottfredson and Hirschi (1986, 1988), and Laub and Sampson (2001).
7 For a discussion on the concept of intermittency, see Carlsson (2013).
8 Fagan (1989) defined desistance as the 'process of reduction in the frequency and severity of (family) violence, leading to its eventual end when 'true desistance' or 'quitting' occurs (p.380, quoted in Bushway et al., 2001).
9 Loeber and LeBlanc (1990 p.409) specified four components of desistance: 'deceleration', 'specialization', 'de-escalation' and 'reaching a ceiling' thus conceptualising desistance overall as a process from more to less serious offending over time (LeBlanc and Loeber, 1998).
10 Weitekamp and Kerner (1994) define termination as the time when the criminal behaviour stops permanently; in contrast, suspension is defined as a break in offending behaviour. They therefore view desistance as a process by which offending decelerates and exhibits less variety.
11 More fully: 'Primary deviation involved the initial flirtation and experimentation with deviant behaviors. Secondary deviation... is deviance that becomes "incorporated as part of the 'me' of the individual"' (Lemert, 1951 p.76, quoted in Maruna and Farrall, 2004).

A critical review of desistance research   35

12 For a critique of the distinction between primary and secondary desistance, see King (2014 p.33).
13 This refers in particular to the Glueck's 15-year longitudinal study of 1,000 juvenile delinquents (see Laub and Sampson, 2001).
14 For a discussion of neurological, psychological, and cognitive development, maturity and maturation see Prior et al. (2011).
15 Wright and Cullen (2004 p.185) replicated Warr's (1998) study but focused on employment rather than marriage. They identified that employment increased opportunities for individuals to interact and associate with pro-social co-workers, which, they reasoned, 'restructure friendship networks by diminishing contact with delinquent peers'. Wright and Cullen (2004 p.200) suggest that the effects of employment on desistance can be attributed to the 'quality of peer associations that occur within the context of work'.
16 It is widely accepted that social bonds include significant intimate or personal relationships, responsibilities and 'stakes in conformity' in a wider sense, and are not confined to the formal institutions of marriage or employment as such.
17 Schroeder and Frana (2009 p.2) draw on Fetzer ([1999] 2003 p.2) to differentiate between religiosity and spirituality. Religiosity is construed as a social experience 'that involves a system of worship and doctrine that is shared with a group' (ibid.). Spirituality is more personal and experiential and 'concerned with the transcendent, addressing ultimate questions about life's meaning, with the assumption that there is more to life than what we see or fully understand' (ibid.).
18 See also Maruna et al. (2006) on conversions to Christianity in prison.
19 See relatedly Bracken et al.'s (2009) study of desistance among Canadian, Aboriginal former gang members.
20 Giordano et al. (2007) relatedly proposed that religion can provide a 'cognitive blueprint for how one is to proceed as a changed individual' (Giordano et al. 2007 p.4); a blueprint found in the prescriptions and teachings associated with that faith, upon which the individual can draw as they embark on the process of desistance and encounter new situations and experiences.
21 Schroeder and Frana (2009) suggest that religion affords emotional comfort, a distraction from current stressors and contributes to demarcating the transition from deviance to conventionality, arguably symbolizing a shift in one's moral status.
22 See similarly Adjorjan and Chui (2011) on Christian faith.
23 For example Barry (2010) draws on Bourdieu's (1986) concepts of capital; Maruna and Farrall (2004), building on Farrall and Bowling (1999), draw on Gidden's (1984) theory of structuration; Giordano et al. (2002; 2003; 2007) draw on Mead's (1964) symbolic interactionist perspective; King (2010, 2012) draws on Archer's (2000; 2003) concept of the 'Internal Conversation' (see also Vaughan [2007] and Emirbayer and Mische's [1998] orientations of agency); Bottoms and Shapland (2010) and Farrall et al. (2010) draw on Mouzelis (2008).
24 As Carlsson (2012, p.4) elaborates, the impact of a 'turning point' is only really understood over time. To be clear, he argues that that it is not the event (i.e. work or marriage) that is in itself the change agent but the 'way such changes under certain circumstances bring about other changes' (Carlsson 2012 p.3). He conceptualises turning points as those 'crucial [processes] in which new lines of individual . . . activity are forged, in which new aspects of the self are brought into being (Becker 1966 p. xiv)'.
25 Symbolic interactionism suggests that people construct their identities as they evaluate others' attitudes towards them (Cooley, 1902/1922; Mead, 1934). This process occurs within and through social interactions which are, in particular, communicative exchanges.
26 Farrall et al. (2011) elucidate the relationship between a desister's actions (their agency, beliefs and identity) and the structural properties of the social system which shape desistance drawing on the conceptual framework elaborated by Mouzelis (2008). Their comprehensive modelling of the interaction between macro- and meso-level structural

influences and individual agency enables a particularly nuanced analysis of the processes that influence the nature, direction and timing of change processes.
27 For a detailed discussion of these findings see Farrall et al. (2014).
28 Goldsmith and Halsey (2013) examined the dynamics of serious and persistent offending of a co-offending network of young Indigenous Australian men dubbed the 'Gang of 49' by the media. Goldsmith and Halsey offer insights into the structural features of the network including issues of network density, mobility and the significance of place as well as the structural-relational features in terms of density of kinship and friendship ties and the sense of belonging and identity such ties engender. They also examine the role of alcohol in amplifying offending – as a 'device for socialisation', as a factor in 'bolstering the criminal proclivities of the group' (p.1170); as the direct/indirect object of acquisitive crime; and in amplifying harm caused.

References

Adjorjan, M., and Chui, W.H. (2011) Making Sense of Going Straight: Personal Accounts of Male Ex-Prisoners in Hong Kong. *British Journal of Criminology*. doi:10.1093/bjc/azr093

Akers, R.L. (1973) *Deviant Behaviour: A Social Learning Approach*. Belmont, CA: Wadsworth.

Akers, R.L. (1998) *Social Learning and Social Structure: A General Theory of Crime and Deviance*. Boston, MA: Northeastern University Press.

Aldridge, J., Medina, J., and Ralphs, R. (2007) *Youth Gangs in an English City: Social Exclusion, Drugs and Violence*. Full Research Report ESRC End of Award Report, RES-000–23–0615. Swindon: ESRC.

Archer, M. (2000) *Being Human: The Problem of Agency*. Cambridge: Cambridge University Press.

Archer, M. (2003) *Structure, Agency and the Internal Conversation*. Cambridge: Cambridge University Press.

Arendell, T. (2000) Conceiving and Investigating Motherhood: The Decade's Scholarship. *Journal of Marriage and Family* 62(4), pp.1192–1207.

Armstrong, R. (n.d.) *The Subdued Beast* (Unpublished PhD thesis, University of Cambridge, UK).

Baier, C.J., and Wright, B.R.E. (2001) "If you love me, keep my commandments": A Meta-Analysis of the Effect of Religion on Crime. *Journal of Research in Crime and Delinquency* 38(1), pp.3–21.

Bannister, J., and Fraser, A. (2008) Youth Gang Identification: Learning and Social Development in Restricted Geographies. *Scottish Journal of Criminal Justice Studies* 14, pp.96–114.

Barry, M. (2007) Youth Offending and Youth Transitions: The Power of Capital in Influencing Change. *Critical Criminology* 15(2), pp.185–198.

Becker, H.S. (1966) *Outsiders: Studies in the Sociology of Deviance*. New York, NY: Free Press.

Bersani, B., Laub, J.H., and Nieuwbeerta, P. (2009) Marriage and Desistance from Crime in the Netherlands: Do Gender and Socio-historical Context Matter? *Journal of Quantitative Criminology* 25(1), pp.3–24.

Bianchi, S.M., Casper, L.M., and King, R.B. (2005) *Work, Family, Health and Well-being*. Mahwah, NJ: Lawrence Erlbaum Associates.

Blokland, A.A.J., and Nieuwbeerta, P. (2005) The Effects of Life Circumstances on Longitudinal Trajectories of Offending. *Criminology* 43(4), pp.1203–1240.

Blumstein, A., and Cohen, J. (1979) Estimation of Individual Crime Rates From Arrest Records. *Journal of Criminal Law and Criminology* 70(4), pp.561–585.

Blumstein, A., and Cohen, J. (1987) Characterising Criminal Careers. *Science* 238(4818), pp.985–991.

Blumstein, A., Cohen, J., and Farrington, D. (1988) Criminal Career Research: Its Value for Criminology. *Criminology* 26(1), pp.1–35.

Blumstein, A., Cohen, J., Roth, J.A., and Visher, C.A. (eds.) (1986) *Criminal Careers and Career Criminals*. Washington, DC: National Academy Press.

Bottoms, A.E. (2014) Desistance from Crime, in Ashmore, Z., and Shuker, R. (eds.) *Forensic Practice in the Community*. Abingdon: Routledge, pp.251–273.

Bottoms, A.E., and Shapland, J. (2011) Steps Towards Desistance Among Male Young Adult Recidivists, in Farrall, S., Hough, M., Maruna, S., and Sparks, R. (eds.) *Escape Routes: Contemporary Perspectives on Life After Punishment*. London: Routledge, pp.43–80.

Bottoms, A.E., Shapland, J., Costello, A., Holmes, D., and Mair, G. (2004) Towards Desistance: Theoretical Underpinnings for an Empirical Study. *Howard Journal of Criminal Justice* 43(4), pp.368–389.

Bottoms, A.E., and Wiles, P. (1992) Explanations of Crime and Place, in Evans, D.J., Fyfe, N.R., and Herbert, D.T. (eds.) *Crime, Policing and Place*. London: Routledge, pp.11–35.

Bourdieu, P. (1986) The Forms of Capital, in Richardson, J. (ed.) *Handbook of Theory and Research for the Sociology of Education*. New York, NY: Greenwood, pp.214–258.

Bracken, D., Deane, L., and Morrissette, L. (2009) Desistance and Social Marginalization: the Case of Canadian Aboriginal Offenders. *Theoretical Criminology* 13(1), pp.61–78.

Burnett, R. (1992) *The Dynamics of Recidivism*. Oxford: University of Oxford Centre for Criminological Research.

Burnett, R. (2004) One-to-One Ways of Promoting Desistance: In Search of an Evidence Base, in Burnett, R., and Roberts, C. (eds.) *What Works in Probation and Youth Justice*. Cullompton: Willan, pp.180–197.

Burnett, R., and McNeill, F. (2005) The Place of the Officer–Offender Relationship in Assisting Offenders to Desist from Crime. *Probation Journal* 52(3), pp.247–268.

Bushway, S.D., Piquero, A., Broidy, L., Cauffman, E., and Mazerole, P. (2001) An Empirical Framework for Studying Desistance as a Process. *Criminology* 39(2), pp.496–515.

Calverley, A. (2013) *Cultures of Desistance: Rehabilitation, Reintegration and Ethnic Minorities*. Abingdon: Routledge.

Carlsson, C. (2012) Using 'Turning Points' to Understand Processes of Change in Offending: Notes from a Swedish Study on Life Course and Crime. *British Journal of Criminology* 52(1), pp.1–16.

Carlsson, C. (2013) Masculinities, Persistence, and Desistance. *Criminology* 51(3), pp.661–693.

Chu, D.C. (2007) Religiosity and Desistance from Drug Use. *Criminal Justice and Behavior* 34(5), pp.661–679.

Clarke, R.V., and Cornish, D.B. (1985) Modeling Offenders' Decisions: A Framework for Research and Policy, in Tonry, M., and Morris, N. (eds.) *Crime and Justice: An Annual Review of Research*, Vol. 6. Chicago, IL: University of Chicago Press, pp.147–185.

Cloward, R., and Ohlin, L. (1960) *Delinquency and Opportunity: A Theory of Delinquent Gangs*. Chicago, IL: Free Press.

Cohen, L.E., and Land, K.C. (1987) Age, Structure and Crime: Symmetry Versus Asymmetry and The Projection of Crime Rates Through the 1990s. *American Sociological Review* 52(2), pp.170–183.

Cooley, C.H. (1922) *Human Nature and the Social Order*. New York, IL: Scribner. (Original work published 1902.)

Cornish, D.B., and Clarke, R.V.G. (eds.) (1986) *The Reasoning Criminal: Rational Choice Perspectives on Offending*. Berlin: Springer-Verlag.

Côté, J. (1997) An Empirical Test of the Identity Capital Model. *Journal of Adolescence* 20(5), pp.577–597.

Cromwell, P.F., Olson, J.N., and D'Aunn, W.A. (1991) *Breaking and Entering: An Ethnographic Analysis of Burglary*. Newbury Park, CA: Sage.

Cusson, M., and Pinsonneault, P. (1986) The Decision to Give Up Crime, in Cornish, D.B., and Clarke, R.V. (eds.) *The Reasoning Criminal: Rational Choice Perspectives in Offending*. New York, NY: Springer-Verlag, pp.72–82.

Deuchar, R. (2009) Urban Youth Cultures and the Re-building of Social Capital: Illustrations from a Pilot Study in Glasgow. *Scottish Youth Issues Journal* 1, pp.7–22.

Dufour, I.F., Brassard, R., and Martel, J. (2013) An Integrative Approach to Apprehend Desistance. *International Journal of Offender Therapy and Comparative Criminology*. doi:10.1177/0306624X13509781

Edin, K., and Kefalas, M. (2005) *Promises I Can Keep: Why Poor Women Put Motherhood Before Marriage*. Berkeley: University of California Press.

Edin, K., Nelson, T.J., and Paranal, R. (2001) *Fatherhood and Incarceration as Potential Turning Points in the Criminal Careers of Unskilled Men*. Evanston, IL: Northwestern University Institution for Policy Research.

Emirbayer, M., and Mische, A. (1998) What Is Agency? *American Journal of Sociology* 103(4), pp.962–1023.

Fagan, J. (1989) Cessation of Family Violence: Deterrence and Dissuasion, in Ohlin, L., and Tonry, M. (eds.) *Crime and Justice: An Annual Review of Research*, Vol. 11. Chicago, IL: Chicago University Press, pp.377–425.

Farrall, S. (2002) *Rethinking What Works With Offenders: Probation, Social Context and Desistance from Crime*. Cullompton: Willan.

Farrall, S. (2004) Social Capital and Offender Reintegration: Making Probation Desistance Focussed, in Maruna, S., and Immarigeon, R. (eds.) *After Crime and Punishment: Pathways to Offender Reintegration*. Cullompton: Willan, pp.57–84.

Farrall, S. (2005) On the Existential Aspects of Desistance from Crime. *Symbolic Interaction* 28(3), pp.367–386.

Farrall, S., Bottoms, A.E., and Shapland, J. (2010) Social Structures and Desistance from Crime. *European Journal of Criminology* 7(6), pp.546–570.

Farrall, S., and Bowling, B. (1999) Structuration, Human Development and Desistance from Crime. *British Journal of Criminology* 39(2), pp.253–268.

Farrall, S., and Calverley, A. (2006) *Understanding Desistance From Crime: Theoretical Directions in Resettlement and Rehabilitation*. Oxford: Oxford University Press: Crime and Justice Series.

Farrall, S., Hunter, B., Sharpe, G., and Calverley, A. (2014) *Criminal Careers in Transition: The Social Context of Desistance from Crime*. Oxford: Oxford University Press: Clarendon Series in Criminology.

Farrall, S., Sharpe, G., Hunter, B., and Calverley, A. (2011) Theorizing Structural and Individual-Level Processes in Desistance and Persistence: Outlining an Integrated Perspective. *Australian and New Zealand Journal of Criminology* 44(2), pp.218–234.

Farrington, D.P. (1983) Randomized Experiments on Crime and Justice, in Tonry, M., and Morris, N. (eds.) *Crime and Justice: An Annual Review of Research*, Vol. 4. Chicago, IL: University of Chicago Press, pp.25–308.

Farrington, D.P. (1986) Age and Crime, in Tonry, M., and Morris, N. (eds.) *Crime and Justice: An Annual Review of Research*, Vol. 7. Chicago, IL: University of Chicago Press, pp.189–250.

Farrington, D.P. (1992) Criminal Career Research in the United Kingdom. *British Journal of Criminology* 32(4), pp.521–536.

Farrington, D.P. (1997) Human Development and Criminal Careers, in Maguire, M., Morgan, R., and Reiner, R. (eds.) *The Oxford Handbook of Criminology* (2nd ed.). Oxford: Clarendon Press, pp.361–408.

Farrington, D.P. (1999) A Criminological Research Agenda for the Next Millennium. *International Journal of Offender Therapy Comparative Criminology* 43(2), pp.154–167.

Farrington, D.P., and West, D.J. (1995) The Effects of Marriage, Separation, and Children on Offending by Adult Males, in Blau, Z.S., and Hagan, J. (eds.) *Current Perspectives on Aging and the Life Cycle: Vol. 4. Delinquency and Disrepute in the Life Course: Contextual and Dynamic Analyses*. Greenwich, CT: JAI Press, pp.249–281.

Fetzer Institute/National Institute on Aging Working Group. (1999, 2003 reprint) Multi-dimensional Measurement of Religiousness/Spirituality for Use in Health Research: A Report of the Fetzer Institute/National Institute on Aging Working Group. Kalamazoo, MI: Fetzer Institute. [13 full text instruments]. Available online at http://www.fetzer.org/resources/multidimensional-measurement-religiousnessspirituality-use-health-research, accessed 16/04/15.

Fleisher, M.S., and Krienert, J.L. (2004) Life-Course Events, Social Networks, and the Emergence of Violence Among Female Gang Members. *Journal of Community Psychology* 32(5), pp.607–622.

Flynn, N. (2010) *Criminal Behaviour in Context: Place, Space and Desistance from Crime*. International Series on Desistance and Rehabilitation. Cullompton: Willan.

Forrest, W., and Hay, C. (2011) Life Course Transitions, Self Control and Desistance from Crime. *Criminology and Criminal Justice* 11(5), pp.487–513.

Gibbens, T.C.N. (1984) Borstal Boys After 25 Years. *British Journal of Criminology* 24(1), 49–62.

Giddens, A. (1984) *The Constitution of Society*. Cambridge: Polity Press.

Giordano, P.C., Cernkovich, S.A., and Holland, D.D. (2003) Changes in Friendship Relations Over the Life Course: Implications for Desistance From Crime. *Criminology* 41(2), pp.293–328.

Giordano, P.C., Cernkovich, S.A., and Rudolph, J.L. (2002) Gender, Crime and Desistance: Toward a Theory of Cognitive Transformation. *American Journal of Sociology* 107, pp.990–1064.

Giordano P.C., Schroeder, R.D., and Cernkovich, S.A. (2007) Emotions and Crime Over the Life Course: A Neo-Median Perspective on Criminal Continuity and Change. *American Journal of Sociology* 112(6), pp.1603–1661.

Giordano, P.C., Seffrin, P.M., Manning, W.D., and Longmorn, M. (2011) Parenthood and Crime: The Role of Wantedness, Relationships With Partners, and SES. *Journal of Criminal Justice* 39(5), pp.405–416.

Glaser, D. (1964) *Effectiveness of a Prison and Parole System*. Indianapolis, IN: Bobbs-Merrill.

Glueck, S., and Glueck, E. (1940) *Juvenile Delinquents Grown Up*. New York, NY: Commonwealth Fund.

Glueck, S., and Glueck, E. (1974) *Of Delinquency and Crime*. Springfield, IL: Thomas.

Goffman, E. (1963) *Stigma: Notes on the Management of Spoiled Identity*. Harmondsworth: Prentice-Hall.

Goldsmith, A., and Halsey, M. (2013) Mobility, Place and Belonging in Indigenous Youth Co-Offending. *British Journal of Criminology* 53(6), pp.1157–1177.

Gottfredson, M., and Hirschi, T. (1986) The True Value of Lambda Would Appear to be Zero: an Essay on Career Criminals, Criminal Careers, Selective Incapacitation, Cohort Studies and Related Topics. *Criminology* 24(2), pp.213–234.

Gottfredson, M., and Hirschi, T. (1988) Science, Public Policy and the Career Paradigm. *Criminology* 26(1), pp.7–55.

Gottfredson, M., and Hirschi, T. (1990) *A General Theory of Crime*. Stanford, CA: Stanford University Press.

Gove, W.R. (1985) The Effect of Age and Gender on Deviant Behavior: A Biopsychosocial Perspective, in Rossi, A.S. (ed.) *Gender and the Life Course*. New York, NY: Aldine, pp.115–144.

Graham, J., and Bowling, B. (1995) *Young People and Crime*. Home Office Research Study No. 145. London: HMSO.

Hagan, J., and McCarthy, B. (1997) *Mean Streets: Youth Crime and Homelessness*. Cambridge: Cambridge University Press.

Haggard, U.A., Gumpert, C.H., and Grann, M. (2001) Against All Odds: A Qualitative Follow-up Study of High Risk Violent Offenders Who Were Not Reconvicted. *Journal of Interpersonal Violence* 16(10), pp.1048–1065.

Hauari, H., and Hollingworth, K. (2009) *Understanding Fathering: Masculinity, Diversity and Change*. York: Joseph Rowntree Foundation. Available at: http://www.jrf.org.uk/sites/files/jrf/understanding-fathering-diversity-full.pdf, accessed 14/05/2010.

Haynie, D.L. (2001) Delinquent Peers Revisited: Does Network Structure Matter? *American Journal of Sociology* 106(4), pp.1013–1057.

Haynie, D.L. (2002) Friendship Networks and Delinquency: The Relative Nature of Peer Delinquency. *Journal of Quantitative Criminology* 18(2), pp.99–134.

Healy, D. (2012) Advise, Assist and Befriend: Can Probation Supervision Support Desistance? *Social Policy and Administration* 46(4), pp.377–394.

Healy, D. (2013) Changing Fate? Agency and the Desistance Process. *Theoretical Criminology* 17(4), pp.557–574.

Healy, D. (2014) Becoming a Desister: Exploring the Role of Agency, Coping and Imagination in the Construction of a New Self. *British Journal of Criminology* 54(5), pp.873–891.

Hirschi, T. (1969) *Causes of Delinquency*. Berkeley: University of California Press.

Hirschi, T., and Gottfredson, M.R. (1983) Age and the Explanation of Crime. *American Journal of Sociology* 89, pp.552–584.

Holt, P. (2000) *'Case Management: Context for Supervision' Community and Criminal Justice: Monograph 2*. Leicester: De Montfort University.

Kazemian, L. (2007) Desistance from Crime: Theoretical, Empirical, Methodological and Policy Considerations. *Journal of Contemporary Criminal Justice* 23(1), pp.5–27.

Keizer, R., Dykstra, P.A., and Poortman, A.R. (2010) Life Outcomes of Childless Men and Fathers. *European Sociological Review* 26(1), pp.1–15.

Kiernan, K. (2004) Unmarried Cohabitation and Parenthood in Britain and Europe. *Law & Policy* 26(1), pp.33–55.

King, R.D., Massoglia, M., and Macmillan, R. (2007) The Context of Marriage and Crime: Gender, the Propensity to Marry and Offending in Early Adulthood. *Criminology* 45(1), pp.33–65.

King, S. (2010) *Going Straight on Probation: Desistance Transitions and the Impact of Probation*. Unpublished PhD dissertation. Available at: http://etheses.bham.ac.uk/3172/5/King_11_PhD.pdf, accessed 09/02/13.

King, S. (2012) Transformative Agency and Desistance from Crime. *Criminology and Criminal Justice*. doi:10.1177/1748895812452282

King, S. (2014) *Desistance Transitions and the Impact of Probation*. Abingdon: Routledge.

Klein, M.W., Weerman, F.M., and Thornberry, T.P. (2006) Street Gang Violence in Europe. *European Journal of Criminology* 3(4), pp.413–437.

Knight, B.J., Osborn, S.G., West, D.J. (1977) Early Marriage and Criminal Tendency in Males. *British Journal of Criminology* 17(4), pp.348–360.

Knight, B.J., and West, D.J. (1975) Temporary and Continuing Delinquency. *British Journal of Criminology* 15(1), pp.43–50.

Kreager, D.A., Matsueda, R.L., and Erosheva, E.A. (2010) Motherhood and Criminal Desistance in Disadvantaged Neighbourhoods. *Criminology* 48(1), pp.221–258.

Laub, J.H., Nagin, D.S., and Sampson, R.J. (1998) Trajectories of Change in Criminal Offending: Good Marriages and the Desistance Process. *American Sociological Review* 63, pp.225–238.

Laub, J.H., and Sampson, R.J. (1993) Turning Points in the Life Course: Why Change Matters to the Study of Crime. *Criminology* 31(3), pp.301–325.

Laub, J.H., and Sampson, R.J. (2001) Understanding Desistance from Crime, in Tonry, M.H., and Morris, N. (eds.) *Crime and Justice: An Annual Review of Research*, Vol. 26. Chicago, IL: University of Chicago Press, pp.1–78.

Laub, J.H., and Sampson, R.J. (2003) *Shared Beginnings, Divergent Lives*. Cambridge, MA: Harvard University Press.

LeBel, T.P., Burnett, R., Maruna, S., and Bushway, S. (2008) The 'Chicken and Egg' of Subjective and Social Factors in Desistance from Crime. *European Journal of Criminology* 5(2), pp.131–159.

LeBlanc, M., and Loeber, R. (1998) Developmental Criminology Updated, in Tonry, M. (ed.) *Crime and Justice: A Review of Research*, Vol. 23. Chicago, IL: University of Chicago Press, pp.115–197.

Leibrich, J. (1993) *Straight to the Point: Angles on Giving Up Crime*. Otago, New Zealand: University of Otago Press.

Leibrich, J. (1994) What Do Offenders Say About Going Straight? *Federal Probation* 58(2), pp.41–46.

Leibrich, J. (1996) The Role of Shame in Going Straight: A Study of Former Offenders, in Galaway, B., and Hudson, J. (eds.) *Restorative Justice: International Perspectives*. Monsey, NJ: Criminal Justice Press, pp.283–302.

Lemert, E.M. (1951) *Social Pathology: Systematic Approaches to the Study of Sociopathic Behavior*. New York, NY: McGraw-Hill.

Lichter, D.T., LeClere, F.B., and McLaughlin, D.K. (1991) Local Marriage Markets and the Marital Behavior of Black and White Women. *American Journal of Sociology* 96, pp.843–867.

Lim, C., and Putnam, R.D. (2010) Religion, Social Networks, and Life Satisfaction. *American Sociological Review* 75(6), pp.914–933.

Loeber, R., and LeBlanc, M. (1990) Toward a Developmental Criminology, in Tonry, M., and Morris, N. (eds.) *Crime and Justice: An Annual Review of Research*, Vol. 12. Chicago, IL: University of Chicago Press, pp.375–473.

Lyngstad, T.H., and Skardhamar, T. (2011) *Understanding the Marriage Effect: Changes in Criminal Offending Around the Time of Marriage*. Gemass Working Paper No.2. https://www.academia.edu/3851257/Changes_in_Criminal_Offending_around_the_Time_of_Marriage, accessed 23/12/14.

Marranci, G. (2006) *Jihad Beyond Islam*. Oxford: Berg.

Marranci, G. (2007, 26 July) *Faith, Ideology and Fear: The Case of Current and Former Muslim Prisoners.* IQRA Annual Lecture: House of Lords.

Marranci, G. (2009) *Faith, Ideology and Fear: Muslim Identities Within and Beyond Prisons.* London: Continuum.

Marsiglio, W., and Pleck, J.H. (2004) Fatherhood and Masculinities, in Kimmel, M.S., Hearn, J., and Connell R.W. (eds.) *Handbook of Studies on Men and Masculinities.* Thousand Oaks, CA: Sage, pp.249–269.

Maruna, S. (1997) Going Straight: Desistance from Crime and Life Narratives of Reform, in Lieblich, A., and Josselson, R. (eds.) *The Narrative Study of Lives,* Vol. 5. Thousand Oaks, CA: Sage, pp.59–93.

Maruna, S. (2001) *Making Good: How Ex-Convicts Reform and Rebuild their Lives.* Washington, DC: American Psychological Association Books.

Maruna, S., and Farrall, S. (2004) Desistance from Crime: A Theoretical Reformulation. *Kolner Zeitschrift für Soziologie und Sozialpsychologie* 43, pp.171–194.

Maruna, S., Immarigeon, R., and LeBel, T. (2004) Ex-Offender Reintegration: Theory and Practice, in Maruna, S., and Immarigeon, R. (eds.) *After Crime and Punishment: Pathways to Offender Reintegration.* Cullompton: Willan, pp.3–26.

Maruna, S., and LeBel, T. (2010) The Desistance Paradigm in Correctional Practice: From Programs to Lives, in McNeill, F., Raynor, P., and Trotter, C. (eds.) *Offender Supervision: New Directions in Theory and Practice.* Cullomptom: Willan, pp.65–89.

Maruna, S., Wilson, L., and Curran, K. (2006). Why God is Often Found Behind Bars: Prison Conversion and the Crisis of Self-Narrative. *Research in Human Development* 3(2&3), pp.161–184.

Massoglia, M., and Uggen, C. (2010) Settling Down and Aging Out: Toward an Interactionist Theory of Desistance and the Transition to Adulthood. *American Journal of Sociology* 116(2), pp.543–582.

Matza, D. (1964) *Delinquency and Drift.* New York, NY: Wiley.

McCulloch, T. (2005) Probation, Social Context and Desistance: Retracing the Relationship. *Probation Journal* 52(1), pp.8–22.

McGuire, J. (ed.) (1995) *What Works: Reducing Reoffending.* Chichester: Wiley.

McNeill, F. (2002) Beyond 'What Works': How and Why Do People Stop Offending? CJSW Briefing Paper 5. http://www.cjsw.ac.uk/sites/default/files/Briefing%20 Paper%205_final.pdf, accessed 8/11/03.

McNeill, F. (2003) Desistance-Focussed Probation Practice, in Chui, W.H., and Nellis, M. (eds.) *Moving Probation Forward: Evidence, Arguments and Practice.* Harlow: Pearson Longman, pp.146–162.

McNeill, F. (2006) A Desistance Paradigm for Offender Management. *Criminology and Criminal Justice* 6(1), pp.37–60.

McNeill, F. (2012) Four Forms of 'Offender' Rehabilitation: Towards an Interdisciplinary Perspective. *Legal and Criminological Psychology* 17(1), pp.18–36.

McNeill, F., Batchelor, S., Burnett, R., and Knox, J. (2005) *Twenty-First Century Social Work: Reducing Re-Offending: Key Practice Skills.* Edinburgh: Scottish Executive.

McNeill, F., and Weaver, B. (2010) *Changing Lives? Desistance Research and Offender Management.* SCCJR Report No. 03/2010. Research Output: Research Report. Published online at: http://www.sccjr.ac.uk/documents/Report%202010_03%20-%20 Changing%20Lives.pdf, accessed 09/07/13.

Mead, G.H. (1934) *Mind, Self and Society.* Chicago, IL: University of Chicago Press.

Mead, G.H. (1964) *Selected Writings.* Indianapolis, IN: Bobbs-Merrill.

Meisenhelder, T. (1977) An Exploratory Study of Exiting from Criminal Careers. *Criminology* 15, pp.319–334.

Meisenhelder, T. (1982) Becoming Normal: Certification as a Stage in Exiting From Crime. *Deviant Behavior: An Interdisciplinary Journal* 3, pp.137–153.

Miller, M.K. (2006) *Religion in Criminal Justice*. New York, NY: LFB Scholarly.

Moloney, M., MacKenzie, K., Hunt, G., and Joe-Laidler, K. (2009) The Path and Promise of Fatherhood for Gang Members. *British Journal of Criminology* 49(3), pp.305–325.

Monsbakken, C.W., Lyngstad, T.H., and Skardhamar, T. (2012a) Crime and The Transition to Parenthood: The Role of Sex and Relationship Context. *British Journal of Criminology* 53(1), pp.129–148.

Monsbakken, C.W., Lyngstad, T.H., and Skardhamar, T. (2012b) *Crime and The Transition to Marriage: The Roles of Gender and Partner's Criminal Involvement*, Discussion Papers Statistics Norway Research Department, No. 678, February 2012. http://www.ssb.no/a/publikasjoner/pdf/DP/dp678.pdf, accessed 23/12/14.

Moore, J.W., and Hagedorn, J.M. (1999) What Happens to Girls in the Gang? in Chesney-Lind, M., and Hagedorn, J.M. (eds.) *Female Gangs in America*. Chicago, IL: Lake View Press, pp.177–186.

Mouzelis, N. (2008) *Modern and Post-modern Social Theorising*. Cambridge: Cambridge University Press.

Nagin, D.S., and Paternoster, R. (1994) Personal Capital and Social Control: the Deterrence Implications of Individual Differences in Criminal Offending. *Criminology* 32(4), pp.581–606.

Newburn, T. (2002) Young People, Crime and Youth Justice, in Maguire, M., Morgan, R., and Reiner, R. (eds.) *The Oxford Handbook of Criminology* (3rd ed.). Oxford: Oxford University Press, pp.531–578.

Nussbaum, M. (2000) *Women and Human Development*. Cambridge: Cambridge University Press.

Osborn, S.G., and West, D.J. (1979) Conviction Records of Fathers and Sons Compared. *British Journal of Criminology* 19(2), pp.120–133.

Osgood, D.W., and Lee, H. (1993) Leisure Activities, Age, and Adult Roles Across the Lifespan. *Society and Leisure* 16, pp.181–208.

Ouimet, M., and LeBlanc, M. (1996) The Role of Life Experiences in the Continuation of the Adult Criminal Career. *Criminal Behaviour and Mental Health* 6(1), pp.73–97.

Owens, B. (2009) Training and Employment in an Economic Downturn: Lessons for Desistance Studies. *Irish Probation Journal* 6, pp.49–65.

Paternoster, R. (1989) Decisions to Participate in and Desist from Four Types of Common Delinquency: Deterrence and the Rational Choice Perspective. *Law and Society Review* 23(1), pp.7–40.

Paternoster, R., and Bushway, S. (2009) Desistance and the 'Feared Self': Toward an Identity Theory of Criminal Desistance. *Journal of Law and Criminology* 99(4), pp.1103–1156.

Paternoster, R., and Pogarsky, G. (2009) Rational Choice, Agency and Thoughtfully Reflective Decision Making: The Short and Long-Term Consequences of Making Good Choices. *Journal of Quantitative Criminology* 25(2), pp.103–127.

Piliavin, I., Gartner, R., Thornton, C., and Matsueda, R. (1986) Crime, Deterrence, and Rational Choice. *American Sociological Review* 51(1), pp.101–119.

Pleck, E.H. (2004) Two Dimensions of Fatherhood: a History of the Good Dad–Bad Dad Complex, in Lamb, M.E. (ed.) *The Role of The Father in Child Development* (4th ed.). New York, NY: Wiley, pp.32–57.

Porporino, F. (2010) Bringing Sense and Sensitivity to Corrections: From Programmes to 'Fix' Offenders to Services to Support Desistance, in Brayford, J., Cowe, F., and Deering, J. (eds.) *What Else Works? Creative Practice With Offenders*. Cullompton: Willan, pp.61–86.

Prior, D., Farrow, K., Hughes, N., Kelly, G., Manders, G., White, S., and Wilkinson, B. (2011) *Maturity, Young Adults and Criminal Justice: A Literature Review*. London: Transition to Adulthood Alliance/Barrow Cadbury Trust.

Pyrooz, D.C., Decker, S.H., and Webb, V.J. (2010) The Ties that Bind: Desistance from Gangs. *Crime and Delinquency*. doi:10.1177/0011128710372191

Pyrooz, D.C., Sweeten, G., and Piquero, A.R. (2012) Embeddedness, Continuity and Change in Gang Membership and Gang. *Journal of Research in Crime and Delinquency*. doi:10.1177/0022427811434830

Rand, A. (1987) Transitional Life Events and Desistance From Delinquency and Crime, in Wolfgang, M.E, Thornberry, T.P., and Figurelio, R.M. (eds.) *From Boy to Man, From Delinquency to Crime*. Chicago, IL: University of Chicago Press, pp.134–162.

Rex, S. (1999) Desistance From Offending: Experiences of Probation. *Howard Journal of Criminal Justice* 36(4), pp.366–383.

Rhodes, J. (2008) Ex-offenders' Social Ties and the Routes into Employment. *Internet Journal of Criminology* 1, pp.1–20.

Robinson, G., and McNeill, F. (2008) Exploring the Dynamics of Compliance with Community Penalties. *Theoretical Criminology* 12(4), pp.431–449.

Rumgay, J. (2004) Scripts for Safer Survival: Pathways Out of Female Crime. *Howard Journal of Criminal Justice* 43(4), pp.405–419.

Rutherford, A. (1992) *Growing Out of Crime: The New Era*. Winchester: Waterside Press.

Rutter, M. (1996) Transitions and Turning Points in Developmental Psychopathology: As Applied to the Age Span Between Childhood and Mid-adulthood. *Journal of Behavioural Development* 19(3), pp.603–626.

Sampson, R.J., and Laub, J.H. (1993) *Crime in the Making: Pathways and Turning Points Through Life*. London: Harvard University Press.

Sampson, R.J., and Laub, J.H. (2004) A General Age-Graded Theory of Crime: Lessons Learned and The Future of Life-Course Criminology, in Farrington, D. (ed.) *Advances in Criminological Theory: Testing Integrated Developmental/Life Course Theories of Offending: Advances in Criminological Theory*, Vol. 14. Edison, NJ: Transaction, pp.165–182.

Sampson, R.J., and Laub, J.H. (2005) A Life-Course View of the Development of Crime. *ANNALS: American Academy of Political and Social Science* 602(1), pp.12–45.

Sampson, R.J., Laub, J.H., and Wimer, C. (2006) Does Marriage Reduce Crime?: A Counter-Factual Approach to Within-Individual Causal Effects *Criminology* 44(3), pp.465–508.

Savolainen, J. (2009) Work, Family and Criminal Desistance. *British Journal of Criminology* 49(3), pp.285–304.

Schroeder, R., and Frana, J. (2009) Spirituality and Religion, Emotional Coping, and Criminal Desistance: A Qualitative Study of Men Undergoing Change. *Sociological Spectrum: Mid-South Sociological Association* 29(6), pp.718–741.

Sen, A. (1985) *Commodities and Capabilities*. Amsterdam: North Holland.

Shanahan, M.J. (2000) Pathways to Adulthood in Changing Societies: Variability and Mechanism in Lifecourse Perspective. *Annual Review of Sociology* 26, pp.667–692.

Shannon, S., and Abrams, L. (2007) Juvenile Offenders as Fathers: Perceptions of Fatherhood, Crime and Becoming an Adult. *Families in Society* 88(2), pp.183–191.

Shapland, J.M., and Bottoms, A.E. (2011) Steps Towards Desistance Among Male and Young Adult Recidivists, in Farrall, S., Sparks, R., Maruna, S., and Hough, M. (eds.) *Escape Routes: Contemporary Perspectives on Life After Punishments*. Abingdon: Routledge, pp.43–77.
Shapland, J., Bottoms, A.E., and Muir, G. (2012) Perceptions of the Criminal Justice System Among Young Adult Desisters, in Lösel, F., Bottoms, A.E., and Farrington, D.P. (eds.) *Young Adult Offenders Lost in Transition?* Abingdon: Routledge, pp.128–145.
Shavit, Y., and Rattner, A. (1988) Age, Crime and the Early Life Course. *American Journal of Sociology* 93(6), pp.1457–1470.
Shover, N. (1983) The Later Stages of Ordinary Property Offender Careers. *Social Problems* 31(2), pp.208–218.
Shover, N. (1985) *Aging Criminals*. Beverly Hills, CA: Sage.
Shover, N. (1996) *Great Pretenders: Pursuits and Careers of Persistent Thieves*. Oxford: Oxford University Press.
Siennick, S.E., and Osgood, D.W. (2008) A Review of Research on the Impact on Crime of Transitions into Adult Roles, in Liberman, A. (ed.) *The Long View of Crime: A Synthesis of Longitudinal Research*. New York, NY: Springer, pp.161–187.
Simons, R.L., Stewart, E., Gordon, L.C., Conger, R.D., and Elder, G.H. (2002) A Test of Life Course Explanations for Stability and Change in Antisocial Behaviour from Adolescence to Young Adulthood. *Criminology* 40(2), pp.401–434.
Skardhamar, T., and Savolainen, J. (2012, November) *Does Employment Contribute to Desistance? Offending Trajectories of Crime-Prone Men Around the Time of Job Entry*. Discussion Papers, Statistics Norway Research Department, No. 716.
Soyer, M. (2014) The Imagination of Desistance: A Juxtaposition of the Construction of Incarceration as a Turning Point and the Reality of Recidivism. *British Journal of Criminology* 54, pp.91–108.
Steffensmeier, D.J., Allan, E.A., Harer, M.D., and Streifel, C. (1989) Age and the Distribution of Crime. *American Journal of Sociology* 94(4), pp.803–831.
Steffensmeier, D.J., and Harer, M.D. (1987) Is the Crime Rate Really Falling? An Aging U.S Population and its Impact on the Nation's Crime Rate 1980–1984. *Journal of Research and Delinquency* 24(1), pp.23–48.
Sutherland, E.H. (1947) *The Principles of Criminology* (4th ed.). Chicago, IL: J.B. Lippincott.
Sviridoff, M., and Thompson, J.W. (1983) Links Between Employment and Crime: A Qualitative Study of Rikers Island Releasees. *Crime and Delinquency* 29(2), pp.195–212.
Topalli, V., Brezina, T., and Bernhard, M. (2012) With God on My Side: The Paradoxical Relationship Between Religious Belief and Criminality Among Hardcore Street Offenders. *Theoretical Criminology*. doi:10.1177/1362480612463114
Trasler, G. (1979) Delinquency, Recidivism and Desistance. *British Journal of Criminology* 19(4), pp.314–322.
Trotter, C. (1999) *Working with Involuntary Clients: A Guide to Practice*. London: Sage.
Uggen, C. (2000) Work as a Turning Point in the Life Course of Criminals: A Duration Model of Age, Employment and Recidivism. *American Sociological Review* 65, pp.529–546.
Uggen, C., and Kruttschnitt, C. (1998) Crime in the Breaking: Gender Differences in Desistance. *Law and Society Review* 32(2), pp.339–366.
Uggen, C., Manza, J., and Behrens, A. (2004). Less Than the Average Citizen: Stigma, Role Transition and the Civic Reintegration of Convicted Felons, in Maruna, S., and Immarigeon, R. (eds.) *After Crime and Punishment: Pathways to Offender Reintegration*. Cullompton: Willan, pp.258–290.

Vaughan, B. (2007) The Internal Narrative of Desistance. *British Journal of Criminology* 47(3), pp.390–404.

Vold, G.B., Bernard, T.J., and Snipes, J.B. (1998) *Theoretical Criminology* (4th ed.). New York, NY: Open University Press.

Warr, M. (1993) Parents, Peers and Delinquency. *Social Forces* 72(1), pp.247–264.

Warr, M. (1998) Life-Course Transitions and Desistance from Crime. *Criminology* 36(2), pp.183–216.

Warr, M. (2002) *Companions in Crime: The Social Aspects of Criminal Conduct*. Cambridge: Cambridge University Press.

Weaver, B. (2012) The Relational Context of Desistance: Some Implications and Opportunities for Social Policy. *Social Policy and Administration* 46(4), pp.395–412.

Weitekamp, E.G., and Kerner, H.J. (1994) Epilogue: Work-shop and Plenary Discussions, and Future Directions, in Weitekamp, E.G., and Kerner, H.J. (eds.) *Cross-National Longitudinal Research on Human Development and Criminal Behaviour*. Dordrecht: Kluwer Academic, pp.439–449.

West, D.J. (1982) *Delinquency: Its Roots, Careers and Prospects*. London: Heinemann.

West, D.J., and Farrington, D.P. (1977) *The Delinquent Way of Life*. London: Heinemann.

Wilson, J.Q., and Herrnstein, R.J. (1985) *Crime and Human Nature*. New York, NY: Simon and Schuster.

Wright, J.P., and Cullen, F.T. (2004) Employment, Peers and Life-course Transitions. *Justice Quarterly* 21(1), pp.183–205.

3 Critical realism and relational sociology
A conceptual framework for theorising desistance[1]

Introduction

The preceding chapter provided a critical analysis of the empirical and theoretical literature on desistance. It was observed that contemporary studies tend to conceptualise the process of desistance as being influenced to various degrees by external factors and/or internal or subjective factors, with different theories proposing that one or the other is of particular influential significance – often at a given time, or in a given situation – to the process of desistance, with variations further seeking to identify the relative influence of one on another or seeking to understand the temporal process wherein one or other becomes more or less prominent in terms of their relative significance to the desistance process (see Farrall and Bowling, 1999; LeBel et al., 2008 for example). What has emerged from this are studies that variously emphasise the role of structural factors in the desistance process, and which portray either an over-socialised perspective of the individual (*homo sociologicus*), or which emphasise the role of agentic factors, and thus which portray an under-socialised, overly cognitive individual (*homo economicus*), who can choose to stop offending at will. In the main, most studies variously integrate structural and agentic factors but, it is argued here, that by relegating social relations to the domain of structures and by neglecting to analyse the dynamics or properties of social relations, they essentially lose sight of the individual-in-relation (*homo relatus*); the reflexive individual in his or her relationally and emotionally textured world.

At its most simplistic level,[2] agency refers to the capacity of individuals to act independently and to 'construct their actions along lines of their own choosing' (Cheal, 2005 p.187). Structure generally refers to the recurrent patterned arrangements in society, such as class for example, which to a greater or lesser degree influence or constrain the choices and opportunities available to the individual (ibid). Many social theorists, however, pursue a balance between the two (see for example Archer, 1995, 2003, 2007a, 2007b, 2010; Berger and Luckmann, 1966; Bourdieu, 1986, 1990; Giddens, 1984, Mouzelis, 1995). Such theories suggest that structures influence human behaviours and humans are, in turn, capable of effecting change in the socio-structural contexts they inhabit. However, the structure-agency coupling itself leads to a series of common problems in that they fail to illuminate *how* social structures shape decisions by ignoring how and why agents are reflexive, such that they seek to influence or alter their socio-structural context.

Archer's critical realist, morphogenetic approach[3] seeks to address these shortcomings. While her approach is discussed more fully below, in brief, she elaborates the way in which structural properties, or conditioning structures, both enable and constrain individual action. She puts forward a theory of personal reflexivity, manifest in the 'internal conversation', which she argues is the mediating force between structure and agency (Archer, 2000, 2003). Archer argues that reflexivity performs this mediating role 'by virtue of the fact that we deliberate about ourselves in relation to the social situations we confront' (2007a p.42). Personal reflexivity is, in her formulation, the means through which people identify and order the ultimate concerns they commit themselves to. She regards a concern as 'an end that is desired, however tentatively or nebulously, and also a notion, however imprecise, of the course of action through which to accomplish it' (Archer, 2003 p.6). The morphogenetic approach is able to account thus for the way in which individuals both receive and respond to conditioning structures. While Archer's morphogenetic approach can offer a richly textured theoretical account of the dynamic relationship between structure and agency, Archer's approach has some significant limitations. In particular, Archer fails to provide an account of the context in which these ultimate concerns arise. This is because her focus remains essentially individualistic and, as such, while she is able to demonstrate that 'who we are is what we care about' (Archer, 2006), she is unable to elaborate on the relational context within which these cares emerge.

It is argued here, following Pierpaolo Donati, that it is our relationships that constitute 'who we are' and are thus the context within which our ultimate concerns arise.

> We are our 'relational concerns', as individuals as well as social agents/actors, since we necessarily live in many different contexts that are social circles (like a family, a network of friends, maybe a civil association, up to a nation) which imply a collective entity.
>
> (Donati, 2011a p.xvi)

Donati argues, contra to current socio-theoretical preoccupations with the agent or the structure, that it is the social relation which is the key to understanding social reality and social changes. The social relation is conceptualised by Donati as those bonds maintained between subjects that constitute their reciprocal orientations towards each other; it is the 'reality in between', that which exists *between* people, which 'are both the product of concrete human beings and also that which helps to forge them' (Donati, 2011a p.61), 'which depend on the[m] . . ., but at the same time goes beyond them and exceeds them' (2011a p.26).

Donati elaborates that social relations have become the 'unknown object' (of theory, research and in practice) even though 'thought becomes more and more "relational"' (2011a p.4). 'Everyone speaks of social relations, as do all social theories. But the fact of the matter is that most people, like most social theorists, think of social relations as a product of the Self or as an external constraint impinging on it.' (2011a p.xv). Indeed, he argues that

> the object of sociology is neither the so-called subject [as in explanations of desistance informed by, for example, rational choice theories], nor the social system [as in explanations of desistance informed by theories that emphasise the role of structures exerting exogenous forces], nor equivalent couplets (structure and agency, life-worlds and social systems) [as in explanations of desistance informed by interactionist efforts that fall short of providing insights into the 'why?' questions so frequently posed by desistance] but . . . the social relation itself.
>
> (Donati, 2011a p.4–5 [this author's insertions])

In order to shed light on social relations, Donati forwards a relational paradigm for sociology which depends and builds upon the social ontology of critical realism. This chapter will thus proceed to outline Archer's 'Morphogenetic Approach' and her concept of the 'Internal Conversation', which informs the conceptual framework employed in this study with which this chapter concludes. However, while a critical realist framework can be utilised to analyse individual contributions to the desistance process, Archer's approach cannot adequately account for the role of social relations in offending and desistance. This chapter thus progresses a conceptual framework that draws on the complementary approaches of Archer's critical realist morphogenetic approach and Donati's relational paradigm. The relational contributions to the desistance process are analysed using an adaptation of Archer's morphogenetic sequence applied to Donati's theory of social relations. In so doing, it is suggested that the relational realist conceptual framework advanced here gives proper recognition to the distinct characteristics, properties and powers of individual actions, social relations and social systems.

The morphogenetic approach and the internal conversation

Archer's morphogenetic approach is essentially a theory of social change which is concerned with explaining how the causal power of social structures and cultural systems is mediated through agency. Her elaboration of the process of morphogenesis comprises three phases; namely, structural conditioning, social interaction, and structural reproduction/elaboration (see Figure 3.1).

As Figure 3.1 illustrates, this three-part cycle of change is temporally sequential in that structure precedes the actions that ultimately alter it and, in turn, structural elaboration inevitably ensues from those actions (Archer, 2010). The conditioning influence of the structural/cultural context (*relation a*) shapes the social environment and, as part of that, people's situations of action such that some courses of action are enabled and others constrained. The properties of the structural/cultural context include the results of past actions, the accessibility of roles and resources and the prevalence of internalised beliefs (Archer, 1995,

Structural Conditioning

T 1

Social Interaction ← Relation A

T 2   T 3

Structural Reproduction (morphostasis) ← Relation B

T 4

Structural Elaboration (morphogenesis)

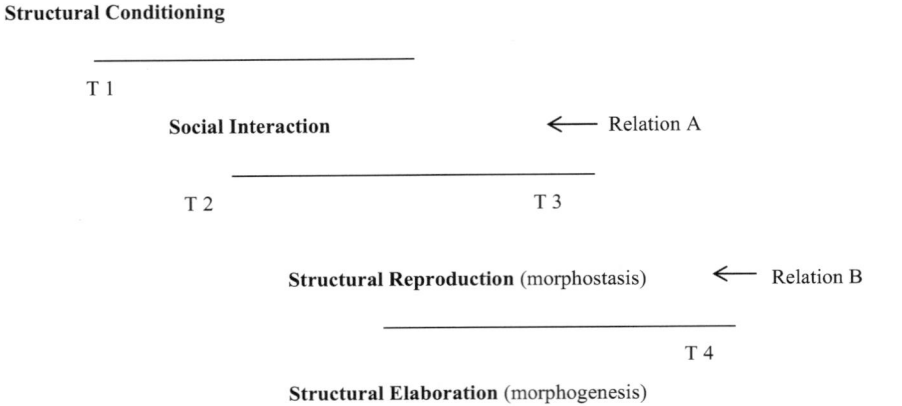

Figure 3.1 The basic morphogenetic sequence (source Archer, 2010)

2010). *Relation b* in Figure 3.1 refers to the process through which conditioning structures are mediated through agency by the application of personal reflexivity. *Relation b* is therefore decisive as to whether conditioning structures exert a similar level of influence on agents as they did at the initial T1 (as would be the case if morphostasis was the outcome) or whether the conditioning structures, and their influence, are modified and altered (as would be the case if morphogenesis were the outcome) (Archer, 2010).

Social structures and cultural systems structure the situations of action through constraints and enablements. However, Archer (2010) theorises that if contextual or structural conditioning exerts an influence through constraints and enablements then this only accounts for how structural and cultural properties objectively impact upon agents (*relation a*). This is because there are no independently operating constraints and enablements to the extent that for anything to exert the power of a constraint or an enablement it has to stand in a relationship such that it constrains or enables the achievement of some specific individual endeavour (Archer, 2010). These endeavours are what Archer refers to as 'projects' which she defines as any end or objective that can be intentionally pursued or considered by human beings. This means that the extent to which conditioning structures operate as either a constraint or enablement depends on how the individual receives or responds to their influence. Individual agents reflexively deliberate about how they will respond and, to a greater or lesser degree, they can endure or evade that influence (Archer, 2010).

In this vein, personal reflexivity (which takes the form of an internal conversation) is the mediating force between conditioning structures and agency. Archer argues that reflexivity performs this mediating role 'by virtue of the fact that we deliberate about ourselves in relation to the social situations we confront, certainly fallibly, certainly incompletely' (2007a p.42). Critically, these concerns, projects and practices need not be virtuous or legal or, like Archer's (2003) 'fractured reflexive', they may reflect an inability to order a set of practices, a way of being in the world. Rather, such people find themselves buffeted and beholden to a life of delinquency and drift rather than expressing an explicit dedication to a life of crime. This framework thus permits a conceptual lens that accommodates processes of both persistence in and desistance from crime.

In the interest of clarity, this understanding of social change is distinct therefore from some influential desistance accounts that claim to lend equal weight to both structure and agency (e.g. Laub and Sampson, 2001, 2003) but which do not operate with this kind of reflexivity. Rather the role of the agent characteristically remains subordinate to the role of structures which are seen to condition (Laub and Sampson, 2001), if not determine (Laub, Nagin and Sampson,1998), human action and thus desistance. As a result, such theories fail to consider 'how the agent originally submitted to these forces and why they remain enthralled by them' (Vaughan, 2007 p.390). While it might be argued that the availability of roles and the accompanying 'scripts' (Rumgay, 2004), behaviours and practices attributed to the role might become habitualised, people do not march through life mechanically responding to or animating fixed role structures. The personification or interiorisation of a role, which is neither pre-determined nor fixed, is accomplished by an individual reflecting on their situation through the lens of their ultimate concerns and the range of actions available to them (Archer, 2003). According to Archer, it is this reflexive internal dialogue about ourselves in relation to society and vice versa that makes active agents, people who can exercise some control over their lives as opposed to passive agents to whom things simply happen. It is argued here that this is what Archer's morphogenetic approach offers to understanding individual contributions to desistance.

Deconstructing Archer's internal conversation

The dynamic process of reflexivity: individual contributions to outcomes

Archer re-deploys the morphogenetic sequence to illustrate the process of reflexivity (Archer, 2003 p.112–16). She distinguishes three phases in the analytical process (see Figure 3.2).

Archer disaggregates the self into the temporal concepts of 'Me', 'I' and 'You'. Generally, 'Me' refers to the pre-existing self; 'I' refers to the present self; 'You' refers to the future self. The conditioning 'Me' phase, and the emerging results of previous reflexive deliberations fed through previous interactions, condition an individual's actions at T1. The 'I' phase (at T2–T3) evokes an internal conversation, conditioned by the pre-existing self, the 'Me', which defines a future direction, and in so doing shapes and influences the 'You' of the future (T4). It is through these means that we decide on courses of actions by deliberating about ourselves, our current concerns and social contexts, and by envisioning and pursuing projects that reflect and define who we are, that enable us to realise our ultimate concerns in circumstances that are, to some extent, pre-defined. This

52 *Critical realism, relational sociology*

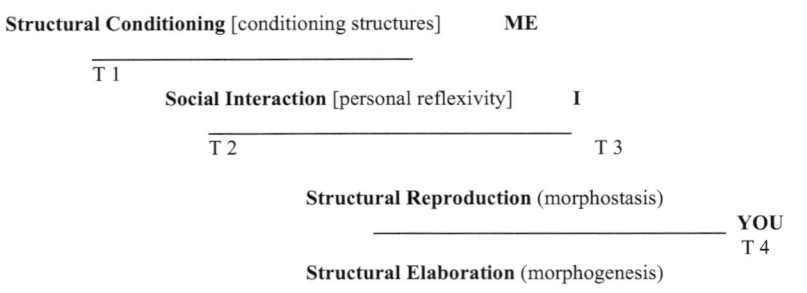

Structural Conditioning [conditioning structures]   **ME**
―――――――――――――――――――――――――――
T 1
             Social Interaction [personal reflexivity]   **I**
             ―――――――――――――――――――――――――――
             T 2   T 3
                          Structural Reproduction (morphostasis)
                          ―――――――――――――――――――――――   **YOU**
                                                          T 4
                          Structural Elaboration (morphogenesis)

Figure 3.2 The morphogenetic sequence applied to the internal conversation (based on Figure 1.1)

internal conversation temporarily concludes when the different parts of the self arrive at a consensus about the projected course of action that best reflects the individual's 'constellations of concerns' (Archer, 2007a p.42), but which is also realisable within the constraints of the individual's social circumstances.

Archer suggests that the internal conversation can be conceptualized as a three-part schema, namely discernment, deliberation and dedication. This internal conversation 'takes place' in the middle stage (T2–T3) of each morphogenetic cycle (Archer, 2000 p.231) (see Figure 3.2).

> At any time a life entails the things we are doing, the things we have done and the things we could do, which relate to the 'I', the 'Me' and the 'You' respectively. Discernment is basically about putting together the reflective, retrospective and prospective through a dialogue which reviews by comparing and contrasting them.
>
> (Archer, 2000 p.233)

'Discernment' (Archer, 2000 p.232–5) is essentially an 'inconclusive moment of review' (ibid p.235) wherein individuals, or the 'I', review their current concerns and, through that lens, their levels of satisfaction or otherwise with their existing circumstances. In this phase, the person also reviews the possible alternative lifestyle choices available to them, in contrast to their current lifestyle, reflecting a 'willing[ness] to consider different options' (Vaughan, 2007 p.394). For the would-be-desister for example, this may manifest in terms of the individual's increased amenability towards the possibility of an alternative way of life that does not include offending and which may be triggered by various factors, for example, the acquisition of employment, which registers with the individual as something desirable, as a personal concern. Where, in this regard, a valued concern is in jeopardy, Archer theorises that the 'You' reproaches the 'I' for endangering it. It says, 'How could you . . .' and runs through a scenario in which continued offending and potential imprisonment might imperil employment for example. But the 'You' also challenges the 'I' by bringing up an agenda where new possibilities are explored, such as 'if you care so much about your job, why are you meeting the boys again?' Archer supposes that in this phase, we review different scenarios of a life that can accommodate the realization or maintenance of our key concerns.

The second phase of the internal conversation, 'deliberation' (Archer, 2000 p.235–7), comprises an evaluative, cost-benefit exploration of the worth of one's ultimate concerns; in this process, various concerns are compared and weighed up against each other and (provisionally) ranked accordingly. To evaluate whether the self has the 'emotional shoving power' (Archer, 2000 p.236) and resolve to initiate and sustain the necessary courses of action required to realize one's concerns, the 'I' and the 'You' contemplate the potential scenarios that might ensue. In this phase of the internal conversation, 'the 'You' reflects upon the 'I's' experiences of itself, the 'Me', and the 'I' assesses the strength of the 'You's' inclinations' (ibid p.237). The outcome of these deliberations is a re-organisation of one's concerns.

The 'final' phase of the internal conversation is 'Dedication'. In this phase, the internal conversation between the 'I' and the 'You' manifests in a prioritization of concerns such that the individual commits him- or herself to an ultimate concern, to that which he or she cares most about (such as a particular job or relationship). In so doing, the 'I' and the 'You' conduct a final appraisal of the terms and conditions of this single concern and its implications for other valued concerns. Where the terms and conditions are mutually accepted by the 'I' and the 'You', other concerns are organised around the agreed ultimate concern in accordance with their relative worth. It is in dedicating one's self to this 'unique pattern of commitments' (Archer, 2000 p.241) that one crafts one's 'individual modus vivendi' (ibid p.238) through which personal identity is forged.

The constraints of the morphogenetic approach: a brief overview

Archer's morphogenetic framework and conceptualisation of the internal conversation enables an exploration of how agency is exercised by individuals in their interaction with conditioning structures, and it is this framework (reiterated at the conclusion of this chapter) that is deployed in this study to analyse individual contributions to the process of desistance. Despite the methodological utility of Archer's framework, in terms of illuminating the dynamic process of desistance, her work may be lacking in three inter-related respects. Firstly, one might question the extent to which these internal conversations and structural elaborations or transformations are conceivable simply as an individual project; as King observes, 'there is a strange loneliness in her sociology where the agent wanders as an isolated figure, engaged in private conversation' (2010 p.257). Secondly, she doesn't theorise *why* certain hooks for change, to use Giordano, Cernkovich and Holland's (2002) expression, are effective upon the agent. There must be a pre-existing orientation there but Archer seems to take this as a given. Relatedly, she fails to offer an account of the context in which ultimate concerns arise. This is because her focus remains essentially individualistic and, as such, while she is able to demonstrate that 'who we are is what we care about' (Archer, 2006), she is unable to elaborate on the relational context within which these cares emerge.

Finally, building on this last observation, it may be that it is not just the individual rationality of the would-be-desister that has to change but also the orientation of the social relation itself. For example, individuals-in-relation who are mutually oriented to the maintenance of the relation may initiate changes, perhaps in the manner of their relating and/or their behaviours, to accommodate the concerns of each individual participating in the relation. In this context, it is the social relation (which is not reducible to the individual in question but resides in between individuals-in-relation) that may be invoked as both a constraint upon offending and an enablement for a new way of living. Donati argues, thus, that Archer's explanation of reflexivity needs to be expanded to account for the form of reflexivity that people apply to their relationships ('relational reflexivity' (Donati, 2008 p.121)) rather than simply to themselves (personal reflexivity), 'to render their relationships with others and with the world reflexive, bringing to bear one's own personal internal reflexivity' (Donati, 2011b p.16).

Donati's relational sociology: an overview

Donati prioritises the social relation as the key to understanding society, and social changes, contra to current socio-theoretical preoccupations with the agent and/or the structure. In Donati's relational paradigm, social relations reflect an order of reality of their own with internal dynamics that require theoretical-practical conceptualisation. The underpinning rationale is that relationality is not a by-product of the person, but is essential to the person's being.

So far, however, the relational context of desistance has been under-explored and under-theorised.[4] Granted, there are numerous qualitative and quantitative studies that illustrate the effects of certain relational forms on desistance (see Chapter 2). However, in these studies, the relationship between, for example, marriage and desistance is variously explained in relation to differential association (Warr, 1998) or the acquisition of social bonds or ties that operate as mechanisms of informal social control that exhibit constraining effects on an individual's behaviour (Laub et al., 1998; Sampson and Laub, 1990, 2003). The point here is that despite the widespread recognition of the role of familial or intimate relationships in the desistance process, the majority of accounts of the desistance process retain an individualistic focus, and where such accounts recognise the role of social relations, these are decontextualised insofar as they are relegated to the domain of conditioning structures to the neglect of any analysis of their unique powers and properties. If, following Donati, we understand the human as relationally constituted, then scholars of the desistance process can no longer elide the relational context within which the subjects of their enquiries are immersed; a context which requires a more nuanced understanding of the properties of social relations. Understanding the phenomenon of desistance means recognising that for the would-be-desister this process is inescapably relational, in that he himself, his actions and so on 'derive from a relational context, [are] immersed in a relational context and bring about a relational context' (Donati, 2011a p.14).

It is argued here that understanding the relational context of desistance is critical to understanding why a 'hook for change' can dig into an individual's psyche and to understanding the way in which social relations can exercise a restraining influence upon offending, which more individualistic accounts of the desistance process omit. For example, Paternoster and Bushway's (2009 p.1106) 'identity theory of criminal desistance' conceptualises the process of change as a 'cognitive, internal and individual' process. They suggest that desistance emerges from a 'crystallisation of discontent' in that people make a conscious decision to change based on increasing dissatisfactions with one's present, which becomes conceptually linked by the person to an anticipated future, and weighed up against self as future non-offender, this induces their motivation to change (ibid p.1103). However, they never really elaborate what provokes this discontent and under what conditions this 'growing sense of dissatisfaction' (ibid p.1123) becomes a trigger for change at a given time and why it might have sustaining powers. Paternoster and Bushway's desister is in this sense every bit as lonely and isolated as Archer's agent. Putting desistance in a relational light could explain both of these although not in the way a social control theorist might suppose, but in recognising that both the individual and the social relation undergo reflexive change in tandem with each other. This is where Donati's relational paradigm has much to offer our understandings of the desistance process.

Donati's approach is concerned with *rel-azione*, that is, reciprocal interaction or action which 'emerges out of mutual interaction' (Donati, 2011a p.124). Social relations are conceptualised as both the '"mediation" of prior structural and cultural conditioning and have *emergent powers of causal consequence in their own right and of their own kind*' (Archer, 2011 p.202, italics added). This means that they cannot be reduced solely to interpersonal relations which are non-emergent (in terms of their causal efficacy) because they can be reduced to the influences of one person on another. Rather, Donati suggests that:

> The relation is made up of diverse components which can be further distinguished by *the effect of ego on the other* (consistency in the behaviour of the ego towards others), *the other on ego* (the responsiveness of a person to different egos), and the effect of their interaction (the behaviour that none of the actors 'brings' to the relation, but which results from their mutual conditioning of each other) . . . These effects can be observed and measured, given suitable methods. The first two effects can be analysed at the level of the individual, the third can only be examined by taking the relation as the unit of analysis.
>
> (Donati, 2011a p.126)

Donati disaggregates the social relation into its two components, the 'refero' and the 'religio'. To explain, its symbolic referent (the 'refero') denotes the cultural norms and means or the 'chains of meaning' (Donati, 2011a p.129) (and the resultant implications) brought to that 'type' of relationship rather than another (to a family for example rather than those that exist between church members), and which need not be identical for all participants. Then there is the specific *kind of bond* (the 'religio') generated between them. Thus, the social relation

> is not merely the product of perceptions, sentiments and empathy, but it is a fact which is both symbolic ('a reference to', i.e. *re-fero*) and structural ('a bond between', i.e. *re-ligio*). As such, it does not depend on the subject even though it can be actualized ('live') only through the subjects. It is in this activity dependence that the relation assumes its particular sense.
>
> (Donati, 2011a p.16)

The implication of this 'activity dependence' (Donati, 2011a p.16) is that 'the relation cannot be reduced to the subjects even though it can only 'come alive' through these subjects' (ibid p.130). Each relation, involving two or more people, has, therefore, irreducible properties arising from the reciprocal orientation of those involved. This notion of reciprocity is central to Donati's conceptualisation of social relations. Donati explains that the social relation 'implies an 'exchange of something', a reciprocal action in which something passes from ego to alter and vice versa, which generates a reciprocal link of some kind between them' (ibid p.73). This mutual exchange is the engine, or what he terms the 'generating mechanism of social relations' (ibid), in that it is the practice of reciprocity that generates and re-generates the bond of the relationship, motivated by the maintenance of the emergent relational goods of trust, confidence or caring for example. Relational goods, which may be defined in communicative and affective terms and which are produced through interaction (Gui, 2000), are generated from relationships linking those involved and are reliant on the endurance of the relational bond. Relational goods cannot be divided among those individuals participating in the relation precisely because they emerge from and reside within the relation and thus are *shared between* individuals-in-relation. If individuals-in-relation withdraw from the relationship they destroy the generative mechanism that produces these goods. In this sense, when a disagreement ensues, individuals-in-relation may reach a compromise that will allow the relationship between them to endure. This reciprocal orientation is also the source of collective intentionality in larger groups.

Particular social relations such as employer to employee or wife to husband, mother to daughter, friend to friend have certain relational characteristics that define them. Even so, the form and shape that the relation takes is not pre-determined but differs between individuals-in-relation depending on how they personify and interiorise the relation; in turn, nor is the form and shape the relation takes between individuals-in-relation permanently fixed. Thus social relations are

> that reference – symbolic and intentional – which connects social subjects as it actualises or generates a connection between them expressive of their reciprocal actions (which consist in the influence that the terms of the relation have on one another and on the effect of the reciprocity emerging between

them. Being in a relation can have a static or dynamic meaning; it can mean remaining in a context (morphostatic sense) or participating in a generative interaction (morphogenetic sense). It is thus necessary to differentiate between *social relations as a context* (i.e. as the cultural and structural connections in a context under investigation) and *social relations as interaction* (as the emergent effects in/of an interactive dynamic).

(Donati, 2011a p.89)

Donati suggests that social relations connect the micro and the macro, defined as the 'phenomena at the level of events' (2011a p.88), in that shifts in the nature and form of social relations can be accounted for by changes in the interpersonal relations between people (i.e. between a father and his son), as well as their interaction with changes in social and cultural structures. Just as interaction takes place in a relational context, social relations themselves are embedded in and shaped by a structural and cultural context. This means 'understanding and explaining social phenomena in their structural-institutional aspects by linking them to events and/or to the subject/ motives of individuals and vice versa' (ibid). Such an analysis could demonstrate where people experience the greatest difficulties in sustaining desistance, and in so doing it could be possible to intervene in order to modify those characteristics of the network which enable or constrain the intended outcomes (as one of the mutually desired ends of this process). Interventions in this regard would mean

acting on [networks of] relationships to produce changes in both context and in behaviour through the modification of existing relations; . . . activ[ating] the natural potential of social networks and mak[ing] use of innovative forms . . . of relationality.

(Donati, 2011a p.95)

Donati's relational paradigm provides an account of social integration based upon people's reciprocal orientation to relational goods (at all levels). Archer (2011a p.205) observes that the focus in social science (to which one might add, criminology) on 'market exchange relations and political command relations' has meant that social relations have been at best marginalised and at worst elided. Yet, in echoes of Habermas' (1987) related argument about the colonization of the lifeworld, Archer (2011a) observes that market exchange and political command relations operate with an instrumental or systems rationality which has the effect of fragmenting and disrupting human relations. Donati (2011a) instead advocates a politics of 'fraternity' (in the form of collective action, cooperation and mutual aid) in the pursuit of the common good in society. Unlike the market (the first sector) and the state (the second sector) (which produce private and public goods respectively) civil society (comprising the 'social-private' (third sector) and the complex of friends and family (fourth sector)) is constituted in and by reciprocal relations (Archer, 2011a) and produces secondary/associational and primary relational goods. How reciprocity is enacted and what it entails will, of course, depend on the nature of the relationship, the form of social relation and the social and cultural context in which it is rooted (Donati, 2014). In general terms, however, Donati (2009) suggests that the manner of relating, characteristic of these relations of reciprocity, manifests as mutual helping performed in accordance with the principles of solidarity and subsidiarity. Subsidiarity is a way to supply the means or a way to move resources to support the other without making him or her passive or dependent but in such a way that it allows and assists the other to do what is required in accordance with his or her ultimate concerns. Subsidiarity cannot work without solidarity (sharing a common or mutual responsibility through reciprocity which implies interdependence) (Donati, 2009). Such an approach, underpinned by Donati's relational theory of reflexivity (below), might be aligned with the aspirations of co-production and the pursuit of such approaches within criminal justice services[5] (Weaver, 2011).

Donati's relational theory of reflexivity

Donati (2011a) draws on Archer's concepts of 'reflexivity', as both a mediatory mechanism between structure and agency and as a mode of collective group orientation, that is, as 'relational reflexivity'. Donati thus progresses Archer's concept of the internal conversation to address the relationship between the internal reflexivity of the person and the social networks s/he belongs to. In so doing, he argues that Archer's (2000, 2003) emphasis on personal reflexivity needs to be connected to the properties and powers of the social networks in which people live, because, he argues, these networks operate with their own distinct form of reflexivity.

Reflexivity is defined by Donati, building on Archer's (2003, 2007a) critical realist formulation, as a social relation between ego and alter within a social context. Reflexivity is conceived as a 'meaningful and consistent way for an entity to refer to itself through/with/within the relationship to the other' (Donati, 2011a p.193). Personal reflexivity refers to that internal conversation the individual conducts within him/herself, and which is 'a relational operation on the part of an individual mind to an 'Other' who can be internal (the ego as an Other) or external (alter)' (Donati, 2011a p.195) in reference to another person or persons, as in relational reflexivity, which has an 'interactive character' (Donati, 2011a p.193) but who also takes the social context into consideration. For Donati, the process of reflexivity is relational insofar as it is shaped by the relational networks in which it emerges. This set of relations affect what can and does fulfil an individual and so the individual brings his/her personal reflexivity to bear with regard to his/her participation in this relational context. Donati further argues that individual action is guided not only by individual concerns but by the good of the relations which matter most to people. In this context, compromises by individuals-in-relation are deliberated over and decided upon in order to sustain these relationships and maintain relational goods. Individuals-in-relation thus make reciprocal adjustments or modifications to their behaviours as an outcome of *relational* reflexivity.

In this way, social relations can motivate individuals to behave in a way that they might not otherwise have done.

An example might be a family trying to keep itself together and ward off criminality of one of its members. The family asks itself 'how can we change in order to stay together', appealing to one of its members through, for example, the reciprocal orientation of parenthood. The family must ask itself what adjustments must we make to our individual lifestyles, behaviour or manner of relating in order to sustain this relation, and maintain the associated relational goods. Here, 'efforts will be made to emerge from the transition producing a new way of 'being' and 'making' the family as a relational good for its members' (Donati, 2011b p.17). Thus, the social relation becomes more reflexive as it seeks to accommodate the concerns of all people participating in it; this is ' "we" reflexivity' (Donati, 2011b p.16). The emergent goods/structural elaborations are therefore the intentional products of individuals who want to create shared relational goods. In this sense these goods/structural elaborations are the products of a relational reflexivity connected to the personal reflexivity of each individual. Nonetheless, while social relations are intrinsically reflexive, the modality of relational reflexivity adopted will be as variable between social relations as is the mode of personal reflexivity adopted by those participating in the relation (Donati, 2014).

Beyond personal (internal conversation) and relational (interactive) reflexivity is what Donati terms system reflectivity. 'If ego and alter are parts of a system, we meet system reflexivity' (Donati, 2011a p.193). Systemic reflectivity refers to the socio-cultural structures and their interactive parts. Thus 'there is a kind of reflexivity pertaining to socio-cultural structures themselves' (ibid p.194), (conceptualised as relational networks) 'which influences individuals and their interactions via the context in which they find themselves, and is bound to reappear in the outcomes (structural elaborations) of the morphogenetic process' (ibid). These outcomes or structural elaborations are, of course, those structures which emerge from the different types of reflexivity of actors in social interaction.

Conceptual schema for the study

The conceptual schema applied in this study (Figure 3.3 below) is an adaptation of Archer's morphogenetic framework to illustrate the conceptual schema progressed by Donati (2011a). This study investigated the way in which social relations are configured in the T2–T3 phase. They have constraints and enablements from outside, as well as their own internal network dynamics, which are distinct from what happens inside individuals (individual contributions) (see Figure 3.4 below) as they autonomously and reflexively evaluate their situation, take decisions and so on (analysed through Archer's internal conversation). The elaborated structure, or outcomes (T4), thus emerge as products of both the individual's application of their personal reflexivity (individual contributions) and of the interactive dynamics of their relational network(s) (relational contributions). This is because social relations have their own powers and qualities in contributing to the final outcome.

60 *Critical realism, relational sociology*

Structural Conditioning [conditioning structures]

T 1
    Interactions in Networks [black box: individual and relational contributions]

T 2   T 3
    Structural Reproduction (morphostasis)   (i.e persistence)

                                                   Outcomes
                                                   T 4
    Structural Elaboration (morphogenesis)   (i.e desistance)

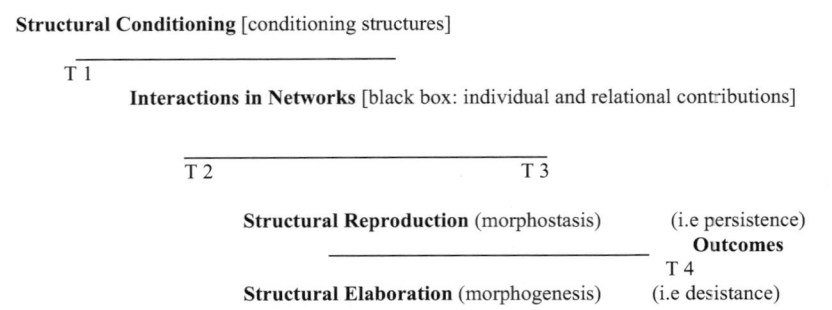

Figure 3.3 Overview of investigative framework

Structural Conditioning [conditioning structures] **ME**

T 1
    Social Interaction [personal reflexivity: individual contributions] **I**

T 2   T 3
    Structural Reproduction (morphostasis)

                                                   YOU   T 4
    Structural Elaboration (morphogenesis)

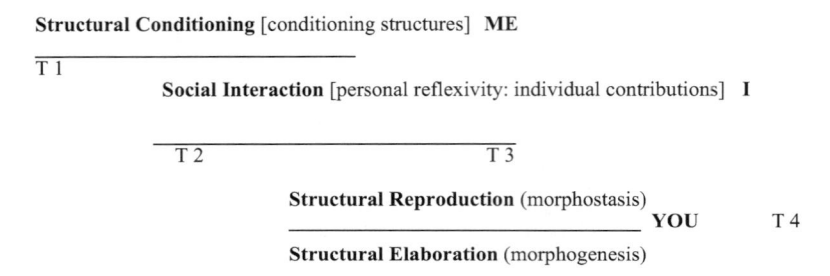

Figure 3.4 The morphogenetic sequence applied to the internal conversation (individual contributions)

Overview of investigative framework

The conditioning influence of the structural/cultural context (T1–T2 in Figure 3.3) shapes the situations of actions – in terms of the accessibility of roles and resources, to the prevalence of internalised beliefs, to the sets of relations in which people find themselves – such that some courses of action would be enabled and others constrained (Archer, 2007a; Donati, 2011a). In this manner, they influence the nature and form a given social relation takes. The conditioning structures can thus be understood as the sets of relational rules prescribing how one should behave in a certain way towards others, according to the cultural norms that the context prescribes, which the individual follows reflexively (Donati, 2011, personal communication). What is normatively expected of a person form the constraints and enablements in their conditioning structures, but these are different in different contexts and social spheres and they may be more or less constraining or enabling, more or less explicit or implicit, requiring more or less reflexivity (Donati, 2011, personal communication).

The intermediary phase (T2–T3 in Figure 3.3) is the 'black box' in which the individual (Figure 3.4) and relational (Figure 3.5) contributions to the outcomes (at T4 in Figure 3.3) are constructed (elaborated separately below). The individual contributions (to outcomes, i.e. Mark does it this way, Kate does it that way) pertain to the redefinition of personal identity and the exercise of reflexivity, and this is analysed through Archer's internal conversation (see Figure 3.4 above). The relational contributions to the outcomes are analysed to identify/observe what happens in the 'me-we-you' circle of interactions with significant others, using an adaptation of the morphogenetic sequence to analyse social relations (see Figure 3.5 below).

The outcomes (at T4 in Figure 3.3) are conceptualised through a relational theoretical lens, rather than a critical realist one. If one thinks in terms of individuals and their aggregative behaviours (as Archer does in *Realist Social Theory* (1995 p.342)) the elaborated structure or outcome depends on the power distribution among the various groups (the proportion of their influence on the process). If one thinks in terms of relational sociology the picture is slightly different in that the elaborated structure depends upon the dynamics of the relational network, which means that relations have their own powers and qualities in determining the final outcome, besides the agential power of the actors and the balance in their power relations (Donati, 2011, personal communication).

Individual contributions

As previously noted, the individual contributions pertain to the redefinition of personal identity and the exercise of personal reflexivity and this is analysed through Archer's internal conversation (see Figure 3.4 above).

In terms of the redefinition of personal identity, Archer's (2000) notion of the 'Me' refers to the identity attributed to a person by virtue of their involuntary placement in the world through, for example, their association with particular collectivities with whom they share certain advantages or disadvantages. This is the context of structural or cultural conditions (at T1). This 'Me' is not, however, reducible to the self or the person – because the 'I' has the capacity to reflect on this conferred identity (T2–T3). Part of this reflection involves a consideration of the wider forces that contribute to the assignment of this identity and this may provide, for example, some of the impetus for the 'You' to think about his or her future through the lens of his/her ultimate concerns (T4).

Archer's account of the process of reflexivity, elaborated earlier in the chapter, clarified that the conditioning 'Me' phase (which includes the results of previous deliberations) enables or constrains an individual's actions (at T1 in Figure 3.4). The 'I' phase (at T2–T3 in Figure 3.4) evokes an internal conversation, conditioned thus by the pre-existing self, the 'Me', which defines a future direction, and in so doing shapes and influences the 'You' of the future (T4 in Figure 3.4). It is through these means that we decide on courses of actions by deliberating about ourselves, our current concerns and social contexts, and by envisioning and pursuing projects that reflect and define who we are, that enable us to realise our ultimate concerns in circumstances that are, to some extent, pre-defined. This internal conversation temporarily concludes when the different parts of the self arrive at a consensus about the projected course of action that best reflects the individual's 'constellations of concerns', (Archer, 2007a p.42) but which is also realisable within the constraints of the individual's social circumstances.

The relational contributions

The relational contributions to the outcomes emerge through people's interactions in networks, as a context in which personal reflexivity is brought to bear or as the manner in which social relations are configured by those participating in the relation as an outcome of the exercise of their relational reflexivity. The relational contributions to the outcomes are analysed using an adaptation of the morphogenetic sequence (see Figure 3.5) to analyse social relations – to identify/observe what happens in the 'me-we-you' circle of interactions with significant others.

'Me' refers to the self as primary agent; this is the identity attributed to him/her by others, specifically the networks of individuals or primary contacts with whom s/he associates. 'We' refers to the individual as a corporate agent and his/her relationships to and with the associational belongings of which s/he is a part – such as a specific workplace, family, or community of believers (T2–T3). When s/he assumes a social role (or assumes certain tasks in society) s/he becomes an actor ('you') in as much as s/he interiorises or personifies a role i.e. as a worker, or parent or partner (T4). Donati (2011a) clarifies that, in all these relational spheres, one's ultimate concerns are progressively defined in relation to how the 'I' (the self) (at T1 in Figure 3.5) defines his/her choices when s/he acts as a 'you' (T4) and must respond both to the needs and requirements of his/her relational contexts and to the deeper aspirations of his/her 'I', when s/he considers whether s/he is satisfied or not with the 'Me' that has been attributed to him/her by others, and when s/he confronts and compares the meaning of his/her belonging (the 'we'/us to which s/he belongs) against that of other membership groups (T2–T3). It is in performing or personifying a role, in carrying out the tasks associated with that role, in acting as a 'You', that the self ('I') asks itself if it is gaining satisfaction from its activities, choices, lifestyle or not. Ultimate concerns are the answers given to the existential questions that people ask of themselves when they attempt to make sense of who they are and the world around them and when they consider

Structural Conditioning [conditioning structures]   **I**
────────────────────────────
T 1
        Interactions in Networks [relational contributions]
        ──────────────────────────────── **Me-We**
        T 2   T 3
                    Structural Reproduction (morphostasis)
                    ──────────────────────────────── **YOU**
                                                      T 4
                    Structural Elaboration (morphogenesis)

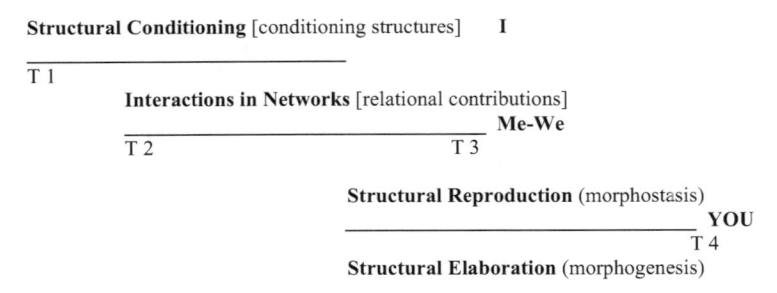

Figure 3.5 The morphogenetic sequence applied to social relations (relational contributions)

their level of satisfaction with their way of life. In this vein, Donati proposes that every way of being a self (as I, Me, We, You) is a dialogue (an internal conversation) with his/her own 'I', his/her personal identity. Social identity is formed from the dialogue between the 'I' and the other relational spheres.

In summation, therefore, this study investigated the way in which social relations, different from conditioning structures, are configured in the T2–T3 phase (Figure 3.5); these too have constraints and enablements from outside as well as their own internal network dynamics which is distinct from what happens inside the individuals who autonomously and reflexively evaluate their situations, take decisions and so on (Figure 3.4) (Donati, 2011, personal communication). This conceptual framework facilitates an exploration of the conditioning structures surrounding individuals, of the individual contributions to the desistance process, and an examination of the powers and properties of social relations and, as part of that, the relational contributions to the desistance process.

Notes

1 Parts of this chapter draw from Donati, P. (2011a) *Relational Sociology: A New Paradigm for the Social Sciences*. Abingdon: Routledge. Reproduced with permission from Routledge.

   Parts of this chapter were previously published in Weaver, B. (2012) The Relational Context of Desistance: Some Implications and Opportunities for Social Policy, *Social Policy and Administration* 46(4), pp.395–412. Reproduced with permission from Wiley.

   Parts of this chapter were previously published in Weaver, B., and McNeill, F. (2015) Lifelines: Desistance, Social Relations and Reciprocity. *Criminal Justice and Behavior* 42(1), pp.95–107. Reproduced with permission from Sage.

   Thanks to the American Sociological Association and to Professor Margaret Archer for their kind permission to reproduce Professor Archer's figure of 'the basic morphogenetic sequence' as it appears in M. Archer (2010), Routine, Reflexivity and Realism. *Sociological Theory* 28(3), pp.272–303.
2 For a more nuanced discussion on the concept of agency and desistance see Bottoms and Shapland (2011), Healy (2013, 2014), and King (2014).
3 'Morphogenesis refers to "those processes which tend to elaborate or change a system's given form, structure or state" (Buckley, 1967 p.58), and morphostasis to processes in a complex system that tend to preserve these unchanged' (Archer, 2010 p.274).
4 Although see, for example, Farrall (2005) on the existential aspects of desistance from crime and Giordano, Schroeder and Cernkovich (2007), who focus on the interpersonal effects of intimate and friend relationships.
5 This relationship is explored further in Chapter 12.

References

Archer, M. (1995) *Realist Social Theory: The Morphogenetic Approach*. Cambridge: Cambridge University Press.
Archer, M. (2000) *Being Human: The Problem of Agency*. Cambridge: Cambridge University Press.
Archer, M. (2003) *Structure, Agency and the Internal Conversation*. Cambridge: Cambridge University Press.

Archer, M. (2006) Persons and Ultimate Concerns: Who We Are Is What We Care About, in Malinvaud, E., and Glendon, M.A. (eds.) *Conceptualization of the Person in Social Sciences*. Proceedings of the Eleventh Plenary Session of the Pontifical Academy of Social Sciences, Vatican City, pp.261–283.

Archer, M. (2007a) *Making Our Way Through The World: Human Reflexivity and Social Mobility*. Cambridge: Cambridge University Press.

Archer, M. (2007b) The Trajectory of the Morphogenetic Approach: An Account in the First Person. *Sociologia, Problemas e Practicas* 54, pp.35–47.

Archer, M. (2010) Routine, Reflexivity and Realism. *Sociological Theory* 28(3), pp.272–303.

Archer, M. (2011) Critical Realism and Relational Sociology: Complementarity and Synergy. *Journal of Critical Realism* 9(2), pp.199–207.

Berger, P.L., and Luckmann, T. (1966) *The Social Construction of Reality*. New York, NY: Anchor Books.

Bottoms, A.E., and Shapland, J. (2011) Steps Towards Desistance Among Male Young Adult Recidivists, in Farrall, S., Hough, M., Maruna, S., and Sparks, R. (eds.) *Escape Routes: Contemporary Perspectives on Life After Punishment*. London: Routledge, pp.43–80.

Bourdieu, P. (1986) The Forms of Capital, in Richardson, J. (ed.) *Handbook of Theory and Research for the Sociology of Education*. New York, NY: Greenwood, pp.214–258.

Bourdieu, P. (1990) *The Logic of Practice*. Stanford: Stanford University Press.

Buckley, W. (1967) *Sociology and Modern System Theory*. Englewood Cliffs, NJ: Prentice-Hall.

Cheal, D. (2005) *Dimensions of Sociological Theory*. London: Palgrave.

Donati, P. (2008) *Oltre il multiculturalismo. La ragione relazionale per un mondo commune*. Rome-Bari: Laterza.

Donati, P. (2009) What Does 'Subsidiarity' Mean? The Relational Perspective. *Journal of Markets and Morality* 12(2), pp.211–243.

Donati, P. (2011a) *Relational Sociology: A New Paradigm for the Social Sciences*. Abingdon: Routledge.

Donati, P. (2011b) Family Transitions: How Can We Treat Them in a Morphogenetic Society? *Disability and the Family* 16(1), pp.1–19.

Donati, P. (2014) Morphogenic Society and the Structure of Social Relations, in Archer, M.S. (ed.) *Late Modernity: Trajectories Towards Morphogenic Society*. Lausanne, Switzerland: Springer International, pp.143–172.

Farrall, S. (2005) On the Existential Aspects of Desistance from Crime. *Symbolic Interaction* 28(3), pp.367–386.

Farrall, S., and Bowling, B. (1999) Structuration, Human Development and Desistance from Crime. *British Journal of Criminology* 39(2), pp.253–268.

Giddens, A. (1984) *The Constitution of Society*. Cambridge: Polity Press.

Giordano, P.C., Cernkovich, S.A., and Rudolph, J.L. (2002) Gender, Crime and Desistance: Toward a Theory of Cognitive Transformation. *American Journal of Sociology* 107, pp.990–1064.

Giordano, P.C., Schroeder, R.D., Cernkovich, S.A. (2007) Emotions and Crime Over the Life Course: A Neo-Median Perspective on Criminal Continuity and Change. *American Journal of Sociology* 112(6), pp.1603–1661.

Gui, B. (2000) Beyond Transactions: On the Interpersonal Dimensions of Economic Reality. *Annals of Public and Cooperative Economics* 71(2), pp.139–169.

Habermas, J. (1987) *Lifeworld and System: A Critique of Functionalist Reason, Vol. 2 of The Theory of Communicative Action*. English translation by Thomas McCarthy. Boston, MA: Beacon Press. (Originally published in German in 1981)
Healy, D. (2013) Changing Fate? Agency and the Desistance Process. *Theoretical Criminology* 17(4), pp.557–574.
Healy, D. (2014) Becoming a Desister: Exploring the Role of Agency, Coping and Imagination in the Construction of a New Self. *British Journal of Criminology* 54(5), pp.873–891.
King, S. (2014) *Desistance Transitions and the Impact of Probation*. Abingdon: Routledge.
Laub, J.H., Nagin, D.S., and Sampson, R.J. (1998) Trajectories of Change in Criminal Offending: Good Marriages and the Desistance Process. *American Sociological Review* 63, pp.225–238.
Laub, J.H., and Sampson, R.J. (2001) Understanding Desistance from Crime, in Tonry, M.H., and Morris, N. (eds.) *Crime and Justice: An Annual Review of Research*, Vol. 26. Chicago, IL: University of Chicago Press, pp.1–78.
Laub, J.H., and Sampson, R.J. (2003) *Shared Beginnings, Divergent Lives*. Cambridge, MA: Harvard University Press.
LeBel, T.P., Burnett, R., Maruna, S., and Bushway, S. (2008) The 'Chicken and Egg' of Subjective and Social Factors in Desistance from Crime. *European Journal of Criminology* 5(2), pp.131–159.
Mouzelis, N. (1995) *Sociological Theory: What Went Wrong?* New York, NY: Routledge.
Paternoster, R., and Bushway, S. (2009) Desistance and the 'Feared Self': Toward an Identity Theory of Criminal Desistance. *Journal of Law and Criminology* 99(4), pp.1103–1156.
Rumgay, J. (2004) Scripts for Safer Survival: Pathways Out of Female Crime. *Howard Journal of Criminal Justice* 43(4), pp.405–419.
Sampson, R.J., and Laub, J.H. (1990) Crime and Deviance over the Life Course: The Salience of Adult Social Bonds. *American Sociological Review* 55(5), pp.609–627.
Sampson, R.J., and Laub, J.H. (2003) Life-Course Desisters? Trajectories of Crime Among Delinquent Boys Followed to Age 70. *Criminology* 41(3), pp.555–592.
Vaughan, B. (2007) The Internal Narrative of Desistance. *The British Journal of Criminology* 47(3), pp.390–404.
Weaver, B. (2011) Co-Producing Community Justice: The Transformative Potential of Personalisation for Penal Sanctions. *British Journal of Social Work* 41(6), pp.1038–1057.
Weaver, B. (2012) The Relational Context of Desistance: Some Implications and Opportunities for Social Policy. *Social Policy and Administration* 46(4), pp.395–412.
Weaver, B., and McNeill, F. (2015) Lifelines: Desistance, Social Relations and Reciprocity. *Criminal Justice and Behavior* 42(1), pp.95–107.

4 The dynamics of co-offending[1]
From formation to fragmentation

Introduction

This chapter represents the first substantive chapter of eight data chapters. This chapter is the story of the group, the Del, from formation to fragmentation and is divided into eight parts. The first part, '*Overview of the sample*', introduces the characters on whose narratives this book is based. The second, '*Overview of context/conditioning structures*', offers a portrait of the historical, social, economic and cultural context which frame the group and which inform their situations of action and influence group identities and their interactions. The third part, '*Becoming and belonging*', examines the first sub-theme derived from the superordinate theme '*The relational context of offending*' and describes how the group met and formed. It explores the significance of the group to the participants in the context of their shared but diverse experience of childhood trauma and disconnection from their families, and observes the various socialising influences on their identities and interactions.

The fourth part examines the second sub-theme derived from the superordinate theme '*The relational context of offending*', entitled '*The nature and dynamics of the group, lifestyle and behaviour*' and reveals the shifting nature of group dynamics, identities, offending behaviour and lifestyles over time. It pursues a discussion on the nature of friendship and in so doing reveals both the nature and form of the group as a social relation and the relational rules which structure and characterise their interactive dynamics and collective action. The fifth part examines the third sub-theme '*Identity and identification to and with the group*'. This part examines the changing meaning of belonging to the group for individuals in the context of their increasingly imprisoning lives. While the group initially met individuals' needs for social interaction and participation, their collective actions and acquired reputations for violence and the ensuing social repercussions constrained opportunities for social participation. This part proceeds to examine how, in this context, the group influenced identity formation and how belonging to the group and participating in their collective actions represented, in the absence of alternative means, a source of respect and social recognition and operated as a point of resistance to stigma.

Building on this discussion of reputations and identities, the sixth part discusses the fourth sub-theme '*The individual and the relational self in a collective context'*. It reveals the heterogeneity of individual experiences of the group and how the group influenced individuals' behaviour. It is suggested that while the perceived need to act in accordance with the expectations of the group is experienced by individuals as a constraint on their autonomy, that acting on the basis of their conviction of the veracity of the relational rules to which they subscribed, not only served to reconcile the ambivalence of agency this engendered in individuals, but can be understood as both an expression of agency and individuals' application of relational reflexivity. The seventh part describes the situational nature of '*The fragmentation of the Del*' and the divergent outcomes for individuals. In so doing it foreshadows the role of the splinter or revised group in mutually supporting the early phases of each other's desistance, elaborated in more detail in subsequent chapters, under the superordinate theme '*Roles, reflexivity, relationality and desistance*'. This chapter thus reveals the story of the Del from formation to fragmentation and serves as a foundation to the individual analyses presented in Chapters 5–10.

Overview of the sample

The Webster brothers, Adam (born 1961), Jay (born 1963) and Seth (born 1965), were born and raised in 'Coaston'. Adam occupied a dominant position in the group, which seemed to relate as much to his intelligence as to his capacity for fighting and prowess in football, which as this chapter will illustrate, were construed as valued qualities to possess. Adam's younger brothers, Seth and Jay, consider themselves to have been socialised into the group due to Adam's involvement with similarly situated others in the neighbourhood, and Jay and Seth, in turn, formed friendships with the younger siblings of these associates because the group also comprised other sibling formations including the Nixon brothers (Desmond, Dennis and Iain) and the Mackenzie brothers (Barry and Graeme) all of whom were close in age. This 'group' originally developed through friendships formed on the streets of their local neighbourhood, where they primarily associated. Jed (born 1961) lived on the same housing scheme in Coaston as the Websters and formed a particularly close friendship with Adam in early childhood. The 'Del', as they came to be known, also included another set of siblings, the Smiths (Ben, Jim and James), whose involvement in the group was established when Ben met Adam, Iain and Jed and others at secondary school.

Harry (born 1961) and Andy (born 1961) similarly developed friendships with the Del when they met at secondary school. However, while centrally involved with the group, they occupied a lower status within the group than some of the other boys, with neither one exhibiting the necessary fighting prowess essential to commanding respect amongst one's peers and critical to one's position within the group. Like Evan (born 1965), who moved into Coaston at the age of 12 from an adjoining town, they did not reside on the same housing scheme as the others. There is consensus across the men's narratives that their associations as a group intensified when the older boys reached the age of 12, coinciding with the commencement of their secondary education. Others, particularly the younger brothers like Seth, were approximately 8 years old at this time.

68 *The dynamics of co-offending*

Only some of these people were interviewed for this study. Those people are Jed, Jay, Seth, Evan, Harry and Andy. Some people's association with the Del was more peripheral or fleeting; they associated with the Del for a while but when the group became more frequently and more seriously involved in offending, they disengaged and drifted away from them. As this chapter will illustrate, groups and the people that comprise them are not fixed, static entities. Given the transient nature of some people's involvement in offending and the Del, tracking them down would have proved a challenge which would not be warranted by what they might be able to contribute to understandings of desistance. Indeed, a few of the men refer to this fluidity in association – in terms of the varying levels of connectedness or attachment between people which were more or less intense, at different times and for different reasons. The people involved here are those who occupied more central and enduring positions within the group. There were, however, other central characters, mentioned above, who declined to participate, for reasons not given; others were inaccessible, living elsewhere or deceased.

Overview of context/conditioning structures

Describing Coaston, Evan said that 'from someone outside looking in, they probably thought it was a nice pretty little seaside town but never understood there was loads of baggage, there were loads of issues going on.' These 'issues' include the impact of de-industrialisation and the attendant economic inequalities and social disadvantage it compounded. In addition, cultural class beliefs and attitudes towards social mobility and gender roles and identities, for example, were significant conditioning influences on the group's developing personal and collective identities, shaping their situations of action through the constraints and enablements they engendered (T1–T2 in Figure 4.1).

The area in which the Del resided was a small town on the west coast of Scotland whose current population totals approximately 12,000. In the 1960s and early 1970s, Coaston, a predominantly working-class town, had the appearance of a pleasant holiday destination, boasting a number of industries which provided

Structural Conditioning[conditioning structures]

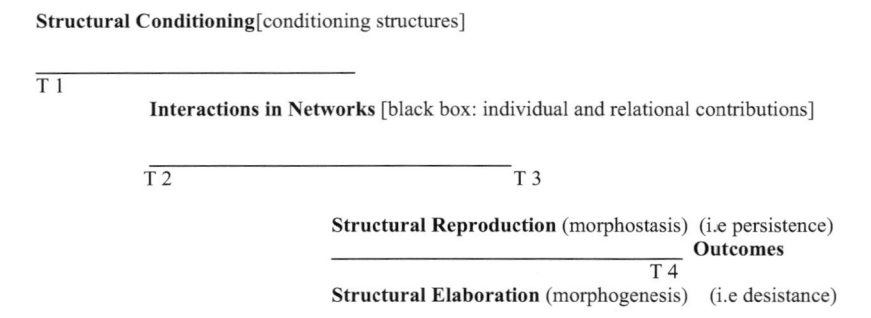

T 1

        Interactions in Networks [black box: individual and relational contributions]

T 2   T 3

        Structural Reproduction (morphostasis) (i.e persistence)
                                              Outcomes
                                             T 4
        Structural Elaboration (morphogenesis) (i.e desistance)

Figure 4.1 Overview of investigative framework

mass employment including shipyards, factories and a local power station. Like many areas, Coaston experienced a decline in heavy industry and manufacturing employment in the 1970s and 1980s, causing unemployment and poverty and aggravating other social problems (McDowell, 2003 in Deuchar, 2009). Indeed, the west of Scotland was particularly affected by de-industrialisation (Torrance, 2009), and 'Scottish industries haemorrhaged jobs' (Craig, 2010 p.301) resulting in a number of industrial closures. By 1983 around three quarter of a million Scots were dependent on benefits and over a fifth of the population of Scotland were living on or below the poverty line (Finlay, 2003). In this era of Thatcherite materialism, where to have was to be, the difference between the haves and the have nots, and thus inequality, rose sharply (Wilkinson and Pickett, 2010). This was the economic and social context characterising the Del's formative years, their adolescence and early adulthood.

Evan: [In terms of] employment . . . I think as the seventies went on things began to decline. The shipyards certainly was going almost very quickly and [name of factory] – it almost went – late seventies, early eighties – suddenly all the jobs lost were there and that had a massive effect I think on the community . . . unemployment rose and there was not much hope.

This collective sense of hopelessness emerging from burgeoning inequalities, increasing poverty and diminishing opportunities arose in the context of a Scottish working class culture which exhibited hostility towards social mobility (Finlay, 2003) and to those seen to be 'rising above their status'. This phenomenon is echoed in Willis' (1977) *'Learning to Labour'*, where young working class male adolescents held themselves back from progress in school for fear of standing out and losing ties to friends if they rose too far, and in turn, their communities. In 'these practices of daily life, "meritocracy" stands for a threat to solidarity [and]. . . . social mobility carries social costs' (Sennett, 2003 p.98). These cultural constraints on motivation and aspiration contributed to the suppression of people's expectations and to a collective resignation towards the structural constraints on opportunity that the worsening economic context heralded (Craig, 2010).

Seth: There was a total feeling of hopelessness that you could never get a job . . . that was instilled in me with my Dad not working . . . there was no hope . . . you could never get a job and . . . you could never go to college . . . It wasn't a kind of thing that was done, going back for education . . . Not to say that nobody ever did but, hey, in our thinking you didnae.

Exacerbated by de-industrialisation, unemployment and poverty framed the economic context for many of the Del, their families and the community, reinforcing their already suppressed aspirations. However, violent crime (often linked with poor housing), environmental degeneration, concentrated poverty, educational under-achievement and religious sectarianism are also prevalent in social histories documenting the structural, cultural and social landscape of the west of Scotland of this era (see, for example, Craig, 2010; Devine, 1999; Dudgeon, 2009; Finlay, 2003). Cultural representations portray a dominant 'macho' patriarchal culture of a large area of West Scotland, with heavy drinking as normal male behaviour, domestic violence a common feature, and frustration an aggravating one as local autobiographies of this era and from this area testify (see for example Galloway 2008; Weaver 2008) and as social histories document (Craig, 2010; Damer, 1990), to which these men's narratives testify.

As this and the following chapters illustrate, many of the Del were influenced and affected by the nature of the 'relationships' and associated social norms or behavioural 'patterns' they were exposed to. This is not to suggest that they passively responded to social, cultural and structural determinants. Indeed, in echoes of Willis (1977), the Del actively and self-consciously appropriated elements of an idealised configuration of hegemonic 'traditional' working class masculinity (Connell, 2002) in their pursuit of status, respect and social recognition, influenced by and responsive to the social, cultural and economic character of the era and area. This somewhat exaggerated representation of masculinity informed the social relations in which they participated as both a context (the cultural and social connections) and as interaction (the emergent effects in, and of, interactive dynamics). As this chapter illustrates, their emergent gender identities and associated practices were intricately infused into relational rules influencing the kinds of bonds generated between them and which guided the form and nature of their relationships, interactions and the actions they gave rise to.

This chapter will proceed to illuminate the complexities and subjectivities of their lives as a group – their lived experiences and relationships with each other and to the wider social frameworks within which they participated – including their families, school and community. These interactions, underpinned by an idealised form of masculinity, in part informed the relational rules which structured and characterised their relationships and the nature and form of their interactions with each other and wider social relations. The tensions in what was conveyed to them, and about them, through their relationships to, and experiences of, increasing alienation within the family, school and community are, as this chapter illustrates, partly mitigated (and in turn exacerbated) by their association with the group. The sense of belonging, recognition and solidarity they found in the group operated as an enclave of security and protection and as a point of resistance to these messages (T2–T3 in Figure 4.1). Herein resides the motivation for individuals' initial and enduring association with the group, the meaning of this association to them and what this represented in the development of their identities, through which lens they ordered and refracted their ultimate concerns as individuals and as a group. In revealing these relational processes, this chapter illustrates the centrality of the relational to the individual and, thus, to processes of change, and illuminates the group trajectory, itself significant to understanding individual trajectories towards desistance from crime.

The chapter proceeds to discuss the dynamics of offending, as it occurred in the context of the conditioning structures elaborated thus far, under the superordinate group theme '*The relational context of offending*'. In so doing, the following sub-themes are elaborated: '*Becoming and Belonging*'; '*The nature and dynamics of the group, lifestyle and behaviour*'; '*Identity and identification to and with the group*' and '*The fragmentation of the Del*'.

The relational context of offending

Becoming and belonging

Experience of childhood trauma and/or emotional disconnection within the family is a dominant theme across the men's narratives, and was cited as a significant influence on individuals' involvement with the group and their subsequent progression to offending behaviour. The earliest memories Jay and Seth Webster recalled were of their father's pervasive violence; when he was not violent, the ubiquitous threat was as oppressive as the fear, disruption and anguish he engendered during violent episodes.

Seth: [I remember] my Dad drunk and causing chaos and the violence and that . . . I remember him smashing the house up constantly when he was drunk . . . You never knew when it was going to happen and . . . you would have to leave the house.

Jay: . . . the domestic violence always sort of hung over us and a lot of our life had been determined round about things like that. Moving out the house at night and . . . having to get away from an abusive Dad and just dreading him coming in at night.

Both Jay and Seth retrospectively perceive their father's violence as a contributory influence on their involvement in the group, and ultimately, their subsequent involvement in offending behaviour.

Jay: I wouldn't be looking to blame certain things but, obviously, all the chaos that was going on in the house – eh but, then, that carried on for years so I wouldn't really know. I wouldn't be able to identify that or say it was x, y or z. But when the chaos was going on in the house, it gave you a wee chance 'cos everybody's mind was on something else. It gave you a window of opportunity to go and do something, I think.

The dubiety appearing in Jay's rumination suggests, in his mind, an uncertain relationship between his experience of his father's violence in the home and his subsequent involvement in offending, one iterated across other narratives where exposure to abuse or trauma was a defining feature of their childhood. However both here, and across other men's narratives, an absence of parental supervision is construed as an enablement to an offending lifestyle. Additionally Seth and others observe a relationship between this 'chaos' in the home and the need to escape. In this context, the streets provided a place of refuge where he and his brothers associated with similarly situated friends. Jay and Seth's father's violence in the home thus influenced the physical places and social spaces they occupied which, ultimately, informed their identities, concerns, projects and practices.

Seth: The whole unsettledness in the house, my Dad drinking, all the crap, having to get away from the house and things like that – it wasn't a normal life . . . Then all the trouble going on round about us, guys getting into trouble, and it was easier to have their company than being home . . . you took comfort in being with your mates.

Both Andy and Evan were subjected to sexual abuse. Andy was victimised in an isolated incident by a male outside the family, heightening his existing feelings of difference and marginality among his peers, which he attributed, in part, to his diminutive physical stature, his red hair and a squint in one eye for which the remedy was to wear an eye patch. Evan perceives that his feelings of vulnerability and powerlessness as a consequence of the sustained sexual abuse he was subjected to by a family member and the emotional disconnection he perceived within his family contributed to his offending behaviour in as much as he, at least in part, perceived that in offending, he was 'acting out'. For these young boys, association with a gang afforded a sense of protection and safety, of control and structure, of belonging and acceptance and, incrementally, power and influence which, to a greater or lesser degree, ameliorated the sense of disconnection and powerlessness they experienced and the trauma they endured.

The need for relatedness reflects the human need to mutually and reciprocally relate to and care for other people and 'involves feeling connected (or feeling that one belongs in a social milieu)' (Vallerand, 1997 p.300). The need to belong is realised through relationships experienced as combining 'stability, affective concern, and continuation into the foreseeable future' (Baumeister and Leary, 1995 p.500). This emotional drive for social relatedness or connectedness is a motivating force underpinning human behaviour (Baumeister and Leary, 1995; Ryan and Deci, 2000). Where people experience emotional disconnection or feel a lack of belonging within the family, they are more likely to develop strong bonds to friendship groups as a means of satisfying their need for belonging. For the Del, the insecurity, fear and threat that typified their personal contexts and the frequency and intensity of their associations with each other, transformed their relationships into a stronger, more reciprocal, fraternal relationship which served to ameliorate their sense of marginality, powerlessness and isolation (Anderson, 2003; Seaman et al., 2006).

Evan: I couldn't really tell anyone [about the abuse] . . . when I started getting about in gangs who seemed to have some sort of loyalty to one another . . . that helped in a way . . . you felt you belonged somewhere . . . you were a part of a crowd – you felt part of belonging to something. I think maybe just feeling that you belonged to something . . . someone . . . was doing that to me, the abuse, so, [the family] wasnae a sort of happy place . . . and when you were with a crowd of people . . . sometimes you felt that was a little bit protective, you were sort of indestructible.

Indeed, much of the research on gangs reveals familial supportive behaviour in explaining the significance of the gang (see, for example, Harris, 1988; Vigil, 1988). Some groups/gangs function similarly to a family, providing young people with a sense of belonging, security and identity and a source of social support. Being part of a group also offers new experiences, protection and, among the Del, opportunities for economic gain and excitement as well as respect, social recognition, fellowship and solidarity. Across the men's narratives, there is consensus that the group provided, or at least represented, a source of support, safety and protection as much as a way of expressing and experiencing belonging and loyalty.

Experiencing trauma, feeling insecure and powerless can also be ameliorated through the adoption and/or expression of exaggerated forms of masculinities, manifesting in risk-taking and violent behaviours which serve as a mechanism for achieving respect, social recognition, influence and power (Matthews, Jewkes and Abrahams, 2011). When young men experience alienation from the family, school and community, exacerbating existing frustrations and distrust towards the adult world, and in the absence of any influential, pro-social older role models, they can seek status and recognition elsewhere. In such contexts, an aggressive street culture is a viable alternative in the absence of success in conventional areas as an expression of masculinity (Messerschmidt, 2000).

So far, this chapter has illustrated the general conditioning structures precipitating individuals' involvement in the group which include exposure to childhood trauma, abuse and/or emotional disconnection within their families. However, the group itself can be conceptualised as a conditioning structure, in that social and cultural contexts (outlined above) influence the nature and form a given social relation takes. This is distinct from what happens during interaction, which can influence the interpersonal, intersubjective relations between two or more people. As illustrated in Chapter 3, conditioning structures include the set of relations in which the individual is involved and on which he acts by reflecting on his position in that context. Conditioning structures can thus be understood as the set of relational rules prescribing how one should behave in a certain way towards others according to the norms that the context implies.

As previously illustrated, the group comprised friend and fraternal relations, which developed through community or educational connections. While some of the men occasionally referred to the group as a gang, unlike some gangs, there was no pre-existing structure which these individuals joined, or what Vigil (1993) calls 'established' gangs. The Del was, however, informally allied with an older 'team' who shared the same identifying name and was associated with the same territorial locale. This process of identification with the 'big team' was both an internal and external phenomenon in that both groups and people outside the groups recognised their mutual allegiance. This allegiance was primarily opportunistic as opposed to reflecting a pre-existing structure into which they assimilated. While the relations between the group and the 'big team' was based on norms of reciprocity and exchange, the relational goods this association engendered were primarily instrumental and included financial exchanges and physical protection through association.

Jed: When we got bigger we started mixing with . . . the big team – Kev and Mugger and all that . . . They used to be dead friendly with us because obviously they knew we must be useful for something. So we used to hang round them and we were thinking we were in with all these big cunts and it was fuckin' great. We used to go up and 'there you go, there's a couple of bob' and that, you know, but we used to give them money too, when we done a turn, when we broke into a shop or whatever . . . If we were ever stuck for anything, anything at all, they would help us out.

Cloward and Ohlin's (1960) differential opportunity theory proposes that younger gang members learn how to behave from older members who operate as role-models. Through this process, younger members learn how to perform and enact masculinities by asserting their physical superiority and dominance, through which status is conferred and reputations and identities established. While the 'big team' were one influence, this socialisation process more frequently occurred within the group, between siblings and older and younger members (see also Matthews et al., 2011).

Evan: [my brother] was tough, he was hard, so I've got to try and do the same as well. And yet deep down I didn't want to be hard and tough and fight but somehow you were kind of moulded into that. And . . . you would stand a fight, you would do things that got you a bit of reputation . . . in gangs you have to fight, in a sense that was your street cred and you had to stand firm and even if you couldn't fight, you had a go.

Seth: I'd three older brothers that were well known locally for fighting, for offending, for violence all that kind of thing, so in a lot of ways I don't think I had a great deal of choice, it was just all there. I just more or less grew into that whole life, same as my brothers and my friends at that time.

Aggressive behaviours associated with a 'working class "tough" masculinity' (Crawshaw, 2004 p.238) were also shared, if not sanctioned, by men who would not otherwise consider themselves 'offenders'. Most participants described the ubiquity and normality of alcohol-related violence among the general male population.

Harry: you always heard everyone coming home at night and fights in the street and all that and you were up looking out your window to see all the fights . . . you'd hear them all shouting and bawling and you'd look out the window you know? It was a big thing then wasn't it?

Jay: You would go down the town at night and there would be . . . fights and we would watch. We knew where [they] were going to happen. Sometimes we started them, and just sat back and watched . . . Obviously there was another element of [Coaston] – maybe a different sort of social life but to us, this was it. We only seen that kind of side to it.

Craig's (2010) social history of Glasgow echoes these men's observations of the ubiquity, normalcy and acceptability of violence, often exacerbated by alcohol. For the Del, violence within the home, between gangs and within the working class male culture surrounding them was a characteristic feature of their childhood and exerted a powerful socialising impact on their gender identities, on what it meant to be a man and how men should interact in relationships with other men.

The nature and dynamics of the group, lifestyle and behaviour

The formation of the Del was largely unstructured and emerged from the informal coming together of various individuals at different stages, and, as with many groups, over time associations within the group shifted and changed reflecting different levels of 'embeddedness' in the group (Hagan, 1993 cited in Pyrooz, Sweeten and Piquero, 2012) in terms of status, identification with the group and involvement in their collective activities (see also Klein and Maxson, 2006). Indeed, some of those who associated with the Del were able to 'resist' involvement in offending (Murray, 2012).

Evan: Know, maybe when . . . we were going to commit a crime, they would say, 'no, this is not for me'. So some of them knew the certain boundaries that they would go to and they would just go away.

Those who resisted involvement in offending tended to occupy more peripheral positions within the group. Murray (2012 p.35), discussing the impact on young people of non-involvement in offending, suggests that non-offenders forego kudos, which she defines as 'an appreciation by young people of particular actions, attributes or possessions of their peers'. She argues that the act or state of non-offending influences an individual's status and in her analysis, abstaining from criminal activities was generally portrayed by non-offenders as a social deficit. While Jay reflects such a perspective in his view of how he perceived non-offenders: '*I thought they were gay if you know what I mean, sissy-ish,*' this perception was of non-offenders who '*stayed home and did their homework*' as opposed to non-offenders associating with the Del. While Evan concedes that they would tease their non-offending associates, they were not excluded unless they were perceived as untrustworthy. Thus, the attribution of kudos seemed to also relate to moral character and was not solely a reflection of one's actions, facilitating a distinction between non-offending associates and non-offending non-associates.

Evan: we would maybe wind them up and say . . . 'ah, what's the matter with you?' – you know what young teenagers are like . . . we wouldn't say, 'well we're not talking to him again', unless he maybe informed on us.

Kudos is, as Murray (2012) suggests, a measure of status and social recognition, reflecting one's possession of valorised virtues of fearlessness, courage and loyalty, and influences one's position in the group (see also Barry, 2006). Non-offenders are relatively poorly positioned to display virtues of courage, loyalty and trustworthiness, where this emerges from the ties and obligations ensuing from shared involvement in offending. Incrementally, some non-offending or less embedded associates naturally 'drifted' away from the group (Matza, 1964) at an earlier stage (on which see Pyrooz et al., 2012) as the Del's involvement in criminality and violence escalated over the years.

Jay: You got some people that dropped off . . . to get a job. They probably thought enough was enough . . . They maybe just stopped hanging out with us or they've may be been working away, so maybe just an opportunity arose for them and they took it – but I wouldnae say that was any of the real, real inner circle of pals – that was the ones that were just there or thereabouts.

Relations between people within the core group would similarly oscillate in intensity:

Evan: There was that many people. Every so often you seemed to make a bond with one of the other people and you . . . were real close buddies for a couple of months and then maybe something would happen, one of them would maybe get sent to prison . . . and you would team up with somebody else and you would become close.

These oscillations in associations, or porous network boundaries, contrast with the formality often associated with images of gangs (Klein, Weerman and Thornberry, 2006). However, in reality, 'gangs are very much like informal friendship networks' (Aldridge, Medina and Ralphs, 2007 p.17). Whilst the group in their original form held many commonalities with what Klein et al. (2006 p.414) define as 'street gangs'[2] and while occasionally referring to themselves as a gang, they also refuted the label, possibly associating the term with images of highly structured, formal groups, with fixed and enduring identities such as those associated with 'American stereotypes' (ibid).

Territorially divided and sectarian gangs and inter-gang violence and conflict are prevalent in social histories (Craig, 2010; Sack, 1986), fiction (McArthur and Long, 1935; Patrick, 1973) and research on Scottish gangs (see Bannister and Fraser, 2008; Deuchar, 2009; Deuchar and Holligan, 2010; Fraser, 2010; Holligan and Deuchar, 2009). While religious identity in West Scotland has historically been a divisive feature among the working class, dictating which school you went to and at times which employment opportunities you could access (Devine, 1999), sectarianism was not a theme that emerged strongly in men's narratives. Intertwined with politics, religion and football – sectarianism in Scotland refers to relations between Protestants and Catholics informed by the wider historical context of 'The Troubles' associated with Northern Ireland and the religious identities associated with the two largest football clubs based in Glasgow: Glasgow Celtic and Rangers F.C (Deuchar, 2009). Although the Del attended schools which reflected their religious affiliation and while inter-school rivalries gave rise to violence, this was not strictly motivated by sectarianism, nor was religious identity a criteria for gang affiliation in Coaston as it was in Glasgow in the 1960s and 1970s (see also Holligan and Deuchar, 2009). In Coaston, territorial divisions between three adjoining towns influenced gang loyalties, particularly in the early stages of the group's life.

Kintrea et al. (2008 p.4) describe territoriality as 'a social system through which control is claimed by one group over a defined geographic area and defended against others'. The meanings and impacts of territorialism are decidedly more complex and multi-faceted than this description directly implies. Territoriality, frequently associated with gangs, masculinity, poverty, deprivation and marginalisation (Davies, 1998; Glaser, 1998; Holligan and Deuchar, 2009; Kintrea et al., 2008; MacLure and Sotelo, 2004; Centre for Social Justice, 2009) can, as Holligan and Deuchar (2009) observe, contribute to or compound social exclusion, which can be reinforced through self-imposed restrictions (Byrne, 1999; Kintrea et al., 2008); the development of 'bonding' social capital (Woolcock and Narayan, 2000) which can be reinforced through territorial behaviours (Marshall et al., 2004; Reynolds, 2007); and the development of personal and collective identity.

Group identities are often embedded in place, and identification with place in turn influences these identities (Bannister and Fraser 2008; Flynn, 2010; Fraser, 2010; Kintrea et al., 2008). For young people, who have limited resources, constrained social and geographical mobility, and who spend a large amount of their time on the streets, territorial spaces become imbued with meaning through individual and collective memory, which informs both personal and collective identities, embedded in, and reinforced by, the relationships which develop there (Fraser 2010). The 'street' becomes a place, or context, in which identities are negotiated, reputations earned and status conferred.

Seth: Everybody kind of hung about our street, an area that was rough. There was a lot of poor families in it, so there was a lot of kids hanging about the streets and getting up to things – a kind of gang culture, from an early age . . . life was on the street then, from an early age, and that was who you were, that was what we all did.

Shared experiences and territorial locales can be an equalising experience wherein acquired status depends less on material accoutrements and more on one's personal and social resources. Friendship bonds developed in first, the neighbourhood and, later, secondary school are facilitated by not only restricted geographical mobility but by perceptions of similarity and processes of identification; people usually select and identify more strongly with friends who are similar to themselves including similar socio-economic backgrounds (Allan, 1989; Cotterell, 1996; Giordano, Schroeder and Cernkovich, 2003; Pahl, 2000). This is because by 'building affinities with others who occupy a similar social and economic location, individuals affirm their own position, cement their status and give substance to their identities' (Allan, 1998 p.693–4). This explains why 'managing ties of friendship when there is status discrepancy can be quite problematic' (Allan, 1998 p.693) (see also Allan, 1996; Reynolds, 2007). Pahl (2000) argues that equality of status is a necessary precondition of a reciprocal friendship characterised by affection and mutuality and the emergent relational goods of reciprocity, solidarity and loyalty, which prompt and guide the actions of those in relation (see also Blau, 1964).

Friendships create obligations and are causally influential. Friendship can mitigate negative emotionality and stigma, give confidence and impetus to act in a way an individual might not undertake alone and, in terms of 'relational bads' (Donati, 2011), they can also be exclusionary and divisive (Archer, 2011). There is an instrumental and an affective dynamic in the social relation of friendship. Emotional properties or goods can be categorised under the affective dimension of relationality. Where relational goods can be construed as benefits or resources in terms of providing status and social recognition, they can be categorised under the instrumental dimension. The presence of relational goods means understanding social capital as a social relation which encourages or discourages certain actions of individuals-in-relation through their mutual orientation towards the maintenance of the co-indivisible relational goods it produces, from which other ends, information or resources can be derived as secondary emergent effects (Donati, 2006). Social capital is not, then, an asset possessed by the individual, nor is it a collective property of a social structure, but a configuration of those social networks which are shared by people who will not be able to produce such goods outside their reciprocal relations (Donati, 2007). The core emergent effects of social capital are the relational goods of social trust, solidarity and social connectedness all of which rest 'implicitly on some background of shared expectations of reciprocity' (Putnam, 2000 p.136).

Pahl (2000) argues that the relational good fraternity, associated with social capital as a social relation, suffuses kin and family relations. Fraternity is not confined to familial relations but denotes a particular type of friendship or social relation based on mutuality and reciprocity; reciprocity is the expression of fraternity. Characteristically friends are viewed as freely chosen and the moral obligations they carry are less binding and important than those relating to kin ties; kin relationships traditionally tend to be more structured and role governed than friend relations (Pahl, 2000). However, shared networks across sibling and friendship groups, as with the Del, means sibling relations can operate more like friend relations and vice versa. The relationships between the Del thus suffused kin relations with norms and expectations associated with the role of friendship, and vice versa, which formed a strong social bond.

Seth: They were more like a family . . . in the end up than what I was getting in the house I suppose.

As previously observed, in the context of their shared experience of trauma, emotional disconnection within the family and alienation from community institutions, friends become more significant than families of origin to self-concept and identity formation (Pahl 2000; Weeks, Donovan and Heaphy, 1999 cited by Reynolds, 2007). All of the men interviewed had high expectations of their friendships in the group and were strongly invested in their maintenance. The significance of these relational goods, of reciprocity, trust, equality, loyalty and solidarity, occurred frequently across accounts and manifested in specific expectations and behavioural obligations – for example – that you would support your friends if they were caught up in a violent incident or that you would take the blame for an offence to offset the impact on someone else, for whom the consequences would be more severe.

Seth: Some of the older ones would take the younger ones with them and, if they got caught, the younger one would put himself up for it 'cos he knew he wouldn't get into as much trouble. That's the same if you're doing something with somebody who hadn't been in a lot of trouble or who hadn't been caught – if they got caught or questioned, they would take the blame for it 'cos they wouldn't get as much of a punishment.

Jed: Everybody looked after each other. I mean if I went out one night and got a doing, well Adam and the whole lot of them . . . would be out the next night looking for them, the people who set about me. If Adam got a doing, we'd be looking for them. Nothing ever went unanswered.

This emphasis on, and impact of, leaving nothing unanswered contributed to an escalation in violent offending and, as much as reflecting a commitment to each other as friends, was underpinned by normative expectations emerging from 'a culture of honour'. This means defending oneself and others in the group against slights or perceived transgressions and not being seen to be afraid. As previously observed, these virtues of loyalty, courage and fearlessness had the effect of commanding respect, and the degree to which they were exhibited in an individual influenced that individual's status amongst his peers.

Territoriality lessened as a focal point for identity and identification between the Del in mid-adolescence. Attending a Catholic secondary school meant that people mixed from different areas; bonds were forged through this new spatial connection, which provided an alternative frame of reference and which crystallised their identity as a group, rather than identification with place as a principal source of personal and collective identity. Simultaneously, the territorial emphasis became less pronounced as a direct source of conflict although the historical context of these feuds often underpinned enduring conflicts between the Del and other individuals and groups during early adulthood, exacerbated by the need to maintain a reputation, to 'let nothing go unanswered'. While, then, the Del as 'an interstitial group originally formed spontaneously' over time they 'then integrated through conflict' which served to inform their identity and solidify their cohesion as a group (Thrasher, 1927 p.57).

Seth: There was a lot of fighting then – when you get to that age, in the pubs and you're all drinking and the territorial squabbles from when yous were kids would be coming up and stupid things. Or fighting with the older ones, you know trying to prove yourself.

Jed: Most of the time it's because of what we've done . . . like if we batter some guy . . . his cousins and fucking brothers are going to get us and then we would get them, and then all their fucking mates are going to get in – it just happened all the time, you know what I mean?

These themes are elaborated more fully in the following sub-section; the remainder of this subsection provides an insight into the shifting dynamic of the Del's offending behaviour and their shared lifestyle. Somewhat reminiscent of Whyte's (1943) 'corner boys', the Del's lifestyles did not entirely cohere around criminality and violence, particularly during their earlier years. Rather, as Matza (1964) suggested, the Del drifted between conventional and criminal activities, although as a group, and consistent with their age and developmental stage, their emphasis or concerns were on the collective context of their shared pursuits, on being together.

Seth: There was carefree times . . . we used to do normal things that kids would do . . . it wasn't all just hanging about and causing trouble. It was kind of normal things – going to school and . . . doing just normal things.
Harry: We used to do things together . . . we used to go to discos . . . with a carry out when you were sixteen and you loved it . . . we used to go to the youth club and that apart from the streets.

However, while their behaviour 'wasnae all bad', as Jay observed (below), over time, their activities were increasingly characterised by anti-social behaviours including mobbing and rioting, fire-raising and vandalism. As they matured through adolescence, the places and social spaces they occupied similarly changed, from streets to pubs, and so did the nature and intensity of their offending.

Jay: We'd play football and hang about the park . . . so it wasnae all bad, but as we got older, most of the time we just spent down the pub, making up plans and drinking. There was loads and loads of fights but I couldn't go into every one of them.
Seth: Being a wee bit more adult then you were starting to go to the pubs and there were some good times in all of that as well, it wasn't all totally bad but it was all based around trouble. You would go out and get into fights through drink or being in a pub and then you'd spend your money so you'd be breaking into things.

Violent and acquisitive offences typified the Del's offending behaviour, assuming prominence over earlier patterns of delinquent or anti-social behaviour. These broad offence categories reflect a range of offences including fraud, theft, reset, and housebreaking, to violent offences of assault, serious assault, and possession of offensive weapons, armed robbery and attempted murder to public disorder offences of breach of the peace and malicious damage. Across the group, there are variations in people's offending profiles, number of convictions and sentencing outcomes, elaborated more fully in subsequent chapters. Jed, for example, amassed in excess of 80 convictions over two decades, although he surmised that his offending total is nearer 500. Like many of the Del, his convictions were principally disposed of through the imposition of frequent, short prison sentences of varying durations, resulting in him spending the equivalent of a decade in jail. Although like Jed, Andy committed in the region of 500 primarily acquisitive offences, he obtained only 13 convictions, reflecting the imposition of increasingly lengthy custodial sentences. At the age of 48, Andy had spent 32 years in adult prisons; his longest period in the community in this time lasted seven weeks and his shortest a few hours.

As a group, their offending varied in the extent to which a given offence was planned or unplanned. While there would be some deliberation over how a given offence should be executed, in the main, their offending might generally be characterised as opportunistic, reactive and impulsive as opposed to organised in any meaningful sense.

Jay: If it was housebreakings it would be sorta planned or semi-planned. If it was serious assaults, it could be planned 'cos it could be somebody you'd a grudge against or somebody you wanted to get. A lot of times it was just random. It was just a consequence of the gang culture . . . so you could be fuelled up with anger, or you could be drunk, or it could be a spur of the moment thing – so it could really range.

Harry: There was no solid pattern to any of them. It was just if it was happening, it was happening you know? So if you were skint, you would say, come on, we will go and tan a house and we done it.

Alcohol also played a significant role in their offending behaviour. Alcohol was intentionally used as a means of overcoming natural inhibitions or reservations to facilitate offending, particularly acts of violence, or being under the influence of alcohol would inadvertently facilitate offending as a consequence or outcome of reduced inhibitions or increased impulsivity. Often, acquisitive offending was engaged in for the purpose of generating income to acquire alcohol for recreational purposes.

Jay: We'd either do something because we were drunk or get drunk because we wanted to do something we couldn't do without a drink.
Andy: It was either we done it to get money to buy drink or we had had a few drinks and that spurred us on, so it was always there somewhere.

Over time, offending became a typical if not definitive feature of their shared lifestyle and, progressively, their individual and collective identities. Of significance here is the apparent near non-reflexivity applied to their offending behaviour at this time, emerging across the men's narratives. Their collective involvement in offending gave rise to an acceptance of the relative normalcy or inevitability of involvement in offending as an emergent effect of their interactive dynamics.

Harry: In they days that's just the way it was . . . I didnae look at myself that way you know? I just went with the flow and that was part of it . . . the people I ran about with . . . they were always at it so I used to go housebreaking with them but I didnae look at myself and say 'what kind of guy am I?' I didnae, you didnae think in they days.

Andy: I don't think I was involved with anybody who wasn't into crime so I never gave it much thought. I never ever had any quiet thoughts, or quiet moments, where I thought, 'wait a moment, this is not right'. Obviously, I knew it wasn't right but that didn't matter to me really. It was just what we did. I never saw myself stopping it. I don't think I ever thought too far ahead. I just lived from day to day.

Involvement in offending was thus accepted as an outcome of their interactive dynamics. Equally, these excerpts could be read as evidence of low self-efficacy, a reduced sense of agency, or a fatalistic view of the development of their offending careers (Maruna, 2001).

Jay: Looking back I suppose there was always a choice but at the time, no I just felt hooked in with the circle and hooked in with the cycle, if you like, the whole atmosphere, the whole environment, the whole lifestyle.

To be hooked perhaps implies a sense of compulsion, of addiction; however, it is not suggested here that offending is an addiction. The concept of 'being hooked' usefully reveals something of the complexities of the relational context of offending. For the individuals comprising the group, as the next sub-theme illustrates, the relational context of offending represents both the expression and erosion of agency, reflecting a series of compromises on the part of individuals-in-relation that enable the relations between people to endure. Individual reflexivity and action must be understood in the relational context within which it manifests. While relationships between individuals comprising the group were mutually valued, individuals were also increasingly dependent on these relationships – which simultaneously prescribed how each should behave according to what is normatively expected by others in the group. These relational rules (conceptualised as conditioning structures at T1 in Figure 4.1) and their individual and collective actions (the outcomes of their interactions at T2–T3 in Figure 4.1) influence outcomes for individuals and the collective (at T4 Figure 4.1) which represent the conditioning structures (at T1) in the next phase of the morphogenetic cycle, influencing their socio-structural contexts, creating new constraints and enablements on both individual and collective action. Issues of both choice and control must be viewed as emerging in the context of the various constraints and enablements in the conditioning structures, discussed above, to which individual reflexivity was brought to bear through the lens of their relational concerns, as the following sub-theme elaborates. The following sub-theme illustrates the primacy of these relationships to individuals and how the maintenance of the emergent relational goods manifested in specific expectations and behavioural obligations which contributed to the maintenance of association with the group and offending.

Identity and identification to and with the group

For narrative flow, this sub-theme has been further sub-divided into: 'Imprisoning lives, reputations and restrictions'; 'On identity'; and 'The individual and relational self in collective context'.

Imprisoning lives, reputations and restrictions

As previously observed, while the group itself offered respite from the trauma and abuse many experienced, the extent to which the group intentionally functioned as a source of security and protection emerged as a consequence of the interpersonal and inter-group conflicts that a life lived on the streets engendered. The group operated as a protective structure, both directly, in terms of exacting retribution and revenge on anyone who was violent towards them, and indirectly through their reputation for violence – a source of symbolic power or 'street capital' (Sandberg, 2008) that commanded respect, conferred status and deterred reprisals against them.

Jay: There was that safety . . . aspect as well. If you run about with the guys that nobody really kind of messed with . . . [also] my pals, they meant everything. Not just to me, it was the same fae them as well. We used to call ourselves 'the boys' and if any of us were in trouble – the rest of us would all go. It was a tight group . . . we had all that commitment to each other.

Jed: It went to the point that nobody would say a word to us. We used to go in the fuckin' pubs, even if I walked in myself . . . as soon as they know who you were, they didnae bother their arse . . . they were scared. They knew if one of them put a hand on me – anyone of them, the whole lot of them would get it the next day . . . It felt fuckin' great man.

As a consequence of their reputation for violence and the cycle of retributive violence this invoked, it was increasingly unsafe for members of the Del to appear in public without the protection of the group which served to intensify their commitments to, or at least dependency on, each other.

Jed: We never went out ourselves. I mean if I was going to sign on or whatever, I would always make sure there was three or four guys with me, the same as the rest of them . . . At first you felt, well – fairly chuffed, no cunt's going to say a word to me but then after a while you start going 'man, this is fucking ridiculous' . . . but . . . it became part of your life, you know . . . you never felt safe unless all your mates were with you.

While it was desirable to maintain the reputation they had developed, reflecting normative expectations emerging from a 'culture of honour' and the relational rules to which they subscribed, the maintenance of this reputation thus gave rise to an increasingly imprisoning and restrictive lifestyle offering little choice or opportunity to be or do anything different. Maintaining a reputation means fulfilling the expectations that others have of you in accordance with an ascribed characteristic, trait or image. The need to maintain an image consistent with a given social role inhibits and promotes certain courses of action as delineated by the relational rules that circumscribe how one should conduct oneself in a given social context. Maintaining a reputation was incompatible with, for example, certain types of social activities and association with people outside their social milieu. Immersion in the 'gang culture' restricted the development of new social ties and engagement in activities that were incompatible with the specific configuration of masculinity they appropriated (Willis, 1977).

Jay: By that time though I had a sort of reputation to keep so you couldnae be seen going to drama classes or anything like that . . . I'd get embarrassed about being seen to do certain things, or being seen with certain people if it didnae fit in with the gang culture.

In the context of existing and self-imposed restrictions on their opportunities to access alternative membership groups or social activities, the group thus represented a site of belonging, or an exclusive enclave of inclusion, which met their needs for social interaction and participation. However, at the same time, their offending, the reputations they acquired and the ensuing interpersonal repercussions further constrained the possibilities and opportunities for alternative means of social participation.

Seth: There was a sense that you were disliked, you know, kind of shunned from normal things. The only place you could really move was in your group. There was certain things you wouldnae do like guys going to cadets and things like that, you just felt you couldnae be part of that. You were getting in to trouble you know and that didn't exactly go hand in hand with things like that.

Jay: It had an effect on relationships with people – just your reputation . . . sometimes we would go to people['s] . . . houses and their mothers wouldnae want them to [be] with us . . . we had quite a bad reputation about the town.

Significantly, their reputations for, as Harry termed it (below), their 'unruly' behaviour and frequent non-attendance also had repercussions for their experience of school and educational outcomes, which were further compounded by regular periods of detention in assessment centres and approved schools. Seth described being segregated with other people with behavioural issues or learning needs and overlooked, which contributed to their disaffection at school and low educational attainment.

Harry: As soon as you've got a reputation the teachers lose interest in you . . . We were flung to the side you know? Probably because we were all unruly. You know what I mean?

Seth: Because of the reputation I went in with – whether that was because of my family or things I had done – they kind of knew us so, once you were pegged in secondary school as a trouble-maker – that was you. You were in all the bad classes . . . They were done so that the trouble-makers were in the bottom class together. So, even if you done well in tests, you were still never moved out the class where all the trouble-makers were.

Having a reputation thus resulted in restricted opportunities for social participation and education, which, in part, can be construed as an outcome of the totality of their collective actions and interactive dynamics as a group. However, the stigma, prejudice and discrimination they experienced emerged as an outcome of their wider social interactions.

On identity

Adolescence and early adulthood is a period of experimentation with identity and at this stage, the peer group plays a critical role in identity formation (Erikson, 1950). Belonging to a group offers a relational web within and through which identities can be acquired, tested and performed. For the Del, the group also operated as a vehicle which facilitated offending, and their offending operated as a means through which group solidarity was realised (Messerschmidt, 1993) and reputations developed. Being able to fight, demonstrating fearlessness in risk taking and exhibiting loyalty are all ways of 'doing masculinity' and developing reputational or 'street capital' (Sandberg, 2008). Reputation can be construed as a reflection of the interpretation of one's social identity. In this vein, as Jay suggests, identities are intricately infused into relational rules which inhibit and promote certain courses of action, and which are learned and performed, appropriated and negotiated over time, through social interaction.

Jay: Well certainly from 13 or 14 . . . you are sort of watching people more, idolising all the older gang members . . . suss[ing] out who was who, what was what, and what you do and what you don't do. So it was a time of learning, about how you were going to get from there to there . . . They were the years when you were sussing everything out and learning how you were going to be the man you were going to be, basically.

Personal and social identities emerge through social interaction and through processes of internal (how people see themselves) and external identification (how people are categorised by others). Donati argues that 'personal identity, that is, the consciousness of the self, interacts with the social identity that is formed through social interaction' (2011 pp.48–49). Every way of being a self, as a primary agent (me), a corporate agent (we) or social actor (you) is a dialogue between one's personal and social identity. Social identity is, then, influenced by processes of *both* internal and external identification in terms of membership of a social category or social role. Social identification constitutes 'a subjective process through which externally assigned category distinctions are accepted [or rejected] and in-group characteristics are adopted to help define and express the self' (Barreto and Ellemers, 2003 p.141 [this author's insertion]). Identification to and with a group thus requires an acceptance and adoption of the norms and rules of associational belonging characteristic of membership of a given group (Hogg and Hardie, 1991).

Recognition and acceptance by the group is a form of personal validation and can shape how people come to see themselves. Young people who experience stigma and marginalisation from mainstream society can gain respect and social recognition from their peers through offending behaviour, association with the group and involvement with the criminal justice system, as a means of proving their masculine attributes (Barry, 2006; Messerschmidt, 1994). In the early stages, involvement with the criminal justice system represented a rite of passage which served to crystallise identities and consolidate reputations.

Jay: It was quite a thing in they days if you got lifted and put in the cells at that age, it was an image thing. There was some kudos you know?

Harry: Well when you're that age, I was only 16, I was coming out and you thought you were great cos you were just out the jail. So it was more of an achievement than anything else you know?

Andy: I thought I was getting respect fae people . . . I can remember sitting round the back of the bookies counting the things I had done . . . I was myself . . . counting the things I had broken into . . . I think I was proud of myself, honestly . . . I was actually feeling good cos I'd done however many things I'd done.

The social recognition (Honneth, 1995) and status conferred by their peers both within and outside the group was also a means of ameliorating and resisting the stigma attributed to their identities in certain public spheres, such as the school and the community. Corrigan and Watson (2002) distinguish between public stigma and self-stigma. Public stigma relates to the negative stereotypes and attributes that society places on the stigmatised individual, which can invoke discrimination and contribute to the stigmatised person's marginalisation. Self-stigma refers to the degree to which individuals internalise and adopt these judgements, stereotypes and attributions (see also Lemert, 1951; Markowitz, 2001; Shih, 2004). Those who closely identify with their group, despite the stigma associated with the group, are more likely to be able to resist negative attributions which do not correspond with the individual or group's views of themselves (Crocker and Major, 1998). Highly identified individuals frequently interact with others from the same group and are more aware of the positive aspects of group membership, which include the imputation of status by association with the group, respect, social recognition and acceptance, which can reinforce related behaviours and the positive aspects of the social identities they inform.

Harry: Well you are in and about a crowd and they are all the hard men of [Coaston] and you were part of that you know?

Seth: I think it was the kind of status . . . and the gang kind of thing – the friendship and the loyalty . . . that you felt then. You were part of something . . . I would say that I probably got nothing from it bar the standing in the eyes of my pals round about me – and respect.

Evan: You got a bit – when you done something notorious – know you were . . . (gestures) and 'that was good [Evan]', know? . . . There was one or two lads you would know who were quite handy and I think they enjoyed that notoriety and you didn't mind being about them know cos you . . . knew this person, this person could handle themselves so you enjoyed that and you encouraged that person into that . . . 'you're the man' know?

Indeed, the credibility or legitimacy of the person conveying positive regard or social recognition, or conversely attributing stigma, is also relevant to the potency of the attribution or judgement (Ikaheimo and Laitinen, 2011; Shih, 2004). As observed earlier, Harry and Andy for example were, initially at least, resolutely unconcerned by the negative views that others outside of the group had of them – indeed they rarely considered how they were perceived by non-group members. Rather, their peer group was the primary influence on their self-concept, and thus the perceptions their peers had of them were more influential than the 'reflected appraisals' of the 'generalised other' (Cooley, 1956). People adopt various self-protective strategies to resist stigma and preserve their self-esteem (Crocker and Major, 1998). Resistance to stigma was also accomplished through the use of rationalisations and justifications or 'techniques of neutralisations' (Sykes and Matza, 1957) as a means of externalising behaviour and, thus, resisting the personification or internalisation of negative attributes as a property of the self. In this context, 'neutralizations are probably best understood as "insulation from labelling" (Covington 1984 p.621)' (Maruna and Copes, 2005 p.257).

Evan: You justify things Beth . . . and I used to say well I don't steal from my own, know, I am stealing from people who can afford it. So I am not really a bad guy . . . but, deep down, I knew that what I was doing was wrong . . . but you justify that and you say 'but I am not a bad guy'.

However, resisting stigma in public spheres is more challenging for an individual to maintain without the protection of the group who can deflect discrediting attributions from the individual. When in the company of the group, for example, Jed's sensitivity to stigma was diffused across the group and therefore diminished in potency and ostensibly depersonalised. He experienced it as particularly troubling outside the company of the group where perhaps it became more apparent, condemnations were more likely to be articulated or were less easily ignored.

Jed: Years ago, every cunt knew what you had done . . . Within a day it was through the whole fucking town and then you'd walk down the town and – I can actually hear them – 'fucking bastards, they should be strung up,' . . . and . . . I thought 'Oh god man'. There were times I didn't go down the town for months . . . It was only when we all got together we'd go down the town and then nae cunt would say a fucking word . . . When you're out with the boys you don't care about anything. Once you're locked up yourself . . . that's when it all comes . . . and you wonder what people think of you. You wonder what the woman across the road is saying every time she sees the polis up at your mother's or what they are going to say next time I walk down the fucking town.

The ability to resist internalising a stigmatised self-concept or discredited identity (for a detailed discussion see Crocker and Major, 1998) also depends in part on the centrality or importance of the stigmatising 'condition' to one's personal identity and to the significance placed on how that aspect of one's social identity is interpreted and responded to in a given social context. Hall (1966) for example found that increased identification with a delinquent subculture in general was associated with higher self-esteem. Nelson Foote (1951 p.17 cited in Hall, 1966) defined the process of identification as appropriation of and 'commitment to a particular identity or series of identities'. As the individual comes to identify with a group, he differentiates himself from those outside the group. This process of identification and differentiation is, Hall argues, basic to the validation of the identity. By engaging in this process, as Jay suggested earlier, the individual learns who he is and who he is not. Since this learning process constitutes the appropriation of a particular identity and identification with a group, Hall suggests that the individual principally identifies with similarly situated others and evaluates himself against the norms, attitudes and standards of this group. Hall argues that higher levels of identification and conformity to the standards of the group results in higher levels of self-evaluation; those who have lower levels of identification with the group or higher levels of identification with conventional standards or values can experience internal conflict as a result of these inconsistent and contradictory identities. As the group is not the primary reference point of self-evaluation, more marginally identified individuals will exhibit lower levels of self-evaluation.

This however is an incomplete picture. While this can tell us something about levels of identification with a delinquent sub-culture and the associated levels of self-evaluation, it remains somewhat individualistic in focus, drawing on conceptions of an atomistic individual and their level of identification with the cultural contexts that frame them. It cannot, for example, provide an explanation as to why a given individual with a lower level of identification with, or internalisation of, the norms and standards of the group may nonetheless be more highly 'embedded' (Granovetter, 1985) in the group than another highly identified individual. There is, therefore, a crucial distinction to be made between an individual's levels of cognitive identification with a deviant sub-culture per se and experience of embeddedness within a particular group who engage in deviant behaviours, which requires an examination of the group as a social relation.

The individual and the relational self in a collective context

Exploring levels of embeddedness in the group as a social relation allows that similarly situated individuals may arrive at different patterns of identification with their shared culture and to other individuals participating in the social relation. Any grouping of individuals-in-relation will necessarily mean variations in the relationships, status, identification, involvement and levels and meaning of belongingness among individual members of a group, which accounts for the heterogeneity of experience of participation in a group. In this vein, Pyrooz et al. (2012) elaborate and extend Hagan's (1993) concept of embeddedness to explain rates of desistance (or extrication) from gang membership; they argue that those with lower levels of embeddedness exit the gang earlier than those more highly embedded. Pyrooz et al. (2012) explain that

> Criminal embeddedness is a multidimensional, emergent property encompassing not only conventional network characteristics such as density of network ties or centrality within a deviant network but also the level of involvement in crime, isolation from pro-social networks, positions of leadership within a deviant network, and adoption of deviant values and identities.
>
> (p. 4)

Concepts of identification and embeddedness can facilitate an understanding of the differential experiences of group membership and, arguably, processes of change. To illustrate, Andy exhibited high levels of identification with a deviant subculture[3] and low levels of embeddedness within the group manifesting in a low status within the group, low levels of influence, and a comparatively marginal position within the group.

Andy: I can remember my Dad sitting saying to me one day 'where do we go from here?' My reply was, I was 16 at the time and I'm in a young offenders', and my reply was 'Barlinnie, Perth' – all these adult prisons I was mentioning. I was too far gone with trying to impress other people and live up to any kind of image I thought I had, and by then my Mum and Dad had probably lost me . . . I was always thinking er easy money, opportunist kind of thieving. I never ever felt I was going to go out and try and get a job and settle down and stuff like that, it never entered my mind . . . every single thought I had in they days was all thieving. I used to get a kick out of breaking into places and going through drawers and finding things.

Yet, in discussing his relationship to the group:

Andy: I don't think I had any influence over anybody. I think I was [pause] I used to do things to please them . . . to keep in with them. I always felt if I didnae do these things I wouldnae be as pally with them or they wouldnae be as pally with me. I think I looked up to quite a lot of them . . . I felt accepted but I always felt I had to try and prove myself among these boys 'cos ... I just felt a wee bit in awe of them. I felt I would need to do things to prove that I was one of them.

Andy's sense of having to 'please' or 'keep in' with the others reveals his sense of the contingency of his acceptance by the Del and is illustrative of his subordinate positioning and status within the group hierarchy. To an extent, as indicated earlier, this reflects his subordinate status manifest in his inability to fight or command respect through intimidation or assertiveness. However, Andy's involvement in petty offending commenced prior to involvement with the Del and his identification with a deviant sub-culture, realised through his association with the Del, underpinned the significance of his involvement with them, and their (albeit contingent) acceptance of him facilitated the realisation of a related identity. By contrast, Seth, assisted by his brother's (Adam) dominant position within the group and, as measured by his own status and centrality to the group, levels of involvement in criminal activity and isolation from pro-social networks, was highly embedded in the Del. While Seth engaged in offending with the group he exhibited low levels of identification with a 'deviant sub-culture'. For Seth, his relationships within the group[4] and the associated relational goods were more significant to him than any gains derived from offending, generating an enduring sense that he 'never really fitted in' to the offending culture despite his immersion in the group.

Seth: I felt that I never really fitted in – even then I kind of knew it was wrong ... I was always kind of watching it from the outside and you realised it wasn't right even then.. I just didn't ever feel part of it ... I never got any real thrill from offending or anything, never any buzz.

The sample size and situational nature of the fragmentation of the group (discussed below) precludes making generalisations about whether differences in levels of identification and embeddedness influence an individual's desistance, or whether more instrumental or affective rationales underpinning both offending and relations with the group influence individual trajectories. It is noteworthy, however, that the fragmentation of the group had no bearing on either the nature or frequency of Andy's offending, whereas it had a significant impact on other people's offending trajectories (discussed below and in subsequent chapters). Moreover, while differentiating between and considering levels of identification with a deviant sub-culture per se and degrees of embeddedness within a group can help illuminate differences in individuals' experiences of the group, by respectively prioritising agentic and structural explanations for human behaviour neither concept can offer a nuanced understanding of the dynamics of individuals-in-relation or how and why participation in a given social relation has powers to feed back on the individual. It is argued here that taking the social relation as the primary unit of analysis can reveal a more nuanced understanding of human behaviour in general and of the relationship between individual and collective action in particular.

As previously suggested the form of masculinities adopted and adapted by the Del was a blend of stereotypical traditional working class and idealised hard man forms which created a model for social relations between men and between men and women (Connell and Messerschmidt, 2005) and the performance of gender identities. The valorisation of this form (and performance of) hegemonic masculinity was influenced by the social and cultural conditions, values and beliefs from which it derived not least as a means of accomplishing respect and social recognition in the face of broader social inequalities. While never perfectly realised or supposed (each knowing his seeming incongruous vulnerabilities, anxieties, fears and insecurities) a successful performance through acts of bravery, courage and violence is recognised and the desired status conferred, and by mutual agreement unchallenged.

In the aftermath of a particularly violent incident, for example, the Del would be reluctant to discuss with each other how they felt about the incident. However, there are numerous examples across the men's narratives of individuals recalling a level of cognitive and moral dissonance over behaviours they had engaged in as a group, relating primarily to whether the victim had 'deserved' it or the extent to which the victim was injured or equipped to defend themselves. In these discussions, emotions of shame, remorse, guilt and fear would be censured in accordance with their normative modes of exchange, where talk of emotions was discouraged. However, these exchanges could perform an important function in suspending or ameliorating the inner conflicts arising from having engaged in behaviours inconsistent with an individual's beliefs or sense of what is right (Festinger, 1957) through the mutual assertion of justifications which could serve as a means of protecting a positive self-image (Cooper and Fazio, 1984) and preserving their view of themselves.

Jed: You start wondering if the person deserved it . . . but you couldnae tell your mates, cos they would think you'd gone soft . . . the next day you'd maybe sit for about an hour before anybody would say anything – like 'that was some doing the cunt got' or somebody would come in and say 'oh his ribs are all broken, his jaw's broken' and then you'd start thinking about it . . . I was always the cunt that said, 'we shouldn't have done that', but the other ones were always like that 'oh shut up, he deserved every fucking blow'.

Given the centrality of the others' views for individuals' self-concepts, mutually agreed and expressed justifications could make it easier for an individual to reconcile or suppress their inner tensions or conflicts by shifting an individual's sense of personal responsibility or accountability for action onto the group and the exigencies of their collective lifestyle. Jed (above) is clearly articulating his own remorse but in the process of doing this is presenting a clear distinction between his reactions and those of the others, which in the context of his own experience of personal shame, allows him to draw a comparison with their seeming unconcern to preserve or protect his own inherent 'goodness' (see relatedly Maruna 2001). Such a position is further rationalised by Jed (below) in locating the impetus and justifications for *his* actions as an individual within the norms and expectations of the group as a means of resolving the ambivalence of agency where one is simultaneously drawn and disinclined towards the same course of action (Ekstrom, 2010).

Jed: Oh I could have said no but most of the time you don't want to say no in case you're called a fucking shitbag . . . You cannae be bothered with that so to prevent all that carry on you just do it . . . I always done it. I think it's more pride than anything else.

Seth: I think once you'd embarked on it you felt there was no turning back . . . the embarrassment you know if you started and then you were too scared to go through with it. That would have been seen as fear then, a weakness. Although you knew it was wrong . . . you had the kind of sense of – you had to do it.

These extracts suggest that the group encourages collective participation in behaviours that individuals might not normally undertake alone, partly motivated by fear of 'losing face', status or the respect of their friends as measured against the extent to which individuals behaved in accordance with the norms, attitudes and standards of the group and fulfilled their relational obligations and expectations. Close friendships generate such reciprocated obligations and expectations; it is the desire to maintain the relation and their shared relational goods of trust, solidarity, loyalty, and social connectedness that prompt and guide individual action, also a mode of collective group orientation. However, these normative expectations and obligations were variously experienced as a constraint on individual autonomy, as Seth illustrates.

Seth: I felt as though I was just swept up in it. I felt I couldn't just step away from it. You were part of the gang, living up to the reputation; you've got to keep going. I just felt that I couldnae step away.

The use of the word 'you' can imply a generalised experience, in this case referring to their shared associational belonging, roles and the relational expectations of group members. Seth's use of the words 'I' and 'You' in this context also betrays ambivalence, an inner tension between his individual and relational concerns. Briefly, however, if, following Donati (2011) where 'I' represents the Self and 'You' represents one's self as a social actor, Seth's 'internal conversation' is discernible in this extract in which he reflects on his commitments to the group and what he perceives as the constraints this commitment placed on his autonomy. In performing or personifying a role, in carrying out the tasks associated with that role, in acting as a 'You', the Self, one's 'I', asks itself if it is gaining satisfaction from one's activities, choices, lifestyle or not. One's ultimate concerns are progressively defined in relation to how the Self defines his choices when he acts as a 'You' and must respond both to the demands of his relational contexts and to the deeper demands of his 'Self'. At this juncture, within the limits of the possibilities and opportunities available to him, Seth's relational concerns pre-dominate as an outcome of his internal conversation, to which he commits himself.

Rather than construing Seth's commitment to his relational concerns, then, as the erosion of agency, it can be understood as the expression of agency in that he acted on his convictions, in the context of his relational concerns, guided by the relationships that mattered most to him, within the constraints of the cultural context. The individual, while not subjugating himself to the relation, makes adjustments and compromises to maintain the relation and the associated relational goods. This process can thus be theorised as evidence of Seth's application of his personal reflexivity, not simply to himself or to his individual concerns, but to his relationships (i.e. in a context which produced certain relational goods), consistent with Donati's (2011) concept of social or relational reflexivity. Issues of both choice and control must thus be understood as emerging in the context of the various constraints and enablements in the conditioning structures, which include the group itself, to which individual reflexivity is brought to bear through the lens of one's relational concerns.

The fragmentation of the Del

During their 20s, a violent and enduring feud effectively divided the group. The feud was triggered by Seth having an affair with Iain Nixon's wife while Iain was in prison. Like Adam, Iain occupied a prominent position within the group. Indeed, just as Seth, Jay and Adam were brothers, two of Iain's brothers were similarly involved in the group, which meant that the group was fractured along sibling lines, with other individuals siding with either the Nixons or the Websters, depending on the strength and intensity of existing relationships in the group at that point. Seth's actions were construed by the Nixon side as a betrayal of the relational rules of friendship and this signalled the demise of the original group, necessarily and irrevocably affecting individual relationships.

Jay: Well [Seth] was going out with one of [the Nixon's] wives and there was bad blood fae then. Then one night, I was in the pub and one of them was arguing – I started arguing with one of them and I hit him, then he hit me and we started a fight and fae there it just . . . got out of control.

As Jay implies, the violence escalated in frequency and intensity over a two year period. Some people, such as Harry, developed alternative social networks rather than align themselves with one faction due to fear of a violent reproach by the other party.

Harry: I never fell out major with any of them because . . . I didn't want to get involved . . . I just spoke to them all and . . . I think they all realised that and they were happier with me. Other ones were getting involved that weren't involved you know?

Harry started associating with his elder brother's friends who were heavily involved in the football culture signalling a shift in his offending towards primarily football-related violence. Evan was in prison throughout this period and retained amicable relations with both factions during periods when they too were incarcerated; on his release he associated with different friends and continued to engage in acquisitive crime. Andy, who had associated with Iain in prison, continued to do so following his release and his return to Coaston. This resulted in a violent reprisal by the Websters and thereafter Andy had no further contact with either faction although, like Evan, he continued to engage in acquisitive crime alone. Jed sided with the Webster brothers with whom he had always been particularly close and supported the Websters in the ongoing violent conflicts.

Although individual narratives of offending and desistance are continued in Chapters 5–10, this chapter concludes with an examination of the way in which the Websters' faction (hereafter revised group) supported each other to change the direction of their lives and, ultimately, desist. In general, at this age and stage in their lives, some of the revised group were in committed intimate or personal relationships and acquired new roles as fathers, which, for some, presented as viable alternative means of accomplishing masculinity, identity and social recognition and which, to varying degrees, triggered a reflexive re-evaluation of their relationships and their lifestyles, through the lens of their ultimate and relational concerns (discussed in individual stories). In the context of enduring economic and structural constraints in the west of Scotland at this time, and as an opportunity to extricate themselves from the seemingly endless and escalating violence, a number of the Del relocated to London to maximise the opportunities presented by the construction boom of the eighties.

From fragmentation to reformation

This section illustrates the role that some of the Del played in triggering a reflexive re-evaluation of their involvement in offending and in mutually supporting the early phases of each other's process of desistance. What follows is a general overview of the role of the revised group in supporting desistance in the context of, and in interaction with, their collective relocation to London. Individual narratives of both continued offending and desistance across the sample are explored in Chapters 5–10 which provide a more nuanced analysis of the dynamics of desistance.

Adam was the first of the revised group to move to London (circa 1987), motivated by a desire to extricate himself from the violence and to access employment in steel-fixing. In Adam's case this was informed by a reflexive intention to desist and distance himself from the 'relational bads' (Donati, 2011) emerging from the feud, further underpinned by his emotional connection to his spouse and a desire to maintain those emergent 'relational goods', which continued offending and its outcomes threatened. Concerned to support his friends to start over, Adam encouraged them to relocate and trained them in steel-fixing, sharing and imparting the skills in which he had been trained by his father-in-law. Among those interviewed in this study, Jed, Seth and Jay followed him to London although others not interviewed included the Smith brothers (Ben, Jim and James) and Mark also moved with them. Adam's concern for his friends can be construed as evidence of his application of his personal reflexivity, not simply to himself or to his individual social mobility, but to his relationships as a way of exercising his leadership in a different way (i.e. in a context which produced relational goods), consistent with Donati's (2011) concept of relational reflexivity. Re-establishing a revised and collaborative relational network in a new location facilitated the re-emergence of the relational goods of social trust, solidarity and social connectedness threatened by the feud, from which other ends, including new knowledge and skills, employment and economic resources, were derived as secondary emergent effects (Donati, 2006).

For most of the revised group, relocating to London represented an opportunity for a lifestyle free from the violence the feud gave rise to, to an area in which they were unknown, and which yielded opportunities for employment in steel-fixing and, thus, legitimate economic gains, all of which generated further change-promotive outcomes. While economic and social changes to their conditioning structures in the form of employment opportunities were enabled by the construction boom of the 1980s, the recognition and pursuit of such opportunities can be construed as an expression of their individual and collective agency. However, the development of the necessary skills in steel-fixing and their capacity to *access* these opportunities and settle in a new area emerged from the mutual and reciprocal exchange of support and resources among the revised group. The changes in their conditioning structures were thus, in part, the outcome of the collaborative efforts of the revised group, to which they brought their personal reflexivity to bear. This move thus offered shared opportunities for change, or changes in their conditioning structures, as an outcome of both their interactive dynamics and the diversified relational contexts the move facilitated, both within and beyond the group, to which individuals responded differently through the lens of their individual and relational concerns.

This new environment, without the legacies of conflict that typified their lifestyle and interactions in Coaston, freed the revised group from the restrictive reputations, imprisoning lifestyles and the cycle of violence that had characterised their lives previously and opened up new possibilities for social participation. Anonymity in a new environment contributed to the development of an alternative social identity for individuals and the group, which, in conjunction with regular employment, represented relative freedom from the restrictions of their former environment, an opportunity to see oneself differently, to be seen differently and to live differently. Relocating to London thus afforded the revised group an opportunity to 'knife off' (Maruna and Roy, 2007) the stigma and reputations they had acquired (and required) in Coaston through the anonymity they collectively enjoyed as a consequence of their new environment and the shifting social spaces they occupied.

Jay: Well when we stayed [in Coaston] we were quite notorious . . . when we went [to London], nobody knew us, so it was like a fresh start. Also we were used to getting the blame of stuff [in Coaston]. We got the blame of stuff we did do and . . . stuff we never done. So [in London], we were . . . breaking free fae the tag, the stigma.

Living and working in a new environment afforded the revised group an opportunity to engage in a wealth of new experiences and an opportunity to connect to different people, which contributed to an enhanced sense of agency and an ability to imagine themselves and their relationships differently, and, thus, capable of actualising things as yet unrealised.

Jay: Going to London . . . opened up a whole new world because I had been cocooned up in here in [Coaston], in my relationships, my friendships . . . when I moved it was just as if the blinkers were taken away . . . I met a whole different range of people and I knew that I could move away from [Coaston] and the life I was in and do things I could never have done before . . . I would say that was definitely a big turning point in my life.

The meanings and outcomes of work for individuals are discussed in Chapters 5–10. Across the revised group, however, employment in steel-fixing required the development of employment-based networks to access further work and, thus, the development of 'bridging' social capital. Bridging social capital involves establishing new social relations; these ties facilitate the reciprocal exchange of resources from one network to a member of another network and in this sense are linked to the development of broader identities and social mobility (Woolcock and Narayan, 2000). In the steel-fixing industry, where work was obtained through 'word of mouth' and was typically distributed within known employment-based networks, bridging social capital was a critical and instrumental means of access to further contractual work for the group. One person, often Adam, would obtain a contract for work and, as foreman, employed his friends and associates to carry out the work. In addition to sustaining employment, the development of new social relationships through work, comprising a diverse range of people, 'afforded a concrete way of enhancing one's own identity as a respectable person' (Giordano et al., 2003 p.311), through the development of a constructive reputation as a 'worker', which was necessary for access to further work. Alongside the male-dominated environment and hyper-masculine, hard-working culture of the steel-fixing industry, work thus represented an alternative means of accomplishing masculinity, and acquiring self-respect and social recognition consistent with their idealised configuration of what it meant to be a man.

Jed: [Men would] be talking about their work and things like that. We were dead proud of them . . . that's the way we thought of guys . . . that were out there working.
Seth: I think realising that if you do work hard there is hope there and I took a kind of pride in it . . . It [also] took that thing away, about how are you going to get money . . . But now it's your working all the hours to buy something

good ... or to put money away for security for your family or go a holiday. Work definitely had a big impact on me – starting work and realising that you could do it without committing crime; you could have a decent life and feel good about yourself.

Participation in regular employment at this stage also provided the revised group with new weekly routines, new social relationships and employment-based networks, economic stability, and concrete opportunities for new experiences which, as Seth suggested previously – and in the context of the hopelessness they had previously felt – generated hope and an enhanced sense of agency. For those, like Seth and Adam, involved in committed intimate relationships, participation in employment also informed their personal and social identities as providers, consistent with their roles as fathers and relationships with partners, which, again, simultaneously provided a conventional means of accomplishing masculinity, a pro-social identity and social recognition.

Personal relationships exerted a distinct change-promotive influence on the behaviour of some of those in the revised group and their lifestyle (see Chapters 5–10). Generally, however, the acquisition of new relationships and associated social roles and practices – in conjunction with an increasing disillusionment with their previous lifestyles and the threat continued offending potentially posed to these roles and relationships, to their shifting identities and to employment opportunities – influenced not only individual behaviour but the interactive dynamics of the revised group. The shifting priorities and concerns of individuals away from the group and towards their families of formation and associated shifts in their behaviour exerted a constraint on the behaviour of others, who found they had less support from their desisting peers for engagement in offending behaviour. This reflected a shift in the relational rules in this revised relational context, to which they responded by modifying their behaviour, motivated by a desire to support each other.

People's receptivity to the influence of their friends arose from the reciprocal bond between them; in turn, what emerged from their interactions and combined resources was a transformation in their conditioning structures underpinned by their shared concern with elaborating a new way of being-in-relation as a reciprocal good. The emergent relational goods were the intentional products both of their social reflexivity and of the personal reflexivity of each individual modifying their relations when they no longer produced the desired outcomes consistent with their ultimate concerns (Donati, 2011).

Conclusion

This chapter introduced the characters on whose narratives this book draws and delineates the history of the Del, from formation, through their lived experiences, early group dynamics and subjectivities, to the ultimate fragmentation of the group. In so doing, this chapter serves as a foundation and a context to the individual stories that follow.

This chapter illustrated how the Del actively and self-consciously appropriated elements of an exaggerated configuration of 'traditional' working class masculinity influenced by, and responsive to, the social, cultural and economic character of the era of their duration. This somewhat idealised representation of masculinity informed the social relations in which they participated as both a context and as interaction. Their emergent gender identities were intricately infused into relational rules influencing the kinds of bonds generated between them and which guided the nature and form of their relations and interactions and the actions they gave rise to. Drawing on Donati's relational sociology, sociologies of friendship and the literature on gangs, the analysis in this chapter illuminated the shifting dynamics of the group, in terms of 'membership' or affiliations, group identities, interactive dynamics and behaviour, and shifts in the meaning of belonging and the operative function of the group over time in the context of existing, self-imposed and emergent or ensuing restrictions on social participation. The chapter concluded by describing the situational nature of the fragmentation of the group and the divergent outcomes this heralded for the men at the centre of this study. Of these outcomes, the role of the 'revised group' in supporting the early phases of each other's desistance was outlined.

Employing the adaptation of Donati's conceptual schema progressed in Chapter 3, this chapter illustrated the way in which the group as a social relation was configured in the T2–T3 phase (Figure 4.1). Social relations have constraints and enablements from outside, in terms of normative expectations of friendship for example, as well as their own internal network dynamics, influenced by the conditioning structures, which inform the situations of actions (T1–T2) and the relational rules to which they subscribe and their modes of interaction. This is distinct from what happens inside the individuals who evaluate their situations, take decisions autonomously, discussed under 'the individual and the relational self in a collective context' and elaborated more substantially in subsequent chapters. The chapter also revealed how the elaborated structure, the outcomes for individuals and the group (at T4) depends upon and is influenced by the dynamics of the relational network, the totality of their collective actions and the ensuing repercussions, which means that relations have their own powers and qualities in determining the final outcome, besides the agential power of the actors and the balance in their power relations which can influence both persistence in and desistance from offending. The outcomes for the individuals and the group at T4 represent the conditioning structures at T1 in the next phase of the morphogenetic cycle, influencing their socio-structural contexts by creating new constraints and enablements on both individual and collective action.

This chapter has further illustrated how both structure and agency are mediated through reflexivity, also a mode of collective group orientation as 'relational reflexivity', to illustrate that both individual and collective action is guided by individual concerns *and* by the good of the relationships which matter most to them. To this end, this chapter illustrated how social relations operate with their own kinds of reflexivity, oriented to the maintenance of the relation, where it is valued by those participating in it, and thus to the maintenance of the emergent relational goods relevant to desistance, but which equally during the life-space of the group contributed to persistent involvement in offending, even where this invoked ambivalence of agency.

Notes

1 Parts of this chapter draw from Donati, P. (2011) *Relational Sociology: A New Paradigm for the Social Sciences*. Abingdon: Routledge. Reproduced with permission from Routledge.
   Parts of this chapter were previously published in Weaver, B. (2012) The Relational Context of Desistance: Some Implications and Opportunities for Social Policy. *Social Policy and Administration*, 46(4), pp.395–412. Reproduced with permission from Wiley.
   Parts of this chapter were previously published in Weaver, B., and McNeill. F. (2015) Lifelines: Desistance, Social Relations and Reciprocity. *Criminal Justice and Behavior* 42(1), pp.95–107. Reproduced with permission from Sage.
2 'Those gangs that meet the criteria of the Eurogang consensus definition (durable and street-oriented youth groups whose involvement in illegal activity is part of their group identity), groups that may alternatively be called "troublesome youth groups"' (Klein et al., 2006 p.414).
3 Hall (1966) elaborates that a highly identified individual would a) think of themselves as a 'delinquent' or 'offender', reflecting the extent to which they interiorised both the associated role and identity; b) hold a negative attitude towards or relationship with their parents; c) invest in or highly value their relationships with not only co-offenders but offending associated and related activities, thus exhibiting an orientation towards a more 'delinquent' peer group as juxtaposed with d) more normative social orientations. Such an individual would e) exhibit or express an internal locus of control in terms of explaining involvement in criminality and f) associate excitement and risk taking behaviours as expressive of their personality.
4 Arguably, relational dynamics require further consideration as a measure of embeddedness alongside the more quantifiable structural indicators discussed by Pyrooz et al. (2012).

References

Aldridge, J., Medina, J., and Ralphs, R. (2007) *Youth Gangs in an English City: Social Exclusion, Drugs and Violence*. Full Research Report ESRC End of Award Report, RES-000–23–0615. Swindon: ESRC.
Allan, G. (1989) *Friendship*. London: Harvester/Wheatsheaf.
Allan, G. (1996) *Kinship and Friendships in Modern Britain*. Oxford: Oxford University Press.
Allan, G. (1998) Friendship, Sociology and Social Structure. *Journal of Social and Personal Relationships* 15(5), pp.685–702.
Anderson, E. (2003) *A Place on the Corner* (2nd ed.). Chicago, IL: University of Chicago Press.
Archer, M. (2011) The Logic of the Gift: Can it Find a Place Within Normal Economic Activity? http://www.secondspring.co.uk/uploads/articles_19_953760526.pdf, accessed 28/8/12.
Bannister, J., and Fraser, A. (2008) Youth Gang Identification: Learning and Social Development in Restricted Geographies. *Scottish Journal of Criminal Justice Studies* 14, pp.96–114.
Barreto, M., and Ellemers, N. (2003) The Effects of Being Categorised: The Interplay Between Internal and External Social Identities. *European Review of Social Psychology* 14(1), pp.139–170.

Barry, M. (2006) *Youth Offending in Transition: The Search for Social Recognition.* Abingdon: Routledge.
Baumeister, R.F., and Leary, M.R. (1995) The Need to Belong: Desire for Interpersonal Attachments as a Fundamental Human Motivation. *Psychological Bulletin* 117(3), pp.497–529.
Blau, P. (1964) *Exchange and Power in Social Life.* New York, NY: Wiley.
Byrne, D. (1999) *Social Exclusion.* Buckingham: Open University Press.
Centre for Social Justice. (2009) *Dying to Belong: An In-Depth Review of Street Gangs in Britain.* London: Author.
Cloward, R., and Ohlin, L. (1960) *Delinquency and Opportunity: A Theory of Delinquent Gangs.* Chicago, IL: Free Press.
Connell, R.W. (2002) *The Men and the Boys.* Cambridge: Polity Press.
Connell, R.W., and Messerschmidt, J.W. (2005) Hegemonic Masculinity: Rethinking the Concept. *Gender & Society* 19(6), pp.829–859.
Cooley, C.H. (1956) *The Two Major Works of Charles H. Cooley – Social Organization and Human Nature and the Social Order.* Glencoe, IL: Free Press.
Cooper, J., and Fazio, R.H. (1984) A New Look at Dissonance Theory, in Berkowitz, L. (ed.) *Advances in Experimental Social Psychology*, Vol. 17. New York, NY: Academic Press, pp.229–266.
Corrigan, P., and Watson, A. (2002) *Understanding the Impact of Stigma on People With Mental Illness.* New York: Wiley.
Cotterell, J. (1996) *Social Networks and Social Influences in Adolescence.* London: Routledge.
Covington, M. (1984) The Self-Worth Theory of Achievement Motivation: Findings and Implications. *Elementary School Journal* 85(1), pp.5–20.
Craig, C. (2010) *The Tears That Made the Clyde: Well-Being in Glasgow.* Argyll: Argyll.
Crawshaw, P. (2004) The 'Logic of Practice' in Risky Community: The Potential of the Work of Pierre Bourdieu for Theorising Young Men's Risk-Taking, in W. Mitchell, R. Bunton, and E. Green (eds.) *Young People, Risk and Pleasure. Constructing Identities in Everyday Life.* New York: Palgrave Macmillan, pp.224–243.
Crocker, J., Major, B., and Steele, C. (1998) Social Stigma, in Gilbert, D.T., Fiske, S.T., and Lindzey, G. (eds.) *The Handbook of Social Psychology* (4th ed.), Vol. 2. Boston, MA: McGraw-Hill, pp.504–553.
Damer, S. (1990) *Glasgow: Going for a Song. (City Cultures).* London: Lawrence & Wishart Ltd.
Davies, A. (1998) Street Gangs, Crime and Policing in Glasgow During the 1930s: The Case of the Beehive Boys. *Journal of Social History* 23(3), pp.251–267.
Deuchar, R. (2009) Urban Youth Cultures and the Re-building of Social Capital: Illustrations from a Pilot Study in Glasgow. *Scottish Youth Issues Journal* 1, pp.7–22.
Deuchar, R., and Holligan, C. (2010) Gangs, Sectarianism and Social Capital: A Qualitative Study of Young People in Scotland. *Sociology* 44(1), pp.13–30.
Devine, T.M. (1999) *The Scottish Nation: 1700–2000.* London: Penguin Books.
Donati, P. (2006). L'Analisi Relazionale: Regole, Quadro Metodologico, Esempi [The analysis of relational rules, methodological framework examples], in Donati, P. (ed.) *Sociologia. Una Introduzione Allo Studi Della Societe* [*Sociology. An introduction to the study of society*]. Cedam, Italy: Padova, pp.195–251.
Donati, P. (2007) L'approccio relazionale al capital sociale. *Sociologia e politiche sociali* 10(1), pp.9–39.
Donati, P. (2011) *Relational Sociology: A New Paradigm for the Social Sciences.* Abingdon: Routledge.

Dudgeon, P. (2009) *Our Glasgow: Memories of Life in Disappearing Britain*. London: Headline.
Ekstrom, L.W. (2010) Ambivalence and Authentic Agency. *Ratio* 23(4), pp.374–392.
Erikson, E.H. (1950) *Childhood and Society*. New York, NY: Norton.
Festinger, L. (1957) *A Theory of Cognitive Dissonance*. Stanford, CA: Stanford University Press.
Finlay, R. (2003) *Modern Scotland 1914–2000*. London: Profile Books.
Flynn, N. (2010) *Criminal Behaviour in Context: Place, Space and Desistance from Crime*. International Series on Desistance and Rehabilitation. Cullompton: Willan.
Foote, N. (1951) Identification as the Basis for a Theory of Motivation. *American Sociological Review* 16, pp.14–21.
Fraser, A. (2010) *Growing Through Gangs: Young People, Identity and Social Change in Glasgow*. Unpublished PhD dissertation.
Galloway, J. (2008) *This Is Not About Me*. London: Granta Books.
Giordano, P.C., Cernkovich, S.A., and Holland, D.D. (2003) Changes in Friendship Relations Over the Life Course: Implications for Desistance From Crime. *Criminology* 41(2), pp.293–328.
Glaser, C. (1998) Swines, Hazels and the Dirty Dozen: Masculinity, Territoriality and the Youth Gangs of Soweto, 1960–1976. *Journal of South African Studies* 24(4), pp.719–736.
Granovetter, M. (1985) Economic Action and Social Structure: The Problem of Embeddedness. *American Journal of Sociology* 91(3), pp.481–510.
Hagan, J. (1993) The Social Embeddedness of Crime and Unemployment. *Criminology* 31(4), pp.465–491.
Hall, P.M. (1966) Identification with the Delinquent Subculture and Level of Self-Evaluation. *Sociometry* 29(2), pp.146–158.
Harris, M.G. (1988) *Cholas: Latino Girls and Gangs*. New York, NY: AMS Press.
Hogg, M., and Hardie, E. (1991) Social Attraction, Personal Attraction, and Self-Categorization: A Field Study. *Personality and Social Psychology Bulletin* 17(2), pp.175–180.
Holligan, C., and Deuchar, R. (2009) Territorialities in Scotland: Perceptions of Young People in Glasgow. *Journal of Youth Studies* 12(6), pp.727–742.
Honneth, A. (1995) *The Struggle for Recognition: The Moral Grammar of Social Conflicts*. Cambridge: Polity Press.
Ikaheimo, H., and Laitinen, A. (2011) Recognition and Social Ontology – An Introduction, in Ikaheimo, H., and Laitinen, A. (eds.) *Recognition and Social Ontology*. Leiden, Netherlands: Brill, pp.1–24.
Kintrea, K., Bannister, J., Pickering, J., Reid, M., and Suzuki, N. (2008) *Young People and Territoriality in British Cities*. York: Joseph Rowntree Foundation.
Klein, M.W., and Maxson, C.L. (2006) *Street Gang Patterns and Policies*. New York, NY: Oxford University Press.
Klein, M.W., Weerman, F.M., and Thornberry, T.P. (2006) Street Gang Violence in Europe. *European Journal of Criminology* 3(4), pp.413–437.
Lemert, E.M. (1951) *Social Pathology: Systematic Approaches to the Study of Sociopathic Behavior*. New York, NY: McGraw-Hill.
MacLure, R., and Sotelo, M. (2004). Youth Gangs in Nicaragua: Gang Membership as Structured Individuation. *Journal of Youth Studies* 7(4), pp.417–432.
Markowitz, F.E. (2001) Modeling Processes in Recovery from Mental Illness: Relationships between Symptoms, Life Satisfaction, and Self-Concept. *Journal of Health and Social Behavior* 42(1), pp.64–79.

Marshall, M., Frazer, S., Smith, I., Fuller, C., Geddes, M., Ardron, R., . . . Robinson, F. (2004) *Young People in NDC Areas: Findings from Six Case Studies*, Research Report 20, New Deal for Communities, National Evaluation. Sheffield: Sheffield Hallam University.

Maruna, S. (2001) *Making Good: How Ex-Convicts Reform and Rebuild Their Lives*. Washington, DC: American Psychological Association Books.

Maruna, S., and Copes, H. (2005). Excuses, Excuses: What Have We Learned From Five Decades of Neutralization Research, in Tonry, M. (ed.) *Crime and Justice*, Vol. 32. Chicago, IL: University of Chicago, pp.221–320.

Matthews, S., Jewkes R., and Abrahams, N. (2011) 'I had a hard life': Exploring Childhood Adversity in Shaping Masculinity Among Men Who Killed an Intimate Partner in South Africa. *British Journal of Criminology*. doi:10.1093/bjc/azr051

Maruna, S., and Roy, K. (2007) Amputation or Reconstruction: Notes on 'Knifing Off' and Desistance from Crime. *Journal of Contemporary Criminal Justice* 23(1), pp.104–124.

Matza, D. (1964) *Delinquency and Drift*. New York, NY: Wiley.

McArthur, A., and Kingsley Long, H. (1935) *No Mean City*. London: Transworld.

McDowell, L. (2003) Masculine Identities and Low Paid Work: Young Men in Urban Labour Markets. *International Journal of Urban and Regional Research* 27(4), pp.828–848.

Messerschmidt, J. (1994) Schooling, Masculinities, and Youth Crime by White Boys, in Newburn, T., and Stanko, E. (eds.) *Just Boys Doing Business? Men, Masculinities and Crime*. London: Routledge, pp.81–99.

Messerschmidt, J. (2000) Becoming 'Real Men': Adolescent Masculinity Challenges and Sexual Violence. *Men and Masculinities* 2(3), pp.286–307.

Messerschmidt, J.W. (1993) *Masculinities and Crime: Critique and Reconceptualisation of Theory*. Lanham, MD: Rowman and Littlefield.

Murray, C. (2012) Young People's Perspectives: The Trials and Tribulations of Going Straight. *Criminology and Criminal Justice* 12(1), pp.25–40.

Pahl, R. (2000) *On Friendship*. Cambridge: Polity Press.

Patrick, J. (1973) *A Glasgow Gang Observed*. London: Eyre Methuen.

Putnam, R.D. (2000) *Bowling Alone: The Collapse and Revival of American Community*. New York, NY: Simon and Schuster.

Pyrooz, D.C., Sweeten, G., and Piquero, A.R. (2012) Embeddedness, Continuity and Change in Gang Membership and Gang. *Journal of Research in Crime and Delinquency*. doi:10.1177/0022427811434830

Reynolds, T. (2007) Friendship Networks, Social Capital and Ethnic Identity: Researching the Perspectives of Caribbean Young People in Britain. *Journal of Youth Studies* 10(4), pp.383–398.

Ryan, R.M., and Deci, E.L. (2000) Self-determination Theory and the Facilitation of Intrinsic Motivation, Social Development and Well-being. *American Psychologist* 55(1), pp.68–78.

Sack, R.D. (1986) *Human Territoriality: Its Theory and History*. Cambridge: Cambridge University Press.

Sandberg, S. (2008) Street Capital, Ethnicity and Violence on the Streets of Oslo. *Theoretical Criminology* 12(2), pp.153–171.

Seaman, P., Turner K., Hill, M., Stafford A., and Walker, M. (2006) *Parenting and Children's Resilience in Disadvantaged Communities*. York: Joseph Rowntree Foundation.

Sennett, R. (2003) *Respect: The Formation of Character in a World of Inequality*. London: Allan Lane.

Shih, M. (2004) Positive Stigma: Examining Resilience and Empowerment in Overcoming Stigma. *Annals of the American Academy of Political and Social Science* 591(1), pp.175–185.
Sykes, G., and Matza, D. (1957) Techniques of Neutralization: A Theory of Delinquency. *American Sociological Review* 22(6), pp.664–670.
Thrasher, F. (1927) *The Gang: A Study of 1,313 Gangs in Chicago*. Chicago, IL: University of Chicago Press.
Torrance, D. (2009) *"We in Scotland": Thatcherism in a Cold Climate*. Edinburgh: Berlinn.
Vallerand, R.J. (1997) Toward a Hierarchical Model of Intrinsic and Extrinsic Motivation, in Zanna, M.P. (ed.) *Advances in Experimental Social Psychology*, Vol. 29. San Diego, CA: Academic Press, pp.271–360.
Vigil, J.D. (1988) *Barrio Gangs: Street Life and Identity in Southern California*. Austin: University of Texas Press.
Vigil, J.D. (1993) The Established Gang, in Cummings, S., and Monti, D.J. (eds.) *Gangs: The Origins and Impact of Contemporary Youth Gangs in the United States*. Albany: State University of New York Press, pp.95–112.
Weaver, A. (2008) *So You Think You Know Me?* Hook, UK: Waterside Press.
Weaver, B. (2012) The Relational Context of Desistance: Some Implications and Opportunities for Social Policy. *Social Policy and Administration* 46(4), pp.395–412.
Weaver, B., and McNeill, F. (2015) Lifelines: Desistance, Social Relations and Reciprocity. *Criminal Justice and Behavior* 42(1), pp.95–107.
Weeks, J., Donovan, C., and Heaphy, B. (1999) Everyday Experiments: Narratives of Non-Heterosexual Relationships, in Silva, E., and Smart, C. (eds.) *The New Family?* London: Sage, pp.83–99.
Whyte, W. (1943) *Street Corner Society*. Chicago, IL: University of Chicago Press.
Wilkinson, R., and Pickett, K. (2010) *The Spirit Level: Why Equality is Better for Everyone*. London: Penguin.
Willis, P. (1977) *Learning to Labour: How Working Class Kids Get Working Class Jobs*. Farnborough: Saxon House.
Woolcock, M., and Narayan, D. (2000) Social Capital: Implications for Development Theory, Research, and Policy. *World Bank Research Observer* 15(2), pp.225–249.

5 Work, family and transitional masculinities[1]
Seth's story

I'm a hard worker, I like that. I like my work and the fact I do work hard to provide for my family. That's about it.

Biographical overview

Seth, aged 43, is the younger brother to Jay and Adam Webster. He was born in 1965 and was raised in Coaston, the youngest of six siblings. His father's violence towards his mother was a definitive feature of his childhood and, as discussed in Chapter 4, was a contributory influence on his involvement with the Del into which he was somewhat socialised through his elder brothers' involvement. Seth offended persistently for a period of 13 years between the ages of 9 and 22 during which time he acquired approximately 50 convictions primarily of an acquisitive or violent nature, although as discussed in Chapter 4, his offending was primarily underpinned by expressive, affective rationales. For Seth, who was highly embedded in the Del but who exhibited low levels of identification with a 'deviant' subculture, his relationships to and with the group and the maintenance of the associated relational goods were more significant to him than any instrumental outcomes of offending.

In the aftermath of the fragmentation of the Del, Seth's involvement in offending comprised violent offences directly related to the feud. With the exception of a brief period on probation during his adolescence, his convictions resulted in custodial sentences of varying lengths. Indeed, he pointed out that between the ages of 14 and 22, he '*never had a birthday outside*'; during this period he 'graduated' through various children's and penal institutions. Between the ages of 22 and 32 Seth did not offend. In his thirties he was convicted for a '*couple of breaches*' of the peace and an assault, for which he was fined. Seth attributes these offences to the unintended outcome of his frequent alcohol binges which characterised this period of his life. In the year preceding the interview, he was convicted for driving whilst under the influence of alcohol. Notwithstanding these lapses, Seth would consider himself to have desisted for over two decades.

Seth met his wife Lesley during his late teens and although they are still married, they separated a few months prior to the interview. The couple has two children; the youngest, a daughter, resides with her mother and the eldest, a son, resides with Seth. Seth continues to work as a steel fixer, the trade he learnt, like many of his friends, in London where he lived with Lesley for three years, between the ages of 22 and 25 before returning to Coaston where he has been resident since. Indeed, Seth's delineation of his life stages following the fragmentation of the Del are structured in accordance with places of residence, namely 'The London Years' (aged 22–25) and 'The [Coaston] Years' (aged 25–42), although his elaboration of these stages are dominated by the significance he placed on work and family.

This chapter commences by describing Seth's response to the feud and his subsequent imprisonment, which is discussed under the superordinate theme '*Experience of punishment*'. The chapter then proceeds, under the superordinate theme '*Roles, reflexivity, relationality and desistance*', to discuss the role of Seth's extant familial, social and personal relationships in supporting desistance over time, commencing with his relocation to London, following his release from prison. The significance of employment in Seth's narrative of change is discussed under the final superordinate theme '*The meanings and outcomes of work*'.

Experience of punishment

A process of investment in the self

As discussed in Chapter 4, the feud among the Del resulted in a series of violent exchanges. Seth '*went on the run . . . for six weeks*', when he learned that he was wanted by the police in connection with his involvement in a serious assault on Dennis Nixon. However, the fragmentation of the Del, the escalating violence, the threat and fear of recriminations, and associated restrictions on his freedom, in conjunction with his developing relationship with Lesley and the impact this was having on her, triggered a reflexive evaluation of his lifestyle, culminating in his decision to hand himself in to the police.

Seth: These guys were looking for me, the police were looking for me and I was holed up in houses for maybe two weeks at a time and I couldn't get out . . . then there's the fear as well . . . in the end up I was relieved to . . . hand myself in. There was definitely a wee bit of taking charge and . . . I think that was the first time I had took other people's feelings into consideration, and I realised how much I had hurt [Lesley] . . . also my mother . . . I think when I was on the run, I spent a lot of time myself and I had a lot of time to think . . . I definitely started changing then.

Seth's reflexive evaluation of his lifestyle resonates with the early stages of the desistance process identified by Bottoms and Shapland (2011), who found that shifts in offending were often linked to a triggering event such as the importance of new and strengthening social relationships or negative turning points, for example, associated with criminal acts (Haggard, Gumpert and Grann, 2001), which can influence an individual's motivation to change. Processes of extrication from gangs are often similarly prompted by an accrual of reasons or events interacting to 'push or pull' the individual away from the gang (Bannister et al., 2010; Decker and Lauritsen, 2002; Vigil, 1988). The reflexive process underpinning individuals' responses to these various triggering events is, however, rarely elaborated in the desistance literature (although see King, 2014; Vaughan, 2007). Archer (2000) suggests that individuals respond to the constraints and enablements that inhere in their conditioning structures by engaging in an internal conversation (personal reflexivity), through which process they deliberate on the social situations they confront through the lens of their ultimate concerns. An ultimate concern is a desired end or goal and a sense, however vague or uncertain, of a course of action that is perceived to be realisable in the given social circumstances the individual inhabits (ibid). At this juncture, in response to shifting conditioning structures influenced by 'between-individual' changes such as the fragmentation of the Del, the increasing interpersonal violence and the development of a new intimate relationship with Lesley, Seth began evaluating his current lifestyle through the lens of his similarly shifting ultimate concerns for a different life. This is not, however, a solely cognitive process, as Seth's extract above suggests; '[e]motional empathy and responsiveness may help initiate a process of self-appraisal from which a different kind of person emerges' (Vaughan, 2007 p.391; see also Bottoms and Shapland, 2011).

Archer (2003) delineates three phases to the process of reflexivity, manifest in an inner dialogue (see Chapter 3). The initial phase is characterised as a period of 'discernment' where the person reviews the possible alternative lifestyle choices available to them, in contrast to their current lifestyle, reflecting a 'willing[ness] to consider different options' (Vaughan, 2007 p.394). Seth was sentenced to three years in prison, which liberated him from the immediate constraints emerging from his relational concerns in the community, and which, in the context of his 'openness to change', he apprehended as an opportunity or 'hook for change' (Giordano, Cernkovich and Rudolph, 2002 p.1000). He started taking action towards realising this through what might be described as a process of investment in the self.

Seth: I started exercising every day, [developing] self-control, starting to do things to take care of myself and start to change. It was the first time I had gone in and done that. I done that through[out] the three year sentence. I think there was a wee feeling of optimism there, that I was going in to deal with it, get it done, and get on with it and that I could come out and do things.

Seth's application of his personal reflexivity to his changing 'conditioning structures' precipitating his imprisonment in turn influenced his responses to the constraints, enablements and expectations that inhere in the 'prisoner society' (Crewe, 2009) and the 'formal' prison culture. Where previously Seth's experience of and response to imprisonment was characterised by immersion in the prisoner community and a sense of hopelessness, compounded by the loss of personal control being in prison represented, his response to this period of imprisonment, influenced by his recent experience of the demise of the Del and informed by a desire for an alternative lifestyle, and '*a growing realisation that there was things out there that you could do. That you're not stuck in that life. That you don't need to run with the crowd all the time*', culminated in his decision to distance himself from the prisoner community.

Seth: It was the first time I hadn't buckled to peer pressure whereas before I'd always just kind of went with the flow. If my mates were getting into trouble, I'd be getting into trouble . . . it was around then I realised, well, they're not going to stick by me forever. It was time to start taking care of myself instead of worrying about them.

Seth's process of investment in the self through participation in education and practicing yoga formed a routine that enabled him to create this distance and which engendered a sense of self-discipline, both of which Seth perceived to be critical to maintaining his resolution to change. In turn, his resolve to change, initiated through the exercise of personal agency and self-reflection, enabled him to resist the provocations that emerged from the prisoner community and to forego the status and social recognition (Barry, 2006) previously conferred on him.

Seth: To make a conscious decision to stay away fae it . . . [takes] strength or self-control. You need self-control if you're going to distance yourself fae that and stay away from it – even in the jail . . . you've got a kind of name to live up to. Some of the guys fell out with me and gave me a hard time because I wasnae hanging out with them or getting into trouble . . . It bothers you but you don't let it. You know you are not just suddenly going to start running about doing what they do again just because they'd like you to . . . so there's a wee bit of self-control there and realisation that you are not wanting that in your life.

Implicit in this retrospective narrative is Archer's second phase of reflexivity, deliberation, which is an evaluative process, in which one reviews the perceived costs, benefits and implications pertaining to a given situation or potential courses of action (Archer, 2000), in this case, Seth's pursuit of self-change against the pressures and implications of dissociation from his former friends in prison. Evidently, this comparative evaluation is not as solipsistic in focus as Archer's exposition implies; as these extracts have illustrated, the decision to distance himself was the outcome of his personal reflexivity applied not solely to himself but to his relationships. This is because one's ultimate concerns are progressively defined in relation to how the 'I', one's self, defines his choices when he acts as a 'you', as a social actor, and must respond both to the demands of his relational contexts and to the deeper demands of his 'I', when he considers whether he is satisfied or not with the 'me' that has been attributed to him by others, and when he confronts and compares the meaning of his belonging (the 'we'/us to which he belongs) to that of other potential membership groups (Donati, 2011). Critically, however, a

108 *Seth's story*

resolve to change manifest in 'enhanced internalized control' (Giordano et al., 2002 p.1001) does not readily translate into its realisation on release (see for example, Soyer 2014). However, Seth's experience of altruistic work through the *'Training for Freedom'* programme in prison (see below) reinforced his dedication (Archer's final phase of reflexivity), or commitment to change, through his involvement with a group of community volunteers.

'Training for Freedom': being normal

Prior to the end of his three year sentence, Seth was placed on a *'Training for Freedom'* programme which included participation in a voluntary placement in a drop-in café run by SACRO,[2] as a means of preparing longer-term prisoners for release. Seth identified his experience of volunteering as a 'turning point' which are those 'crucial [processes] in which new lines of individual . . . activity are forged, in which new aspects of the self are brought into being' (Becker 1966 p.xiv, cited in Carlsson, 2012 p.4), and that hold particular significance for offending and desistance. The understanding of a 'turning point' employed here recognises that it is not a given event or experience in itself that exogenously (Laub, Nagin and Sampson, 1998) or 'abruptly' brings about desistance, but rather the way such events or experiences under certain circumstances, and, thus in the context of the surrounding processes in which they are embedded, are imbued with significance, or otherwise, and which directly influence their potential to bring about other changes (Carlsson, 2012). Understood in this context, a turning point can consolidate or reinforce initial motivations to change and engender, as it did for Seth, Archer's final phase of reflexivity, dedication. In this phase, the individual engages in a prioritisation of concerns such that they commit themselves to an ultimate concern, to that which he or she cares most about (such as a particular job or relationship). It is in dedicating one's self to this 'unique pattern of commitments' (Archer, 2000 p.241) that one crafts one's 'individual modus vivendi' (ibid p.238) through which one's identity is forged. In this vein, reflexivity incorporates notions of transcendence through which we can imagine ourselves and our relations differently from what we/they are and thus capable of actualizing things as yet unrealized (Donati, 2011). This is the process through which people come to commit themselves, or otherwise, to desistance.[3]

For Seth, it was the interactive dynamics between him and his co-workers that imbued his experience of volunteering with particular significance, in terms of the impact this had on his self-concept and social identity. Drawing on his prior experiences of imprisonment and recidivism, Seth was aware of the precariousness of his intentions to sustain the positive self-change he had initiated during his period of imprisonment on release. During the early stages of desistance, early aspirations are often shrouded in uncertainty (Farrall and Calverley, 2006). Seth's experience of volunteering, however, engendered a realisation that '*I could function*' (see extract below) which served to crystallise his hopes that another way of being was achievable, which consolidated his commitment to desistance. Feeling accepted by 'normal' people enabled him to transcend his stigmatised status as 'an offender' and communicated to him that his aspirations for a 'normal' life were 'a realizable possibility' (Farrall and Calverley, 2006 p.115; see also Burnett and Maruna, 2004; Maruna, Immarigeon and LeBel, 2004).

The experience of 'fitting in', of feeling a sense of belonging and being 'normal' (Goffman, 1963), was particularly significant to Seth whose narratives of his earlier life (see Chapter 4) were characterised by an acute awareness that not only did he exist on the margins of society but, despite the belonging and social connectedness he experienced in the Del, he never really 'fitted in' with the deviant subculture. Through participation in volunteering alongside 'normal' people who both accepted and respected him, and in experiencing anew the relational goods of social trust and social connectedness that he valued, a new experience of self was brought into being.

Seth: I would say [volunteering] was definitely a turning point . . . I had done everything in the jail, the self-control and you're doing all these things, determined to stay away from trouble, but you've always got that doubt when you go out that things aren't going to go well or you'll fall back into it. I think working there . . . in that period I realised that I could function. They were all normal people . . . and they were taking me home to meet their kids and we'd go to the art galleries and museums . . . and do all different things together. That was probably about the normalest period, just being in society and just doing normal things that I hadn't done before . . . It was just being normal after all they years of trouble, you realise that you can fit in . . . you're not a leper and that was definitely a turning point . . . [They would] treat you with total respect . . . and the trust showed in me . . . You were totally trusted.

Trust is closely related to concepts of responsibility and mutual respect (Edgar, Jacobson and Biggar, 2011). Respect essentially implies the mutuality associated with social recognition (Sennett, 2003). In turn, responsibility taking and being invested with responsibility is a means of social recognition and is the result of being trusted, which can engender a sense of responsibility on the part of the person feeling trusted. 'Social recognition . . . expresses the capacity and need that . . . people have for longer-term *reciprocal* relations of trust and responsibility in the wider society' (Barry, 2006 p.136, italics in original). Actions associated with active citizenship[4] have been constructively associated with desistance precisely because they establish or reinforce notions of reciprocity and mutuality (Drakeford and Gregory, 2010) and, in that, social recognition (Barry, 2006), which can positively influence an individual's self-concept. In particular, '[a]n emergent pro-social self-conception is . . . sensitive to 'messages' from others about the self . . . People may see themselves in a new way in the 'looking glass' that is provided by the views of others, whether through direct comment or via non-verbal responses during interaction' (Burnett and Maruna, 2006 p.95; see also Maruna et al., 2004). In this vein, volunteering alongside others in relation with whom these relational goods may emerge can provide a relational web within and through which shifts in identities can be elicited and/or reinforced.

The drop-in café served people who were homeless and experiencing problems with alcoholism. '*Being on the other side of the fence*', as a helper, also imbued this 'turning point' with significance for Seth. On the one hand, in the act of helping alongside other volunteers, 'whatever status and role differences exist pale into insignificance compared to the contribution the joint effort is making' (Toch, 2000 p.271), generating 'a sense of belonging and an esprit de corps' (Pearl and Riessman, 1965 p.83, cited in Burnett and Maruna, 2006 p.89). On the other hand, through the satisfaction of making a valued contribution to the well-being of others through engagement in helping (LeBel, 2007) or advocacy behaviours (LeBel, 2009) people can acquire or recapture self-esteem and satisfaction with life, and such behaviours can reinforce or maintain a person's pro-social identity. Moreover, through participation in altruistic endeavours, the person giving help can internalise and express the idea that it is not a contradiction to one's masculinity to exercise or express compassion and that one can feel effective and competent when helping those less advantaged, whose own problems can diminish the salience of one's own (Toch, 2000).

Seth: It was good just being on the other side of the fence helping people . . . that aren't having a good time of life. It felt good, aye, it definitely did . . . Some of them were that right far gone with the drink and you could see the hopelessness in their situation, falling in the door drunk, bus passes pinned to their [jackets] so that when they got drunk you just put them on the bus. Just helping them, and the compassion the staff showed to them, was just unbelievable.

The significance of Seth's engagement in volunteering as a turning point resided in the impact that collaborative engagement in altruistic acts exerted on his self-concept and social identity (Burnett and Maruna, 2006; Toch, 2000; Uggen, Manza and Behrens, 2004). Beyond making a contribution to society, feeling part *of* society and earning the trust of others through the assumption of responsibility were particularly significant in reinforcing his commitment to desistance in the early stages.

Roles, reflexivity, relationality and desistance

The role of extant social networks in supporting desistance

While Seth was in prison, Adam and some of the 'revised group' had relocated to London to extricate themselves from the 'relational bads' emerging from the feud and to access the employment opportunities afforded by the construction boom in London in the late 1980s. On Seth's release, Adam encouraged him to join them, which Seth apprehended as an opportunity to consolidate the process of change he had begun in prison, not least because '*it was the first time . . . that there was a prospect of work in front me. That gave me hope*'. An argument was progressed in Chapter 4 that while employment in a new environment heralded economic and social changes to the 'revised group's' conditioning structures that enabled change, the recognition and pursuit of these opportunities can be construed as an outcome of the exercise of reflexivity and as an expression of their individual and collective agency. In particular, however, individuals' capacities to access and thus realise and sustain these opportunities emerged from the mutual and reciprocal exchange of support and resources among the revised group, as an outcome of their collaborative efforts, of shifts in their interactive dynamics and the diversified relational contexts the move facilitated, both within and beyond the group, to which individuals responded differently through the lens of their individual and relational concerns. It is Seth's individual experience that this chapter is concerned to reveal.

As part of the '*Training for Freedom*' programme, Seth was granted 'leave' in the community for ten hours a week. He used this to spend time with Lesley who, towards the end of his sentence, advised him that she was pregnant with their first child. The impact of intimate or personal relationships and parenthood is discussed in the following subsection, however, at this stage, some of the revised group had also formed stable personal relationships and become fathers, which further impacted their internal network dynamics.

Individuals comprising the revised group diverged in terms of what was going on in their individual lives, and, thus, in terms of how they responded to the opportunities the move represented. For Seth, who was committed to change, in a stable personal relationship and about to become a father for the first time, the move to London and access to employment presented as an opportunity to realise his desire for a different way of living, to be 'normal', and a means through which he could personify and interiorise this new social role. Critically, for Seth, who was concerned to distance himself from peers that were still offending as a strategy to resist any potentially negative influence they might exert, rather than withdraw from social interaction as he had in prison, he associated with those among the revised group who were similarly situated.

Seth: Adam was there and Marie [Adam's wife], and some of the others and we'd do things with them . . . maybe go shopping for the day . . . car boot sales and that – just normal things.

Shifts in the interactive dynamics between the revised group were also discernible in the explicit support and reinforcement of efforts to change. Seth described how Adam acted as a type of mentor, using his own experiences to advise him on the possibilities and pitfalls ahead.

Seth: When I came out of [prison] we went down to London and [Adam] got me work and when we went down there . . . he'd stepped away fae [offending] and settled down with [Marie] . . . and he'd say to me about doing this or not doing that . . . It's almost as if [Adam] knew . . . what sort of . . . pressures would come up . . . and he could help me overcome that.

In this revised group, then, the desisting friends benefited from the reciprocal support and reinforcement of their efforts to change that their mutual recognition of each other's efforts implied.

Seth: It's not like you just had to . . . not see people . . . there was people about you that were wanting the same things, so that helped. We all . . . got to that point where we wanted out of it round about the same time . . . we all stayed pretty close and we were working together and living together at different times.

Giordano et al. (2002) suggest that people learn from those whose behaviour represents a contrast to their own. However, it is suggested here that this is particularly so of people whose behaviour previously mirrored theirs and has since changed. They not only have less support from peers for engaging in offending but the observation of change in a credible person is particularly influential where they can identify with the individual and internalize the benefits of responding to this influence (Kelman, 1958), in the hope of achieving similar outcomes.

Seth: I think that [Adam] probably made a significant difference to my situation as well. He always discouraged me from getting into trouble and . . . I suppose he gave me that insight that you can see that it can be done. As I say, growing up and that hopelessness you felt that you were stuck in it. To see [Adam] getting on and staying out of trouble and go on to work and things like that well it was a good influence.

This *seems* consistent with Giordano, Cernkovich and Holland's (2003) findings that those open to change can make agentic moves to become closer to those within their own networks they believe will be a positive influence while distancing themselves from those who continue to offend. They argue that shifts in receptivity to the influence of anti-social friends (see also Monahan, Steinberg and Cauffman, 2009) and in the nature of friendship choices, as a movement towards pro-social peers, can explain this progression. However, as observed in Chapter 2, the literature discussing the role of peers in relation to onset and persistence (see for example Farrington, 1992; Haynie, 2001, 2002; Warr, 1993, 2002) and desistance (see for example Calverley, 2013; Giordano et al., 2003; Graham and Bowling, 1995; Massoglia and Uggen, 2010; Uggen and Kruttschnitt, 1998) polarises peers into 'anti-social' pressures or 'pro-social' influences, with each category representing different groups. Discussion surrounds the would-be-desister's decisive (Paternoster and Bushway, 2009) or developmental (Giordano et al., 2003) disassociation from 'negative' influences and either re-connection with pro-social former associates or development of new pro-social relationships (Giordano et al., 2003; Knight and West, 1975) with further explanations deriving from social learning, differential association (Akers, 1973; Sutherland, 1947; Warr, 1993) or social control theories (Sampson and Laub, 1993). These studies are usually refracted through the lens of the individual desister (Cromwell, Olson and D'Aunn, 1991; Warr, 1998) or more infrequently from the standpoint of the individual situated in a structural network of relations in a given context (Haynie, 2001). However, a focus on individuals who comprised a naturally forming group reveals that consistent with the reciprocal character of peer influence or friendship (Cairns and Cairns, 1994; Pahl, 2000), the friends benefited from the mutual support the revised group afforded. Moreover, that Adam, in particular, had *become* a positive influence is what imputed his influence with credibility and which in turn generated hope in Seth that he too could realise related outcomes. Where once, then, these relationships and reciprocities contributed to their collective involvement in offending, these particular friends also supported each other, albeit to differing degrees and with different effects and at different stages, to pursue constructive changes in their lifestyles and relationships.

The role of intimate relationships and families of formation in supporting desistance

This sub-theme illustrates the role of intimate relationships and families of formation in the desistance process. The associations between marriage (or intimate relationships) and/or parenthood and desistance emerging from empirical studies of desistance were elaborated in Chapter 2; in the process of illustrating the influence that Seth's relationship with Lesley, his partner, then wife, and his role as a father had on his life, this sub-theme will draw selectively on the central arguments emerging from this research.

Sampson, Laub and Wimer (2006) suggested that marriage is not only associated with desistance, but has a causal effect. Lyngstad and Skardhamar (2011 p.2) alternatively argue that it is possible to 'treat marriage as an *outcome* of rather than a causal agent in the process of criminal desistance' (see also Kiernan, 2004; Monsbakken, Lyngstad and Skardhamar, 2012b). In Seth's case, however, this relationship was not causative of desistance nor was it conditional on his desistance. While both differential association (Warr, 1998) and social control theories (Laub and Sampson, 2001) suggest that an intimate relationship can limit criminal involvement by reducing opportunities for crime or access to peers (Warr, 1998) or by exerting mechanisms of informal social control over the individual (Laub and Sampson, 2003), this does not hold true for Seth who acknowledges that during the earlier stages of this relationship, prior to his final period of imprisonment, discussed above, he continued to offend and to associate with the group despite Lesley's 'normative orientation' which is generally considered to positively influence behaviour (Giordano et al., 2003 p.306).

Seth: She obviously wasnae happy about [me offending] but we got on that well, we were just happy to be together when we were together. We didn't see it as a problem then. [Offending] just seemed to be a part of life.

114 *Seth's story*

Critically, a partner or spouse can only exert influence where the individual is receptive to that influence, consistent with the individual's ultimate and relational concerns. A control theorist would suggest that 'if the marriage is . . . characterized by weak or non-existent attachment, continued offending will occur' (Laub and Sampson, 2003 p.44). That Lesley and Seth remained in this relationship for approximately two decades suggests that this relationship was of considerable significance in incremental effect to both of them, and indeed Seth's narrative emphasises this.[5] As observed, however, in Chapter 4, during the early stages of his relationship with Lesley, Seth's primary attachments were to the Del, and whilst he was emotionally attached to Lesley, the historical significance and depth of his attachment to the Del meant that he would structure his time in a way that facilitated the maintenance of these two separate relational spheres:

Seth: We were close but I was still going out and getting into trouble at the same time . . . I would see [Lesley] to up to maybe 8 o'clock and then I was going out after that and just fighting constantly.

In contrast to control and differential associational theorists, who emphasise the actions of the change agent to explain the significance of transitional events such as marriage, Giordano et al. (2003) progress an agentic and cognitive analysis of this phenomenon as the outcome of motivational and attitudinal changes in the would-be-desister, which they explain in reference to 'developmental changes in the nature of interpersonal ties as actors move into adulthood' and the accumulation of social experiences (Giordano et al., 2003 p.297). The developmental perspective they articulate attends to the ascendancy of intimate relationships over peer relationships as individuals move into adulthood and thus to distance from and resistance to the negative influence of peer relations, and this analysis does have some credence here. Seth recalls how both he and his relationship to Lesley matured and intensified over the years:

Seth: Realising the hurt I was causing – for yourself as well . . . going in the jail all the time, and you feel all that hopelessness and loneliness and you just knew you had to get away from it all. With [Lesley] as well . . . you're definitely starting to think about . . . what your actions were doing . . . thinking about other people instead of just yourself. Things that mattered to you, that you thought were important, changed.

This does seem to provide support for the idea that shifts in the direction and nature of interpersonal ties with age, reflective of 'changes in ways of thinking about the self in relation to others', can influence an individual's behaviour (Giordano et al., 2003 p.307). Indeed there is evidence across the men's narratives of them becoming more other-focused in their outlook. However, despite their assertion that their cognitive emphasis provides a more conditional perspective (or context) on change and on the pro-social impact of the specific change agent (Giordano et al., 2011), such an analysis is limited in its capacity to illuminate the internal processes and relational dynamics that contribute to or sustain desistance over time or why someone becomes more or less open to the possibility of change. Applying Donati's (2011) theory of relational reflexivity can shed some light on these processes. It is the deepening emotional connection and the associated shifts in the dynamic of the relation between Lesley and Seth in early adulthood that is relevant to understanding the shifting significance of the outcomes of his offending on this relationship which threaten the emergent relational goods to which both parties are reciprocally oriented. Crucially, however, these relational concerns need to be positioned in the context of changes in the dynamics of his social network. It is thus changes in the nature of the dynamics of these social relations, in conjunction with a growing dissatisfaction with the outcomes of his offending for both himself and Lesley, that trigger Seth's reflexive internal conversation and re-prioritisation of his concerns that manifest in a shift in practices that will enable him to realise these relational concerns. Desistance in this regard emerged from Seth's reflexive evaluation of the outcomes of his current lifestyle choices, which he weighed up against his shifting sense of what mattered to him, reflecting a reorientation of his ultimate concerns as they emerge in their relational contexts which underpin the motivational and attitudinal changes to which Giordano et al. (2003) refer.

The point here is that it is Seth's constellation of relational concerns that triggers a reflexive re-evaluation of what is important to him; his personal reflexivity is brought to bear on the social relations in which he participates and this reflexive evaluation is thus 'derived from a relational context, is immersed in a relational context and brings about a relational context' (Donati, 2011 p.14). His reflexive evaluation of certain peer relations brought about a realisation that they no longer generated the reciprocal relational goods they once enjoyed, of trust, loyalty and concern. When viewed in the context of a burgeoning intimate relationship which yielded such relational goods, but which were threatened by his continuous imprisonment, Seth became aware that his ultimate concerns resided in becoming a better partner and his continued association with certain friends in the context of the feud could generate relational 'bads' that would undermine this relation.

Becoming a father shortly after his release from prison and relocation to London further cemented Seth's relationship with Lesley and imbued it with additional significance. Seth placed particular emphasis on becoming a father in consolidating his commitment to desistance on his release. Over time, *being* a father emerged as a significant social role identity and his participation in employment (elaborated in the following sub-section) contributed to this. There is a distinct difference between becoming a father and being a father, between having a child and raising a child. There is also considerable individual variation in how the role of parenthood is both exercised and experienced (Marsiglio and Pleck, 2004) such that generalisations about the impact of parenting on one's behaviour, and thus desistance, are inherently problematic. Indeed, both parenting and parenthood are likely to be influenced by the context or form of an individual's relationship to the other parent (see for example Giordano et al., 2011; Massoglia and Uggen, 2010; Monsbakken, Lyngstad and Skardhamar, 2012a), just as the relational or interactive dynamics between parents will influence the experience of parenting. In turn, becoming parents is likely to influence the interactive dynamics between people in an intimate relation. The father-child relation thus needs to be viewed in the context of a network of mutually interdependent relations within the family, which exert a direct and reciprocal influence through interaction, and an indirect influence, mediated by the behaviour of third parties, such as the mother (Marsiglio et al., 2000). In this vein, one's identity as a father emerges 'as part of a reciprocal process negotiated by men, children, mothers and other interested parties' (ibid p.1173).

What it means to be a parent is further influenced by one's own experience of being parented (see for example Hauari and Hollingworth, 2009; Moloney et al., 2009). Seth's intention to '*not be like my Dad*' manifested in his desire to be involved in and provide for his family, further reflecting his wider, internalised cultural and class values and beliefs regarding his role as partner and parent, which influenced his appropriation of the 'traditional' nature and form of the social relation of family and the associated sets of relational rules that prescribe how one should behave in certain ways towards others according to the norms that the context prescribes (Donati, 2011). As Marsiglio and Pleck (2004 p.260) observe, 'the provider role continues to be an important feature of hegemonic images of masculinity and men's fathering experience'. In this vein, the meaning and experience of fatherhood exists through specific socio-cultural processes, and, thus, is influenced by one's conditioning structures, which shape the situations of actions for individuals to which individuals bring their personal reflexivity to bear. Fatherhood does not, then, represent a static or stable identity, experience or behavioural pattern (Marsiglio et al., 2000). For example, even during episodes of binge drinking (discussed further below), ensuring he did not expose his children to any negative experiences and continued to provide for his family marked a significant departure between Seth's experience of being fathered and his own role and impact as a father.

Seth: I never brought it home. The weans never seen me drunk or anything . . . I always made sure there was enough money coming in and that [Lesley] got enough money. It was never a problem there . . . I wasn't like my father, if I wasn't bringing it home.

Masculinity is negotiated and enacted differently in different situations and different social spaces (Connell and Messerschmidt, 2005) and is experienced and expressed differently at various stages in an individual's life course (Collier, 1998; Robinson and Hockey, 2011). Becoming a father represents another way of realising masculinity or brings a new dimension to one's sense of masculinity, which is implied in Seth's discussions of providing for family, and his enduring commitment to ensure '*they never went without*'.

In Seth's case, his experience of fatherhood during the early stages of his release needs to be positioned in the emergence and coalescence of a variety of influences and changes exerting a cumulative effect on his self-concept, his social identity and his lifestyle. While fatherhood undoubtedly afforded Seth a new source of self-respect and an alternative social identity, it was the aforementioned changes in his conditioning structures that enabled the activation of this new social role. Indeed, the impact of fatherhood on desistance is difficult to disentangle from the influence of wider social relations (Monsbakken et al., 2012a) and is not always direct but is rather mediated through shifts in peer relationships, intimate relationships and employment which interact to open up new possibilities (Moloney et al., 2009). For Seth, investment in a significant intimate relationship, participation in employment, a fresh start in a new environment and the support of a revised peer group network with similarly established relational attachments enabled his assumption of this new social role. While certain lifestyle changes can ensue as a consequence of the transition to parenthood, in the form of increased responsibilities, perhaps influenced by normative social expectations, these transitional processes cannot sufficiently account for abstinence from offending over time. While Seth placed significance on fatherhood in reinforcing his commitment to desistance, his narrative of desistance does not centre on becoming a father in and of itself. Rather, it was the interaction of becoming and being a father, or family man, at this particular time, and in the context of this intimate relationship, which provided an alternative circle of belonging and connectedness, and which was facilitated by shifts in the relational dynamics of the revised group and involvement in stable employment. The mutually reinforcing interaction of these processes thus enabled him to fulfil the requirements of the role, and strengthened his sense of self-efficacy and control in those early years.

Seth: When [Andrew] was born – that was a turning point. That was probably about the best period of my life . . . definitely the most settled, the most focused I was. I knew what was happening and I was in control. Then it just seemed to be that if I said I was going to do something, I would do it. That period fae getting out of prison right through to when [Andrew] was a toddler.

The meanings and outcomes of work

As discussed in Chapter 2, while employment has generally been associated with desistance, employment in and of itself does not produce or trigger desistance; rather it is the meaning and outcomes of either the nature or quality of the work or participation in employment and how these influence an individual's self-concept and social identity and interact with a person's priorities, goals and relational concerns. Moreover, research has revealed some conditional interaction between various transitional events and experiences, such as, for example, the links between employment and investment in significant intimate relations and/or parenthood (see for example Bianchi, Casper and King, 2005 cited in Bersani et al., 2009; Edin, Nelson and Paranal, 2001; Farrall, 2004; Laub and Sampson, 2001; Maruna, 2001; Owens, 2009; Rhodes, 2008; Rumgay, 2004; Savolainen, 2009; Visher and Travis, 2003). The natures of these interacting life transitions further influences the various impacts they exert on people's identities, behaviours and social contexts, which directly or indirectly influence their potential to enable or constrain processes of change, at different stages in a given individual's life (Weaver, 2012).

The desistance promotive meanings and outcomes of work

Informal social networks are the predominant means through which people with convictions access paid employment (Farrall, 2002, 2004; Niven and Stewart, 2005; Rhodes, 2008; Visher and Courtney, 2007). As discussed in Chapter 4, Adam was pivotal in training and affording Seth, and others comprising the revised group, access to employment in steel-fixing. As foreman, Adam regularly obtained contracts for work and employed his friends and associates to carry out the work, which enabled them to circumnavigate the otherwise exclusionary practices of the labour market (Rhodes, 2008), and which Seth suggested '*took that thing away, about how are you going to get money . . . if you're not earning a wage and going out working, then its crime isn't it?*'. Moreover, working together as a team became a definitive feature of their lifestyles which reinforced a sense of common purpose amongst the revised group and which enabled the internalisation of identities, both individually and as a collective, in which participation in work occupied a central place. However, sustaining employment in steel-fixing also required the development of employment-based networks to access further work and, thus, the development of 'bridging' social capital.

Bridging social capital involves establishing new social relations; these ties facilitate the reciprocal exchange of resources from one network to a member of another network and in this sense are linked to the development of broader identities and social mobility (Woolcock and Narayan, 2000). In the steel-fixing industry, where work was obtained through 'word of mouth' and was typically distributed within known employment-based networks, bridging social capital was a critical and instrumental means of access to further contractual work. In addition to sustaining employment, the development of new social relationships through work, comprising a diverse range of people, 'afforded a concrete way of enhancing one's own identity as a respectable person' (Giordano et al., 2003 p.311), through the development of a constructive reputation as a 'worker', which was also necessary for access to further work.

Seth: At first, I done a few weeks of labouring and then [Adam] got me a job steel fixing with him. I was earning decent money then, well not at the start but I was learning and . . . [Adam] set me up with this other guy working – we were working so many different jobs – so I went away with this guy and he was kind of teaching me . . . Now, my friends are mostly work guys. Some I see regular, outside work as well. You get to know a lot of people in the building trade and they're the ones who will seek you out when there's another job on. I'm seen as quite a good steel fixer and quite a lot of guys seek me out for work.

Employment is not static in nature but denotes a vast array of 'different working conditions, skill requirements, values and rewards' (Owens, 2009 p.58) and, thus, divergences in experiences of participation in work, all of which have a bearing on the potential influence and impact of employment on an individual. Moreover, the employment relation is, as the foregoing analysis and extract imply, constitutive of various networks of social relations (Baron, 1988). People's social relationships within their working environment exert a significant influence on their experience of and satisfaction in work (Morgeson and Humphrey, 2006; Humphrey, Nahrgaug and Morgeson, 2007). This implies that we need a relational vision of work if we are to understand its meaning and outcomes. While some studies have suggested that the quality of employment is more strongly associated with desistance (Shover, 1996; Uggen, 1999), elsewhere, social relations in work have been shown to be more significant than the nature of the work with regard to job satisfaction (Morgeson and Humphrey, 2006).

The four significant social characteristics of work identified by Morgeson and Humphrey (2006) are apparent in the steel-fixing industry and are evident in Seth's extract above, namely social support, interdependence, interaction with people outside of the organisation and feedback from others. Working with existing friends created a sense of camaraderie and along with other co-workers, they collectively created a working alliance and culture within which Seth could access social support, or advice and assistance. Steel-fixing requires the reciprocal interaction with, or interdependence between, co-workers in order to complete tasks which, in turn, facilitated the transmission and sharing of knowledge and skills, which has the potential to realise generative motives and bolster both human and social capital, thus enabling people to feel a 'connection to' or 'embeddedness' in the world (Maruna, 2001 p.119; Morgeson and Humphrey, 2006). Moreover, the contractual nature of steel-fixing required the maintenance of work-based networks that increased his access to a broader range of contacts, beyond the revised group, within the wider construction industry. As Seth suggests above, he is '*seen as quite a good steel fixer*' which implies that he internalised constructive messages about his capacities as a steel fixer, which Morgeson and Humphrey (2006) suggest has a positive effect on people's satisfaction levels and well-being, and which, in turn, may reinforce the internalisation of an identity, in which work assumes an essential role (Rhodes, 2008).

The relationship between work, self-esteem and identity is well established (Crisp, 2010). Indeed, as Owens states, 'employment is part of the idea of what is acceptable' (Owens, 2009 p.50), symbolic of, as Giordano et al. (2002) observe, a level of respectability. In this sense there is a level of interdependence and interaction between employment and investment in significant intimate relations and/or parenthood. Employment and family roles form the basis of 'a general 'law-abiding adult citizen' identity construct' (Uggen et al., 2004 p.263). For Seth, the interaction of these processes provided a 'skeleton script' as to how to proceed as a changed individual on release (Rumgay, 2004 p.410) and has endured as an identity construct since.

Seth: I'm a hard worker, I like that. I like my work and the fact that I do work hard to provide for my family. That's about it.

While employment did not motivate or trigger desistance for Seth, it assisted him to sustain it in the context of broader enabling shifts in his conditioning structures, which, in turn, endowed his participation in work with meaning. Just as experiencing a sense of belonging and normalcy imbued his earlier experience of volunteering with particular significance, the 'normalising' and stabilising outcomes of participation in employment were particularly salient for Seth, representing a departure from the chaos and instability that characterised his life previously (see Chapter 4).

Seth: I would say being settled and working all the time and just doing normal things with my family has been, probably, the most important thing to me.

Seth's concerns for stability and normalcy were both realised through and represented by his participation in employment and his assumed role as provider in his family of formation. Social relationships play a constitutive part of a responsible and legitimate identity and employment represents an important means through which these aspects of one's identity might be performed, realised and recognised (Rhodes, 2008). Providing for one's family through participation in employment, then, represents a visible and tangible symbol of change and reformation.

The role of breadwinner or provider remains central to masculine identity for many men; in this vein, fatherhood links the world of work to the world of family (Hauari and Hollingworth, 2009; Robinson and Hockey, 2011; Young, 2007). The ability to provide financially for and protect one's dependents have popularly defined working class manhood in Scotland (Craig 2010; Young, 2007), and physical work or manual labour in particular is perceived as an expression of masculinity (Willis, 1977). Alongside the male-dominated environment and hyper-masculine, hard-working culture of the steel-fixing industry, work thus represented an alternative means of accomplishing masculinity and acquiring self-respect and social recognition consistent with Seth's idealised configuration of what it meant to be a man.

Seth: I felt proud to go out and earn money and work hard and doing all the hours going and things like that. You felt good when you done seven days and come in and give [Lesley] the money. Even the guys round about me, they were all blowing their money every week... and I'd save the money or just go out buying normal things for our house. I was kind of learning that there was hope, that there was a chance there. I think fae getting out of [prison] to me having bought my own house was only a period of 18 months. It was a good time wi' nae chaos or anything.

The concept of 'hope' emerges as a dominant theme in much desistance research (see for example Burnett and Maruna, 2004; LeBel et al., 2008) and is considered to be particularly influential in the early stages of desistance (Farrall and Calverley, 2006; Lloyd and Serin, 2011) although it is equally recognised that unless it is embedded in realistic and tangible social opportunities to change the direction of one's life, it is not sustainable; rather, 'hope, expectation and confidence fade quickly on an empty stomach' (McNeill and Weaver, 2010 p.4). Hope is further associated with an increased sense of personal agency and confidence, particularly where people can discern or access the means through which they can realise their goals, and where, as Seth had, they have access to supportive, reflexive relational networks. On release from prison, work thus consolidated Seth's commitment to desistance and provided concrete opportunities through which his hopes for another way of being were realised and through which, in conjunction with his assumed roles within his family of formation, an alternative sense of self was brought into being and reinforced.

Constraints and limitations

A retrospective analysis enables the identification of patterns of continuity and change over time. As previously observed, participation in employment is no more universally experienced than it is static in nature. Even within the same job, the perception and value of this job will vary in accordance with an individual's priorities, concerns and experience. Moreover, how a single type of work is experienced by a given individual will vary in different economic contexts reflected, in part, in shifting working conditions. As the recession descended on London in the early 1990s, Seth returned with his family to Coaston. Changes to his conditioning structures generated by the impact of the recession on the construction industry (see for example Gordon, 2011) meant that he was increasingly working away from home, no longer principally with the revised group, which ultimately restricted the normalising and stabilising outcomes that his participation in employment initially enabled.

Seth: If the work wasn't great here or if I came across a job . . . like in Germany, you could go over there and earn some really good money. I'd be more settled now if I had just done a decent job with less money [rather than] always unsettling yourself, up and down the country.

Seth responded to strains of this itinerant lifestyle and the male dominated, hard-drinking, hard-working and highly competitive culture of the steel-fixing industry (Iacuone, 2005) by resuming his use of alcohol, from which he had abstained since his release from prison.

Seth: I started drinking at first just to show my [work] mates and it was alright at the start . . . I didn't really get into trouble or anything but I was starting about the pubs again and meeting up with the guys'.

Masculinity is negotiated and performed differently in different situations and in different relational spheres and social spaces (Connell and Messerschmidt,

2005; Robinson and Hockey, 2011). The experience and expression of masculine identity with one's workmates on building sites, which are traditionally masculinized environments, for example, differs from that which is normatively expected within the domestic environment with one's wife and children manifest in and accomplished through differing social behaviours (Robinson and Hockey, 2011). Alcohol consumption has traditionally been symbolic of masculinity (Lemle and Mishkind, 1989; Plant, Plant and Mason, 2002) and the pub performs an important social function as the primary social space for men in the construction industry, who are working away from their families and hometowns, living in crowded, often insubstantial, accommodation in unfamiliar geographical locations (Tilki, 2006). Moreover, opportunities for construction jobs are often discussed and negotiated in pubs, further adding to the social pressures to conform to this pub culture; isolation from these social and economic networks risks jeopardising social connections on which continued access to work is reliant (Tilki, 2006).

Seth: There was periods when I was working away from home and I'd drink . . . mostly out of boredom . . . that's the kind of culture . . . you finish your work and then everyone goes for a pint . . . [which led to] a couple of stupid things but nothing major, drink related breaches of the peace and . . . an assault.

Seth's involvement in these isolated offences, arising as a consequence of unanticipated interpersonal or situational dynamics did not, however, herald a return to an offending lifestyle. At that stage, in his thirties, his attitudes, values, beliefs, and lifestyle broadly conformed to 'conventional society' where several acceptable conformities, in terms of lifestyles and values, may co-exist (Maruna et al., 2004 p.274). Indeed alcohol related aggression and violence both amongst and by males in the west of Scotland is something of a cultural, if not class, 'norm', as discussed in Chapter 4 (see also Craig, 2010). However, over time, Seth's repeated episodes of binge drinking served as a respite from, and thus a means of coping with, his financial, employment and relational concerns.

Seth: If things like money and work were getting on top of me or if I wasn't getting on with [Lesley], I would use that as an excuse to stay out the house [drinking] for a couple of days . . . that's been me right up to the day for at least ten years.

While, as this chapter has illustrated, Seth had embarked on and sustained a process of change, some continuity in his cognitive and behavioural patterns are evident. Alcohol and the pub respectively provided the means of and social space to which he was able to 'flee' or escape from the pressures bearing down on him. Seth conceptualises the development of these avoidant coping mechanisms as a process that began in childhood which he attributes to repeated experiences of 'fleeing' with his family from his father's violence and his subsequent pattern of repeatedly absconding from various young offender institutions. Echoing research on coping socialisation processes in response to stress internalised during earlier developmental stages (Kliewer, Fearnow and Miller,1996), Seth suggested, '*that's probably how I flee from things the now*'. Men's desires to regulate and suppress emotionality can also be located in gender socialisation processes, through which young men learn that they should not display 'feminine' traits such as emotionality, vulnerability or weakness (Connell, 1995, 2002; Doyle and Paludi, 1991; McClure, 2006; Wallace, 2007; White and Cones, 1999). For Seth, alcohol use, conversely associated with expressions of masculinity, had long represented a means of suppressing his unwanted emotions. This behavioural pattern was established in his early years and reinforced in peer interactions at different stages in his life (see also Chapter 4).

In the early stages, then, participation in work enabled change by contributing to a range of desistance promotive outcomes, including the activation and personification of his role identity as a good provider and family man. Subsequent changes to his working conditions manifest in working away from home, and his related immersion in the hard-drinking, hard-working culture of the steel-fixing industry, while enabling the maintenance of social relations within his working environment, ultimately interfered with his capacity to sustain direct family involvement. In turn, Seth's pattern of binge drinking in response to various stressors '*got out of control*' and contributed in cumulative effect to his later separation from Lesley.

Conclusion

This chapter has discussed Seth's life beyond the fragmentation of the Del, and, in that, his process of desistance. The role of the revised group, his family of formation and his participation in employment in enabling and reinforcing his commitment to desistance characterised his narrative of change and has formed the principal focus of analysis in this chapter. What this analysis has revealed is that it was the complex and contingent interaction of these various transitional processes and ensuing opportunities for change (within his conditioning structures) as mediated through the lens of his personal priorities, values, aspirations and relational concerns, which imbued these particular opportunities, events and experiences with significance and which directly influenced their potential to enable or constrain processes of change, at different stages in his life.

In particular, this chapter illustrated how the fragmentation of the Del and the resultant interpersonal conflicts, in conjunction with his deepening emotional attachment to Lesley and the realisation of the impacts of his then lifestyle on the emergent relational goods, triggered his initial reflexive re-evaluation of his lifestyle. This evaluative process continued throughout his subsequent prison sentence, which he had apprehended as an opportunity for change, in so far as it liberated him from the constraints in his conditioning structures, and enabled him to begin a process of investment in himself. His experience of '*Training for Freedom*', in particular his relationships and interactions with his co-workers and his experience of helping others, was particularly significant in communicating an alternative experience of self, and in turn, the possibility that another way of

Structural Conditioning [conditioning structures]

T 1
───────────────────────────────

          Interactions in Networks [black box: individual and relational contributions]

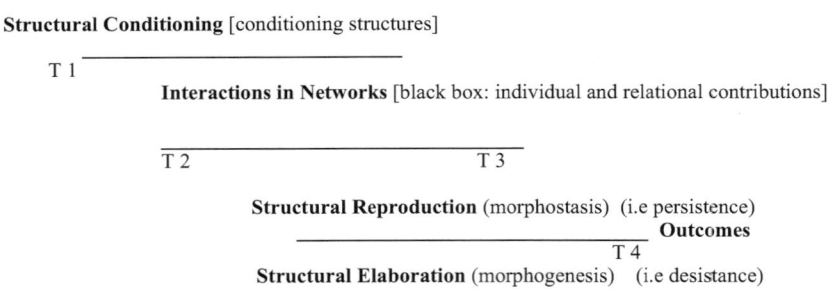

    T 2   T 3
─────────────────────────────────────

          Structural Reproduction (morphostasis) (i.e persistence)
                                                           Outcomes
          ─────────────────────────────
                                                        T 4
          Structural Elaboration (morphogenesis)   (i.e desistance)

Figure 5.1 Overview of investigative framework

being was realisable. This chapter then illustrated the contributions of the revised group, Seth's relationship with Lesley and his family of formation in supporting desistance, and the centrality of work to his changing self-concept, social identity, and to the nature and form of these social relations and their interactive dynamics.

As discussed in Chapter 2, quantitative research tends to focus on the degree to which intimate relationships or parenthood are causative or conditional on desistance, in terms of the relative sequencing of relational investments and desistance. In contrast, qualitative analyses tend to focus on revealing the relative contribution of the identified change agent to the outcomes, be it the role of the partner, for example, as change agent (as in social control theories), or the role of the individual as change agent (as in more agentic or cognitive theories of desistance). Applying Donati's theory of relational reflexivity allows for a more nuanced analysis. For Seth, it was the incremental significance of his relationship with Lesley in the context of shifts in his conditioning structures (at T1 in Figure 5.1), triggered by the fragmentation of the Del to which he applied his personal reflexivity, resulting in a reprioritisation of his ultimate concerns (T2–T3), manifesting in a shift in practices that enabled him, in incremental effect, to realise his interconnected individual and relational concerns with which continued offending was incompatible (T4). The mutually reinforcing interaction of becoming and being a father or family man during the early stages of his release and changes in the relational dynamics of the revised group and involvement in stable employment (T4–T1 in the next stage of the morphogenetic sequence), strengthened his sense of hope, self-efficacy and resolve to desist. Assuming and activating the role of family man was enabled by his participation in work (T2–T3), which contributed to changes, in cumulative effect, to his self-concept, social identity and lifestyle (T4). Employment essentially represented a concrete opportunity for realising change, through which his hopes for another way of being were realised and through which, in conjunction with his assumed role in his family of formation, an alternative sense of self was once more brought into being. However, what this chapter has also illustrated is that the outcomes of these processes are not static but are influenced by changes in conditioning structures, which can, depending on the individual's response to these changes, engender constraints and limitations.

What this in turn reveals, then, is that desistance can be a complex, contingent, individualised, reflexive and relational process.

Notes

1 Parts of this chapter draw from Donati, P. (2011) *Relational Sociology: A New Paradigm for the Social Sciences*. Abingdon: Routledge. Reproduced with permission from Routledge.
   Parts of this chapter were previously published in Weaver, B. (2012) The Relational Context of Desistance: Some Implications and Opportunities for Social Policy, *Social Policy and Administration* 46(4), pp.395–412. Reproduced with permission from Wiley.
   Parts of this chapter were previously published in Weaver, B., and McNeill, F. (2015) Lifelines: Desistance, Social Relations and Reciprocity. *Criminal Justice and Behavior* 42(1), pp.95–107. Reproduced with permission from Sage.
2 SACRO, the Scottish Association for the Care and Resettlement of Offenders, is a third sector, community justice organisation.
3 As previously noted in Chapter 3, the internal conversation is ongoing; in the face of setbacks, temptations or provocations (Bottoms and Shapland, 2011), or where certain courses of action, events or experiences lead to undesired consequences, individuals may begin to lose motivation and commitment (Archer, 2000).
4 There is no universally agreed definition of Active Citizenship. Crick (2002 p.2) argues that it represents a focus on 'the rights to be exercised as well as agreed responsibilities'. Activity in this sense is often associated with engagement in public services, volunteering and democratic participation (see for example Crick, 2000; Lister, 2003).
5 It is acknowledged, however, that even if it a relationship ends, it can still have a transformative effect.

References

Akers, R.L. (1973) *Deviant Behaviour: A Social Learning Approach*. Belmont, CA: Wadsworth.
Archer, M. (2000) *Being Human: The Problem of Agency*. Cambridge: Cambridge University Press.
Archer, M. (2003) *Structure, Agency and the Internal Conversation*. Cambridge: Cambridge University Press.
Bannister, J., Pickering, J., Batchelor, S., Burman, M., Kintrea, K., and McVie, S. (2010) *Troublesome Youth Groups, Gangs and Knife Carrying in Scotland*. Edinburgh: Scottish Government.
Baron, J.N. (1988) The Employment Relation as a Social Relation. *Journal of the Japanese and International Economies* 2(4), pp.492–525.
Barry, M. (2006) *Youth Offending in Transition: The Search for Social Recognition*. Abingdon: Routledge.
Becker, H.S. (1966) *Outsiders: Studies in the Sociology of Deviance*. New York, NY: Free Press.
Bersani, B., Laub, J.H., and Nieuwbeerta, P. (2009) Marriage and Desistance from Crime in the Netherlands: Do Gender and Socio-historical Context Matter? *Journal of Quantitative Criminology* 25(1), pp.3–24.
Bianchi, S.M., Casper, L.M., and King, R.B. (2005) *Work, Family, Health and Well-Being*. Mahwah, NJ: Lawrence Erlbaum Associates.
Bottoms, A.E., and Shapland, J. (2011) Steps Towards Desistance Among Male Young Adult Recidivists, in Farrall, S., Hough, M., Maruna, S., and Sparks, R. (eds.) *Escape*

Routes: Contemporary Perspectives on Life After Punishment. London: Routledge, pp.43–80.

Burnett, R., and Maruna, S. (2004) So Prison Works Does It?: The Criminal Careers of 130 Men Released from Prison Under Home Secretary Michael Howard. *Howard Journal of Criminal Justice* 43(4), pp.405–419.

Burnett, R., and Maruna, S. (2006) The Kindness of Prisoners: Strength-Based Resettlement in Theory and in Action. *Criminology and Criminal Justice* 6(1), pp.83–106.

Cairns, R.B., and Cairns, B.D. (1994). *Lifelines and Risks: Pathways of Youth in Our Time*. Cambridge: Cambridge University Press.

Calverley, A. (2013) *Cultures of Desistance: Rehabilitation, Reintegration and Ethnic Minorities*. Abingdon: Routledge.

Carlsson, C. (2012) Using 'Turning Points' to Understand Processes of Change in Offending: Notes from a Swedish Study on Life Course and Crime. *British Journal of Criminology* 52(1), pp.1–16.

Collier, P. (1998) *Social Capital and Poverty*, Social Capital Initiative Working Paper No 4. Washington, DC: World Bank.

Connell, R.W. (1995) *Masculinities*. Cambridge: Polity Press.

Connell, R.W. (2002) *The Men and the Boys*. Cambridge: Polity Press.

Connell R.W., and Messerschmidt, J.W. (2005) Hegemonic Masculinity: Rethinking the Concept. *Gender & Society* 19(6), pp.829–859.

Craig, C. (2010) *The Tears That Made the Clyde: Well-Being in Glasgow*. Argyll: Argyll.

Crewe, B. (2009) *The Prisoner Society: Power, Adaptation and Social Life in an English Prison*. Oxford: Oxford University Press, Clarendon Studies in Criminology.

Crick, B. (2000) *Essays on Citizenship*. London: Continuum.

Crick, B. (2002) *Education for Citizenship: The Citizenship Order*. Parliamentary Affairs 55, pp.488–504.

Crisp, R. (2010) *Work, Place and Identity: The Salience of Work for Residents in Four Neighbourhoods*. Research Paper No. 10. Sheffield: Centre for Regional Economic Social Research.

Cromwell. P.F., Olson. J.N., and D'Aunn, W.A. (1991) *Breaking and Entering: An Ethnographic Analysis of Burglary*. Newbury Park, CA: Sage.

Decker, S.H., and Lauritsen, J. (2002) Leaving the Gangs, in Huff, C.R. (ed.) *Gangs in America* (3rd ed.). Thousand Oaks, CA: Sage, pp.51–67.

Donati, P. (2011) *Relational Sociology: A New Paradigm for the Social Sciences*. Abingdon: Routledge.

Doyle, J., and Paludi, M. (1991) *Sex and Gender: The Human Experience*. New York, NY: William C. Brown.

Drakeford, M., and Gregory, L. (2010) Transforming Time: A New Tool for Youth Justice. *Youth Justice* 10(2), pp.143–156.

Edgar, K., Jacobson, J., and Biggar, K. (2011) *Time Well Spent*. London: Prison Reform Trust.

Edin, K., Nelson, T.J., and Paranal, R. (2001) *Fatherhood and Incarceration as Potential Turning Points in the Criminal Careers of Unskilled Men*. Evanston, IL: Northwestern University Institution for Policy Research.

Farrall, S. (2002) *Rethinking What Works With Offenders: Probation, Social Context and Desistance from Crime*. Cullompton: Willan.

Farrall, S. (2004) Social Capital and Offender Reintegration: Making Probation Desistance Focussed, in Maruna, S., and Immarigeon, R. (eds.) *After Crime and Punishment: Pathways to Offender Reintegration*. Cullompton: Willan, pp.57–84.

Farrall, S., and Calverley, A. (2006) *Understanding Desistance From Crime: Theoretical Directions in Resettlement and Rehabilitation*. Crime and Justice Series. Oxford: Oxford University Press.

Farrington, D.P. (1992) Criminal Career Research in the United Kingdom. *British Journal of Criminology* 32(4), pp.521–536.

Giordano, P.C., Cernkovich, S.A., and Holland, D.D. (2003) Changes in Friendship Relations Over the Life Course: Implications for Desistance From Crime. *Criminology* 41(2), pp.293–328.

Giordano, P.C., Cernkovich, S.A., and Rudolph, J.L. (2002) Gender, Crime and Desistance: Toward a Theory of Cognitive Transformation. *American Journal of Sociology* 107, pp.990–1064.

Giordano, P.C., Seffrin, P.M., Manning, W.D., and Longmorn, M. (2011) Parenthood and Crime: The Role of Wantedness, Relationships With Partners, and SES. *Journal of Criminal Justice* 39(5), pp.405–416.

Goffman, E. (1963) *Stigma: Notes on the Management of Spoiled Identity*. Harmondsworth: Prentice-Hall.

Gordon, I. (2011) *The Economic Recession: Why London Escaped Lightly*. LES London Briefing. http://www.lse.ac.uk/geographyAndEnvironment/research/london/events/HEIF/HEIF4b_10–11%20-newlondonenv/briefs/gordon.pdf, accessed 20/6/13.

Graham, J., and Bowling, B. (1995) *Young People and Crime. Home Office Research Study No. 145*. London: HMSO.

Haggard, U.A., Gumpert, C.H., and Grann, M. (2001) Against All Odds: A Qualitative Follow-up Study of High Risk Violent Offenders Who Were Not Reconvicted. *Journal of Interpersonal Violence* 16(10), pp.1048–1065.

Hauari, H., and Hollingworth, K. (2009) *Understanding Fathering: Masculinity, Diversity and Change*. York: Joseph Rowntree Foundation. Available at: http://www.jrf.org.uk/sites/files/jrf/understanding-fathering-diversity-full.pdf, accessed 09/02/2011.

Haynie, D.L. (2001) Delinquent Peers Revisited: Does Network Structure Matter? *American Journal of Sociology* 106(4), pp.1013–1057.

Haynie, D.L. (2002) Friendship Networks and Delinquency: The Relative Nature of Peer Delinquency. *Journal of Quantitative Criminology* 18(2), pp.99–134.

Humphrey, S.E., Nahrgaug, J.D., and Morgeson, F.P. (2007) Integrating Motivational, Social and Contextual Work Design Features: a Meta-Analytic Summary and Theoretical Extension of the Work Design Literature. *Journal of Applied Psychology* 92(5), pp.1332–1356.

Iacuone, D. (2005) 'Real Men Are Tough Guys': Hegemonic Masculinity as Safety in the Construction Industry. *Journal of Men's Studies* 13(2), pp.247–266.

Kelman, H.C. (1958) Compliance, Identification and Internalization: Three Processes of Attitude Change. *Conflict Resolution* 2(1), pp.51–60.

Kiernan, K. (2004) Unmarried Cohabitation and Parenthood in Britain and Europe. *Law & Policy* 26(1), pp.33–55.

King, S. (2014) *Desistance Transitions and the Impact of Probation*. Abingdon: Routledge.

Kliewer, W., Fearnow, M.D., and Miller, P.A. (1996) Coping Socialization in Middle Childhood: Tests of Maternal and Paternal Influences. *Child Development* 67(5), pp.2339–2357.

Knight, B.J., and West, D.J. (1975) Temporary and Continuing Delinquency. *British Journal of Criminology* 15(1), pp.43–50.

Laub, J.H., Nagin, D.S., and Sampson, R.J. (1998) Trajectories of Change in Criminal Offending: Good Marriages and the Desistance Process. *American Sociological Review* 63, pp.225–238.

Laub, J.H., and Sampson, R.J. (2001) Understanding Desistance from Crime, in Tonry, M.H., and Morris, N. (eds.) *Crime and Justice: An Annual Review of Research*, Vol. 26. Chicago, IL: University of Chicago Press, pp.1–78.

Laub, J.H., and Sampson, R.J. (2003) *Shared Beginnings, Divergent Lives*. Cambridge, MA: Harvard University Press.

LeBel, T.P. (2007) An Examination of the Impact of Formerly Incarcerated Persons Helping Others. *Journal of Offender Rehabilitation* 46(1–2), pp.1–24.

LeBel, T.P. (2009) Formerly Incarcerated Persons' Use of Advocacy/Activism as a Coping Strategy in the Reintegration Process, in Veysey, B., Christian, J., and Martinez, D.J. (eds.) *How Offenders Transform Their Lives*. Cullompton: Willan, pp.165–187.

LeBel, T.P., Burnett, R., Maruna, S., and Bushway, S. (2008) The 'Chicken and Egg' of Subjective and Social Factors in Desistance from Crime. *European Journal of Criminology* 5(2), pp.131–159.

Lemle, R., and Mishkind, M.E. (1989) Alcohol and Masculinity. *Journal of Substance Abuse Treatment* 6(4), pp.213–222.

Lister, R. (2003) *Citizenship: Feminist Perspectives* (2nd ed.). Basingstoke: Palgrave Macmillan.

Lloyd, C., and Serin, R. (2011) Agency and Outcome Expectancies for Crime and Desistance: Measuring Offenders and Personal Beliefs About Change. *Psychology, Crime and Law* 18(6), pp.543–565.

Lyngstad, T.H., and Skardhamar, T. (2011) *Understanding the Marriage Effect: Changes in Criminal Offending Around the Time of Marriage*. Gemass Working Paper No.2. https://www.academia.edu/3851257/Changes_in_Criminal_Offending_around_the_Time_of_Marriage, accessed 23/12/14.

Marsiglio, W., Amato, P., Day, R.D., and Lamb, M. (2000) Scholarship on Fatherhood in the 1990s and Beyond. *Journal of Marriage and Family* 62(4), pp.1173–1191.

Marsiglio, W., and Pleck, J.H. (2004) Fatherhood and Masculinities, in Kimmel, M.S., Hearn, J., and Connell R.W. (eds.) *Handbook of Studies on Men and Masculinities*. Thousand Oaks, CA: Sage, pp.249–269.

Maruna, S. (2001) *Making Good: How Ex-Convicts Reform and Rebuild Their Lives*. Washington, DC: American Psychological Association Books.

Maruna, S., Immarigeon, R., and LeBel, T. (2004) Ex-Offender Reintegration: Theory and Practice, in Maruna, S., and Immarigeon, R. (eds.) *After Crime and Punishment: Pathways to Offender Reintegration*. Cullompton: Willan, pp.3–26.

Massoglia, M., and Uggen, C. (2010) Settling Down and Aging Out: Toward an Interactionist Theory of Desistance and the Transition to Adulthood. *American Journal of Sociology* 116(2), pp.543–582.

McClure, S. (2006) Improvising Masculinity: African American Fraternity Membership in the Construction of a Black Masculinity. *Journal of African Studies* 10(1), pp.57–73.

McNeill, F., and Weaver, B. (2010) *Changing Lives? Desistance Research and Offender Management*. SCCJR Report No. 03/2010, published online at: http://www.sccjr.ac.uk/documents/Report%202010_03%20-%20Changing%20Lives.pdf, accessed 09/07/13.

Moloney, M., MacKenzie, K., Hunt, G., and Joe-Laidler, K. (2009) The Path and Promise of Fatherhood for Gang Members. *British Journal of Criminology* 49(3), pp.305–325.

Monahan, K.C., Steinberg, L., and Cauffman, E. (2009) Affiliation with Antisocial Peers, Susceptibility to Peer Influence, and Antisocial Behavior During the Transition to Adulthood. *Developmental Psychology* 45(6), pp.1520–1530.

Monsbakken, C.W., Lyngstad, T.H., and Skardhamar, T. (2012a) Crime and the Transition to Parenthood: The Role of Sex and Relationship Context. *British Journal of Criminology* 53(1), pp.129–148.

Monsbakken, C.W., Lyngstad, T.H., and Skardhamar, T. (2012b) *Crime and The Transition to Marriage: The Roles of Gender and Partner's Criminal Involvement*, Discussion Papers Statistics Norway Research Department, No. 678, February 2012. http://www.ssb.no/a/publikasjoner/pdf/DP/dp678.pdf, accessed 23/12/14.
Morgeson, F.P., and Humphrey, S.E. (2006) The Work Design Questionnaire (WDQ): Developing and Validating a Comprehensive Measure for Assessing Job Design and the Nature of Work. *Journal of Applied Psychology* 91(6), pp.1321–1339.
Niven, S., and Stewart, D. (2005) *Resettlement Outcomes on Release from Prison in 2003*. London: Home Office.
Owens, B. (2009) Training and Employment in an Economic Downturn: Lessons for Desistance Studies. *Irish Probation Journal* 6, pp.49–65.
Pahl, R. (2000) *On Friendship*. Cambridge: Polity Press.
Paternoster, R., and Bushway, S. (2009) Desistance and the 'Feared Self': Toward an Identity Theory of Criminal Desistance. *Journal of Law and Criminology* 99(4), pp.1103–1156.
Pearl, A., and Riessman, F. (1965) *New Careers for the Poor: The Nonprofessional in Human Service*. New York, NY: Free Press.
Plant, M., Plant, M., and Mason, W. (2002) Drinking, Smoking and Illicit Drug Use Among British Adults. *Journal of Substance Use* 7, pp.24–33.
Rhodes, J. (2008) Ex-offenders' Social Ties and the Routes Into Employment. *Internet Journal of Criminology* 1, pp.1–20.
Robinson, V., and Hockey, J. (2011) *Masculinities in Transition*. London: Palgrave Macmillan.
Rumgay, J. (2004) Scripts for Safer Survival: Pathways Out of Female Crime. *Howard Journal of Criminal Justice* 43(4), pp.405–419.
Sampson, R.J., and Laub, J.H. (1993) *Crime in the Making: Pathways and Turning Points Through Life*. Cambridge, MA: Harvard University Press.
Sampson, R.J., Laub, J.H., and Wimer, C. (2006) Does Marriage Reduce Crime?: A Counter-Factual Approach to Within-Individual Causal Effects. *Criminology* 44(3), pp.465–508.
Savolainen, J. (2009) Work, Family and Criminal Desistance. *British Journal of Criminology* 49(3), pp.285–304.
Sennett, R. (2003) *Respect: The Formation of Character in a World of Inequality*. London: Allan Lane.
Shover, N. (1996) *Great Pretenders: Pursuits and Careers of Persistent Thieves*. Oxford: Oxford University Press.
Soyer, M. (2014) The Imagination of Desistance: A Juxtaposition of the Construction of Incarceration as a Turning Point and the Reality of Recidivism. *British Journal of Criminology* 54, pp.91–108.
Sutherland, E.H. (1947) *The Principles of Criminology* (4th ed.). Chicago, IL: J.B. Lippincott.
Tilki, M. (2006) The Social Contexts of Drinking Among Irish Men in London: Evidence From a Qualitative Study. *Drugs, Education, Prevention and Policy* 13(3), pp.247–261.
Uggen, C. (1999) Ex-offenders and the Conformist Alternative: A Job Quality Model of Work and Crime. *Social Problems* 46(1), pp.127–151.
Uggen, C., and Kruttschnitt, C. (1998) Crime in the Breaking: Gender Differences in Desistance. *Law and Society Review* 32(2), pp.339–366.
Uggen, C., Manza, J., and Behrens, A. (2004). Less Than the Average Citizen: Stigma, Role Transition and the Civic Reintegration of Convicted Felons, in Maruna, S., and

Immarigeon, R. (eds.) *After Crime and Punishment: Pathways to Offender Reintegration*. Cullompton: Willan, pp.258–290.

Vaughan, B. (2007) The Internal Narrative of Desistance. *British Journal of Criminology* 47(3), pp.390–404.

Vigil, J.D. (1988) *Barrio Gangs: Street Life and Identity in Southern California*. Austin: University of Texas Press.

Visher, C.A., and Courtney, S.M.E. (2007) *One Year Out: Experiences of Prisoners Returning to Cleveland; Returning Home Policy Brief*. Washington, DC: Urban Institution Justice Policy Center.

Visher, C.A., and Travis, J. (2003). Transitions from Prison to Community: Understanding Individual Pathways. *Annual Review of Sociology* 29(1), pp.89–113.

Wallace, D.M. (2007) 'It's a M-A-N Thing': Black Male Gender Role Socialization and the Performance of Masculinity in Love Relationships. *Journal of Pan African Studies* 1(7), pp.11–22.

Warr, M. (1993) Parents, Peers and Delinquency. *Social Forces* 72(1), pp.247–264.

Warr, M. (1998) Life-Course Transitions and Desistance from Crime. *Criminology* 36(2), pp.183–216.

Warr, M. (2002) *Companions in Crime: The Social Aspects of Criminal Conduct*. Cambridge: Cambridge University Press.

Weaver, B. (2012) The Relational Context of Desistance: Some Implications and Opportunities for Social Policy. *Social Policy and Administration* 46(4), pp.395–412.

Weaver, B., and McNeill, F. (2015) Lifelines: Desistance, Social Relations and Reciprocity. *Criminal Justice and Behavior* 42(1), pp.95–107.

White, J.L., and Cones, J.H. (1999) *Black Man Emerging: Facing the Past and Seizing a Future in America*. New York, NY: Freeman.

Willis, P. (1977) *Learning to Labour: How Working Class Kids Get Working Class Jobs*. Farnborough: Saxon House.

Woolcock, M., and Narayan, D. (2000) Social Capital: Implications for Development Theory, Research, and Policy. *World Bank Research Observer* 15(2), pp.225–249.

Young, J. (2007) *The Vertigo of Late Modernity*. London: Sage.

6 Fighting, football and fatherhood[1]
Harry's story

To get my son brought up. Once I see him settled, married and has his family, then I will be happy. That's my purpose in life.

Biographical overview

Harry, aged 47, was born in Glasgow in 1961 but has resided in and around Coaston for the past 39 years. His experience of emotional disconnection within and towards his family during his childhood, discussed in Chapter 4, was a contributory influence on his involvement with the Del. Both of his parents worked every day; his father worked four jobs and his mother worked in a pub and while this meant that they were comparatively financially comfortable they were often emotionally and physically unavailable. His relationship with his family of origin remains fractious and they have limited contact.

Harry offended persistently for two decades (aged 13–33) during which time he acquired an extensive number of convictions '*running to three pages*' primarily of an acquisitive or violent nature, all of which resulted in short prison sentences of varying lengths. Harry's offending was primarily situational, spontaneous and opportunistic and, as discussed in Chapter 4, his high level of identification with the 'deviant' subculture enabled him to resist the public stigma and negative attributions conferred on the Del. However, whilst he exhibited high levels of identification with, or internalisation of, the norms and standards of the group he was less highly embedded in the group than Seth, for example. While exhibiting a willingness to fight afforded Harry a measure of credibility and his association with the Del lent him 'street capital' (Sandberg, 2008), his lack of competence in fighting meant that he had a lesser status in terms of his role and position within the Del.

In the aftermath of the fragmentation of the Del, Harry extricated himself from the feud by alternatively associating with his elder brother's friends who were heavily involved in the football culture which heralded a shift in his offending towards primarily football related violence from which he has desisted for fifteen years. Harry met his wife Millie during his late teens and their son was born in 1994, when Harry was 33, shortly after he acquired his first job in a factory, aged 32. He has worked as a side loader driver in a local steel works for the past seven years.

Harry's delineation of his life stages following the fragmentation of the Del are structured in accordance with the salient experiences and concerns constitutive of his identity during these life stages, namely 'The Football Years' (aged 25–33) and 'Fatherhood' (aged 33–47). This chapter commences by describing Harry's response to the feud and elucidates these experiences and concerns under the superordinate theme '*Roles, reflexivity, relationality and desistance*' which discusses the role of Harry's familial, social and personal relationships in supporting desistance over time. The role of employment in Harry's narrative of change is discussed under the final superordinate theme '*The meanings and outcomes of work*'.

Roles, reflexivity, relationality and desistance

The role of extant familial and new social networks in supporting desistance

In response to the feud, Harry made a prudential decision to distance himself from the ensuing intra-group enmities.

Harry: I never fell out major with any of them, because . . . I didn't want to get involved . . . so I just spoke to them all and I was happier that way and I think they all realised that and they were happier with me.

His ability to extricate himself from the feud was facilitated by the availability of an alternative social network with whom his elder brother associated and which was deeply immersed in football fan culture. In this sense, while his brother provided a gateway to an alternative social network, football fandom was the conduit through which Harry developed an alternative personal and social identity.

Harry: It was the crowd that was next in line . . . that I went with. My brother . . . went to football regularly . . . and initially it was his pals I was jumping about with . . . they were different kind of friends you know, mostly workers, you know they didn't get into bother. So I gradually started going with them . . . to every game, home and abroad, and . . . that was me basically, football was my life from then on.

Football and the associated 'fan' culture and social life structured Harry's social relationships, lifestyle and identity for eight years after the fragmentation of the Del. His new friendship group shared his devotion to Celtic football club and the intensity of his immersion in this 'associational belonging' informed both his personal and social identity. Personal and social identities emerge through social interaction and, in that, through processes of internal and external identification in terms of membership of a social category or social role. Social identification constitutes 'a subjective process through which externally assigned category distinctions are accepted [or rejected] and in-group characteristics are adopted to help define and express the self' (Barreto and Ellemers, 2003 p.141 [this author's insertion]). Identification to and with this new group thus required an acceptance and adoption of the norms and rules of associational belonging (Hogg and Hardie, 1991) characteristic of the membership of this group manifest in attendance at each football game and an explicit and unwavering support of the club. The football team was the focus of men's solidarity, and relationships with other men are affirmed through their commitment to the team. The time invested in it, according to King (1997), symbolises the values and friendships which exist between supporters in general and the group in particular. On this common ground, men share a sense of collective identity, community, solidarity, camaraderie and associational belonging (see also Holden and Wilde, 2004; King, 1997; Poulton, 2012; Social Issues Research Centre [SIRC], 2008; Spaaij, 2008) which for these very reasons, in the aftermath of the fragmentation of, and his subsequent extrication from, the Del, was particularly significant to Harry.

In particular, association with the '*football crowd*' represented a *credible* alternative to association with the Del. Masculinity is substantially defined through football and the 'world of the football fan is organised around typically male-oriented social spaces – pubs, bars and large-scale sports arenas' (SIRC, 2008 p.6). Perhaps more pertinently, pride in the club's success and their support brings social recognition from other men who are football supporters.

> Since masculine relations are substantially concerned with status . . . the pride [attained] from football is important. It assists him in asserting himself in relations with other men in his community. Consequently, a fundamental part of the lads' support is emphasising the rivalry of his club and the superiority of his club.
>
> (King, 1997 p.334).

One aspect of the norms of football fandom and an unwritten rule of associational belonging is a willingness to defend the honour of one's club (Spaaij, 2008). As Harry states in the extract above, while the people he associated with were '*mostly workers, [who] didn't get into bother*' the relationship between football fandom and allegiance to a club, not least in the context of 'Old Firm'[2] rivalries, often manifested in violent conflicts with members of the opposing club.

Harry: I started to get a few more assaults on my card then because I was a Celtic man and that could cause a lot of fights you know? So I got a few [convictions] with that an' all.

In Scotland, football allegiance plays a significant part in the respective social identities for Protestants and Catholics (Holden and Wilde, 2004) and 'symbolic pride . . . is therefore frequently made into a "matter of honour"' (Hognestad, 1997 p.194). Whether this reflects 'substantive sectarian hatred that reaches beyond the confines of football or . . . merely ritualised forms of abuse intended to 'wind-up' rival supporters' is debatable (Hamilton-Smith and Hopkins, 2012 p.3).

Nonetheless, echoing gang-related rivalries (see Chapter 4), 'hard masculinity, territorial identifications, individual and collective management of reputation, a sense of solidarity and autonomy . . . are central to expressions of football-related violence' (Spaaij, 2008 p.369). However, precisely because these violent interpersonal clashes occur between groups of rival supporters, football-related aggression and violence has historically been viewed by supporters as '"doing wrong" rather than "doing crime"' (Presdee, 1994 cited in Poulton, 2012 p.7).

Whilst, then, there is much continuity within Harry's transition from association with the Del to football fandom, not least in relation to the maintenance of alcohol-fuelled violent behaviour, and the defence of associated reputations, the context within which this shift occurred arguably symbolised a shift in his moral status (Gusfield, 1967) from offender to fan, reflected in his identity migration from one social network and set of relations to another. His new associates were not typically classed as 'offenders' although they too participated in football-related violence. In the 1980s through 1990s, attributions of 'deviance' to football-related violence were muted compared to the more recent criminalisation and increasing regulation of sectarianism and associated disorderly conduct occurring in contemporary Scottish football (Waiton, 2012). This transition itself reflects a passage from one moral status to another, through which the same behaviour in different social contexts is associated with greater or lesser degrees of deviance (Gusfield, 1967).

Prior to the fragmentation of the Del, then, Harry had been immersed in an offending lifestyle to which acquisitive and violent related crime was central. Thereafter, his lifestyle cohered around football fandom in which violence played a part, but which was, at that time, more socially acceptable than the violence he had participated in with the Del. The changes in his conditioning structures manifest in the fragmentation of, and his extrication from the Del and his association with a new group enabled changes in his personal and social identity in the transition from offender to football fan. However, whilst representing a measurable break from his former lifestyle, not least in terms of shifts in the frequency and context of, and thus justifications and motivations for, his offending, there is evidence of some continuity in terms of his immersion in an alternative subculture which afforded him a source of status, recognition, masculinity, community and belonging in which anti-social and violent behaviours were variously tolerated and expected.

Role of intimate relationships and families of formation in supporting desistance

This sub-theme illustrates the role of intimate relationships and families of formation in the desistance process. As observed in preceding chapters, the relative contribution or influence of these social relations on an individual's offending (or desistance) is subject to much debate. In contrast to social control theorists who place explanatory weight on the actions or influence of the partner, Giordano, Cernkovich and Holland (2003) cast the individual, not the partner, as the primary change agent. In particular they construe shifts in receptivity to a partner's normative influence as the outcome of motivational and attitudinal changes reflecting developmental changes based on the accumulation of experience and the ascendancy of intimate over peer relationships. However, although the constructive influences of a pro-social partner seem self-evident, attachment to a pro-social partner does not explain why someone becomes more amenable to change at one time rather than another, particularly where, as in Harry's case, attitudinal changes do not automatically translate into a reorientation of values. Despite the disintegration of the Del, his emotional connection to Millie, and her exhortations to change, like Seth, this relationship was neither causative of nor conditional on his desistance. As elaborated above, Harry engaged in football-related violence until he was 33, of which Millie was aware, although he ceased house-breaking in his '*late 20s*' reflecting his deepening concern to maintain the relationship with Millie and to limit the shame and stigma this might afford her.

Harry: I didn't want [Millie] to get a reputation . . . I didn't want [her] to think that she was going with a housebreaker. It would be embarrassing when it was in the paper . . . When you get more mature you realise it's an embarrassment to your family . . . you don't like to see your loved ones hurt.

Similarly, while Millie disapproved of his offending, her forbearance reflected her concern to maintain the relationship, which challenges a strict social control (Laub and Sampson, 2001) or differential association (Warr, 1998) perspective.

Harry: She put up with a hell of a lot . . . she tried for years to get me on the straight and narrow but it just didnae happen. She let me know that I should maybe change and start doing this and that . . . but she stood by me for all they years . . . even though I was in the jail regularly . . . I mean why would she do that?

What these extracts illustrate are the reciprocal and collaborative adjustments made by both parties to maintain the relationship, emerging from their mutual concern, oriented to the sustenance of the emergent relational goods which they both valued, consistent with Donati's (2011) theory of relational reflexivity. Yet, despite their emotional connectedness and the value placed on the relationship, it was fatherhood that encouraged Harry's desistance, in incremental effect.

Harry: I think that made a major difference – being a father you know? That kind of changed my whole life completely. That is when I stopped drinking and . . . started to settle down . . . I knew then I had to get my life in order . . . but it didnae happen overnight.

For Harry, then, desistance emerged as one among many wider shifts in practices or behaviours, emerging from a re-prioritisation of his ultimate concerns; like Seth, the initial impetus for change was thus consolidated by his continuous reflection. To illustrate, previously Harry had engaged in an internal conversation (personal reflexivity) which acknowledged, but was not significantly altered by, being in a new role position in relation to Millie; it was not until after his son was born that he engaged in a more socially expanded form of reflexivity. At this point, Harry's reflexive evaluation of his lifestyle against his shifting sense of what mattered to him, informed by his own values and beliefs surrounding fatherhood (more on which below), reflected a reorientation of his relational concerns, the realisation of which required a shift in his practices. Desistance was one shift in practice emerging from Harry's perception of the impact his offending would have on this social relation, underpinned by a desire to maintain a constructive paternal image, which was critical to his self-concept.

Harry: You don't want your child brung up knowing that you're in jail do you? That's the thing that would have hurt me the most. He doesn't know nothing of what I've done in my past – not a thing.

Here, then, it is the social relation of the family (which is not reducible to the individuals involved, as existing explanations of desistance would suppose, but which refers to that which emerges from their reciprocal orientation) that is being invoked as both a constraint upon offending and an enablement for a new way of living. Thus, it is changes in the social relation and how *it* becomes more reflexive that underpins this process of change for Harry.

The impact of intimate relationships and fatherhood on individual behaviour emerges from the nature and intensity of the bond *between* individuals-in-relation and the chains of meanings that these particular types of social relation entail for individuals, who bring their own personal reflexivity to bear in a manner consistent with their ultimate concerns (Donati, 2011). The chains of meanings that characterise the social relations of father and partner are 'the complicated tissue of relations between culture, personality, social norms' and lived experiences (Donati, 2011 p.130). As previously observed in 'Seth's story' (Chapter 5), social and cultural expectations and his own experience of being parented (see for example Hauari and Hollingworth, 2009; Moloney et al., 2009) influenced his appropriation of the 'traditional' nature and form of the social relation of family. Where Seth's intention to '*not be like my Dad*' manifested in his desire to be involved in and provide for his family, conversely, given Harry's experience of his father as provider, he similarly embraced this aspect of the fathering role echoing his father's economic contribution to family life. However, just as fatherhood is only one aspect of an individual's multiple identities (Kimmel, Hearn and Connell, 2004) so fatherhood encompasses multiple roles including breadwinner, good provider, protector and educator (Hauari and Hollingworth, 2009) and in this sense, Harry's personification of this social role was more multi-faceted than Seth's. Harry drew on the repository of his personal experiences of being fathered and chose to be intensively and directly involved in raising his son, representing a departure from his father's absence, and a departure from Seth's comparatively more circumscribed and distant role as 'good provider'. He also adopted aspects of his positive experiences of being fathered, which centred on his father's football fanaticism and his own introduction to the world of football at an early age.

Harry: My father was a Celtic fanatic and he run a Celtic supporter's bus in Glasgow . . . Every Saturday we were at the football; me, my father and my brother . . . And that's the reason my mother moved [us] from Glasgow because she wanted to get him away from the football because that's all he done apart fae work. But it didn't work!

Football fandom is often inherited through a process of socialisation wherein the son is introduced to football by his father (SIRC, 2008). In this sense, football is 'strongly rooted in a sense of belonging to a place – and to a people' (SIRC, 2008 p.34). These formative experiences can influence the transmission of social identities from one generation to another, and Harry's family of origin and formation were no exception to this, in that football structured the interactive dynamics between father and son and played an important role 'in the inter-generational relationships between male members of families' (SIRC, 2008 p.35). In addition, Harry viewed his son's engagement in playing football as a means of diverting him from a life lived on the streets which, in his experience, carried with it a risk of involvement in offending.

Harry: I am hard on [my son] because of his football which is probably wrong . . . but I don't want him to pack his football in and go back on those streets because I know what lays ahead because I have been through it. I want him to do something in life. I don't want him to have the life I had.

Football is a mechanism for 'perform[ing] elements of 'good fathering', spend[ing] quality time with children (Coakley 2009), and develop[ing] bonds and visibly demonstrat[ing]' support of and nurturing towards children (Jeanes and Magee, 2011 p.275). It provides 'a platform for fathers to perform the '"involved" ideal' (ibid p.275) and to form relationships with their sons and, critically, to 'foster communication within a setting in which they are familiar and comfortable (Coakley 2009)' (Jeanes and Magee, 2011 p.279). Being a football father became an intrinsic element of Harry's fathering as did encouraging his son's participation in education to ensure his son had access to meaningful employment opportunities that Harry considers are unavailable to him due, in part, to his lack of qualifications. This resonates with Maruna's (2001) association between generative commitments and desistance. Contributing to the well-being of the next generation provided Harry with a sense of purpose and meaning, allowing him to redress the balance of his past by using his own experiences to inform his approach to parenting to safeguard his son's future, thus shaping or influencing the conditioning structures, and, thus the situations of actions, for the next generation.

For Harry, his role in and experience of fathering, as the principle mechanism supporting his process of desistance, resided in the connection between these individuals-in-relation, the relationships themselves (between Harry and Millie and between Harry and his son) and the chains of meanings that these types of social relation (as partner and father) encompassed. It is not, then, simply the effects of one individual on another; rather it is the application of Harry's (and arguably Millie's) personal reflexivity which is brought to bear on these social relations, consistent with their ultimate or relational concerns that are critical in contributing to the outcomes.

While fatherhood triggered a reflexive reappraisal of his ultimate concerns, resulting in a gradual shift in practices which included abstinence from further offending, it was the centrality of *being* a father to Harry's self-concept and to his life's purpose that is distinct from Seth's experience of becoming a father, which, in the context of his changing conditioning structures, *reinforced* Seth's already established commitment to desist, but for whom desistance was not directly attributable to becoming and being a father in and of itself. To be clear, it is not suggested that fatherhood was *causative* of Harry's desistance (see for example Monsbakken et al., 2012). As Harry suggested above, '*I knew then I had to get my life in order . . . but it didnae happen overnight*'. Rather, this gradual shift in practices reflected his concerns surrounding the potential impact and consequences that continued offending would have on this social relation and his assumption of parenting responsibilities, not only as a football father and educator but as a provider to which his participation in employment contributed.

The meanings and outcomes of work

As previously observed, the relationship between employment and desistance resides in the way in which the meaning and outcomes of either the nature or quality of the work or participation in employment influence an individual's self-concept and social identity and interact with a person's priorities, goals and relational concerns. Moreover, the nature of any interaction between employment and wider transitional events and experiences, including parenthood, can affect the various impacts they exert on people's identities, behaviours and social contexts (see for example Bianchi et al., 2005 cited in Bersani et al., 2009; Edin et al., 2001; Farrall, 2004; Laub and Sampson, 2001; Maruna, 2001; Owens, 2009; Rhodes, 2008; Savolainen, 2009; Visher and Travis, 2003), which directly or indirectly influence their potential to enable or constrain processes of change, at different stages in an individual's life.

The desistance promotive meanings and outcomes of work

Like numerous people with convictions, Harry's entry into employment, in his early thirties, was facilitated through informal social networks (Calverley, 2013; Farrall 2002, 2004; Niven and Stewart, 2005; Rhodes, 2008, Visher and Courtney, 2007). As the following subsection elaborates, his capacity to access employment was constrained by his limited education and absence of experience of employment, further compounded by his criminal record, and therefore employers' attitudes and discrimination, in an area which, having never recovered from the decline in heavy industry and manufacturing employment in the 1970s and 1980s, remains characterised by high unemployment rates (discussed in Chapter 4).

Harry: I never ever had a chance [to work] until I was in my thirties and that was a friend that got me that job in a factory. I ended up there for ten years.

Initially, Harry's participation in work enabled a reduction in his football-related violent offending consequent to the alteration employment necessitated in his routine social activities and the social spaces he occupied, which would appear, prima facie, consistent with social control theories and the notion of 'desistance by default' (Laub and Sampson (2003 p.278). This line of reasoning implies that people do not make a conscious or deliberate decision to stop offending but desist as a consequence of participation in employment or involvement in marriage which 're-order short-term situational inducements to crime and . . . re-direct long-term commitments to conformity' (Laub and Sampson, 2001 p.51).

Harry: Getting work was a big thing. I was away in a different environment then. I wasn't going out like normal and meeting [my friends] in the pubs – it was just a whole change in my life. I was mostly working weekends and I started going in to my wife rather than going out with the crowd. When you're working you start to take a back seat from all of that because you want to keep your job.

This does not, however, explain why people choose to submit themselves to these institutions in the first place, or why one institution rather than another at one time exerts this effect, or why people remain in jobs or marriages during challenging times when their investment in them has dwindled (Vaughan, 2007). While it might be argued that the availability of roles and the accompanying 'scripts' (Rumgay, 2004), behaviours and practices attributed to the role might become habitualised, people do not march through life mechanically animating fixed role structures. The personification or interiorisation of a role, which is neither pre-determined nor fixed, is accomplished by an individual reflecting on their situation through the lens of their ultimate concerns and the range of actions available to them (Archer, 2003). Indeed, while Harry's participation in employment certainly constrained his participation in social activities and the places and spaces within which his offending occurred, it was the meanings and outcomes of participation in employment refracted through the lens of his individual and relational concerns that underpinned his shift in practices.

Participation in work is a normative adult transition in that 'employment is part of the idea of what is acceptable' (Owens, 2009 p.50). As the extract below suggests, initially gaining employment was as much about fitting in with what the people that mattered to him were doing at that time, and thus, what they apprehended as 'normal' as he perceived it, through the 'looking-glass self' (Cooley, 1902/1922). Even though, as discussed above, his friends were involved in football-related violence, they were all working; without any 'pro-social' practices to counterbalance his involvement in these behaviours, such that would suggest that one is capable of being more than, for example, a football fan, would be to expand the circles within which one perceives one does not fully belong (see relatedly Massoglia and Uggen, 2010). It is precisely through this reflexive evaluative process that we decide on courses of actions by ruminating on ourselves, our concerns and our relational and social contexts, envisioning and pursuing projects that reflect and define who we perceive ourselves to be, that enable us to realise our ultimate concerns, in circumstances that are to a greater or lesser degree pre-defined (Archer, 2003). The initial impetus to change his lifestyle through participation in work emerged as an outcome of his individual reflexivity influenced by his relational concerns.

Harry: I *wanted* to get a job basically. As you get older and all your friends and your wife is all out working, all you want is a decent job with decent money . . . When you get more mature you realise all that carry on, well, it's an embarrassment to your immediate family and to your friends and you don't want that.

Participation in work, and the sense of personal progression it engendered, provided Harry with a sense of self-respect, self-worth and self-esteem and, as the extract below implies, the formal recognition of his efforts and capacities through promotion communicated to him that his efforts were acknowledged, recognised and respected. Taking responsibility and being invested with responsibility is, as observed in 'Seth's story', a means of social recognition and is the result of being trusted, which can similarly engender a sense of responsibility on the part of the person feeling trusted. 'Social recognition . . . expresses the capacity and need that . . . people have for longer-term *reciprocal* relations of trust and responsibility in the wider society' (Barry, 2006 p.136, italics in original), which can positively influence an individual's self-concept. For Harry, however, it was 'not so much a matter of getting ahead as of becoming inside' (Sennett, 2003 p.14) which is as much about the respect one earns from others by doing something well, as it is about the realisation of self-achievement which provides a 'profound pleasure in and of itself' (ibid).

Harry: I started off as a machine operator and worked myself up to a supervisor you know, so I took my work serious. It was the first job I ever had and I wanted to do well.

Critically, the meaning of and impetus to sustain employment was further altered by the birth of his son shortly after starting work. Fulfilling his role as a 'good provider' by making a financial contribution to the family reinforced Harry's commitment to maintaining his employment over time even though he derived little satisfaction from the nature of his employment.

Harry: You learn that when things are important in life you've got to keep them up – like my job's important so I have got to stay in that job although

I hate it and I just want to leave the place . . . money is more important to me now because it is to keep a family whereas when it was to keep myself I didn't bother.

Constraints and limitations

While fatherhood ultimately triggered Harry's reflexive re-prioritisation of his ultimate concerns manifest in affective changes in his perspective and priorities and effectual changes in his practices, which included abstaining from offending, this process of change was reinforced by continued participation in employment, which enabled him to provide for his family and thus contributed to his personification of this new social role. People characteristically define themselves in relation to their occupational identity (Deci and Ryan, 1985). However, Harry's occupational identity was less embedded than Seth's in his social identity and self-concept, perhaps reflecting the comparatively unskilled and repetitive nature of his employment, which held less meaning and affective satisfaction (Moorman, 1993) for him. Where the culture and conditions of Seth's work limited the desistance promotive outcomes of participation in employment, the nature and conditions of Harry's employment constrained both the instrumental and affective outcomes that work can provide, not least in relation to the standard of living it enabled but also with regard to the degree of personal satisfaction and meaningful purposiveness it afforded over time (as the preceding extract makes clear). Moreover, Harry's limited educational and employment experience, compounded by a criminal record, in a geographical location characterised by high levels of unemployment, exerted a significant constraining effect on his occupational mobility and thus his capacities to influence his conditioning structures in this context.

Harry: I can only go for a job with low wages because I've not got an education and I understand that though there's nae jobs about here anyway. Having a record doesn't help with that mind you.

Conclusion

This chapter has discussed Harry's life beyond the fragmentation of the Del, and his process of desistance. The interactions between his participation in an alternative social network, his family of formation and his participation in employment in incrementally triggering and enabling his desistance from offending characterised his narrative of change, the detail and dynamics of which have formed the principal focus of analysis in this chapter. What this analysis in particular has revealed is that it was the interaction of these social relations as mediated through the lens of his personal priorities, values, aspirations and relational concerns, which imbued these particular transitional opportunities, events and experiences with significance and which informed their potential to enable or constrain processes of change.

Unlike cognitive or agentic theoretical explanations of desistance, Harry did not make a conscious decision to desist but nor did he desist by default or react instinctively to structural changes in his conditioning structures, as social control theories tend to suggest. Rather, Harry's desistance gradually surfaced alongside other shifts he initiated in his practices or behaviours, in the context of his conditioning structures, which emerged from a reflexive re-prioritisation of his ultimate concerns as a means of actualising his individual and relational concerns with which continued offending was incompatible.

The shifts in Harry's conditioning structures as a consequence of the fragmentation of the Del and his association with an alternative 'subculture' (at T1 in Figure 6.1) enabled him to continue offending. Collectively, their interactive dynamics and shared projects and practices (T2–T3) heralded a diversification in the context in which his violent offending behaviour occurred which represented a transition from one moral status to another. Through his association with this new group Harry became immersed in an alternative culture which influenced his identity, behaviour and lifestyle but one in which violence and anti-social behaviour were tolerated (T4). While Harry's relationship with Millie was neither causative nor conditional on his desistance (T1) as an outcome of his application of his personal reflexivity (T2–T3), he desisted from housebreaking (T4), motivated by his concern to limit the shame and embarrassment this might engender for her. In turn, she tolerated his continued offending and stood by him, despite her normative orientation, whilst continuing to attempt to influence his behaviour. This illustrates that it was the reciprocal and collaborative adjustments (T2–T3) made by both parties to maintain the relation, emerging from their mutual concern, oriented to the maintenance of the emergent relational goods (T4), which they both valued, consistent with Donati's (2011) concept of reflexivity. Harry's concerns surrounding the shame and embarrassment that his offending might incur for those who mattered to him is in itself an outcome of the application of his (relational) reflexivity, not applied solely to himself but guided by the good of the relationships which mattered to him. Previously, as noted in Chapter 4, Harry was unconcerned by the views others outside the group had of him, which related to the primacy of the influence of the Del, who were, then, his primary reference

Structural Conditioning [conditioning structures]

T 1

    Interactions in Networks [black box: individual and relational contributions]

T 2   T 3

    Structural Reproduction (morphostasis)   (i.e persistence)

                                                           Outcomes

                                                    T 4

    Structural Elaboration (morphogenesis)   (i.e desistance)

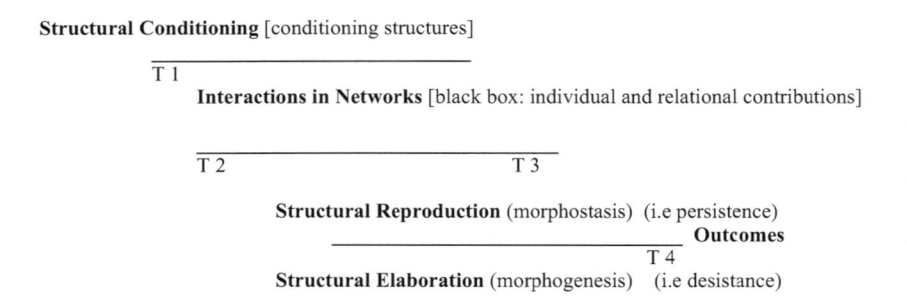

Figure 6.1 Overview of investigative framework

group. Where once this reputation was an asset to him, as his attachments shifted it became a liability, to which he responded by making adjustments to his behaviours. In a similar vein, it was Harry's reflexive evaluation of himself against his new friendship group (the football crowd) and how he perceived they might view him that had initiated his pursuit of employment.

Ultimately, it was fatherhood (T1) which provided the impetus to initiate and sustain changes in his practices (T4) as an outcome of his concern surrounding the potential impact that offending and its outcomes would have on this social relation and the assumption and realisation of his parental role and responsibilities (T2–T3). While Harry attributes a central role to fatherhood in his narrative of desistance, to differing degrees, the various relational spheres in which he participated contributed to changes in his conditioning structures and his identity and behaviour at different stages. The relational contexts within which Harry's desistance was both triggered, enabled and sustained, then, is not analytically reducible to the effects of one individual on another; rather it is the application of Harry's (and arguably others') individual and relational reflexivity which is brought to bear on these social relations, consistent with his/their ultimate or relational concerns that are critical in contributing to the outcomes.

Notes

1 Parts of this chapter draw from Donati, P. (2011) *Relational Sociology: A New Paradigm for the Social Sciences*. Abingdon: Routledge. Reproduced with permission from Routledge.

   Parts of this chapter were previously published in Weaver, B. (2012) The Relational Context of Desistance: Some Implications and Opportunities for Social Policy. *Social Policy and Administration* 46(4), pp.395–412. Reproduced with permission from Wiley.

   Parts of this chapter were previously published in Weaver, B., and McNeill, F. (2015) Lifelines: Desistance, Social Relations and Reciprocity. *Criminal Justice and Behavior* 42(1), pp.95–107. Reproduced with permission from Sage.

2 The 'Old Firm' is the collective name for Celtic and Rangers Football Clubs, both based in Glasgow. The rivalry between the clubs is legendary and embedded in Scottish culture.

References

Archer, M. (2003) *Structure, Agency and the Internal Conversation*. Cambridge: Cambridge University Press.

Barreto, M., and Ellemers, N. (2003) The Effects of Being Categorised: The Interplay between Internal and External Social Identities. *European Review of Social Psychology* 14(1), pp.139–170.

Barry, M. (2006) *Youth Offending in Transition: The Search for Social Recognition*. Abingdon: Routledge.

Bersani, B., Laub, J.H., and Nieuwbeerta, P. (2009) Marriage and Desistance from Crime in the Netherlands: Do Gender and Socio-historical Context Matter? *Journal of Quantitative Criminology* 25(1), pp.3–24.

Bianchi, S.M., Casper, L.M., and King, R.B. (2005) *Work, Family, Health and Well-Being*. Mahwah, NJ: Lawrence Erlbaum Associates.

Calverley, A. (2013) *Cultures of Desistance: Rehabilitation, Reintegration and Ethnic Minorities*. Abingdon: Routledge.
Coakley, J. (2009). The Good Father: Parental Expectations and Youth Sports, in Tess K. (ed.) *Fathering Through Sport and Leisure*. New York, NY: Routledge, pp.40–50.
Cooley, C.H. (1922) *Human Nature and the Social Order*. New York, NY: Scribner. (Original work published 1902.)
Deci, E.L., and Ryan, R.M. (1985) *Intrinsic Motivation and Self-Determination in Human Behaviour*. New York, NY: Plenum.
Donati, P. (2011) *Relational Sociology: A New Paradigm for the Social Sciences*. Abingdon: Routledge.
Edin, K., Nelson, T.J., and Paranal, R. (2001) *Fatherhood and Incarceration as Potential Turning Points in the Criminal Careers of Unskilled Men*. Evanston, IL: Northwestern University Institution for Policy Research.
Farrall, S. (2002) *Rethinking What Works with Offenders: Probation, Social Context and Desistance from Crime*. Cullompton: Willan.
Farrall, S. (2004) Social Capital and Offender Reintegration: Making Probation Desistance Focussed, in Maruna, S., and Immarigeon, R. (eds.) *After Crime and Punishment: Pathways to Offender Reintegration*. Cullompton: Willan, pp.57–84.
Giordano, P.C., Cernkovich, S.A., and Holland, D.D. (2003) Changes in Friendship Relations Over the Life Course: Implications for Desistance From Crime. *Criminology* 41(2), pp.293–328.
Gusfield, J.R. (1967) Moral Passage: The Symbolic Process in Public Designations of Deviance. *Social Problems* 15, pp.175–188.
Hamilton-Smith, N., and Hopkins, M. (2012) The Transfer of English Legislation to the Scottish Context: Lessons from the Implementation of the Football Banning Order in Scotland. *Criminology and Criminal Justice*. doi:10.1177/1748895812447083.
Hauari, H., and Hollingworth, K. (2009) *Understanding Fathering: Masculinity, Diversity and Change*. York: Joseph Rowntree Foundation. Available at: http://www.jrf.org.uk/sites/files/jrf/understanding-fathering-diversity-full.pdf, accessed 09/02/11.
Hogg, M., and Hardie, E. (1991) Social Attraction, Personal Attraction, and Self-Categorization: A Field Study. *Personality and Social Psychology Bulletin* 17(2), pp.175–180.
Hognestad, H.K. (1997) The Jambo Experience – An Anthropological Study of Hearts Fans, in Armstrong, G., and Giulianotti, R. (eds.) *Entering the Field – New Perspectives on World Football*. Oxford: Berg, pp.193–210.
Holden, P.R., and Wilde, N. (2004) *Defense or Attack? Can Soccer Help Tackle Social Exclusion*. ISTR Conference, Toronto, Canada.
Jeanes, R., and Magee, J. (2011) 'Come on My Son!' Examining Fathers, Masculinity and Fathering Through Football. *Annals of Leisure Research* 14(2–3), pp.273–288.
Kimmel, M.S., Hearn, J., and Connell, R.W. (eds.) (2004) *Handbook of Studies on Men and Masculinities*. Thousand Oaks, CA: Sage.
King, A. (1997) The Lads: Masculinity and the New Consumption of Football. *Sociology* 31(2), pp.329–346.
Laub, J.H., and Sampson, R.J. (2001) Understanding Desistance from Crime, in Tonry, M.H., and Morris, N. (eds.) *Crime and Justice: An Annual Review of Research*, Vol. 26. Chicago, IL: University of Chicago Press, pp.1–78.
Laub, J.H., and Sampson, R.J. (2003) *Shared Beginnings, Divergent Lives*. Cambridge, MA: Harvard University Press.
Maruna, S. (2001) *Making Good: How Ex-Convicts Reform and Rebuild Their Lives*. Washington, DC: American Psychological Association Books.

Massoglia, M., and Uggen, C. (2010) Settling Down and Aging Out: Toward an Interactionist Theory of Desistance and the Transition to Adulthood. *American Journal of Sociology* 116(2), pp.543–582.

Moloney, M., MacKenzie, K., Hunt, G., and Joe-Laidler, K. (2009) The Path and Promise of Fatherhood for Gang Members. *British Journal of Criminology* 49(3), pp.305–325.

Monsbakken, C.W., Lyngstad, T.H., and Skardhamar, T. (2012) Crime and the Transition to Parenthood: The Role of Sex and Relationship Context. *British Journal of Criminology* 53(1), pp.129–148.

Moorman, R.H. (1993) The Influence of Cognitive and Affective Based Job Satisfaction Measures on the Relationship Between Satisfaction and Organizational Citizenship Behavior. *Human Relation* 46(6), pp.759–776.

Niven, S., and Stewart, D. (2005) *Resettlement Outcomes on Release From Prison in 2003*. London: Home Office.

Owens, B. (2009) Training and Employment in an Economic Downturn: Lessons for Desistance Studies. *Irish Probation Journal* 6, pp.49–65.

Poulton, E. (2012) 'Not Another Football Hooligan Story?' Learning From Narratives of 'True Crime' and Desistance. *Internet Journal of Criminology*, pp.1–20.

Presdee, M. (1994) The Story of Crime: Biography and the Excavation of Transgression, in Ferrell, J., Hayward, K., Morrison, W., and Presdee, M. (eds.) *Cultural Criminology Unleashed*. London: Glasshouse Press, pp.41–48.

Rhodes, J. (2008) Ex-offenders' Social Ties and the Routes Into Employment. *Internet Journal of Criminology* 1, pp.1–20.

Rumgay, J. (2004) Scripts for Safer Survival: Pathways Out of Female Crime. *Howard Journal of Criminal Justice* 43(4), pp.405–419.

Sandberg, S. (2008) Street Capital, Ethnicity and Violence on the Streets of Oslo. *Theoretical Criminology* 12(2), pp.153–171.

Savolainen, J. (2009) Work, Family and Criminal Desistance. *British Journal of Criminology* 49(3), pp.285–304.

Sennett, R. (2003) *Respect: The Formation of Character in a World of Inequality*. London: Allan Lane.

Social Issues Research Centre. (2008) *Football Passions: Report of Research*. Oxford: Author.

Spaaij, R. (2008) Men Like Us, Boys Like Them: Violence, Masculinity, and Collective Identity in Football Hooliganism. *Journal of Sport and Social Issues* 32(4), pp.369–392.

Vaughan, B. (2007) The Internal Narrative of Desistance. *British Journal of Criminology* 47(3), pp.390–404.

Visher, C.A., and Courtney, S.M.E. (2007) *One Year Out: Experiences of Prisoners Returning to Cleveland; Returning Home Policy Brief*. Washington, DC: Urban Institution Justice Policy Center.

Visher, C.A., and Travis, J. (2003) Transitions from Prison to Community: Understanding Individual Pathways. *Annual Review of Sociology* 29(1), pp.89–113.

Waiton, S. (2012) *Snobs' Law: Criminalising Football Fans in an Age of Intolerance*. Scotland: Take a Liberty.

Warr, M. (1998) Life-Course Transitions and Desistance from Crime. *Criminology* 36(2), pp.183–216.

Weaver, B. (2012) The Relational Context of Desistance: Some Implications and Opportunities for Social Policy. *Social Policy and Administration* 46(4), pp.395–412.

Weaver, B., and McNeill, F. (2015) Lifelines: Desistance, Social Relations and Reciprocity. *Criminal Justice and Behavior* 42(1), pp.95–107.

7 From delinquency to desistance and back again?[1]
Jed's story

> *It [desistance] takes other people, Beth. If you're [by] yourself, you'll always think of yourself as a nobody. The more people you've got round about you that care about you ... people that's interested, well that's when you start thinking, well, fuck it. I'm just the same as that guy over the road ...*

Biographical overview

Jed, aged 48, was born in Coaston in 1961 into a working class family of six. His upbringing was marked by significant deprivation and social disadvantage, even relative to his friends. For the main part, his family was dependent on benefits as their sole income and, although he was raised in a loving family, he experienced limited parental supervision. Jed committed his first offence of shoplifting at 14. Over the course of his offending career, he amassed in excess of 80 convictions over a period of two decades. However, he surmised that the number of offences he committed is nearer 500. The majority of Jed's offending behaviour occurred in the context of the Del and ranged from acquisitive offences (of fraud, stealing and housebreaking) to violent offences (of assault, serious assault and attempted murder) to public disorder offences (of breach of the peace and malicious damage). Jed exhibited high levels of identification with the 'deviant' subculture[2] and was highly embedded in the group as measured by his status and centrality to the group, levels of involvement in criminal activity and isolation from pro-social networks. The instrumental outcomes of offending in terms of the acquisition of money, material goods and social status were of equal significance to him as his relationships within the group and the emergent relational goods.

Jed's convictions were primarily disposed of through the imposition of frequent, short prison sentences of varying durations. As he put it, '*I was always in the jail. I used to go home for a couple of days at a time and then I was back in*'. Jed desisted from offending completely for a period of 14 years, approximately between the ages 30 to 44. For most of this period he resided in London, where he had relocated to join the 'revised group' in his late twenties, and where, for the most part, he lived with his partner, Rachel, and their two children. This relationship concluded when he was in his mid-forties, and he currently has no contact with either Rachel or their children. Prior to this, however, the family returned to Scotland for a brief period before Jed returned to London alone. Jed was convicted four times over the three years prior to interview for breach of the peace (primarily domestic); he had not offended in the year preceding the interview. At the time of interview, Jed had been unemployed for a couple of years; his prior occupation was, like Seth, as a steel fixer and construction worker.

Prior to interview, Jed was hospitalised with cirrhosis of the liver and chronic pancreatitis; his arrest on an outstanding warrant was the reason for his recent return to Coaston, although his subsequent hospitalisation and ill-health was his reason for remaining. He described himself as being in the early stages of recovery from a prolonged period of alcohol abuse. At the time of interview, he lived alone in temporary local authority accommodation in Coaston. Although his family of origin, with whom he has daily contact, resides within close proximity, he has no contact with his five children (from his two marriages).

Jed's delineation of his life stages following the fragmentation of the Del are structured in accordance with the salient places and experiences structuring these life stages namely 'The London Years with Rachel' (aged 30–44) and 'The Drinking Years' (aged 44–47), although his elaboration of these stages is dominated by the significance he placed on work and family. This chapter commences by describing Jed's response to the feud and elucidates these experiences and concerns under the superordinate theme '*Roles, reflexivity, relationality and desistance*' which discusses the role of Jed's extant familial, social and personal relationships in supporting desistance over time. The significance of employment in Jed's narrative of change is discussed under the final superordinate theme '*The meanings and outcomes of work*'.

Roles, reflexivity, relationality and desistance

The role of extant social networks in supporting desistance

Jed, like Seth, Adam and Jay, became heavily embroiled in the feud; however, he did not relocate to London with 'the revised group' for a further 18 months. Jed was married at the age of 19 to Mary and, by this time, they had three daughters. Following the relocation of the revised group to London, Jed associated with other friends who engaged in low level alcohol-related offending which constrained his involvement in acquisitive offending due to differences in the interactive dynamics of this alternative friendship group and their collective concerns. With the subsequent demise of his marriage, and after a brief period in prison, Jed relocated to London, and in this sense his story echoes that of Seth's in that he too drew on the mutual and reciprocal exchange of support and resources among the revised group to resettle in a new environment and enter the steel-fixing trade.

Jed: Everybody had moved . . . to London and I was in [Coaston]. It was just me and [Red] and a few others. We started hanging out together but it wasn't the same, they were a bunch of fucking alkies. They would . . . drink all day long and cause mayhem and I wasn't into that. I wanted to go and get money. Then I got the jail. I got five months for something . . . and then the day I got out I met [Ben] and he told me to come down to London. He said 'I've got a job for you; you can stay with us.' So . . . I went down and that was when it all changed.

The revised group were instrumental in enabling licit opportunities for conformity including employment, accommodation and the development of both human capital, in the form of a trade, and bridging social capital, in the form of employment based networks, which, as discussed in Seth's story, were critical to maintaining employment in the steel-fixing industry. In the initial stages, 'opportunities' were exactly what these developments represented. At first Jed continued to get involved in unplanned, alcohol-related violent offending, although he '*didnae get lifted once*'. The extent to which the move to London was initially apprehended as an opportunity to give up crime thus varied across the group (Giordano, Cernkovich and Rudolph 2002). Unlike Seth, Jed had no conscious intention to desist on his relocation to London.

Jed: I went down to London and I started work the next day. I thought 'Fucking hell, its fucking knackering' and I was thinking then, 'cos I had five warrants out on me, 'I wonder if I should just hand myself in, and go back to the jail' 'cos it's a lot better in the jail than it is here, you know, working like a cunt.

Although on his relocation to London, Jed was not '*planning on stopping getting into bother*', incrementally, the economic outcomes of participation in employment were sufficient to trigger a process in which he began reflexively weighing up the pros and cons of engaging in offending and the consequences of a jail sentence on the opportunities he had acquired, through a review of new opportunities for an alternative lifestyle that had been previously unavailable to him.

Jed: I wasn't planning on stopping getting into bother. I went down at first and I wasnae giving a fuck . . . and I just started thinking 'wait a minute I'm getting 5 or 600 pound a week here, I've got a cracking wee place to live, what the fuck am I wanting to get the jail for?' . . . You could see the bigger picture and you'd start thinking, 'oh I could make money down here without stealing it'. You start thinking about going on holiday. I'd never been on holiday in my life.

Participation in employment thus presented as a chance for change. Giordano et al. (2002) suggest that such opportunities can catalyse desistance when they encourage a new sense of self to emerge and when they alter the meaning that participation in acts of offending hold for a given individual – in terms of both its allure and its outcomes. Arguably, what Giordano et al. (2002) are signifying is the individual's reflexive response to the constraints and enablements that inhere in their conditioning structures. It is through this process that they deliberate on the social situations they confront, through the lens of their ultimate concerns,

(Archer, 2003) which necessarily challenges the 'exteriority and constraint assumptions' characteristic of informal social control theories (Giordano et al., 2002 p.992).

The initial phase of Archer's (2003) process of reflexivity (elaborated in Chapter 3) is characterised as a period of 'discernment' where, as Jed's retrospective narrative above illustrates, the person reviews the possible alternative lifestyle choices available to them, in contrast to their current lifestyle, reflecting a 'willing[ness] to consider different options' (Vaughan, 2007 p.394). This phase is essentially a commentary on current and potential concerns in the light of other possibilities and opportunities which evoke a review of possible future scenarios and their outcomes. For Jed, both relocation and employment reduced any perceived need to engage in acquisitive crime, and diminished the allure of this type of offending, although these changes to his conditioning structures did not in and of themselves engender any significant identity transformations at this stage. They did, however, provoke a prudential amenability to the idea of change consistent with Giordano et al.'s (2002) first phase of cognitive transformation. What this suggests, then, is that one does not necessarily have to be open to change to be receptive to a hook for change[3] in the way that, for example, Seth was. For some people, hooks for change can be apprehended as an opportunity (or triggering event) that *engenders* an openness to change (as Bottoms and Shapland's (2011) model of the desistance process would allow) by triggering a period of discernment (Archer, 2003), which can, as it did with Jed, lead to a diminution of the desirability of the offending behaviour in the early stages of change, thus generating a shift in a person's priorities and practices. Ultimately, however, it was the shifting priorities, practices and relational dynamics among the revised group and the eventual dissolution of these significant relationships that was a significant catalyst in Jed's change process, provoking Archer's (2003) second phase of reflexivity 'deliberation'.

Jed: Once all your mates go their separate ways get married off and do all different things and then you start thinking you know? That's when it starts hitting you and you go, well, right, fuck it. It's my turn now. If they can do it so can I.

Archer's second phase of reflexivity, deliberation, is an evaluative process, in which one considers the perceived costs, benefits and implications pertaining to a given situation or potential courses of action against sticking with what one knows (Archer, 2000). 'What ultimately emerges is a comparison of selves – who one is and who one wishes to be' (Vaughan, 2007 p.394). This process also includes envisaging how one's current identity is perceived by others. Unlike Adam and Seth's desire to desist, manifest in intentional and deliberative shifts in their practices, Jed's initial abstinence from acquisitive offending was conformist with that of his friends, resonant with the concept of primary desistance (Maruna and Farrall, 2004). Jed's relocation to London and the acquisition of employment had the effect of constraining his desire to offend while simultaneously enabling a new lifestyle, one within which '*going out all the time and in pubs fighting*' was a part. The shifting priorities and concerns of individuals away from the group and towards their families of formation and associated shifts in their behaviour similarly exerted a constraint on the behaviour of others like Jed, who found they had less support from their desisting peers for engagement in offending behaviour reflecting a shift in the relational rules and expectations in this revised relational context. Just as Harry had reflexively evaluated his lifestyle against that of his football friends, Jed's rumination on the changes occurring within and between individuals comprising the revised group was the catalyst for him to construct a new modus vivendi, as an outcome of his reflexivity influenced by his relational concerns. However, after a short period in London, Jed's involvement with the revised group abruptly concluded over a disagreement over wages, fracturing the trust and norms of reciprocities on which their relationships had been founded, and this ultimately led to his disengagement from them.

Jed: I had a big fall out with them . . . That was that finished and we all went on to different things.

Critically, what this sub-theme has revealed, then, is that differences between individuals' responses to these similar changes in their conditioning structures cannot be explained in terms of external forces exerting an exogenous effect; rather it reflects their varying receptivity and response to these changes as reflexively mediated through the lens of their individual and relational concerns.

The role of intimate relationships and families of formation in supporting desistance

Explanations of desistance as ensuing from life-course transitions such as marriage or parenthood are often theorised as structures or institutions in that they are considered to be 'external' to the individual. These transitions are thought to alter the socio-structural context of an individual's life, sometimes rendering offending incompatible with the acquired lifestyle and roles that the individual occupies; or the individual is cast as perhaps yielding to a new set of routines that inhibit offending behaviour (see for example Farrington and West, 1995; Glueck and Glueck, 1940; Hirschi, 1969; Laub and Sampson, 1993, 2001, 2003). However, such explanations fail to illuminate *how* social structures shape decisions by ignoring how individuals perceive and respond to such influences (Vaughan, 2011). Other explanations that give prominence to the role of agency in desistance suggest that these relationships can provoke shifts in attitudes, values and identities which render offending incompatible with these changes in the self (see for example Giordano et al., 2002). While such theories explain the onset of desistance, they do not explain how it is sustained (Vaughan, 2011). Moreover, by conceptualising spousal contributions as interactional effects, they elide an analysis of the dynamics or properties of social relations, and thus cannot adequately account for the role that social relations play in variously enabling or constraining change. Taking the social relation as the primary unit of analysis facilitates exploration of the shifting meanings and influences of these social relations both over time and in interaction with other social relations. This yields interesting differences as to how, when and why these relationships are significant in supporting an individual's desistance. This subordinate theme thus explores the role that Jed's relationship with Rachel and their family of formation played in supporting and maintaining his desistance from offending over approximately 14 years.

Jed met Rachel within about four years of his relocation to London and they went on to have two children together. His emotional connectedness to Rachel was reciprocated, and his desire to spend time with her manifested in a shift in his routine social activities and the social spaces he occupied. In turn, this enabled the development of an alternative lifestyle which constrained his opportunities to offend. As suggested above, differential association and social control theorists argue that these lifestyle changes exert a grounding effect, which, over time, with an individual's increasing investment in these relationships, renders involvement in crime (which might threaten their investment) less likely (see for example Horney, Osgood and Marshall, 1995; Laub and Sampson, 2003; Warr, 1998). This process is thought to be particularly encouraged by the normative orientation of the spouse (Sutherland, 1937). However, as Jed's extract suggests below, it was the bonds forged between him and Rachel that constituted their reciprocal orientation towards each other, itself a source of their mutual intentionality towards the maintenance of the ensuing relational goods, of love, support and loyalty for example. It was, then, the pursuit and maintenance of these relational goods that prompted and guided their actions, a process reflexively guided not only by individual concerns but by the good of the relationship, in which compromises by the individual are deliberated over and decided in order to sustain these relationships and maintain the associated relational goods (Donati, 2011).

In Archer's (2003) final phase of reflexivity, in dedicating ourselves to those things about which we are most concerned (such as an intimate relationship or an associated role), the internal conversation conducts a final review as to whether the life imagined is indeed worthwhile and realisable. This is the process through which Jed came to commit himself to desistance, in the pursuit of the realisation of his ultimate concerns, towards the maintenance of this significant relationship, through which lens going out to pubs and fighting was rendered undesirable.

Jed: Once you get people round about that care about you and you care for, then that makes a difference. I think if you live yourself, you just want to go out all the time but if you've got a partner or a wife or something, there's always somebody there for you, there's always somebody to talk away your problems and they give you their problems and you try and sort things for them.

Yet, as previously observed, Jed had been married previously, to Mary, at the age of 19. However, although the marriage lasted for several years, he had no emotional investment in the marriage. Throughout the duration of the marriage he continued associating with the Del, uninhibited by any marital expectations that his wife might have held, reflecting the then primacy of these relationships to his individual concerns. Indeed, his decision to marry was the outcome of his comparative positioning of himself against the Del, his primary reference group, through the 'looking-glass self' (Cooley, 1902/1922). It was through this process that he concluded that 'being married' performed a symbolic function as a normative adult transition and status to which he should similarly progress but to which he was weakly attached. Thus he was unreceptive to its influence.

Jed: Everybody was getting married . . . so I thought I might as well join the fuckin' club and get married – so I did. I can barely remember even spending a whole week with her. I'd been married for three weeks and she was pregnant and I got six months. Then, I got out after the six months and I was out for two weeks and then I got another four months. Every time I got out of the jail she would moan at me . . . and I couldn't be bothered with her.

Similarly, Jed conceptualised his progression to fatherhood at this time as a further normative, developmental transition that he should aspire to. Again, however, Jed did not interiorise or personify his role as a father any more than he did that of husband; his ultimate concerns continued to cohere around maintaining his shared lifestyle with the Del, and his family of formation were at worst a burden and at best of little consequence to him.

Jed: Well when I first had the weans I wasnae really interested in them, it was just a thing you do . . . It's a horrible thing to say when you think about it . . . messing about with a life like that – I'll have a wean 'cos every other cunt's got weans . . . I went to the first one [the birth]. The others were just like too many sweeties in the pack – you're like that 'oh fuck, what am I going to do with these ones?' . . . I was too busy going out, I wanted to enjoy myself all the time and do what all the boys were doing.

There is a clear distinction, then, between the meanings and outcomes of the intimate relationships Jed held with Mary and Rachel, and in his transitions to fatherhood in both contexts, a role that, in his second marriage, Jed interiorised into his personal and social identity. Critically it was the interaction of becoming a family man, at this developmental stage, and in the context of this significant intimate relationship, which provided a sense of social connectedness, against the backdrop of the dissolution of his relationships with the revised group. The mutually reinforcing interaction of these processes coupled with his involvement in stable employment enabled him to fulfil the requirements of the role. However, it was not simply the birth of their children that facilitated the interiorisation of the role, but the dynamics of the relationship itself and the 'chains of meanings' that these particular types of social relation entail for those participating in it (Donati, 2011). Jed's relationship with Rachel was demarcated along traditional gender roles; by working to acquire the necessary economic capital to provide for his family, like Seth and Harry, Jed was able to perform and personify the role of partner and father consistent with his internalised views as to what this role constituted, specifically fulfilling the masculine role of 'good provider' (Messerschmidt, 1993 p.70).

Jed: That's the way we were all brought up and that's the way women see men . . . it was always your father went out to work and your mother done all the housework and the men had to just go out there, do your work, come in and fling the money on the table . . . You felt great then. I've done my bit.

In turn, Rachel's adoption and personification of her role as a homemaker reinforced his role, and these interactive dynamics further informed his role and identity as a traditional family man. Where he provided for the family, she took care of him consistent with their shared expectations of this social relation.

Jed: She wanted to do everything right you know? . . . Every week, every time you woke up there was hundreds of electricity, hundreds of gas, the fridge was always full – she done everything, know what I mean? I thought 'this is fucking great man'. It was like hundreds of Maws all piled into the one Maw.

Jed's association, through Rachel, with a new social network further consolidated the emergence of a non-stigmatized identity as a '*normal guy*' based on his perception of how others viewed him in his role of '*family man*' consistent with the notion of secondary desistance which refers to 'the assumption of the role or identity of a "changed person"' (Maruna, Immarigeon and LeBel, 2004 p.19). Whereas personal identity refers to the consciousness of the self, social identity is formed in relation with others. Social identity is our capacity to express what we care about in social roles and it is one's personal identity that personifies it. Thus, the relationship between personal and social identity is a dialectical one, underpinned by the self-consciousness of the individual (Donati, 2011).

Although Jed's new social networks reinforced his shifting self-concept, as a way of managing his social identity, on which his self-concept was contingent, Jed concealed his past offending. This reflects his consciousness and internalization of negative social discourses surrounding offenders (discussed in Chapter 4) and the perceived contingency of his acceptance by others on the presentation of a self as a non-offender.

Jed: I made loads and loads of fucking mates and I knew every single person in the street that we stayed in . . . they just thought I was . . . out working all the time and buying the weans lovely clothes . . . and they just thought I was a great guy. [If] they don't know your past, they've got nothing to judge you on . . . They can just take you as they see you . . . You could never tell people . . . They wouldn't talk to you again . . . they [would] just see you as some kind of thug.

For Jed, maintaining his social identity meant distancing his present self from his past self in interaction with others and in so doing separating who he had become from his former 'spoiled identity' (Goffman, 1963). Rather than experiencing a process of 'de-labelling' (Maruna et al., 2004 p.275), his self-presentation as a non-offender in a new relational sphere might reflect a process of re-labelling. His acceptance by people on the basis of his present self implies that he experienced a shift in societal reaction towards him based not on the recognised change in his behaviour but (in a new social network where he was free from his history) on the basis of his changed behaviour alone.

While Giordano et al. (2002 p.1055) suggest that particular roles can provide a *'cognitive blueprint'* to inform a new way of being and doing, this provides a relatively short-term perspective that neglects to attend to shifting dynamics in relations and the meaning of a given social role to an individual over time, as a result of individual dispositions and/or changing conditioning structures, and individuals' responses to them, which can, in turn influence the relational dynamics between a couple and/or within a family. Where Jed once appreciated that Rachel was like *'a hundred Maws piled into the one Maw'*, over time, he became increasingly disillusioned with this relationship and the routine and pressures of parenting, which he increasingly experienced as a constraint on his autonomy.

Jed: The reason it changed was because of her – Rachel, and the weans. I was right into going [abroad] every year and I was getting pissed off. For the last two or three years . . . I was like that, I cannae be fucked with this . . . You'd walk in the door and the weans would be all running about and 'know what he done', 'know what she done', 'know what he done' [imitating Rachel] and she is up like that [makes nagging impression], I felt like going back out the fucking door you know? I couldn't be bothered with it.

Jed's disillusionment with family life was further compounded by their relocation to Scotland, circa 2006, instigated by Jed's longstanding desire to return. However, the changes to his conditioning structures that this engendered manifested in a series of losses for Jed, notably in relation to employment (discussed below) and with that his role as 'provider', which in turn negatively influenced his sense of self-worth. Given the centrality of employment to his role in providing for the family, and thus to his sense of masculine identity, the accumulating strain and pressures had a profound effect on Jed, who, overwhelmed by constraints over which he felt he was unable to exert control or influence, reverted to acquisitive crime, which, in the context of an increasingly fractious relationship, ultimately heralded the demise of his marriage.

Jed: That's just when it all went downhill. I came up here and I couldn't get a job, it was back to living without any money, going out stealing things you know just to do us. I was out trying to get a job all the time, I was out looking for work and I couldn't get a job. I wanted to get back to the way it was but I just couldn't get it.

The meanings and outcomes of work

The desistance promotive meanings and outcomes of work

As discussed under the preceding superordinate theme, the meaning and outcomes of Jed's participation in work shifted over time, and this superordinate theme builds on the foregoing analysis. It is suggested that it is the meaning and outcomes of either the nature of the work or participation in employment, and how these influence an individual's self-concept and social identity and interact with a person's priorities, goals and relational concerns, that influence how, when and why employment is more or less meaningful or facilitative of desistance.

Following his relocation to London, it was the initial economic outcomes of participation in employment that were significant in contributing to Jed's abstinence from acquisitive crime. Employment represented an alternative, licit and less risky means of acquiring economic capital, and, as discussed, this provoked his reflexive deliberation on the pros and cons of involvement in acquisitive crime, through the lens of the alternative opportunities and lifestyle that a frequent and substantial income offered. Yet, for Jed, given the primacy and significance of his attachment to his peers and his enduring tendency to compare his progress and measure his behaviour against that of his friends, the meaning of working alongside them played a significant role in his openness towards and motivation to sustain this particular work, despite the challenges he encountered and the limited personal satisfaction he gained from the nature of this work.

Jed: I couldnae get the hang [of steel-fixing] but everybody else got it dead quick . . . but I said, right, I'll keep going. I used to go every day and people would [say] 'Ah you've fucked it up' . . . and you felt dead degraded. I could've just walked off but I said, no, fuck it, and every day I went in there and I was making a cunt of it and building things wrong and – for fucking months . . . but eventually . . . I got the hang of it. I was all chuffed . . . it's the only thing I've ever known how to do but I hate it.

As noted in 'Seth's story' working together as a team became a definitive feature of the lifestyles of the revised group which reinforced a sense of common purpose and which enabled the internalisation of identities, both as individuals and as a collective, in which participation in work occupied a central place (Rhodes, 2008). In the early stages, working alongside the revised group in steel-fixing represented an important means of re-establishing his sense of identification with and belonging and conformity to the revised group, which, in view of their shifting priorities, practices and relational dynamics, further exerted a constraining effect on his offending behaviour. As previously observed, however, a disagreement over wages led to Jed's disassociation from the revised group, although he continued working in steel-fixing. At this stage, he continued to abstain from acquisitive crime, but his partying lifestyle led to frequent alcohol-fuelled fights. However, the meanings and outcomes of participation in work were imbued with further significance when his children were born, enabling his role of 'good provider' and, in turn, his personification of his identities as a man, a father and a partner, with which his former lifestyle and offending was both undesirable and incompatible. However, the meaning of employment was so integral to the performance and maintenance of these identities that subsequent shifts in his conditioning structures on his return to Scotland, manifest in his inability to obtain work, heralded his return to acquisitive crime as a means of sustaining his role of provider and alleviating the pressures this engendered (see also Moloney et al., 2009; Wakefield and Uggen, 2008 cited in Savolainen, 2009).

Constraints and limitations

This sub-theme examines the constraints on and of employment, or the lack thereof, in enabling change. As the foregoing analysis suggests, unemployment undermined Jed's capacity to provide financially for his family and, as a consequence, he reverted to acquisitive crime. However, the meaning and outcomes of worklessness in this context extend beyond the financial pressures this engendered to the psychological and affective outcomes that unemployment exerted on his self-concept. It posed challenges to his masculine identity, itself informed by his internalisation of cultural representations of the 'successful man' as measured by his participation in employment and his capacity to provide for his family (Willott and Griffin, 1997). As the extract below illustrates, Jed experienced his sudden financial dependency on Rachel as disempowering and shameful and, as such, as a threat to his masculine pride, which for Jed was intimately connected to a man's capacities for economic independence, autonomy and self-sufficiency. As previously observed, he also believed that was *'the way women see men'*.

Jed: I felt like a tramp because I never had any money and she was having to supply all the money because I couldn't sign on because the [police] were looking for me. . . . but there was never enough . . . We were arguing all the time, and I was out trying to get a job and I couldn't . . . so if I needed anything I would just steal it.

Following the demise of his marriage to Rachel, and despite acquiring further employment in London, the meaning and outcomes of participation in employment changed again. The economic outcomes that had, in his late twenties, been a motivation to sustain employment were no longer sufficient; given his dissatisfaction with the nature of the employment, participation in employment represented nothing more than engagement in a purposeless and cyclical routine that generated money that he didn't know what to do with. This suggests that an individual's priorities and relational concerns, influenced by the pre-existing self, have a significant bearing on the meaning and outcomes of work.

Jed: I was working . . . but I couldn't be fuckin' bothered. I was going to work in the morning and I thought I'm working here like a cunt and when I get my money on Friday night I'm always skint by the Sunday cos I bought hundreds of clothes and all that – I just kept buying things to get rid of the fuckin' money and, eh, once the money was gone it was gone . . . So I went to work, another week's money, and I said right, here we go again.

At this stage, where work was previously imbued with the meaning and purpose of providing for his family, participation in employment for its own sake or for economic or material gain was rendered meaningless. Following his separation from Rachel, Jed relied on employment as a means of accessing new social networks. Jed returned to share an overcrowded flat with nine men who were similarly occupied and immersed in the steel-fixing social culture. However, the hyper-masculine, hard-drinking culture of the construction industry brought its own challenges for Jed, manifest in a prolonged period of chaotic alcohol use that ultimately threatened his health, and which, necessarily, constrained his capacity to continue working.

Jed: I moved into this place, it was full of fucking guys. It was a flat but there was 4 rooms in it and it was all these labourers and . . . [I was] just bevvied all the time. I was working but every night I was drunk . . . It got to a point that I was being sick and there was blood and all that and I wasn't eating or fuck all.

Although now unemployed and with limited financial resources, Jed managed to avoid offending in London due to the reciprocal exchange of resources between him and his flatmates which facilitated a continuous supply of alcohol, which was their collective primary concern. However, this period too came to a conclusion when he was arrested for drinking in the street and was returned to Scotland to answer outstanding warrants for breaches of the peace (domestic) for which he received fines. Initially he continued drinking, but in the absence of employment and an established network with whom he could share resources, Jed reports that he robbed a man, for which he did not get caught, but which evoked in Jed a sense of personal shame and self-disgust.

Jed: I set about him, took his fucking ring and his chain and everything but see when I was doing it, I felt fucking rotten. Years ago I'd have gone 'money, money, money' but this guy, he was a dead nice guy and I felt that size [gestures] . . . I said 'I shouldnae have done that'. It was an absolute mistake. It was the stupidest thing I have ever done in my life. It was just I'll need to get some fucking money somewhere . . . then this clown walked by with a handful of money.

Shortly afterwards, Jed was hospitalised with advanced cirrhosis of the liver and pancreatitis which triggered a period of reflexive assessment of his current concerns through the lens of the past, and, in particular, the litany of loss he had experienced over the years. Through this lens he reviewed possible future scenarios and their outcomes, reminiscent, to an extent, of Paternoster and Bushway's (2009) 'identity theory of criminal desistance'. This resulted in a reprioritisation of his concerns and a shift in his practices, and, now 'in recovery', Jed views both his former lifestyle and offending to be incompatible with his sense of who he now is, which he likens to the person he was when he was with Rachel.

Jed: See the way I am just now, that's the way I was with her and I couldn't go back to [offending] . . . I'll never go back to that, never. I've lost too many things through it . . . I've lost a lot. I keep thinking about all the guys we hung about with. Most of them all lying in that graveyard the now. You think 'am I going to be fucking next?' Then you think, there's too much to do . . . there's too many things you want to do . . . You start thinking things a lot clearer.

Conclusion

This chapter has discussed Jed's life beyond the fragmentation of the Del, and, in that, his process of desistance. The contributions of and interactions between the revised group, his family of formation and his participation in employment in incrementally triggering and enabling his desistance from offending characterised his narrative of change, the detail and dynamics of which have formed the principal focus of analysis in this chapter. What this analysis in particular has revealed is that it was the interaction of these social relations as mediated through the lens of his personal priorities, values, aspirations and relational concerns, in response to the constraints and enablements inhering in his changing conditioning structures, which imbued these particular transitional opportunities, events and experiences with significance and which informed their potential to enable or constrain processes of change at various stages in his life.

Contrary to cognitive or agentic theoretical explanations of desistance, Jed did not make a conscious decision to desist on his relocation to London. Neither did he desist by default, or react instinctively to structural changes manifest in the availability of employment nor, in turn, marriage and family life, as social control theories tend to suggest. Rather, Jed's desistance gradually surfaced alongside other shifts he had initiated in his practices or behaviours, in the context of his conditioning structures, which emerged from a reflexive re-prioritisation of his ultimate concerns as a means of actualising his individual and relational concerns with which continued offending was variously undesirable and incompatible.

The shift in Jed's conditioning structures following his relocation to London and his participation in employment (T1–T2 in Figure 7.1) both constrained his participation in offending and enabled a new way of living to which, in the context of the shifting priorities and practices (and interactive dynamics) of the revised group, he applied his personal reflexivity (T2–T3), responding by refraining from acquisitive offending and modifying his behaviours (T4). While Jed attributes a central role to Rachel and to his role as a family man in his narrative of desistance, a retrospective analysis enables an understanding of how shifting dynamics in social relations and the meaning of a given social role to an individual over

Structural Conditioning [conditioning structures]
―――――――――――――――――――
T 1
        Interactions in Networks [black box: individual and relational contributions]
        ―――――――――――――――――
        T 2   T 3
                Structural Reproduction (morphostasis) (i.e persistence)
                ――――――――――――――――――― **Outcomes**
                                                    T 4
                Structural Elaboration (morphogenesis) (i.e desistance)

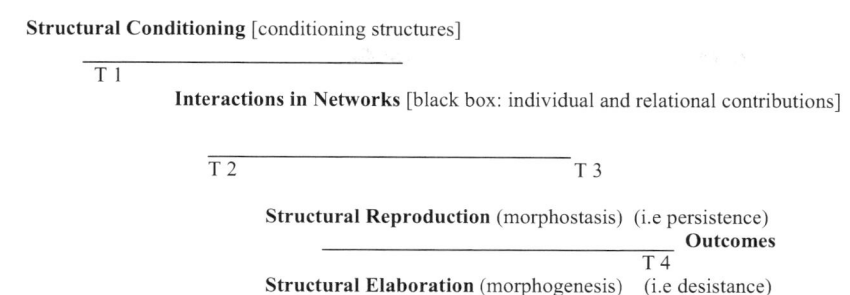

Figure 7.1 Overview of investigative framework

time (at T2–T3), as a result of individual dispositions and/or in response to changing conditioning structures (at T1), influence the outcomes (T4) and thus shape the conditioning structures (at T1) in the next phase of the morphogenetic cycle, creating new constraints and enablements. Moreover, the significance of Jed and Rachel's relationship to his self-concept and on his behaviour and social identity cannot be reduced to the effects of one individual on another but rather are the outcome of the application of their relational reflexivity. As this chapter has illustrated, the bonds forged between Jed and Rachel constituted their reciprocal orientation towards each other and, in turn, their desire to maintain the emergent relational goods prompted and guided their actions in which compromises by the individuals-in-relation were deliberated over and decided in order to sustain these relationships and maintain the associated relational goods (Donati, 2011). Jed's increasing disillusionment with family life over time, however, compounded by their eventual return to Coaston, generated new constraints and pressures as a consequence of his inability to obtain employment (T1), to which he responded by reverting to acquisitive crime as a means of sustaining his role as provider and alleviating the pressures this engendered, but which, cumulatively, led to the emergence of relational problems, including interpersonal conflict and distrust (T2–T3) and which contributed to the demise of his marriage and the loss of these social roles (T4) and his return to London alone (at T1 in the next phase of the morphogenetic cycle). Such an analysis thus marks a departure from current explanations for desistance that fail to illuminate *how* social structures shape decisions, ignoring how the individual perceives and responds to such influences. But it also extends agentic and cognitive explanations by moving beyond their explanations of the onset of desistance, and offering an elaboration of how relations sustain or hinder desistance over time.

Notes

1 Parts of this chapter draw from Donati, P. (2011) *Relational Sociology: A New Paradigm for the Social Sciences*. Abingdon: Routledge. Reproduced with permission from Routledge.

Parts of this chapter were previously published in Weaver, B. (2012) The Relational Context of Desistance: Some Implications and Opportunities for Social Policy. *Social Policy and Administration* 46(4), pp.395–412. Reproduced with permission from Wiley.

Parts of this chapter were previously published in Weaver, B., and McNeill, F. (2015) Lifelines: Desistance, Social Relations and Reciprocity. *Criminal Justice and Behavior* 42(1), pp.95–107. Reproduced with permission from Sage.

2 As discussed in Chapter 4, Hall (1966) elaborates that a highly identified individual would a) think of themselves as a 'delinquent' or 'offender', reflecting the extent to which they interiorised both the associated role and identity; b) hold a negative attitude towards or relationship with their parents; c) invest in or highly value their relationships with not only co-offenders but offending associated and related activities, thus exhibiting an orientation towards a more 'delinquent' peer group as juxtaposed with d) more normative social orientations. Such an individual would e) exhibit or express an internal locus of control in terms of explaining involvement in criminality and f) associate excitement and risk taking behaviours as expressive of their personality.

3 Giordano et al. (2002) argue that the different components of the cognitive transformations they delineate follow sequentially.

References

Archer, M. (2000) *Being Human: The Problem of Agency*. Cambridge: Cambridge University Press.

Archer, M. (2003) *Structure, Agency and the Internal Conversation*. Cambridge: Cambridge University Press.

Bottoms, A.E., and Shapland, J. (2011) Steps Towards Desistance Among Male Young Adult Recidivists, in Farrall, S., Hough, M., Maruna, S., and Sparks, R. (eds.) *Escape Routes: Contemporary Perspectives on Life After Punishment*. London: Routledge, pp.43–80.

Cooley, C.H. (1922) *Human Nature and the Social Order*. New York, NY: Scribner. (Original work published 1902.)

Donati, P. (2011) *Relational Sociology: A New Paradigm for the Social Sciences*. Abingdon: Routledge.

Farrington, D.P., and West, D.J. (1995) The Effects of Marriage, Separation, and Children on Offending by Adult Males, in Blau, Z.S., and Hagan, J. (eds.) *Current Perspectives on Aging and the Life Cycle: Vol. 4. Delinquency and Disrepute in the Life Course: Contextual and Dynamic Analyses*. Greenwich, CT: JAI Press, pp. 249–281.

Giordano, P.C., Cernkovich, S.A., and Rudolph, J.L. (2002) Gender, Crime and Desistance: Toward a Theory of Cognitive Transformation. *American Journal of Sociology* 107, pp.990–1064.

Glueck, S., and Glueck, E. (1940) *Juvenile Delinquents Grown Up*. New York, NY: Commonwealth Fund.

Goffman, E. (1963) *Stigma: Notes on the Management of Spoiled Identity*. Harmondsworth: Prentice-Hall.

Hall, P.M. (1966) Identification With the Delinquent Subculture and Level of Self-Evaluation. *Sociometry* 29(2), pp.146–158.

Hirschi, T. (1969) *Causes of Delinquency*. Berkeley: University of California Press.

Horney, J., Osgood, D.W., and Marshall, I.H. (1995) Criminal Careers in the Short Term: Intra-individual Variability in Crime and Its Relation to Local Life Circumstances. *American Sociological Review* 60, pp.655–673.

Laub, J.H., and Sampson, R.J. (1993) Turning Points in the Life Course: Why Change Matters to the Study of Crime. *Criminology* 31(3), pp.301–325.

Laub, J.H., and Sampson, R.J. (2001) Understanding Desistance from Crime, in Tonry, M.H., and Morris, N. (eds.) *Crime and Justice: An Annual Review of Research*, Vol. 26. Chicago, IL: University of Chicago Press, pp.1–78.

Laub, J.H., and Sampson, R.J. (2003) *Shared Beginnings, Divergent Lives*. Cambridge, MA: Harvard University Press.

Maruna, S., and Farrall, S. (2004) Desistance From Crime: A Theoretical Reformulation. *Kolner Zeitschrift für Soziologie und Sozialpsychologie* 43, pp.171–194.

Maruna, S., Immarigeon, R., and LeBel, T. (2004) Ex-Offender Reintegration: Theory and Practice, in Maruna, S., and Immarigeon, R. (eds.) *After Crime and Punishment: Pathways to Offender Reintegration*. Cullompton: Willan, pp.3–26.

Messerschmidt, J.W. (1993) *Masculinities and Crime: Critique and Reconceptualisation of Theory*. Lanham, MD: Rowman and Littlefield.

Moloney, M., MacKenzie, K., Hunt, G., and Joe-Laidler, K. (2009) The Path and Promise of Fatherhood for Gang Members. *British Journal of Criminology* 49(3), pp.305–325.

Paternoster, R., and Bushway, S. (2009) Desistance and the 'Feared Self': Toward an Identity Theory of Criminal Desistance. *Journal of Law and Criminology* 99(4), pp.1103–1156.

Rhodes, J. (2008) Ex-offenders' Social Ties and the Routes Into Employment. *Internet Journal of Criminology* 1, pp.1–20.

Savolainen, J. (2009) Work, Family and Criminal Desistance. *British Journal of Criminology* 49(3), pp.285–304.

Sutherland, E.H. (1937) *The Professional Thief by a Professional Thief*. Chicago, IL: University of Chicago Press.

Vaughan, B. (2007) The Internal Narrative of Desistance. *British Journal of Criminology* 47(3), pp.390–404.

Vaughan, B. (2011) Review: Pierpaolo Donati, *Relational Sociology: A New Paradigm for the Social Sciences*, London: Routledge. *Journal of Critical Realism* 11(2), pp.255–261.

Warr, M. (1998) Life-Course Transitions and Desistance From Crime. *Criminology* 36(2), pp.183–216.

Weaver, B. (2012) The Relational Context of Desistance: Some Implications and Opportunities for Social Policy. *Social Policy and Administration* 46(4), pp.395–412.

Weaver, B., and McNeill, F. (2015) Lifelines: Desistance, Social Relations and Reciprocity. *Criminal Justice and Behavior* 42(1), pp.95–107.

Willott, S., and Griffin, C. (1997) Wham Bam, Am I a Man?: Unemployed Men Talk About Masculinities. *Feminism and Psychology* 7(1), pp.107–128.

8 Being, becoming and belonging – from gangs to God[1]
Jay's story

> *The whole way I looked at everything, my outlook on life, of what I thought about everything round about me, and what I thought about myself took on a different slant when I became a Christian . . . everybody round about me became different . . . one of the biggest things I felt a change in was how to treat people . . . and it was really about caring about people.*

Biographical overview

Jay, aged 46, is Seth's elder brother. He was born in 1963 and was raised in Coaston, the second youngest of six siblings. His father's violence towards his mother was a definitive feature of his childhood and, as discussed in Chapter 4, was a contributory influence on his involvement with the Del, influenced by his elder brothers' involvement. Jay offended persistently for a period of 12 years (aged 13–25) diminishing in both severity and frequency thereafter. While his 20 convictions are significantly less in number than those of Seth and Jed, he surmises that his offending total is nearer to 300. Like the rest of the Del, Jay's offending was primarily of an acquisitive or violent nature. Assisted by his elder brother's (Adam) dominant position within the group and, as measured by his own status and centrality to the group, levels of involvement in criminal activity and isolation from pro-social networks, Jay was highly embedded in the Del and exhibited high levels of identification with a deviant subculture.[2] In this vein, his relationships to and with the group and the maintenance of the associated relational goods were as significant to him as the instrumental outcomes of offending in terms of the acquisition of money, material goods and social status. Jay's involvement in the criminal justice system, however, is substantially less but more varied than that of Jed, Seth, Harry, Andy and Evan, comprising a period on supervision under the Children's Hearing System, a deferred sentence and fines and around nine periods of imprisonment, which include periods on remand.

Jay met his first wife Harriet at the age of 17; two years later they were married and they had one daughter together. This relationship was characterised by conflict and violence and ended abruptly when Jay was 25 at which time he went to London to join the 'revised group'; this marked the conclusion of his contact with his first wife and their daughter, Sarah. Following his relocation to London, Jay desisted from violent and acquisitive crime but his discovery of amphetamine at this time led to a four year addiction, and, progressively, his involvement in drug dealing and poly-drug misuse which he maintained upon his return to Scotland a couple of years later. Jay considers his conversion to Christianity, aged 29, to be the principal mechanism triggering and sustaining his desistance from offending. Although he acquired no convictions following his relocation to London, he considers himself to have desisted from offending for approximately 17 years prior to interview. He currently works in a residential school with young offenders. Jay remarried in his thirties and he and his wife Peggy, who is also a 'born again Christian', have a daughter together, Emily, aged 8.

Jay's delineation of his life stages following the fragmentation of the Del are structured in accordance with the principal experiences that characterised each period, namely 'The Work, Drugs and Terrorism Years (aged 23–29) and 'The Enlightened Years' (aged 25–42). Spanning these eras, this chapter discusses the role of Jay's extant familial, social and personal relationships in supporting desistance over time, commencing with his relocation to London under the superordinate theme '*Religiosity, reflexivity, relationality and desistance*'. The role of employment in Jay's narrative of change is discussed under the final superordinate theme '*The meanings and outcomes of work*'

Religiosity, reflexivity, relationality and desistance

The role of extant and new social networks in supporting desistance

Like Adam, Jed and Seth, Jay became heavily embroiled in the feud. Following the demise of his marriage to Harriet (discussed under the following sub-theme), Jay relocated to London to join the 'revised group' and in this sense his story echoes those of Jed and Seth in that he too drew on the mutual and reciprocal exchange of support and resources among the revised group to resettle in a new environment and enter the steel-fixing trade. Like Jed, Jay had no conscious 'intention' to desist at this juncture. However, not only did a regular and substantial income remove any need to engage in acquisitive offending, his introduction to amphetamines reduced his tendency to engage in alcohol-related violence while similarly offering an alternative 'buzz' to that which he had previously obtained from offending (Katz, 1988). While Jay would not suggest he had 'desisted' at this stage, his offending comprised the possession, purchase and consumption of illicit drugs, which marked a significant shift in the nature of his offending and the end of his involvement in the criminal justice system.

Jay: I was always violent on the drink but somebody introduced me to speed . . . and then that was me fae then. Every weekend I got full of it but I didn't want to fight with anybody . . . the whole violent thing went away. It was just party time. I still did get into situations . . . with certain things. So although the speed stopped me fighting and being aggressive and stuff, it didn't stop me getting into other forms of crime.

Both the move and participation in employment created new constraints and enablements in Jay's conditioning structures which, in (re-)structuring his situations of action, enabled opportunities for an alternative lifestyle. In particular, Jay's reflexive deliberation over the economic outcomes of participation, which he weighed up against the outcomes of offending, reduced both the need for and desirability of participation in acquisitive crime. Jay's receptivity to the possibility of a new lifestyle thus diminished the appeal and significance of participation in certain types of offending behaviour while enabling participation in an alternative form of 'deviant' behaviour, which itself diminished his tendency to participate in violent offending. Moreover, living and working in a new environment afforded Jay an opportunity to participate in new experiences and an opportunity to connect to different people, which, as Jay implied in the extract below, contributed to an enhanced sense of agency and in that, the ability to imagine himself and his relationships differently, and thus capable of actualising things as yet unrealised.

Jay: London . . . opened up a whole new world because I had been cocooned up in here in [Coaston], in my relationship, my friendships and when I eventually moved it was just as if the blinkers were taken away . . . I met a whole different range of people and I knew that I could move away from [Coaston] and the life I was in and do things I could never have done before . . . I would say that was definitely a big turning point in my life. We tasted a lot of money there with they jobs. It was good money as well and realising that all that [offending] didn't get you anywhere. It didn't get you what that [steel-fixing] could get you. You had a chance of something better.

As Jay explains below, this new environment, without the legacies of conflict which typified their lifestyle and interactions in Coaston, freed the revised group from the restrictive reputations, imprisoning lifestyles and the cycle of violence that had characterised their lives previously and opened up new possibilities for social participation. Their relative anonymity further enabled the development of an alternative social identity for individuals and the group, which, in conjunction with regular employment, represented relative freedom from the restrictions of their former environment, an opportunity to see oneself differently, to be seen differently and to live differently. Jay, in particular, developed ties to a group of Irish Republican sympathizers. Taken together, these co-occurring shifts enabled Jay to restructure his lifestyle, his social network and, ultimately, his sense of self which at this stage, and for the following two years, was principally characterized by participation in work, frequent recreational drug use and his association with and support of a group of Irish Republican sympathizers.

Jay: Well when we stayed [in Coaston] we were quite notorious . . . when we went [to London], nobody knew us, so it was like a fresh start . . . So [in London], we were . . . breaking free fae the tag, the stigma . . . I developed a wider group of friends through the pub so there was a bit of intermingling [between the revised group and the new friendship group] 'cos some of the pubs we went to were Republican pubs in north London and then we went to a certain pub and we met these guys and we just got to know them fae there as a friendship group. Then I went over to Ireland a few times and I got into supporting terrorism.

While some of the 'revised group' remained in London, Jay, like Seth and Adam, returned to Coaston when the recession descended on London in the early 1990s. On their return, Seth's and Adam's ultimate concerns, and thus lifestyles, cohered around employment and their families of formation. On Jay's return, although he sporadically participated in employment, his drug use became increasingly chaotic, and for the following two years, subsidising and sustaining his addiction was his ultimate concern.

Jay: Over a period of time, my life just got worse and worse and I ended up injecting speed and it escalated . . . and that was me – hooked.

Peter, a close friend of Jay's who associated with the Del in their late teenage years, converted to Christianity while living in London. Like Adam, Seth and Jay, he too had returned to Coaston. As a new convert to Pentecostal Christianity, he was keen to share the story of his conversion with others, and played a pivotal role in Jay's conversion two years later.

Jay: [Peter] was a significant person earlier on in my life – maybe 17, 18 onwards . . . He had had an experience in the jail and he had become a Christian. I couldnae believe it . . . He was a very violent person [before]. He came down fae Glasgow and I was sort of intrigued by the way he used to run about with swords . . . and . . . I was took on with him and I wonder if, because of that, God chose him specifically to share with me or . . . to help me because I used to listen to him a lot as well. There was something about him, even in . . . that violent circle. I always trusted him. As much as he was a nutcase, stabbing and slashing people, he cared about people as well. I think if any of my other pals told me about God – I would probably have just laughed. I just watched him over a period of time and there was something totally dramatically changed about him . . . He definitely had a big influence on me.

In echoes of Seth's receptivity to the influence of his elder brother Adam, Jay was particularly receptive to Peter's testimony or narrative of conversion due to the existing reciprocal bond between them. As previously observed, the recognition of change in a credible person is particularly influential where an individual can identify with the change agent and internalise the benefits of responding to this influence (Kelman, 1958) in the hope of achieving similar outcomes. Peter's concern for Jay, whose narrative of this period is characterized by his addiction and the desperation this progressively engendered, can be construed as evidence of Peter's application of his personal reflexivity, not simply to himself, but to this relationship, consistent with Donati's (2011) concept of social or relational reflexivity. Informed by his own faith, Peter's concern for and 'ministry' to Jay was further underpinned by Christian relational ethics of subsidiarity (to relate to the other in a manner that assists the other to do what must be done) and solidarity (sharing a responsibility through reciprocity) (Donati, 2009). These principles consign mutual responsibilities on each person for supporting change and in taking responsibility for personal change.

Jay: [Peter] took me to a church . . . and the guy that was speaking . . . I felt as if he was preaching just to me alone. I told him I wanted to become a Christian and I felt great for a couple of days but that's when I ended up worse. When I went away again I ended up injecting . . . but [from that time] I kept asking people – do you believe in the Bible? I suppose I was kind of searching. I just felt I was either going to die or something like that if I didnae find what I was looking for.

While Jay was open to the idea of changing (Giordano, Cernkovich and Rudolph, 2002), such was the nature of his addiction that the initial fervour inspired by his identification with the speaker's message waned and his addiction accelerated. It was only after he was (literally) stabbed in the back by his, then, similarly chaotic partner that he asked Peter, with a sense of urgency, to take him to church again. It was then that Jay made a public declaration of faith (discussed below) and it was his *internalization* of this faith, reinforced by his subsequent immersion in Bible study, ministry and association with the Christian community, which heralded a rapid transformation in both his personal and social identity; a transformation with which continued offending and substance use was incompatible.

Pentecostalism emphasizes the importance of conversion, construed as a transformative experience in which one's life is dedicated to God and one is 'born-again' (van Klinken, 2012), often necessitating and symbolizing a complete break with the past (Meyer, 1998). The structure of Jay's narrative of transformation, of salvation from a sinful past following a traumatic event, echoes that of Pentecostal conversion narratives in general[3] (van Klinken, 2012). The traumatic event is the catalyst that provokes or compounds a sense of existential loneliness and lostness, a deep-seated dissatisfaction with the person they have become and an isolation from the person they feel they are or would like to be, often characterized by, or narrated as, a fear of dying (van Klinken, 2012). In a similar vein, Maruna, Wilson and Curran (2006) suggest that rather than construing the catalyst for conversion as a life crisis, it may be alternatively construed as an identity crisis, in which one's sense of self is called into question. Quoting Gillespie (1973 p.93), Maruna et al. (2006) observe,

> 'Wishing you were one thing and knowing you were another is severe and produces tension that may find release in the religious conversion experience' (p. 93) . . . James (1902/1985) described the 'sense of dividedness' that dominates the pre-conversion phase . . . as the contrast between what is and what might be me.
>
> (p. 177)

This is, however, distinct from the cognitive theory of identity change progressed by Paternoster and Bushway (2009). While they similarly suggest that dissatisfaction with life may be a precursor to change, they argue that the impetus for change is motivated by an aversion to a projected 'feared self' (Paternoster and Bushway, 2009 p.1106). However, as the preceding extract from Maruna et al. (2006) suggests and as Jay clarifies above and below, his motivation to change was in anticipation of a hoped for self, of *'what I wanted to become'* inspired by the positive change he had witnessed in Peter. Jay's process of reflexivity was, then, triggered by existential doubt, and refracted through the prism of the promise of salvation; through discussions on Christianity with Peter, Jay became aware of the presence of another Being, close to him (immanence), yet also other (transcendence). The spiritual connection that is forged between the believer and God is experienced as a personal relationship which transcends all others. He who was lost is found. In the act of repentance for their sinful past, the convert is forgiven and is born again in Christ and the world is experienced anew.[4]

Jay: The whole way I looked at everything, my outlook on life, of what I thought about everything round about me and what I thought of myself took on a different slant when I discovered Christianity. Because my outlook on life then became different – everybody round about me became different and then obviously I was different because I was changing fae what I had been in the past to what I wanted to become and to what I felt I would need to become. I think I valued things more, valued people more, valued life more – just valued even the simple things in life – like even looking at nature, seeing it different. But one of the biggest things I felt a change in was how to treat people. To treat people differently and view them differently fae what I did before. I just started to see things on a whole different level and it was really about caring about people.

This transformation through conversion, characterized by a change in worldview (Maruna et al., 2006) is then commonly narrated and communicated through public testimony, which has its roots in biblical teachings.[5] The Christian testimonial is a powerful expression of God's redemption and an opportunity to bear witness to one's experience of transformation to others. In so doing, the establishment and identification of shared values and beliefs provides a basis for social trust, mutual respect and social recognition among the community of believers. In particular, the act of giving testimony can be regarded as a 'rite of passage' (Maruna, 2011 p.21) or a ritual of redemption (Maruna, 2001) wherein 'some recognized member(s) of the conventional community must publicly announce and certify that the offender has changed and that he is now to be considered essentially non-criminal' (Meisenhelder, 1977 p.329). In the context of faith-based communities, the individual is redeemed or saved. However, the act of testifying had particular significance for Jay. On the one hand, as the extract below illustrates, in testifying to his commitment to God, and in realising God's forgiveness for past wrongs, Jay dedicated himself to this new identity and faith, and through this process, his perception of himself altered. On the other hand, drawing on his own prior preconceptions of and attitudes towards religiosity, how his identity transition from addict and offender to that of the differently stigmatized identity of 'Christian' would be apprehended by his peers had preoccupied him; it was only in the act of making a public declaration that he testified to himself that he could withstand the risk of social rejection and ridicule that this might engender.

Jay: . . . and that's when I made a public sort of commitment. I felt I had to do that because . . . I'd had all they sort of thoughts, what will people think. I'd always been embarrassed [being seen] with certain people or doing certain things and knew then if I done that – if I stood up in front of everybody – I knew that was real to me. If I was ever going to be a Christian, I had to declare it in front of everybody else. Then that was me, I felt God was in my life; he'd forgave me and I was born again. I knew then that I was changed.

The term 'born-again' is expressed 'as a process of "dying to self." . . . [in which] the person they were in the flesh dies, and they are born again . . . To be born again means a separation from the old self' (Bielo, 2004 p.277–8), which for Jay was expressed through his immediate initiation of significant lifestyle changes, as the extract below suggests.

Jay: I stopped overnight hanging with all my pals but I didnae feel pulled towards them and I didnae feel I had to pull myself back from them. I just thought I don't like what they are doing. It's not right to do it. So I just made a conscious choice not to go there. I met a lassie a couple of years later and she said 'It was as if you'd died'. She said 'We used to see every weekend, at every party, you were there, and it's just as if you'd died' and I said 'Well I did die. I died to my old life' – and that's the only way to describe it. When I became a Christian I stopped drink and drugs, swearing, watching the telly, offending, everything. I just stopped everything.

Jay's internal changes in his beliefs, values and attitudes were thus expressed in external lifestyle changes characterised by the relinquishment of what he had come to regard as his past sinful behaviours, in pursuit of a moral or 'good life'. However,

> some scholars indicate that becoming born-again for men can be a threat to their male identity. By giving up drinking . . . and other activities that – according to the dominant norms of masculinity . . . are considered 'manly', born-again men run the risk of being labelled as 'sissies' (Brereton 1991, 98–101; Gooren 2010, 103–105)
>
> (van Klinken, 2012 p.221).

Indeed, such concerns may have informed Jay's initial reservations or concerns surrounding how he might be seen by his peers. However, van Klinken's research (2012) suggests that Pentecostal Christian males redefine masculinity through the exercise of self-control, self-discipline, resistance of temptations and the assumption of responsibility for oneself and for others. Thus, in the process of being born again, it is not only the individual's sense of morality that is reconfigured, but his sense of what it means to be a man (van Klinken, 2012). As the following sub-themes illustrate, this is connected to notions of leadership, whether within the family or in ministry.

Jay recalls that he was immediately welcomed by the church wherein he developed new and enduring social relationships through his affiliation to various Christian groups and organisations. The common bond of Christianity can serve to dismantle some of the social barriers that (ex-)offenders can encounter and the Christian ethic of fellowship and mutual obligation can offer access to relational networks which can generate crucial emotional, spiritual and practical supports (Giordano et al., 2002; Giordano, Schroeder and Cernkovich 2007).

Jay: People were open, warm, friendly, loving and caring . . . I met policemen, doctors and lawyers and they treat you just the same as everybody else . . . any questions I ever had . . . they would help me and also financial assistance at times . . . as well as spiritual support there was emotional support.

His capacity to relate to this broad church of people from markedly different social backgrounds was enabled by a sense of social equality which, as Maruna et al. (2006) comment, applies as much to degrees of wrongdoing as to need for forgiveness, encapsulated in the idea that all men are created equal under God. The emotional, spiritual and practical assistance they provided communicated acceptance and social recognition and reinforced a sense of belonging which was critical to sustaining his commitment in the early stages, and which reinforced his shifting self-concept as someone of worth. Conversion stories are often seen in and of themselves as success stories (van Klinken, 2012). However, there is a significant difference between *becoming* and *being* a Christian; being a Christian is a dynamic and evolving project of the self that requires maintenance and ongoing reflection. Jay's recent experience of a diminution in the intensity of his religious zeal after sixteen years, manifest in a temporary withdrawal from church attendance, reinforced to him the centrality of his participation in religious practices and involvement in church in sustaining and maintaining his faith.

Jay: I didnae stopped believing . . . but I would say that I wasnae as enthusiastic and I wasnae as kind of going out and doing some of the things that I would do as a Christian . . . I don't think I can explain it totally, but . . . I was in a place I know I don't want to go back in again. It was a kind of cold period for a few months but . . . I got back to church and I just started getting rekindled again.

Jay's experiences reinforce the findings of previous studies (discussed in Chapter 2) that emphasise the significance of internalized faith to processes of change, which can be reinforced through participation in religious practices and communities (see for example Armstrong, n.d.; Schroeder and Frana, 2009). However, for Jay, continued association with a community of believers with whom he could identify and among whom he felt a sense of belonging was as important as the internalisation of his faith in sustaining his religious zeal and subjective well-being over time (Lim and Putnam, 2010). Jay's immersion in the Christian faith through evangelism and ministry following his conversion is discussed further under the final superordinate theme '*The meaning and outcomes of work*'. The following subtheme discusses the dynamics of Jay's involvement in his families of formation and intimate relationships and their role in constraining and/or sustaining change.

The role of intimate relationships and families of formation in supporting desistance

In Jed's chapter, it was suggested that taking the social relation as the primary unit of analysis facilitates an exploration of the shifting meanings and influences of the social relations of marriage and family over time and yields interesting differences as to how, when and why these relationships are significant in constraining, enabling or sustaining desistance. This subordinate theme explores the differences in the role of Jay's two significant intimate relations and their families of formation in constraining or sustaining change at different stages in his life.

Jay met his first wife Harriet at the age of 17; two years later they were married when Harriet became pregnant with Jay's first child. Unlike Seth's, Jed's and Harry's partners, Harriet, whose family of origin were involved in the criminal justice system, was similarly involved in offending behaviour. There is a wealth of empirical evidence that suggests that the partner's participation in criminality constrains the more desistance promoting effects that investment in an intimate relationship can generate (see for example Cusson and Pinsonneault, 1986; Giordano et al., 2002; Osborn and West, 1979; Ouimet and LeBlanc, 1996; Shavit and Rattner, 1988; Simons et al., 2002). Unlike Harry's partner Millie, far from discouraging Jay's involvement in offending, Harriet would herself, at times, participate in offending alongside Jay.

Jay: [Harriet] was brought up . . . round about stuff . . . certainly her brother was a violent character and got into trouble . . . I suppose like everybody else, she didnae want to see you getting caught [but] she was a shoplifter and she was with me a couple of times, fighting and stuff like that.

Nonetheless, while, as previously noted, Jay did not desist from offending at this stage, his investment in this relationship did influence his attitude towards offending at this time.

Jay: When I [was with Harriet], I still offended but I had a different outlook on things and I tried to be responsible. I just wanted to be what I seen as normal. Just, like, in a relationship, settle down, stuff like that. I wouldnae consciously [offend] then, just if I was drunk, whereas [before that] I would say a lot of it just came instinctively. I just think the relationship to me was more of a goal and I didn't want anything to interrupt that if I could help it.

While, then, at this stage, Jay did not desist from offending, in the early stages of the relationship, his reflexive orientation towards the maintenance of his relationship with Harriet emerged as Jay's ultimate concern, which led to a diminution of the desirability of offending in this relational context, to which he responded by initiating adjustments in his behaviours, in accordance with his shifting priorities. In this sense, despite her participation in offending, being in this relationship provoked a desire in him to change his behaviours. While he recognised the benefits of changing, this did not, however, ultimately translate into cessation of offending. What this seems to suggest is that the impacts and outcomes (intended and actual) of social relations are not solely reducible to interpersonal effects. Despite her participation in offending, the relationship still generated in Jay an amenability to the idea of change (Giordano et al., 2002). However, as the preceding extract suggests, Jay's orientation towards this relationship, and, thus, openness to change, was in anticipation of the realisation of an ideal type relationship which would bring about a sense of normalcy. While her participation in offending is not irrelevant, critically the ideal type relationship to which Jay initially oriented himself never materialised. Rather Jay and Harriet's relationship was mutually experienced as divisive and destructive. The asymmetry of their attachments and expectations of the relationship influenced the nature of their interactive dynamics which progressively emerged as reflexively oriented towards actions which generated the emergent 'relational bads' (Donati, 2011) of jealousy, betrayal, conflict and violence.

Jay: I was violent in that relationship, just the same as what my Dad was . . . Although I did do it I really find it hard to accept. Neither one of us was faithful but I was obsessed with her. It was one of they ones, you're not really in control . . . You think its love but she was domineering – do you know what I mean – but I just thought she was the best thing.

The point is that it is not simply Harriet's participation in and attitudes towards offending that constrained change, but the dynamics of the social relation itself. The social relation is conceptualised here as those bonds maintained between subjects that constitute their reciprocal orientations towards each other; it is the 'reality in between', that which exists *between* people, which 'are both the product of concrete human beings and also that which helps to forge them' (Donati, 2011 p.61), 'which depend on the[m] . . ., but at the same time goes beyond them and exceeds them' (2011 p.26). Thus, 'social relations are those maintaining *between* agent-subjects that – as such – 'constitute' their reciprocal orientations and actions as distinct from all that characterizes single actors' (Donati, 2011 p.60). The impact of a given social relation on individuals' behaviour thus emerges from the nature and intensity of the bond *between* individuals-in-relation and the chains of meanings that these particular types of social relation entail for individuals, who bring their own personal reflexivity to bear in a manner consistent with their ultimate concerns (Donati, 2011). As observed in preceding chapters, the chains of meanings that characterise a given social relation can be conceptualised as 'the complicated tissue of relations between culture, personality, social norms' and lived experiences (Donati, 2011 p.130). As with Seth, Jed and Harry, Jay's internalised configuration of hegemonic 'traditional' working class masculinity (Connell, 2002) influenced his expectations of the marital relationship and their associated gender roles; expectations which were not reciprocated by Harriet. When his efforts and expectations were frustrated, he drew on the repository of his personal experiences of his father's violence towards his mother as a means of exercising his control and asserting his masculinity. Ultimately, the relationship concluded when he was 23.

After Jay's conversion to Christianity, he met and married Peggy after six months of dating, to whom he remains married and with whom he has a daughter, Emily. Peggy is also a born-again, Pentecostal Christian.

Jay: I just wanted to marry somebody with shared values and the same beliefs as myself which I thought was very important because my thinking was that if we'd had any children, that I would want my children brought up in the faith.

As previously stated, leadership and the assumption of responsibility for oneself and for others are definitive features of Pentecostal Christian interpretations of and discourses on masculinity. Fatherhood and the husband role in Pentecostalism is thus associated with being the head of household and the principal provider (van Klinken, 2012) which for Jay marked some continuity with his previously internalised beliefs surrounding cultural norms of masculinity relating to gender roles. In turn, Peggy's adoption and personification of her role as a homemaker enabled his personification of his role. Where he provided for the family, she took care of the family and, in the main, recognised his assumed authority in accordance with their shared beliefs, values and expectations of the nature of this social relation. In this context, compromises between them were deliberated and decided in order to sustain these relationships and maintain the emergent relational goods (Donati, 2011).

Jay: I think the man is the head of the house, should be, even though at times to stop arguing . . . you give up the role from time to time, but I would say the man is the authority figure. There's a place for men, there's a place for women. I think the man's got more responsibility. I would say it should come naturally to a man and I think it should come naturally to a woman to let the man.

Despite the intimacy, strength and endurance of their relationship, Peggy barely features in Jay's life story, which may, in part, be attributable to the impact that being 'born again' can exert on peoples' personal and social identities, and their relations with their partners, in that God becomes the relationship of ultimate concern (see also 'Evan's Story'). The marked differences in the meanings and outcomes of Jay's relationships with Harriet and Peggy are thus attributable to a variety of factors, not least differences in age and maturity, differences in the nature of these social relations and their interactive dynamics and differences in Jay's shift in identity and behaviour as a consequence of his conversion to Christianity. In similar vein, Jay's approach to fathering his daughter Emily is a significant departure from his approach to parenting Sarah (his daughter with Harriet).

Jay: I used to get [Sarah] to swear and . . . shout at the polis . . . I still loved her and looked after her for those first 2 or 3 years that I was with her, but I was just – I don't know, but with [Emily] just now, I'm more protective. I think Emily was my second chance . . . I try and shield her from things. From anything I've learnt from the past negative. I always tell her wee stories about people doing good, with good values, and I'm trying to instill good values into her . . . because I feel that's important, but I would never ever want her to go down any of the roads that any of us have been down.

Like Harry, Jay's approach to fatherhood now encompasses multiple generative roles including breadwinner, good provider, protector and educator (Hauari and Hollingworth, 2009). As the extract above suggests, in shielding her from harm and teaching her the ways of his faith, Jay apprehends this both as an opportunity to practice his faith and an opportunity to redress the balance of his past by doing things differently this time around. Moreover, by using his own life experiences to inform his approach to parenting to safeguard his daughter's future and spiritual development, he is actively and intentionally shaping and influencing the conditioning structures, and, thus, the situations of actions, for the next generation.

The meanings and outcomes of work

The desistance promotive meanings and outcomes of work

In preceding chapters, it has been suggested that the relationship between employment and desistance resides in the way in which the meaning and outcomes of either the nature of the work and/or participation in employment influence an individual's self-concept and social identity and interacts with a person's priorities, goals and relational concerns. As previously observed, Jay's first significant experience of participation in employment was in London when, like the rest of the revised group, he entered the steel-fixing trade. While neither the nature of the work nor participation in work were causative of desistance, the economic outcomes diminished any perceived need to engage in acquisitive offending, and his introduction to amphetamines, at this time, reduced his tendency to engage in alcohol-related violence. That said, while he did not need to offend to procure drugs, and while he obtained no convictions, Jay considers his procurement, possession and consumption of drugs to be contiguous with his offending lifestyle, and a precursor to his later involvement in dealing drugs. Thus, while participation in work enabled behavioural and lifestyle changes, he experienced no significant pro-social shift in his values or in his personal and social identity that altered his attitude to offending, which only occurred later – following his conversion to Christianity.

Jay's faith permeates every aspect of his life; it informs his relationships with his wife and daughter, and his role within the family. Since his conversion, it has also been expressed through the nature of the work in which he has participated, which has been oriented to supporting individuals and communities in need. Jay conceptualises his work as an expression of his faith, in terms of a life lived in service to others, informed by the Christian relational ethics of subsidiarity and solidarity referred to previously. Jay's impetus for participation in generative works of this nature, then, was and is informed less by a desire to make good on his past in a reparative sense, and more by a desire to minister or be of service to others, by trying to divert others from the life he has lived, and in so doing fulfilling the word of God. In this sense, Jay's participation in this work, most of which has been of a voluntary nature, neither directly constrained nor enabled his desistance in a causative sense; rather, it is the meaning and outcomes of the work that is of enduring significance in consolidating his new, 'born-again' identity and thus his subjective well-being.

Jay: I [volunteered in a Christian Rehabilitation Centre] for between 3 and 4 years. I also went into a lot of prisons speaking to prisoners, telling them about Christianity . . . so I was involved in that for a couple of years as well. And there was a local drop-in-centre and I used to help [Evan] and we worked in the local community with young people . . . just trying to point young people in the right direction and away from trouble. It felt very fulfilling and also it could get people away fae going down the same roads that [we] went down. I also done some street work . . . in [Coaston]. So, I worked voluntary until I was 37 and that's when I went to college and done my HNC in social care and since then I've worked in [a residential school for young offenders].

Jay not only engaged in generative works, then, but practiced evangelistic outreach, which is the preaching of the Christian Gospel to others with the object of converting them and is an expectation of participation in the Pentecostal church (Anderson, 2004). While his faith imbued the nature of this work with meaning, participating in this work thus contributed to and realised his religious identity. His participation in these works, then, can be construed as an outcome of both his conversion and of desistance; both of which have shaped his generative commitment to diverting others from offending. Moreover, as Jay suggests below, the visible nature of some of this work had the unintentional effect of operating as a tangible symbol of his reformation to the wider community, which, through the social recognition of change this implied, contributed to his changing personal and social identity.

Jay: Word got about because I was . . . well-known . . . me and [Peter] and [Dennis Nixon] went to a church in [Coaston] and people used to come, people that were maybe troubled or in trouble and they used to come to the Church to see us because they heard that we became Christians. I think then they knew we were serious about it.

Constraints and limitations

Where the culture and conditions of Seth's work limited the desistance promotive outcomes of participation in employment, the nature and conditions of Harry's employment constrained both the instrumental and affective outcomes that work can provide, not least in relation to the standard of living, but also with regard to the degree of personal satisfaction, meaning and purpose it afforded over time. Jay identified no significant constraints or limitations in these areas and experienced both the nature and conditions of his work as enabling and empowering both in terms of his role as provider within the family, and in terms of practicing his ministry. Nonetheless, while drawing on his prior experiences of offending to inform his approach to practice, Jay considers that the professional nature of his current occupation places a constraint on the use of self-disclosure in his work with young people, which would seem to suggest that a professional (rather than a religious) identity is harder to reconcile with a previously spoiled identity (Goffman, 1963). Anticipating the judgements and negative stereotypes that people with convictions are often subjected to, Jay considers that others' perceptions of his past may diminish his professional standing and authority, which he suspects would unnecessarily obstruct or distract from the contributions he can make to their outcomes.

Jay: I do believe that my experience can help me in how I deal with these boys and I feel with the experience I've had it can be helpful, but . . . I don't say to them [about my past], not that I'm trying to hide it but I just want to be the person that I'm are with the boys. I mean, they could go to a Children's Hearing and they could turn round and say 'aye, he done that as well' so there's a professional side of things where if you're trying to work with somebody they could try and bring it back on you. Or their family could – like 'what's he doing working with my boy and he's been charged with assault' or whatever.

Conclusion

This chapter has discussed Jay's life beyond the fragmentation of the Del, and, in that, his process of desistance. What this analysis in particular has revealed is the centrality of Jay's conversion to Pentecostal Christianity and his internalisation of the Christian faith to his narrative of change. His initial conversion was reinforced and sustained by his participation in Christian relational networks and through religiously informed practices which enabled the expression of his faith and generative commitments and which contributed to the transformation in his personal and social identity with which continued offending was incompatible. In concert with the preceding individual stories, this chapter has illustrated the ways in which desistance is co-produced between individuals-in-relation, foregrounding a conceptualization of a reflexive individual whose ultimate concerns emerge from, are immersed in and shape their relational worlds. Where Jed's, Seth's and Harry's desistance emerged as a means to realising their relational concerns with, to varying degrees, their families of formation, in which participation in employment played a part, Jay's relationship of ultimate concern was of a spiritual form and his principle role identity emerged as a Christian.

Although Jay considers his conversion to be the catalyst to change, Jay's earlier participation in employment in a new environment heralded a shift in Jay's conditioning structures (T1–T2 in Figure 8.1) which constrained his participation in offending and enabled a new way of living to which he applied his personal reflexivity (T2–T3) and responded by refraining from acquisitive offending and modifying his behaviours, assisted by his introduction to amphetamine (T4). Following his subsequent return to Coaston, although Jay sporadically participated in employment, Jay's addiction and association with similarly situated others structured the situations of action (T1 in the next phase of the morphogenetic cycle) and generated new constraints and enablements. In the context of his increasing desperation about his escalating drug use and its outcomes, he became progressively receptive to Peter's faith-based intercessions. His internalisation of the teachings of Pentecostal Christianity influenced by his interactions with Peter (T2–T3) ultimately shaped his identity, behaviour and lifestyle (T4), and, in turn, the sets of relations in which he was involved (at T1 in the next phase of the morphogenetic cycle), which, bringing his personal reflexivity to bear with regard to his position in this new relational context (T2–T3), motivated his participation in evangelism and ministry (T4).

The analysis progressed in this chapter thus marks a departure from current explanations for desistance that fail to illuminate *how* social structures shape decisions, ignoring how the individual perceives and responds to such influences. But it also extends agentic and cognitive explanations by moving beyond their explanations of the onset of desistance, and offering an elaboration of how relations sustain or hinder desistance over time. In particular, 'Jay's Story' builds on and

Structural Conditioning [conditioning structures]

T 1

      Interactions in Networks [black box: individual and relational contributions]

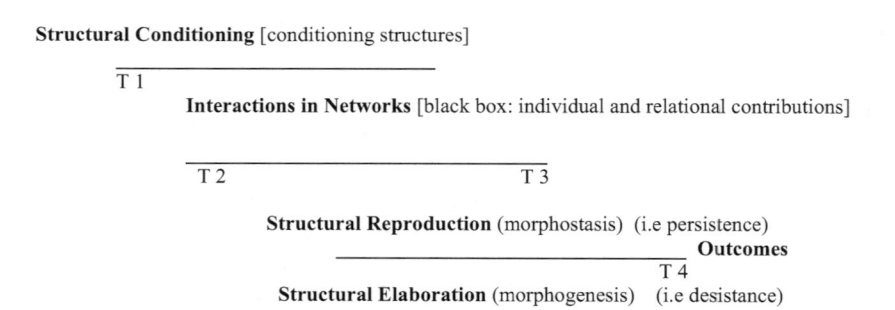

T 2   T 3

      Structural Reproduction (morphostasis) (i.e persistence)
                                                                Outcomes
                                                          T 4
      Structural Elaboration (morphogenesis)   (i.e desistance)

Figure 8.1 Overview of investigative framework

contributes to the burgeoning, yet limited, literature on the contributions of religiosity and spirituality to desistance. The existing literature places emphasis on the significance of internalized faith to processes of change, which can be reinforced through participation in religious practices and communities (see for example Armstrong, n.d., Schroeder and Frana, 2009). However, for Jay, continued association with a community of believers with whom he could identify and among whom he felt a sense of belonging was as important as the internalisation of his faith in sustaining his religious zeal and subjective well-being over time (Lim and Putnam 2010). In particular, and in recognition of Calverley's apposite observation, this analysis has examined the ways in 'the nature of the religion adopted, as opposed to religiosity per se, alters or modifies in some way the trajectory associated with desistance' (Calverley, 2013 p.102) and in particular, the way in which Pentecostal Christianity shaped Jay's personal and social identity, and, in turn, his interactions, behaviours and lifestyle.

Notes

1 Parts of this chapter draw from Donati, P. (2011) *Relational Sociology: A New Paradigm for the Social Sciences*. Abingdon: Routledge. Reproduced with permission from Routledge.
    Parts of this chapter were previously published in Weaver, B. (2012) The Relational Context of Desistance: Some Implications and Opportunities for Social Policy, *Social Policy and Administration* 46(4), pp.395–412. Reproduced with permission from Wiley.
    Parts of this chapter were previously published in Weaver, B., and McNeill, F. (2015) Lifelines: Desistance, Social Relations and Reciprocity. *Criminal Justice and Behavior* 42(1), pp.95–107. Reproduced with permission from Sage.
2 Hall (1966) elaborates that a highly identified individual would a) think of themselves as a 'delinquent' or 'offender', reflecting the extent to which they interiorised both the associated role and identity; b) hold a negative attitude towards or relationship with their parents; c) invest in or highly value their relationships with not only co-offenders but offending associated and related activities, thus exhibiting an orientation towards a more 'delinquent' peer group as juxtaposed with d) more normative social orientations. Such an individual would e) exhibit or express an internal locus of control in terms of explaining involvement in criminality and f) associate excitement and risk taking behaviours as expressive of their personality.
3 The structure of conversion narratives are broadly contiguous with Alcoholics Anonymous testimonial narratives (see for example Marsh, 2011; Warhol and Michie, 1996) and the 'redemption scripts' of the reformed ex-offender self-narrative (Maruna, 2001).
4 See for example The Parable of the Lost Sheep; The Parable of the Lost Coin; The Parable of the Lost Son. Luke 15.
5 See for example Mark 5:19: 'And he did not permit him but said to him, "Go home to your friends and tell them how much the Lord has done for you, and how he has had mercy on you."'

References

Anderson, A. (2004) *An Introduction to Pentecostalism: Global Charismatic Christianity*. Cambridge: Cambridge University Press.
Armstrong, R. (n.d.) *The Subdued Beast*. (Unpublished PhD thesis, University of Cambridge).
Bielo, J.S. (2004) Walking in the Spirit of Blood: Moral Identity Among Born-Again Christians. *Ethnology* 43(3), pp.271–289.

Brereton, V.L. (1991) *From Sin to Salvation: Stories of Women's Conversions, From 1800 to the Present*. Bloomington: Indiana University Press.

Connell, R.W. (2002) *The Men and the Boys*. Cambridge: Polity Press.

Cusson, M., and Pinsonneault, P. (1986) The Decision to Give Up Crime, in Cornish, D.B., and Clarke, R.V. (eds.) *The Reasoning Criminal: Rational Choice Perspectives in Offending*. New York, NY: Springer-Verlag, pp.72–82.

Donati, P. (2009) What Does 'Subsidiarity' Mean? The Relational Perspective. *Journal of Markets and Morality* 12(2), pp.211–243.

Donati, P. (2011) *Relational Sociology: A New Paradigm for the Social Sciences*. Abingdon: Routledge.

Gillespie, V.B. (1973) *Religious Conversation and Personal Identity: How and Why People Change*. Unpublished doctoral dissertation. University of Alabama, Birmingham.

Giordano, P.C., Cernkovich, S.A., and Rudolph, J.L. (2002) Gender, Crime and Desistance: Toward a Theory of Cognitive Transformation. *American Journal of Sociology* 107, pp.990–1064.

Giordano, P.C., Schroeder, R.D., Cernkovich, S.A. (2007) Emotions and Crime Over the Life Course: A Neo-Median Perspective on Criminal Continuity and Change. *American Journal of Sociology* 112(6), pp.1603–1661.

Goffman, E. (1963) *Stigma: Notes on the Management of Spoiled Identity*. Harmondsworth: Prentice-Hall.

Gooren, H. (2010) *Religious Conversion and Disaffiliation: Tracing Patterns of Change in Faith Practices*. New York: Palgrave Macmillan.

Hall, P.M. (1966) Identification With the Delinquent Subculture and Level of Self-Evaluation. *Sociometry* 29(2), pp.146–158.

Hauari, H., and Hollingworth, K. (2009) *Understanding Fathering: Masculinity, Diversity and Change*. York: Joseph Rowntree Foundation. Available at: http://www.jrf.org.uk/sites/files/jrf/understanding-fathering-diversity-full.pdf, accessed 09/02/2013.

James, W. (1985) *The Varieties of Religious Experience*. Harmondsworth: Penguin. (Original work published 1902.)

Katz, J. (1988) *Seductions of Crime: Moral and Sensual Attractions in Doing Evil*. New York, NY: Basic Books.

Kelman, H.C. (1958) Compliance, Identification and Internalization: Three Processes of Attitude Change. *Conflict Resolution* 2(1), pp.51–60.

Lim, C., and Putnam, R.D. (2010) Religion, Social Networks, and Life Satisfaction. *American Sociological Review* 75(6), pp.914–933.

Marsh, B. (2011) Narrating Desistance: Identity Change and the 12-Step Script. *Irish Probation Journal* 8, pp.49–68.

Maruna, S. (2001) *Making Good: How Ex-Convicts Reform and Rebuild their Lives*. Washington, DC: American Psychological Association Books.

Maruna, S. (2011) Reentry as a Rite of Passage. *Punishment and Society* 13(1), pp.3–28.

Maruna, S., Wilson, L., and Curran, K. (2006) Why God Is Often Found Behind Bars: Prison Conversion and the Crisis of Self-Narrative. *Research in Human Development* 3(2&3), pp.161–184.

Meisenhelder, T. (1977) An Exploratory Study of Exiting From Criminal Careers. *Criminology* 15, pp.319–334.

Meyer, B. (1998) 'Make a Complete Break With the Past': Memory and Post-Colonial Modernity in Ghanian Pentecostalist Discourse. *Journal of Religion in Africa* 28(3), pp.316–349.

Osborn, S.G., and West, D.J. (1979) Conviction Records of Fathers and Sons Compared. *British Journal of Criminology* 19(2), pp.120–133.

Ouimet, M., and LeBlanc, M. (1996) The Role of Life Experiences in the Continuation of the Adult Criminal Career. *Criminal Behaviour and Mental Health* 6(1), pp.73–97.

Paternoster, R., and Bushway, S. (2009) Desistance and the 'Feared Self': Toward an Identity Theory of Criminal Desistance. *Journal of Law and Criminology* 99(4), pp.1103–1156.

Schroeder, R., and Frana, J. (2009) Spirituality and Religion, Emotional Coping, and Criminal Desistance: A Qualitative Study of Men Undergoing Change. *Sociological Spectrum: Mid-South Sociological Association* 29(6), pp.718–741.

Shavit, Y., and Rattner, A. (1988) Age, Crime and the Early Life Course. *American Journal of Sociology* 93(6), pp.1457–1470.

Simons, R.L., Stewart, E., Gordon, L.C., Conger, R.D., and Elder, G.H. (2002) A Test of Life Course Explanations for Stability and Change in Antisocial Behaviour From Adolescence to Young Adulthood. *Criminology* 40(2), pp.401–434.

Van Klinken, A. (2012) Men in the Remaking: Conversion Narratives and Born-Again Masculinity in Zambia. *Journal of Religion in Africa* 42(3), pp.215–239.

Warhol, R.R., and Michie, H. (1996) Twelve-Step Teleology: Narratives of Recovery/Recovery as Narrative, in Sidonie, S., and Watson, J. (eds.) *Getting a Life: Everyday Uses of Autobiography*. Minneapolis: University of Minnesota, pp.327–349.

Weaver, B. (2012) The Relational Context of Desistance: Some Implications and Opportunities for Social Policy. *Social Policy and Administration* 46(4), pp.395–412.

Weaver, B., and McNeill, F. (2015) Lifelines: Desistance, Social Relations and Reciprocity. *Criminal Justice and Behavior* 42(1), pp.95–107.

9 Reflexivity, relationality, religiosity and recognition[1]
Evan's story

> *For the first year [post conversion to Christianity] . . . they were always with me night and day, people like Peter and Jay . . . they almost sort of mentored me and gave me good advice . . . they were very influential in the early days.*

Biographical overview

Evan, aged 43, was born in 1965 in a small town neighbouring Coaston where he and his family remained until he was 12 when they relocated to Coaston. Evan's father worked overseas as a pipe-fitter and, whilst this meant that the family were relatively affluent, Evan's contact with his father was sporadic during his childhood. Evan recalls experiencing limited parental supervision while his father was away, as his mother struggled to raise five children single-handedly. As discussed in Chapter 4, Evan perceives that his feelings of vulnerability and powerlessness as a consequence of the sustained sexual abuse he was subjected to by a family member, along with the emotional disconnection he perceived within his family, contributed to his offending behaviour in as much as he, at least in part, perceived that in offending, he was 'acting out'. In the Del he found a sense of belonging, security, protection and acceptance and incrementally power and influence, which, to a greater or lesser degree, ameliorated the sense of disconnection and powerlessness he experienced and the trauma he endured.

Evan was highly embedded in the Del as measured by his status within and centrality to the group, levels of involvement in criminal activity and isolation from pro-social networks. He also exhibited high levels of identification with a 'deviant' subculture.[2] In this vein, his relationships to and with the group and the maintenance of the associated relational goods were as significant to him as the instrumental outcomes of offending in terms of the acquisition of money, material goods and social status. The majority of Evan's offences were acquisitive in nature, and included safe-breaking, housebreaking, theft, fraud and shoplifting. In total, he surmised that he acquired in the region of 100 convictions although he speculated that his offending total was *'probably at least twice that amount'*. While his early offending took place in the context of the Del, following the fragmentation of the Del he tended to offend alone for the sole reason that any economic gains he made would not have to be distributed amongst co-offenders.

In the early stages, his offending was motivated by the acquisition of money to facilitate what he refers to as '*a party lifestyle*'. However, following the fragmentation of the Del and owing to his later involvement in substance misuse, over time, he diversified into selling drugs and offending to acquire the necessary economic capital to finance his addiction. As with Jed, Andy, Seth, Harry and Jay, Evan's convictions primarily resulted in custodial sentences of varying lengths. In total, between the ages of 14 and 28, he spent twelve years in prison serving short prison sentences. Like Jay, Evan considers his conversion to Christianity, aged 29, to be the principal mechanism triggering and sustaining his desistance from offending. He therefore considers himself to have desisted from offending approximately 14 years prior to interview. He currently works as an evangelist in London where he resides with his wife, Evie, to whom he has been married since he was aged 31. Although they have no children, Evan has two children from two previous relationships.

Evan's delineation of his life stages following the fragmentation of the Del is structured in accordance with the principal experiences that characterised each period, namely 'The Prison Years' (aged 22–29[3]) and 'The Christian Years' (aged 29–43). Spanning these eras, this chapter discusses the role of Evan's extant and new social networks and intimate relationships in supporting desistance over time under the superordinate theme '*Religiosity, reflexivity, relationality and desistance*'. This chapter thus commences at the stage of his release from prison, aged 22, after serving a three and a half year prison sentence. The role of employment in Evan's narrative of change is discussed under the final superordinate theme '*The meanings and outcomes of work*'.

Religiosity, reflexivity, relationality and desistance

The role of extant and new social networks in supporting desistance

Like Harry, Evan made a prudential decision to distance himself from the ensuing intra-group enmities that the feud between the Del gave rise to, which was assisted by his imprisonment during this period for three and a half years. By the time he was released, the revised group had moved to London. Following his release from prison, aged 22, Evan sought out and acquired temporary, short-term employment in a local power station. At this stage, the impetus for his pursuit of employment was both prudential and instrumental. It represented an alternative yet licit means of acquiring the economic capital he required to maintain the '*party lifestyle*' he enjoyed. This did not so much reflect a desire to desist as a desire to avoid further imprisonment; '*I was very consciously thinking let's be careful*'.

Participation in work enabled Evan to abstain from acquisitive crime and to sustain his first significant relationship with Monica, whom he met at this time and which consolidated his desire to avoid re-imprisonment and the potential outcomes this might have on their relationship. This period of 'primary desistance' (Maruna and Farrall, 2004) thus emerged as an outcome of Evan's reflexive evaluation of the effects of continued offending and imprisonment, mediated through the lens of his shifting individual and relational concerns, which were progressively oriented towards the maintenance of the relational goods emerging from his relationship with Monica (discussed below). However, within several months, and following the conclusion of his employment and his temporary separation from Monica, he '*got involved in the drug scene*' and his poly-drug use progressively spiralled into a chronic addiction that endured for a further seven years. In this sense, Evan's early attempts to desist correspond with Bottoms and Shapland's (2011) model of the desistance process which recognises that despite taking action towards desistance, failure to maintain these changes in the face of obstacles or temptations may lead to relapse (see also Burnett, 2004).

Evan developed new friendships through his involvement in the 'drug scene' most of whom were similarly experimenting with various 'Class A' drugs. Evan temporarily desisted from acquisitive crime and diversified into drug dealing as a means of subsidising his own drug use, which was, at that time, his ultimate concern. Drug dealing presented as a viable course of action that would enable him to realise this concern, one that carried less risk of apprehension than housebreaking, for example, and which enabled him to maintain his lifestyle while avoiding imprisonment.

Evan: I began to just get involved with more drugs and began to sell and deal in drugs and use [drugs]. I think probably that's what kept me out of prison because I didn't have to do so many crimes because . . . I was making money from [drugs] and I didn't have to take as much risks to live that lifestyle.

Over time, however, as his drug use escalated, and he consumed more than he was selling, he reverted to acquisitive crime to fund his increasingly chaotic drug use and the cycle of repeat imprisonment that had characterised his earlier life resumed. By his mid-twenties, Evan believed that he had 'knifed off' any opportunities to be anyone other than what he had become (Caspi and Moffitt, 1993). Like Harry and Jed, as the extract below illustrates, Evan engaged in a reflexive process in which he compared and measured his own progress and behaviour against his friends' desistance from crime and normative developmental transitions. It is worth noting that by this time, Evan had fathered two sons. However, unlike Harry and Jed, this did not provide the impetus to initiate change. Resonating with Maruna's (2001) notion of a 'condemnation script', Evan felt powerless to influence his conditioning structures and exercise control over his behaviour. Such is the nature of addiction that it can progressively lead to a sense of diminished agency and self-efficacy (Tieu, 2010). Reflecting Archer's (2010, 2012) concept of fractured reflexivity, his internal conversation reinforced to him that positive change was unlikely. In this context, then, the internal conversation does not lead to a purposeful course of action and only intensifies personal distress leading to (albeit temporarily) passive agents who feel unable to effect change in their conditioning structures.[4]

Evan: I thought [prison] was an occupational hazard, this is what I did. This is who I was. The majority of my friends have got themselves jobs, and by their twenties, marrying, settling down . . . I used to wonder, where have I gone wrong? . . . and I would say to myself why am I still doing time? Why am I still doing crime? And I would think maybe this is who I am meant to be . . . I didn't know anything else and by this time I am 26, 27. I am thinking who is going to employ me? I was kind of losing it completely, thinking . . . 'Who is going to give me a second chance?' . . . I thought I had the break at first when I finished that three and a half year and I met [Monica] and I thought this is it, this is what I want, this is what I am going to do with my life . . . and I think after that I thought this is me, this is what I've to be, this is it, this is my sort of destiny in life and I'm going to be a criminal.

Evan's narrative of this era is characterised by his involvement in chaotic poly-drug use, acquisitive crime and frequent short prison sentences. His continuing substance use led to a significant deterioration in his physical and mental well-being, and he became increasingly isolated. Peter and Jay, who had become 'born-again' Christians, persistently tried to engage Evan by sharing their experiences of personal transformation through their conversion to Pentecostal Christianity and by offering him support. In Pentecostal Christianity, new converts are encouraged to testify about what they have experienced – both as a means of consolidating their faith and to encourage others to convert (Anderson, 2004). At this stage, Evan tolerated their interventions but he was not receptive to their testimonies. Jay and Peter nevertheless continued to support him and show him compassion, consistent with the Christian relational ethics of subsidiarity (to relate to the other in a manner that assists the other to do what must be done) and solidarity (sharing a responsibility through reciprocity) (Donati, 2009).

Evan: [Peter], [Jay] and Tom would always talk to me in the street and show me some compassion and care because by this time I'm an addict and not many people want to know addicts. Most of my old friends would just steer clear of me. By this time I'm a mess Beth. I'm 9 stone. I'm out my face all the time and they would constantly show me some friendship and take me for a meal and talk to me.

Evan was released from another short prison sentence on Hogmanay 1993; these co-occurring events, both of which can generate reflection and self-examination, combined to create the conditions which triggered Evan's rumination over the direction in which his life was heading. At first reading, the extract below might appear to resonate with Paternoster and Bushway (2009) who suggest that a perception of 'the positive possible self' can influence a desire to change, but reason that the 'feared self', 'what one does not want to become rather than a sense of what one wants to become' (ibid p.1116) provides 'the initial motivation to change the self' (Paternoster and Bushway, 2009 p.1103) (see relatedly Harris, 2011). However, like Jay, Evan's motivation to initiate change ultimately emerged from his desire to realise a hoped for self, triggered by his association with and observations of change in his friends. As with his earlier reflexive self-evaluations, however, at this juncture, despite his anticipation of an imminent 'feared self', Evan felt powerless to initiate such change.

Evan: 1993 must have been the worst year of my life because I was using Opiates, Heroin, anything, I was using any kind of drug to get high . . . I was just losing it completely, totally, and really in a mess. I wasn't really caring, my appearance was gone, I was lying, stealing, anything to get a fix. I remember I got out from another prison sentence on Hogmanay, 1993 going into 1994. Everybody was partying and I'm sitting there with a can of beer thinking what am I going to do in life? . . . I'd began to lose a few of my friends from overdoses and I'm thinking I'm either going to be next or there's going to be a long prison sentence. And I was thinking those things through, but the drugs were controlling my life.

Of particular significance and echoing Jay's narrative of transformation, the structure of Evan's narrative (above and below) reflects those of Pentecostal conversion narratives in general (Cartledge, 2010; Rambo, 1993; van Klinken, 2012). To recapitulate the observations developed in 'Jay's story', in the pre-conversion phase a traumatic event or series of crises (Rambo, 1993) compounds a sense of existential loneliness and lostness, a deep-seated dissatisfaction with the person they have become and an isolation from the person they feel they are or would like to be, often characterized by, or narrated as, a fear of dying (van Klinken, 2012). There is a cumulative effect of events (which for Evan further included the death of his best friend to an overdose four days prior to him committing himself to Christianity) and interactions with people (primarily Jay and Peter) which precede conversion. The traumatic events or 'crises' (Rambo, 1993) create an amenability to the idea of change (Giordano, Cernkovich and Rudolph, 2002), or 'quest' for meaning, aided by 'encounters' with an advocate of the faith and 'interactions' with the religious community which precedes the individual's 'commitment' and its 'outcomes' (Rambo, 1993; see also Cartledge, 2010).

Indeed, Evan's association and interactions with Jay and Peter in the context of these cumulative events and experiences imbued Christianity with plausibility as an opportunity for change (Giordano et al., 2002) through his observation of the effects of their transformation following their conversion to Christianity. As observed previously, the recognition of change in a credible person is particularly influential where an individual can identify with the change agent(s) and internalize the benefits of responding to this influence (Kelman, 1958) in the hope of achieving similar outcomes. Jay and Peter's continuing compassion, support and recognition of him as someone of worth had the effect of triggering a process of personal reflexivity through an appraisal of *their* behaviour and how different they and their lives had become, which created in him an increasing openness to their encouragement that he accompany them to church. This is distinct, then, from more cognitive or individualistic accounts of the desistance process that place explanatory weight on the *individual's* agentic role in fashioning an alternative identity, and which suggest that social relationships 'are not accessed until after offenders *first decide to change*' (Paternoster and Bushway, 2009 p.1106, italics in original). In the context of his experiences of powerlessness, hopelessness, loss, suffering and social rejection, Evan was particularly receptive to the empowering

Christian discourse that through God he could be forgiven, find hope and a new direction. The *'compassion and care'* conveyed by this community of believers made him feel that he could belong amongst them.

Evan: It was the 29th of January 1994 [aged 29] . . . a preacher spoke . . . about Jesus . . . and he says that he came so that we could be forgiven . . . and he came so that he could give us direction and hope. And I thought that's what I need . . . I looked at Tom and [Jay] and [Peter] and I looked at their lives. I had examined their lives, I had watched their lives and I knew they were different . . . their lives were in order . . . they weren't just saying something, I had seen it had an impact on their life so I thought I need this Jesus that they are talking about . . . I went to church the next day . . . and I remember walking into church and . . . a big massive guy . . . gave me a massive hug. He says 'John welcome to the family of God' and I felt I had come home. I felt I would belong somewhere.

The next day, Evan was sentenced to four months in prison for an outstanding conviction of fraud. Like Jay, Evan's internalisation of his faith was expressed through his immediate initiation of significant lifestyle changes, in particular his detoxification from Heroin, which he considered was enabled by his immediate incarceration.

Evan: Looking back on those 4 month in prison I thank God for them, I really do. I think that in that time I was able to deal with big issues – I could walk away [from provocation], I stopped swearing and smoking. I dealt with my, with God's help, I dealt with my drug addiction because I had to go cold turkey.

Religion traditionally encapsulates particular beliefs, values, attitudes and practices that, in conjunction with the relational ties formed through religious institutions and communities, creates a new world for the convert to inhabit (Rambo, 1993). The reflexive practical reasoning involved in the process of change, or conversion, from *becoming* to *being* a Christian, heralded a re-prioritization of Evan's ultimate concerns. This process of reflexivity, through which projects (courses of action) and practices (a way of being in the world) (Archer, 2007) are decided on, realized and sustained, is relational in so far as it is shaped by the relational networks within which it emerges. These sets of relations affect what does, and can, satisfy the individual and what can be sustained by each, on which the individual brings his/her personal reflexivity to bear with regard to his/her position in this new relational context (Donati, 2011). In the first year following Evan's conversion and subsequent release, Peter and Jay assumed what might be construed as an informal 'circle of support'[5] in terms of socializing Evan into Pentecostal Christian values, beliefs and practices and providing an informal helpful and encouraging environment to reinforce his fledgling Christian identity. In so doing, this 'helping collective' role-modeled Pentecostal Christian identities and generated the relational goods (of love, friendship, devotion, caring) through which this process of re-socialisation was enabled. As Donati observes:

> There is a certain correspondence between personal identity ('who I am is what I care about') and collective identity (who we are is what we care about) . . . this correspondence does not mean that we – as individual persons – are subjugated or subordinated by any holistic entity whatsoever . . . [We] are what we care about not because we (as a group, network or any collective entity) think in the same way or because we share external commitments, or because we have mutual intentionality, or because we are conditioned by the same structures, but because we are in a special relation, and *that* relation is what makes us reflexive in a social, instead of an individual way.
>
> (Donati, 2011 p.xvi)

It is thus through these relations of reciprocity which recognise the dignity of the human person that those participating in it find a shared intrinsic commitment to '[their] communal experiential basis as beneficiaries of worth [in reference to the relational goods these relationships produce] unobtainable in any other way' (Archer, 2010 p.10 [this author's insertions]). Moreover, drawing on Maruna and LeBel's (2009 p.66) research which suggests that when a person is voluntarily involved in a helping collective he/she is 'thought to obtain a sense of belonging', or solidarity, through the 'sharing of experience, strength and hope', it might be inferred that through the experience of supporting Evan, Jay and Peter also benefited from the reinforcement of their Christian identities and evangelistic roles that their mutual recognition of each other's transformations implied.

Evan: for the first year [post conversion] . . . they were always with me night and day, people like Peter and Jay . . . we would meet together . . . they almost sort of mentored me and gave me good advice . . . These guys put a lot of time into me, encouraged me and supported me until I almost could stand on my feet myself in a sense, until I could walk as a Christian and make the right choices and the right decisions; they were very influential in the early days.

Having this circle of support following his conversion was particularly important to Evan whose relationship with Monica and his former networks concluded because he had become a Christian. Evan described this series of rejections as a significant challenge, whilst simultaneously recognising the challenges that living in a criminal milieu without participating in it would have represented in the early stages of desistance and recovery.

Evan: I didn't say to my friends, 'I am not talking to you because I'm a Christian', I suddenly realised that because I had become a Christian, people almost kept away from me. Nobody seemed to come and visit me after that . . . I was disappointed . . . [but] I don't know if it would have been wise to hang about with the same people at that time because I might have been vulnerable at that time, just coming off drugs and doing things and falling back into that kind of lifestyle, but it still hurt.

Like Jay, Evan developed new social relationships through his association with and involvement in various faith-based organisations and institutions. The contribution of these new social relationships in enabling Evan's participation in employment, and the contribution of employment in supporting his process of change, are discussed further under the superordinate theme '*The meanings and outcomes of work*'. The following sub-theme discusses the dynamics of Evan's involvement in his families of formation and intimate relationships and the individual and relational factors which variously influenced his experience of these roles and relationships.

The role of intimate relationships and families of formation in supporting desistance

This sub-theme explores differences in the role of Evan's two significant intimate relations in constraining or sustaining change at different stages in his life and the constraints that a range of factors exerted on the impact and significance of his experience of becoming a father at the ages of 17 and 25.

As discussed in Chapter 2, it is likely that a coalescence of factors will affect the dynamic experience of parenthood (see for example Arendell, 2000; Hauari and Hollingworth, 2009; Marsiglio and Pleck, 2004) including age, maturity, one's experience of being parented, the status, nature and dynamics of the relational context within which a given form of parenting occurs, and individual personal, cultural and socio-economic contexts – all of which variously constrain or enable the realisation of this role and social identity. Evan's first son, David, was born when Evan was seventeen years old, the outcome of a very brief relationship with David's mother, Jane. As previously noted, at this point in his life, Evan's lifestyle cohered around socialising with his friends and engaging in acquisitive crime, interrupted only by the imposition of frequent short prison sentences, all of which necessarily curtailed Evan's level of involvement with his son. At this stage, Evan's ultimate concerns surrounded the acquisition of money and the pursuit of this lifestyle, with which both intimate relationships and fatherhood were incompatible. Although he had seen David as a baby, by the time Evan was released from his three and a half year prison sentence, aged 22, his son was aged 5.

Evan: I had seen him once or twice when he was a baby but I had been in prison for the last three or four years . . . I didn't want to have the responsibility of the relationship but I would go up and demand to see the baby at inappropriate times. I lived for the weekend and . . . I wasn't going to be nailed into that relationship. I didn't have any real concern for [Jane] . . . so that probably had an effect on me not taking responsibility for [David].

For Evan, then, becoming a father at this time, in the context of his relationship with Jane (or lack thereof), engendered no reflexive re-orientation of his ultimate concerns, nor did his subsequent abstinence from offending influence his inclination towards assuming parental responsibilities towards his son, which were overshadowed by his disinterest in Jane. Rather, Evan's disengagement from offending at this time was motivated by his aversion to further imprisonment and was enabled by his participation in temporary employment which restricted his perceived need to engage in acquisitive crime. His relational commitments to Monica, in turn, further diminished the desirability of offending behaviour, and its consequences. Moreover, spending time at work and with Monica had a significant impact on his formerly routine social activities and the social spaces he occupied, which further enabled his abstinence from crime. While, then, these self-initiated changes to his conditioning structures had the effect of enabling his abstinence from offending, it was Evan's reflexive re-prioritisation of his individual and relational concerns, which motivated his pursuit of a different lifestyle, underpinned by his desire to maintain the relational goods emerging from his relationship with Monica, to which they were mutually oriented. Evan observed that this was his first experience of stability and normalcy and maintaining this significant relationship became his ultimate concern.

Evan: It was the first time in my life I'd had any stability and I felt I had found my soul mate. I'd found somebody I could really express love [with] and [who] I really cared about and really wanted to be with and I'd poured out my heart. She was the first person I had told about the abuse . . . It was good, it was great that I could share that . . . That went on for 7 month . . . then the bombshell came when she told me at Christmas time that she wanted me to move out.

In the context of the termination of both his employment and this relationship, Evan responded by immersing himself once more in '*the party lifestyle*', through which he was introduced to recreational drug use. What this seems to suggest then is that Evan's initial abstinence from offending at this stage was contingent on the maintenance of this relationship, which had triggered a re-prioritisation of his ultimate concerns and which, in turn, underpinned the ensuing changes he initiated in his projects and practices. While the separation between Monica and Evan was short-lived it had an enduring effect on their interactive dynamics and on the nature of the bond between them which, for Evan, diminished the salience of this relationship in the context of his shifting constellation of concerns.

Evan: something happened and I think I lost trust . . . so that was [1988] and by this time I had started dabbling in drugs and by September had mainlined . . . I felt the relationship was never really the same again and I was playing away from home, taking drugs, selling drugs and I was clubbing Thursday, Friday, Saturday.

Evan remained in a relationship with Monica for several years thereafter, but the nature and form of the relationship had been altered by his experience of betrayal and loss, and while the relationship was of significance to him, it was no longer his relationship of ultimate concern. He was associating frequently with others who were similarly involved in recreational drug use and its attendant social scene, which, as previously explained, ultimately heralded his resumption of offending. The diminution of the relational goods he had been motivated to maintain thus influenced the meaning and significance of this relationship, which irrevocably diminished the satisfaction he had initially derived from this relationship (Donati, 2011).

In 1990, Evan and Monica had a son, Jake. In this markedly different relational context, Evan's involvement with Jake was thus more intense than his involvement with David. However, by this time, Evan had developed an addiction to Amphetamine, which resulted in increasingly frequent periods of imprisonment, diminishing his capacity to parent and to personify this role identity. While, as previously discussed, he engaged in an internal conversation (personal reflexivity) at this time, particularly during periods of imprisonment, his concerns acknowledged but were not altered by being in a new role position in relation to either Jake or Monica.

Evan: I loved [becoming a father] but I knew I was an addict . . . I did try and make a go of it but I was losing it . . . the drugs were controlling my life . . .

Ultimately, Monica terminated the relationship with Evan, following his conversion to Christianity. Monica did not share his faith, and the alteration in his attitudes, expectations and behaviours, and the disjuncture between their ultimate concerns, compounded by the cumulative effect that his addiction and frequent imprisonment had exerted on the nature of the bond between them, contributed to the demise of the relationship.

A year after his conversion, Evan met and married Evie, to whom he remains married. Evie is also a 'born-again' Christian, and as such she shares his religious commitments to be of service to others. The recognition and reinforcement of Evan's transformation that his relationship with Evie implied, and her encouragement to realise these generative concerns, contributed to his personification of his religious identity. While, then, his relationship with Evie was not causative of desistance, she was a critical support to him following his conversion and remains central to his emotional well-being.

Evan: I think we married quickly [because] we had the same passion; we had the same drive in life; the same goals; we wanted to be effective Christians, reaching out to people, particularly the marginalised, and she encouraged me all the way . . . Knowing there's a girl here who's committed herself to me, loves me, supports me, was there for me when life was tough as well and I am there for her, to love and support her.

Despite the intimacy, strength and endurance of their relationship, like Peggy in Jay's story, Evie barely features in Evan's narrative, which may, in part, be attributable to her involvement in his life subsequent to his conversion and the impact that being 'born-again' can exert on peoples' personal and social identities, and their relations with their partners, in that God becomes the relationship of ultimate concern.

The meanings and outcomes of work

The desistance promotive meanings and outcomes of work

As previously observed, Evan's first significant experience of participation in employment occurred following his release from a three and a half year prison sentence at the age of 22. At this stage, the economic outcomes diminished any perceived need to engage in acquisitive offending, which, in the context of his relationship with Monica, enabled behavioural and lifestyle changes. However, as previously observed, the maintenance of these changes was primarily contingent on his commitment to this relation of concern. Despite his temporary abstinence from offending, at this stage, he experienced no significant pro-social shift in his values or in his personal and social identity that altered his attitude to offending, which only occurred later – following his conversion to Christianity.

Like Jay, Evan's faith is expressed through the nature of his work, which since his conversion to Christianity has been oriented to supporting individuals and communities in need. Evan conceptualises his work as an expression of his faith, in terms of a life lived in service to others, informed by the Christian relational ethics of subsidiarity and solidarity referred to previously. For both Jay and Evan, it is the meaning and outcomes of the work that is of enduring significance in consolidating their new, 'born-again' identity and thus their subjective well-being. While Evan's faith imbued the nature of this work with meaning, participating in this work contributed to and enabled the realization of his religious identities. His participation in these works, then, can be construed as an outcome of both his conversion and of desistance; both of which shaped his generative commitments.

Evan obtained work alongside Jay which was oriented to supporting individuals and communities in need and which generated access to a broader network of Christians. Within two months of his conversion to Christianity, Evan began volunteering for the Prison Fellowship with which he continued for the next two years. In the early stages, his involvement in a 'helping collective' with other volunteers enabled the generation of new social relationships and provided 'a sense of belonging', or solidarity, through the 'sharing of experience, strength and hope' (Maruna and LeBel, 2009 p.66).

Evan: We used to do things like have barbecues and away days for families of prisoners . . . and some of their friends. And you got the volunteers who came together as well . . . we would try to support [each other].

As a prison mentor, like Jay, Evan shared his story of personal transformation. McAdams (2008) conceptualizes the life story as a narrative of personal identity, which is realized in the telling. In particular, the Christian testimonial provides an opportunity to bear witness to one's experience of transformation to others, which, for Evan, also facilitated a shift in his social identity. Thus, unlike Jed's suppression of his past self, this narrative [re]construction of the self supports the integration of a past self into one's present self (Maruna, 2001) which can itself be empowering and therapeutic in certain contexts, particularly when it enables one's past to be reconceptualised as a strength.

Evan: I began to go into prisons . . . to share . . . how God had changed my life – and it was offering hope to some of the guys and . . . I got that little bit more respect 'cos they knew I had been in their shoes . . . [I] enjoyed it because I felt I was being effective, people were listening to me and I came back feeling . . . I had helped someone.

His involvement in this 'generative' role (Maruna, 2001) thus not only reinforced his own process of change but was oriented to supporting others as he had been supported. However, during this period, Evan married Evie and, in *this* relational context, the constraints of not generating an income surfaced. As observed in 'Jay's Story', leadership and the assumption of responsibility for oneself and for others are definitive features of Pentecostal Christian interpretations of and discourses on masculinity and are associated with being the principal provider (van Klinken, 2012) which, as the extract below suggests, marked some continuity with his internalised beliefs surrounding cultural norms of masculinity relating to gender roles.

Evan: Evie was working [and] I had that sense that I need to work, know she shouldn't be working herself, I should be working know – that's a prominent mentality for the West of Scotland, you know, you should be the provider and the woman should be the home nester or whatever know.

Sharing his frustration, the Church leaders employed him to engage in community outreach and to attend a theological college. Over several years, Evan established a drop-in centre and a food and furniture bank for distribution to people in need and engaged other young people, whom he had been mentoring, to assist him in his ministry. However, while both his participation in paid employment and the nature of the work had a significant role in, respectively, contributing to his position of provider, and in realising his religious commitments, the constraints of working in Coaston exacted particular constraints and limitations on his sense of, and opportunities for, personal progression from which he only felt liberated following his relocation to London in 2005, where he continues to reside.

Constraints and limitations

Evan currently works as an Evangelist in London, which, in particular, he considers has enabled him to '*grow and develop and to be the person you are really meant to be*'. Despite the recognition of his transformation he received through his association with a community of believers, and despite the recognition of change he experienced from people in the community, the enduring proximity of a previously 'spoiled identity' (Goffman, 1963) embedded in this sense of place, and in the memories of the community, constrained his sense of personal progression.

192 *Evan's story*

While, on the one hand, he was recognised as a reformed individual, he perceived that the recognition he received reflected the distance he had travelled from his past self, which remained the dominant identity through which lens the positive social recognition he received was refracted. Moving to a new location enabled him to be recognised as the person he had become, as an Evangelist.

> *Evan:* I felt I was a bit restricted in [Coaston] . . . I tried to become transparent and say 'well you know where I have been people . . . I have blown it and I have done this and I've done that – however this is who I am now and this is what I do and this is what I believe'. But, since coming to London, I feel like I don't have . . . the baggage of the community. I have grown up in [Coaston], [and everyone knows] what is going on – it's such a small community. The issues of people are so well known. I don't have that [now]. Sometimes it smothers you. I think in London it's as if I had been given wings and I could fly in a sense – really blossom and grow and develop.

Conclusion

This chapter has discussed Evan's life beyond the fragmentation of the Del, and, in that, his process of desistance. Echoing Jay's narrative of change, this analysis has revealed the centrality of his conversion to Pentecostal Christianity and his internalisation of the Christian faith both to his narrative of change and to every aspect of his life. His initial conversion was supported, reinforced and sustained by his extant social relationships with Peter and Jay and his participation in new Christian relational networks, which enabled the expression of his faith and generative commitments and which contributed to the transformation in his personal and social identity with which continued offending was incompatible. In concert with the preceding individual stories, this chapter has illustrated the ways in which desistance is co-produced between individuals-in-relation, foregrounding a conceptualization of a reflexive individual whose ultimate concerns emerge from, are immersed in and shape their relational worlds. Where Jed's, Seth's and Harry's desistance emerged as a means to realising their relational concerns with, to varying degrees, their families of formation, in which participation in employment played a part, like Jay, Evan's relationship of ultimate concern was of a spiritual form and his principal role identity emerged as a Christian.

Although Evan considers his conversion to be the catalyst to change, Evan's earlier participation in employment following his release from prison, in the context of a significant intimate relationship (T1–T2 in Figure 9.1), enabled a new way of living. The significance of Evan's relationship with Monica in diminishing his desire to offend cannot be reduced to the effects of one individual on another but rather is the outcome of the application of their relational reflexivity. As this chapter has illustrated, the bonds forged between them constituted their reciprocal orientation towards each other (T2–T3) and, in turn, their desire to maintain the emergent relational goods prompted and guided their actions in order to sustain this relationship and maintain the associated relational goods (Donati, 2011), to which Evan applied his personal reflexivity and responded by refraining from

Structural Conditioning [conditioning structures]

```
 T 1
```

      Interactions in Networks [black box: individual and relational contributions]

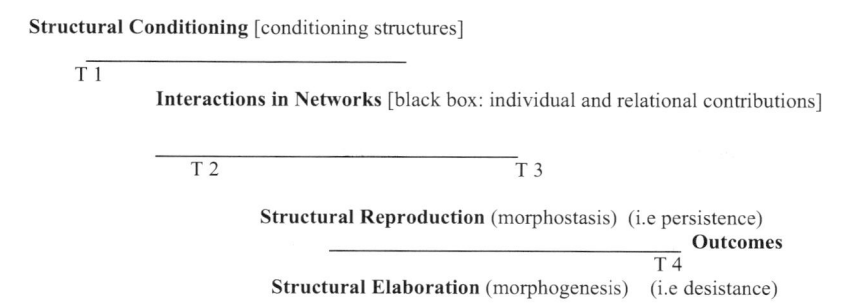

```
     T 2                              T 3
```

           Structural Reproduction (morphostasis) (i.e persistence)
                                                               Outcomes
                                                                T 4
           Structural Elaboration (morphogenesis) (i.e desistance)

Figure 9.1 Overview of investigative framework

acquisitive offending and modifying his behaviours (T4). His separation from Monica, the loss of his employment, his participation in an alternative social network and addiction combined to influence his conditioning structures (T1 in the next phase of the morphogenetic cycle).

In the context of the increasing deleterious outcomes of his addiction on his physical and mental well-being, his frequent imprisonment, and increasing social isolation (at T4–T1), he became progressively receptive to Peter and Jay's faith-based interventions and testimonies of change. His internalisation of the teachings of Pentecostal Christianity influenced by his interactions with Peter and Jay (T2–T3) ultimately shaped his identity, behaviour and lifestyle (T4), and, in turn, the sets of relations in which he was involved (at T1 in the next phase of the morphogenetic cycle). Bringing his personal reflexivity to bear with regard to his position in this new relational context (T2–T3) motivated his participation in evangelism and ministry (T4).

As with preceding chapters, this chapter thus marks a departure from current explanations for desistance that fail to illuminate *how* social structures shape decisions by ignoring how the individual perceives and responds to such influences. But it also extends agentic and cognitive explanations by moving beyond their explanations of the onset of desistance, and offering an elaboration of how relations sustain or hinder desistance over time. In particular, 'Evan's Story' – like Jay's – builds on and contributes to the burgeoning, yet limited, literature on the contributions of religiosity and spirituality to desistance.

Notes

1 Parts of this chapter draw from Donati, P. (2011) *Relational Sociology: A New Paradigm for the Social Sciences*. Abingdon: Routledge. Reproduced with permission from Routledge.

   Parts of this chapter were previously published in Weaver, B. (2013) Desistance, Reflexivity and Relationality: A Case Study. *European Journal of Probation* 5(3), pp.71–88. Reproduced with permission from Sage.

2 Hall (1966) elaborates that a highly identified individual would a) think of themselves as a 'delinquent' or 'offender', reflecting the extent to which they interiorised both the associated role and identity; b) hold a negative attitude towards or relationship with their parents; c) invest in or highly value their relationships with not only co-offenders

but offending associated and related activities, thus exhibiting an orientation towards a more 'delinquent' peer group as juxtaposed with d) more normative social orientations. Such an individual would e) exhibit or express an internal locus of control in terms of explaining involvement in criminality and f) associate excitement and risk taking behaviours as expressive of their personality.
3 This chapter tells Evan's story following the fragmentation of the group and thus from the mid-1980s, when Evan was 22. In his narrative, the years in custody extend from age 14 to 28, during which time he served 12 years in short-term prison sentences of varying lengths in various penal institutions (including list E schools, Assessment Centres, Detention Centres, Young Offenders Institutions and prisons).
4 This leads to morphostasis or structural reproduction at T4 – see Figure 9.1.
5 The term 'circle of support' is an allusion to a specific restorative practice operating across the world, variously named Citizen Circles (in Ohio) or Circles of Support and Accountability for example (e.g. Armstrong et al., 2008). Essentially, the circle is comprised of volunteer community members who provide a network of social support to an individual to help prevent re-offending and enable reintegration.

References

Anderson, A. (2004) *An Introduction to Pentecostalism: Global Charismatic Christianity.* Cambridge: Cambridge University Press.

Archer, M. (2007) *Making Our Way Through the World: Human Reflexivity and Social Mobility.* Cambridge: Cambridge University Press.

Archer, M. (2010) Routine, Reflexivity and Realism. *Sociological Theory* 28(3), pp.272–303.

Archer, M. (2012) *The Reflexive Imperative in Late Modernity.* Cambridge: Cambridge University Press.

Arendell, T. (2000) Conceiving and Investigating Motherhood: The Decade's Scholarship. *Journal of Marriage and Family* 62(4), pp.1192–1207.

Armstrong, S., Chistyakova, Y., MacKenzie, S., and Malloch, M. (2008) *Circles of Support and Accountability: Consideration of the Feasibility of Pilots in Scotland.* Report No. 01/2008, Scottish Centre for Crime and Justice Research, Glasgow.

Bottoms, A.E., and Shapland, J. (2011) Steps Towards Desistance Among Male Young Adult Recidivists, in Farrall, S., Hough, M., Maruna, S., and Sparks, R. (eds.) *Escape Routes: Contemporary Perspectives on Life After Punishment.* London: Routledge, pp.43–80.

Burnett, R. (2004) One-to-One Ways of Promoting Desistance: In Search of an Evidence Base, in Burnett, R., and Roberts, C. (eds.) *What Works in Probation and Youth Justice.* Cullompton: Willan, pp.180–197.

Cartledge, M.J. (2010) *Testimony in the Spirit: Rescripting Ordinary Pentecostal Theology.* Aldershot: Ashgate.

Caspi, A., and Moffitt, T.E. (1993) When Do Individual Differences Matter? A Paradoxical Theory of Personality Coherence. *Psychological Inquiry* 4, pp.247–271.

Donati, P. (2009) What Does 'Subsidiarity' Mean? The Relational Perspective. *Journal of Markets and Morality* 12(2), pp.211–243.

Donati, P. (2011) *Relational Sociology: A New Paradigm for the Social Sciences.* Abingdon: Routledge.

Giordano, P.C., Cernkovich, S.A., and Rudolph, J.L. (2002) Gender, Crime and Desistance: Toward a Theory of Cognitive Transformation. *American Journal of Sociology* 107, pp.990–1064.

Goffman, E. (1963) *Stigma: Notes on the Management of Spoiled Identity*. Harmondsworth: Prentice-Hall.
Hall, P.M. (1966) Identification With the Delinquent Subculture and Level of Self-Evaluation. *Sociometry* 29(2), pp.146–158.
Harris, A. (2011) Constructing Clean Dreams: Accounts, Future Selves, and Social and Structural Support as Desistance Work. *Symbolic Interaction* 34(1), pp.63–85.
Hauari, H., and Hollingworth, K. (2009) *Understanding Fathering: Masculinity, Diversity and Change*. York: Joseph Rowntree Foundation. Available at: http://www.jrf.org.uk/sites/files/jrf/understanding-fathering-diversity-full.pdf, accessed 09/02/2011.
Kelman, H.C. (1958) Compliance, Identification and Internalization: Three Processes of Attitude Change. *Conflict Resolution* 2(1), pp.51–60.
Marsiglio, W., and Pleck, J.H. (2004) Fatherhood and Masculinities, in Kimmel, M.S., Hearn, J., and Connell R.W. (eds.) *Handbook of Studies on Men and Masculinities*. Thousand Oaks, CA: Sage, pp.249–269.
Maruna, S. (2001) *Making Good: How Ex-convicts Reform and Rebuild Their Lives*. Washington, DC: American Psychological Association Books.
Maruna, S., and Farrall, S. (2004) Desistance From Crime: A Theoretical Reformulation. *Kolner Zeitschrift für Soziologie und Sozialpsychologie* 43, pp.171–194.
Maruna, S., and LeBel, T. (2009) Strengths-Based Approaches to Reentry: Extra Mileage Toward Reintegration and Destigmatization. *Japanese Journal of Sociological Criminology* 34, pp.58–80.
McAdams, D.P. (2008) American Identity: The Redemptive Self. *General Psychologist* 43(1), pp.20–27.
Paternoster, R., and Bushway, S. (2009) Desistance and the 'Feared Self': Toward an Identity Theory of Criminal Desistance. *Journal of Law and Criminology* 99(4), pp.1103–1156.
Rambo, L.R. (1993) *Understanding Religious Conversion*. New Haven, CT: Yale University Press.
Tieu, M. (2010) Understanding the Nature of Drug Addiction. *Bioethics Research Notes* 22(1), pp.7–11.
Van Klinken, A. (2012) Men in the Remaking: Conversion Narratives and Born-Again Masculinity in Zambia. *Journal of Religion in Africa* 42(3), pp.215–239.
Weaver, B. (2013) Desistance, Reflexivity and Relationality: A Case Study. *European Journal of Probation* 5(3), pp.71–88.

10 An imprisoned life
Andy's story[1]

All my conversations, all I know, is prison. I've no memories. All my memories is prison.

Biographical overview

Andy was born in Coaston in 1961 and, as discussed in Chapter 4, his involvement with the Del began when he commenced secondary school. The impact of Andy's initial social marginalisation by his peers, as a result of his distinctive physical appearance, was aggravated by his experience of sexual abuse and, while partly mitigated by his association with the Del, was nonetheless evident even within these relationships, manifest in low levels of influence, and a comparatively marginal position within the group, and persists as a prominent theme throughout his life story. Although Andy was involved in truanting from school and some minor incidences of offending behaviour at a young age, his involvement with the Del marked the acceleration of his offending behaviour. As a physically diminutive man, Andy acknowledges his inability and reluctance to fight, which, whilst contributing to his peripheral status in the group, also accounts for his limited involvement in violent offending compared to others in the group. Indeed, most of his offending between the ages of 13 and 17 comprised offences of housebreaking or burglary of private houses, pubs and shops.

Following the fragmentation of the group, Andy continued to offend, either alone or with one co-offender (not from the Del) on a daily basis. While there were various instrumental and affective reasons underpinning Andy's earlier offending and involvement with the Del, his later offending was primarily motivated by economic gain. From the age of 17, influenced by conversations with people he met in prison, Andy's offending escalated to assault and robbery. While Andy surmises that he committed in the region of 500 offences, he acquired only 13 convictions, which, owing to increasing severity and persistency, resulted in lengthy custodial sentences. At the age of 48, Andy had spent 32 years in prison, with his longest period in the community lasting 7 weeks and his shortest a few hours. At the time of interview, he was nearing the end of a ten year sentence.

Andy's life has been lived in prison, and as a consequence, Andy's delineation of his life beyond the group comprised a unitary stage '*a life lived in prison*', perhaps reflecting the 'liminality' and monotony typical of the monolithic experience of long-term imprisonment (Jewkes, 2005). 'Time in prison is something, which is lived through but not in the real sense lived' (Wahidin, 2006 p.8), but which is rather more of an existence in a state of 'limbo' (Sapsford, 1978). In this vein, Andy's life story is a narrative of crime and punishment, or, in his words, '*it's all been crime and prison*'. Reflecting this, this chapter discusses his experiences of long-term imprisonment and the various effects this had on him, and his opportunities for resettlement. Andy's story is, thus, structured and analysed under the superordinate theme: '*Experiencing punishment*', which is divided into three sub-themes: '*Experience of prisoner community*'; '*Effects of prison*'; and '*Experiencing and anticipating release*'.

Experiencing punishment

Experience of prisoner community

The experience of prison has been captured by various autobiographical accounts (see for example Boyle, 1977; Collins, 1997; James, 2003) and by numerous academic studies (see for example Clemmer, 1958; Cohen and Taylor, 1972; Crewe, 2009; Jewkes, 2005; Sykes, 1958; Toch, 1975, 1992; Zamble and Porporino, 1988). These, and other works, grant insight into how prison is subjectively experienced and how prisoners perceive and respond to the institutional and interpersonal environment of prison. While early writings (i.e. Clemmer, 1958; Sykes, 1958) sought to reveal the dynamics of socialisation into the prisoner culture or community,[2] Crewe's (2009) more recent work explored divergences within prisoner populations and their experiences and perceptions of interpersonal interactions in prison. This sub-theme explores Andy's experience of the prisoner community. While, as Crewe and Bennett (2012 p.xxi) suggest, first-hand accounts of prisoner experience are 'imperfect guides to the general experience of imprisonment', in terms of understanding individual experiences of and adaptive responses to prison, 'a situation-by-person approach' is required (Bonta and Gendreau, 1990 p.347).

Prisoners enter prison with their existing personalities, values, attitudes, beliefs, experiences, social status and norms of social interactions (Jewkes, 2012), and these 'conditioning structures' (Donati, 2011) contribute to differences between prisoners' experiences in terms of their interactions with other prisoners and their responses to the constraints, enablements and expectations that inhere in the 'prisoner society' (Crewe, 2009) and the 'formal' prison culture. As previously noted, Andy is a diminutive man who, by his own admission, is unable to fight. Emulating his established patterns of interaction with the Del, Andy learnt to ingratiate himself with other prisoners as a means of avoiding conflict.

Andy: A prison officer said to me: 'You keep in with the bad ones because the good ones will never do you any harm'. I knew he meant being two-faced . . . a lot of prisoners cannae reason very well, they don't like to lose arguments so they get showed up in front of other people. So, I developed a skill at learning how to keep in with people.

Neither disinclination towards conflict nor strategically managing one's social interactions in prison are unusual, although, as Andy suggests in relation to other prisoners, defending one's image, particularly in front of other prisoners, is critical to maintaining status and avoiding exploitation, and these tensions structure norms of engagement (Crewe, 2009). Prisoners are alert to perceived slights. Allowing expressions of disrespect to pass opens one up to the risk of victimisation; in turn, responding to threats requires a credible capacity to back this up with violence (Edgar and Martin, 2002) which, Crewe (2012) observes, can ward off exploitation. How one receives and responds to these interactive dynamics is an important factor in determining one's status in the hierarchical prisoner community. Andy ingratiated himself with more dominant prisoners who could offer him a measure of protection. Instrumental alliances among prisoners are not uncommon; relationships in prison tend to be pragmatic and characterised by material and social support but exhibit little emotionality or affection (Crewe, 2012). However, status and stigma in prison can be mutually compounding and, as Crewe (2009 p.282) observes, 'prisoners who could not 'handle themselves' . . . were generally scorned . . . and men who succumbed to intimidation or failed to stand up for themselves were vulnerable to more intense forms of victimization' (see also Edgar, O'Donnell and Martin, 2003). This was Andy's experience as the following extract illustrates:

Andy: It probably made me less of a man because I became a kind of 'Yes man'. I just agreed with people simply to keep the peace. I've never ever stood up for myself in prison . . . I don't think I will ever be able to . . . I'm terrified of fights . . . I don't know if that makes you less of a man . . . but the least wee person . . . will want a fight with me and . . . its hard to get by because it's all about images in prison, hard men, and I'm probably known as a wee bit of a daftie . . . a person of irrelevance . . . it makes me feel inadequate.

The impact of Andy's subordinate status and his associated experiences in prison are discussed in the following sub-theme. In terms of managing his experience of prison, in the early stages of his prison life (aged 21), Andy discovered that selling and smuggling drugs into the prison for influential prisoners afforded him a level of protection.

Andy: I've always been involved . . . well for the first 20 years . . . I was always involved in . . . either selling drugs or bringing drugs into prison. So it was just a continuation from the outside, inside. I was running about with guys I felt would protect me . . . that's how I got through my time.

By 1986, aged 25, Andy started injecting Heroin and his involvement in the drug scene dominated the first two decades of his prison life. Drug use was a means of psychologically transcending the realities of his existence in prison and suppressing his emotions. In prison, where the performance of a masculine identity is associated with emotional resilience, suppressing the expression of (particularly negative) emotion is central to managing reputations and social interactions (Crewe, 2009, 2012; Sim, 1994; Sykes, 1958).

Andy: It [injecting Heroin made] my time go easier and block[ed] out the existence I was having ... You know, you very rarely get prisoners opening up to each other and I suppose I've found it very hard over the years. It's an image you've got to uphold in prison as a man – of being in control, and not show any weakness – especially don't cry! Don't talk about things that lassies would talk about. Emotions and stuff like that. It's probably been harder for me because I've never been a macho guy – I've never had any fights in my life apart from doings. It's been difficult to maintain for years ... I have lost face so many times in prison it's unbelievable, which also knocks your confidence and self-esteem – I probably havenae got any.

While drug use can offer a means of escape, alleviating frustration, boredom and anxiety (Larner and Tefferteller, 1964; Pearson, 1987; Crewe, 2009, 2012), dependency on drugs in prison breeds contempt and compounds the stigma of addiction. Crewe (2012) explains that this contempt not only reflects an aversion to drug users' pre-prison behaviour (not least their exploitation of their family members) but also because they

> breach a number of norms that make collective living more manageable ... they scavenge for goods that they can trade for drugs and sometimes steal from other prisoners and they are considered untrustworthy, manipulative and generally unreliable. The debts that they build up create friction.
>
> (p.33)

These debts can also place additional strain on prisoners' families on whom prisoners' often depend for financial support (see for example Condry, 2012; Smith et al., 2007) and, in Andy's case, continual demands for subsidies ultimately severed the only relationships he had outside prison by then.

Andy: [I was] getting myself into debt ... I used to phone my Mum, ask her to send £30 here and £20 there and it got to the stage where they wouldnae answer the phone ... I could understand, obviously, and I lost all contact with my family then.

Already vulnerable to exploitation, Andy's dependency on Heroin, loss of financial assistance and rising debts meant that he had to carry out chores for more powerful prisoners who supplied drugs as a means of settling his debts and acquiring drugs (see also Crewe, 2009). However, such an apparent display of subordination attracted victimisation and the withdrawal of the protection he had previously engineered when his utility diminished and his dependence increased. The form of victimisation Andy endured was years of humiliating treatment, psychological torment and social isolation.

Andy: Because I've been a drug addict over the years, I've obviously had to chase drugs in prison and . . . I started getting a bit of a using off a couple of guys. I . . . collecting their meals for them, bringing it up to their cells and just running after [them] – so as I could get drugs off them. Years ago, a couple of guys [said] to a certain guy I was doing it for – 'Is that your dog running after you?' So, not long after that, people started whistling like a dog to me and clicking their fingers . . . [then] more people were doing it . . . I finally said something to1 somebody . . . so, it became common knowledge that I would react to this noise – then screws started doing it. It still happens today. Everywhere I go, everybody knows about it [voice cracking] . . . Years that's been happening Beth. [crying] . . . Anytime I walk by, every day. I had to put myself in the digger [segregation] just to get away fae it all. Then they started doing it in the digger as well. It's a living nightmare man. I can cope with it but there's times when I cannae and I don't even go out for my meals because I'm too embarrassed to show my face.

While bullying vulnerable prisoners is generally apprehended with contempt, those who ' "allow" [it] . . . receive little sympathy' (Crewe, 2012 p.35). Moreover, suffering as a consequence of addiction and drug debt is viewed as self-inflicted; rarely does anyone intervene as they might otherwise (Crewe, 2009). With a ten year sentence ahead of him in 1993, physically and emotionally spent and desperate and fearful of his capacity to continue to cope with his enduring victimisation, in the absence of alternative coping mechanisms (Jeglic, Vaudernoff and Doriovick, 2005) Andy engaged in an isolated incident of serious self-harm. The mental health social worker who subsequently offered him support suggested he engage in '*something creative*'; and this inspired Andy to practice art. Art in prisons offers numerous individual and institutional benefits (see Djurichkovic, 2011; McNeill et al., 2011) and can contribute to better relationships between prisoners and between prisoners and staff (Goddard, 2005; Menning, 2010; Silber, 2005). For Andy, however, it was, initially, a means of escape (Belton and Barclay, 2008), a means of transcending the psychological and emotional trauma he was experiencing, and coping with the social environment that caused it (Cohen and Taylor, 1972).

Andy: [Art] served two purposes for me in that . . . I could just switch myself off – it was an excuse not to listen to people [or] . . . talk to people . . . plus I was finding out the more I done it, the more it was making me feel good about myself and I was getting quite good at it.

Art offers numerous therapeutic benefits to people in prison. It offers an acceptable means of emotional self-expression (Johnson, 2008), and, as Andy suggests, by building a sense of positive achievement (Heenan, 2006; McNeill et al., 2011) it can increase self-esteem (see Cohen, 2009; Cox, and Gelsthorpe, 2008; Currie, 1989; Dean and Field, 2003; Gussak, 2004, 2007, 2009; Silber, 2005). Critically, his interest and immersion in art and art history also contributed to the development of a more constructive personal identity (Currie, 1989; Dean and Field, 2003) through, a perhaps seemingly unlikely, identification with the dedication and endurance that Van Gogh's life symbolised, and in whom he found parallels with his own self-concept and stigmatized social identity in prison.

Andy: I remember reading about Van Gogh and I felt a wee bit of affinity towards him . . . people thought he was mad. He committed suicide . . . but I felt there was a bit of my life in his story. He was a bit of a loner . . . [but he] never gave up. Although people didn't rate him as a painter, he still painted every day of his life. He had such a hard life . . . was shunned by the other artists of the time . . . he was in an asylum, he was depressed for a bit of his life but he was a fantastic artist.

While still 'shunned' by the prisoner community, existing in self-imposed exile on segregation and refusing to attend the workshops, art and his identification with Van Gogh provided a scaffold for Andy to re-frame his self-concept and personal identity. This was further reinforced by other prisoners who sought him out to paint cards and 'scrolls' for their families and by prison staff who requested he paint murals on prison walls, which also provided an 'independent' income. It is important to note, however, that this did not elevate his status in the prisoner community; his victimisation persisted, but it offered a means of coping with, and an alternative lens through which to reframe, this social rejection. In prison, a talent or skill that is valued can be a means of garnering respect. Art, however, is often viewed as a natural ability, rather than a reflection of character, and one that benefits the individual who possesses it, rather than the prisoner community as a whole and is therefore limited in generating respect (Crewe, 2009). However, what Sennett (2003 p.16) terms 'craft love', or doing something well for its own sake rather than to 'compete with or earn the regard of others' (ibid p.14), provides the individual with inner self-respect; 'it's not so much a matter of getting ahead as of becoming inside' (ibid). Thus, there is a distinction to be drawn between 'the respect one earns from others for doing something well' and 'the act of exploring how to do something', 'between . . . being respected and feeling what one does is inherently worthwhile' (ibid). It is this latter sense of achievement and mastery that captures the significance of art for Andy, and which provided 'a profound pleasure in and of itself, and a sense of self-worth which didn't depend on others' (ibid).

Effects of prison

'Fear, anxiety, loneliness, trauma, depression, injustice, powerlessness, violence, rejection and uncertainty are all part of the experience of prison' (Liebling, 1999 p.341). However, the extent to which this does lasting harm is disputed (see for example Bonta and Gendreau, 1990; Haney, 2003; Zamble and Porporino, 1988). The effects of prison vary as widely as experiences of prison, and do so in accordance with individuals' characteristics, age at imprisonment, length of imprisonment and the cumulative or progressive effects of repeat or enduring imprisonment (see for example Armstrong and Weaver, 2013; Crawley and Sparks, 2006; Haney, 2003; Liebling and Maruna, 2005; Maruna and Toch, 2005; Zamble and Porporino, 1988). This sub-theme focuses on the psychological and relational effects of Andy's experience of imprisonment.

Andy has been imprisoned almost continuously since he was 15 years old, in 1977. At this age and stage, an individual's identity is un-established and unformed (Erikson, 1950) and those imprisoned at this age, with limited experience of exercising autonomy, choice and control over their own lives, are more susceptible to the psychological and social effects of prison (Haney, 2003). Moreover, research has shown that longer periods of imprisonment are also more likely to exert an enduring impact on individuals' self-identity and self-esteem (Flanagan,1981) although this conclusion is not consistently upheld (Bonta and Gendreau, 1990). While long-term imprisonment may not necessarily translate into enduring mental health, psychiatric or psychological problems, it can cumulatively and gradually engender negative psychosocial effects. The various psychological mechanisms and behaviours that prisoners develop to adjust to the formal and informal culture of prison can become increasingly natural and, in some cases, internalised (Haney, 2003), which can have far-reaching effects on self-concept, identity and patterns of interactions, and, ultimately, prospects for desistance. Given the duration of Andy's incarceration, coupled with the age at which he was incarcerated, and the absence of any prior or subsequent alternative social roles, it is unsurprising that Andy defines his 'master status' (Goffman, 1963) as that of prisoner:

Andy: I find it hard to be anything other than a guy who's spent 32 years in prison. I've spent all my adult life in prison. The longest period I been out since the age of 15 is 7 weeks, so I'm institutionalised. I know I am.

The concept of 'institutionalisation' (Goffman, 1961) refers to the psychosocial effects of long-term imprisonment, which can include the loss of contact with, or absence, of non-prisoner relationships and loss of prospects outside of the prison (Barton, 1966 cited in Liebling and Maruna, 2005).The 'institutionalised' prisoner generally views himself entirely within the institutional context (Ham, 1980). This process of change involves a number of psychological adaptations including an increasing dependence on the structural regime and the internalisation of interpersonal norms structuring the formal and informal prison culture, which undermine autonomy and incrementally erode prisoners' capacities to make their own decisions and choices, assume personal responsibility and deal with the pressures of life outside prison (Cornwell, 2009; Haney 2003). While the effects of long-term imprisonment vary, prolonged exposure to, or embeddedness in, the prisoner community can give rise to atypical patterns and norms of social interaction (Haney, 2003), which have implications for relationships within prison and following release. Haney (2003 p.41) observes that 'hyper-vigilance, interpersonal distrust and suspicion', or what Andy refers to as paranoia, underpinned by fear, structure thought processes and interactions (see also Crewe, 2009), as a defence against victimisation and exploitation.

Andy: It's made me feel alienated. I feel . . . because of what's been happening . . . it has made me a complete paranoid wreck. I'm going to find it very hard to be in company outside.

In this volatile culture, prisoners regulate, control and suppress their emotions, which over time can result in an 'emotional flatness' or 'emotional over-control' which can be debilitating in future, post-prison relationships (Haney, 2003 p.42). As Crewe (2012) observes, echoed by Andy below, prisoners who are exposed to such a culture of many years often fear that they may never recover their innate emotionality and capacity for intimacy.

Andy: I've lost all my emotions in prison. I don't know how I feel at times. I find it very, very hard to express my feelings, my emotions, because I've spent all my life in prison.

Andy's response to his prolonged experience of exploitation and victimisation was self-containment and social withdrawal. While art helped to ameliorate his diminished sense of self-worth, these combined experiences and effects have resulted in a deep-seated social anxiety, further compounded, as he explains below, by his 'loss of a coherent and satisfactory life narrative' (Crawley and Sparks, 2006 p.63) as a consequence of the aggregate length of his imprisonment.

Andy: I feel I don't mix well, I find it hard to talk, simply because all my memories is prison, even with other prisoners who've got a life that they've come fae and are going back to . . . I find myself sitting in silence most of the time when I'm in company with other prisoners. All my conversations, all I know is prison. I've no memories. All my memories is prison. I just feel so cut off fae the human race.

The loss of a non-prisoner identity, personal relationships, and limited opportunities for personal progression within prison, prolonged periods of isolation from the outside world, in conjunction with the psychosocial effects of imprisonment and the coping or adaptive responses that prisoners can develop pose particular challenges to many former prisoners following release (Crawley and Sparks, 2006; Grounds and Jamieson, 2003; Haney, 2003; Harrington and Spohn, 2007; Liebling, 2004). These challenges are particularly acute for long-term prisoners like Andy who have limited experience of 'being in the world' as an adult, for whom the world to which they return is barely recognisable and for whom a substantial part of their life, when they might otherwise have been invested in employment, relationships and raising families, has passed (Grounds and Jamieson, 2003).

Anticipating and experiencing release

At the time of interview, in 2009, Andy was in the final weeks of his recall to prison, serving out the remainder of his original sentence, which means that he will be released at the age of 48 after 32 years in prison without any statutory or formal supports. Andy expressed a strong desire to desist on release, which was informed primarily by the desire to avoid returning to prison. Arguably, long-term prisoners may not only find their lives have been suspended in prison but the spectre of the prison wall casts a long shadow over their futures. For Andy, whose life had been lived almost entirely in prison and unable to envisage a life beyond prison, his ultimate concerns or hopes for his release were almost exclusively defined by the avoidance of prison, or at least, staying out longer than he had previously been able to.

Andy: I've never been out longer than 7 weeks, so that's going to be a milestone if I get over 7 weeks. I reckon once that happens things will just get better and better for me . . . I just want to live outside prison. . . . I would like to just be who I am the now only not in prison. I find it very difficult to talk about the future because I have never been out longer than 7 weeks in the last 32 years and for me all of a sudden to start saying I'm going to be out for five years – it's difficult for me to comprehend. Obviously I want that to happen but because of the life I've led for so long I find it very difficult . . . to say with belief that it's going to happen.

Andy only made cursory reference to his two periods on parole in 2000 and 2007; given his monolithic experience of imprisonment and his pre-occupation with his existing experiences in prison and his, then pending, release, this is, perhaps, to be expected. On both occasions, motivated to desist, Andy sought to distance himself from Coaston and any former social networks and temptations that might arise. In 2000, he was released to supported accommodation in a large Scottish town, but, with a long-standing, untreated and undisclosed heroin addiction, within the space of a few weeks, he committed armed robbery to subsidise his addiction and returned to prison.

Andy: I didn't want to come back to [Coaston]. I just felt . . . I would always get myself into trouble. I felt that if I was going to try and start a new life that it would need to be somewhere . . . new but . . . I hadnae told anyone that I was a drug addict by this time . . . I ended up robbing the place where I cashed my giros along [and] . . . got myself six years.

In 2007, Andy was again released to supported accommodation in a different town in the same local authority. Although his addiction was, by then, stabilised by Methadone he spent his time drinking in pubs. His lifestyle was so chaotic that he failed to attend appointments and rarely returned to his accommodation. Ultimately he breached the conditions of his licence and was recalled to serve the remainder of his sentence in prison.

Andy: I got myself involved with alcohol and all the local drinkers . . . I was actually living in pubs . . . I got recalled for missing appointments basically and not staying at the address I was meant to stay in . . . although I didn't re-offend . . . I walked away from a hit and a chance of robbing a bookies. That's a big step for me because ten year ago I'd have probably have went and done both.

It has been said that 'while men are in prison their outside behavior patterns remain, in effect, frozen in time . . . until their release' (Zamble and Porporino, 1988 p.152). While Andy's behaviour on release mirrors his earlier behavioural patterns, his resumption of alcohol and drug use on release could equally be construed as a means of managing the trauma of years of victimization and suppressing the anxiety and insecurity of an unfamiliar sense of freedom. Equally, in the absence of any significant relationships on the outside, associating with '*all the local drinkers*' might have been his only means of social interaction, or perhaps he simply surrendered to temptation in the sudden absence of external restrictions and controls. Whatever the reasons, to Andy, despite his recall to prison, his resistance of an opportunity to offend during his last period of release represented a significant departure from earlier behavioural patterns and is central to his belief that he will not re-offend on release this time.

Andy: Although I was drinking I was desperately determined not to re-offend. I knew I was going to get the jail for not going to my appointments but I kept thinking as long as I don't re-offend I am not going to get any added time . . . I still know to this day, that I'll not re-offend as long as I can curb this drink . . . My life is over if I get another sentence.

Andy's desire to avoid imprisonment during his most recent period on release resulted in him resisting an opportunity to offend and is, as he suggested, evidence of his articulated orientation towards desistance. Andy's strategies for pursuing a life free from crime and prison are informed by his previous experiences of release and are solely comprised of 'avoidance goals' (Elliot, 1999), echoing Burnett's (1992 p.187) 'avoider-veterans', whose motivation to desist seemed to be rooted in repeated experiences of imprisonment and the subsequent ramifications. His sole strategies for realising this are the avoidance of Coaston, former associates, involvement in offending and substance use. Critically, however, the desire to avoid further imprisonment does not readily translate into its realisation (Armstrong and Weaver, 2013, Soyer, 2014), as Burnett (1992) observed. Indeed, despite the misappropriation of this study by the then Home Secretary, Michael Howard, to claim that 'Prison Works' (see Burnett and Maruna, 2004), a ten year follow up study of the same people, over 60 percent of whom subsequently recidivated, 'contradict[ed] the easy assumption that a distaste for imprisonment, itself, leads to a lifestyle that avoids repeating the experience' (Burnett and Maruna, 2004 p.401). Leaving to one side that prison might be more accurately described as 'an expensive way of making bad people worse' (Home Office, 1990 p.6 cited in Burnett and Maruna, 2004) (see also Gendreau, Goggin and Cullen, 1999), and even indulging the unlikely possibility that prison might exert a deterrent effect (McGuire, 1995), that this might happen for only a few, and even then for some after one or two sentences while for others only after twenty or thirty years makes clear that prison is an expensive and unpredictable technique for triggering reflection and change (Armstrong and Weaver, 2010; Burnett, 1992). The reality is that, despite a desire to desist, vulnerable prisoners, such as Andy, 'often return to prison quickly between sentences, showing evidence of poor coping in the community as well as in prison' (Liebling, 2012 p.65).

If, as discussed in Chapter 2, desistance is connected to positive identity transformations, the development of agency, supportive social relationships and concrete opportunities to live differently, then the 'pains of imprisonment'[3] (Sykes, 1958) represent a profound challenge to former prisoners' on release. Moreover, avoiding risky behaviours and associates is generally insufficient to overcome the considerable challenges to social integration that former prisoners face, including obtaining and sustaining accommodation, managing restricted finances and limited supportive social networks or opportunities to develop them (Burnett and Maruna, 2004). Long-term prisoners, particularly those imprisoned at an early age, are often released with few independent living skills, limited experience of employment or basic possessions which essentially means that they are 'starting from scratch' (Crawley and Sparks, 2006 p.75) from a position of significant disadvantage. Unaccustomed to exercising personal responsibility, and with few inner resources or constructive coping mechanisms to deal with unanticipated life challenges, when the external structures and controls they have been accustomed to rely on have been removed, former prisoners can resort to tried and tested behaviours to manage the stress, anxiety and loneliness they experience (Haney, 2003).

Conclusion

This chapter has discussed Andy's life beyond the fragmentation of the Del, which has been lived almost exclusively in prison. His experiences and the effects of imprisonment have thus formed the principal focus of the analysis, concluding with a discussion of his experiences and aspirations for his, then pending, release. In particular, this chapter illustrated that in the early stages of imprisonment, Andy imported the previous norms of interaction that he had employed with the Del, as a means of negotiating the relational rules and modes of interactions that inhere in the prisoner community, all of which, in addition to the formal culture of the prison, comprise 'conditioning structures' in that they shape the situations of action through the constraints and enablements they engender

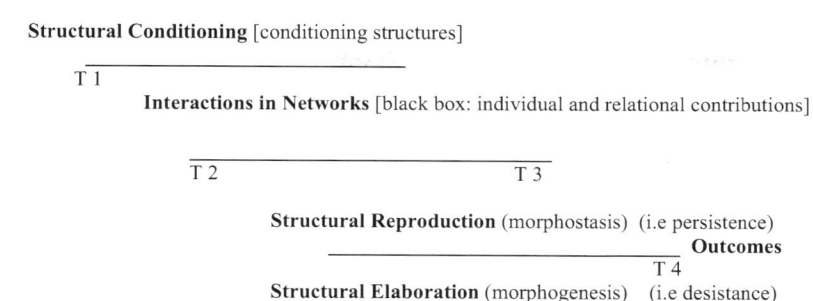

Structural Conditioning [conditioning structures]
──────────────────────────────
T 1
        Interactions in Networks [black box: individual and relational contributions]
       ──────────────────────────────
       T 2   T 3
               Structural Reproduction (morphostasis) (i.e persistence)
               ──────────────────────────────── **Outcomes**
                                                       T 4
               Structural Elaboration (morphogenesis) (i.e desistance)

Figure 10.1 Overview of investigative framework

(T1–T2 in Figure 10.1). The conditioning structures can be further conceptualised, then, as the set of relational rules in the prisoner community, which are informed by, replicate or perhaps exaggerate those characteristic of their interactions outside (Wacquant, 2000) which Andy followed reflexively or, in other words, the constraints which he negotiated in a relational way. Andy's responses to the relational rules and constraints of the prisoner community contributed to his stigmatized status, which, in turn, influenced the nature of his interpersonal interactions with other prisoners, which then shaped and influenced his experience of prison (T2–T3). His involvement in the drug scene and subsequent drug use and the ensuing interpersonal repercussions (T2–T3) contributed to the outcomes, his social withdrawal, self-harm and ultimate investment in art (T4), which represent the conditioning structures (at T1) in the next phase of the morphogenetic cycle, creating new constraints and enablements.

The experience and effects of long-term imprisonment significantly compromise prospects for desistance but, as this chapter has also illustrated, individual level factors are also important (Burnett, 1992). In the early stages of his imprisonment, Andy highly identified with a deviant subculture, and, at an impressionable age, he quickly internalized the norms of the prisoner community (Clemmer, 1970); while his method of adaptation to the prison culture contributed to the pains of his experience of imprisonment, this did nothing to 'deter' him or encourage him to realise a lifestyle that avoided a return to prison. Over time the cumulative experience and effects of a life lived in prison have not only appreciably weakened his prospects for desistance but, while no longer identifying so explicitly with a deviant subculture, in removing all memory or knowledge of another way of living, prison has served to crystallise his implicit identification with prison, where identification in this latter context translates into recognition and familiarity, and where prison represents the only way of being in the world he can tangibly envisage.

Notes

1 Sadly, Andy passed away suddenly on Sunday 11th January 2015. His contribution to this book is an extremely important one and I hope this chapter is able to honour his memory in some way.

2 Where Clemmer (1958) discussed the conditions determining the degree of socialisation into prisoner culture, such that one can be said to exist, Sykes (1958) discussed the conditions explaining the existence of a prisoner culture (Mathiesen, 1966).
3 The pains of imprisonment include the deprivation of autonomy, relatedness and security, involve the suppression of emotion and the adoption of dysfunctional norms of social interaction (Sykes, 1958) and, in Andy's case, include exposure to systematic and enduring victimization and exploitation.

References

Armstrong, S., and Weaver, B. (2010) *What Do the Punished Think of Punishment? The Comparative Experience of Short Prison Sentences and Community Based Punishments*. SCCJR Research 04/10. Available at http://www.sccjr.ac.uk/documents/Report%202010%2004%20-%20User%20Views%20of%20Punishment(1).pdf, accessed 14/07/11.

Armstrong, S., and Weaver, B. (2013) Persistent Punishment: User Views of Short Prison Sentences. *Howard Journal of Criminal Justice* 52(3), pp.285–305.

Barton, R. (1966) *Institutional Neurosis* (2nd ed.). Bristol: Wright.

Belton, S., and Barclay, L. (2008) *J Block Women of Art Project Report: Evaluating Community Education in a Prison Setting*. Dawn House in association with Ruby Gaea. Darwin, Australia: Charles Darwin University, http://www.cdu.edu.au/gshp/documents/JBlockWomenofArtProjectReport.pdf, accessed 09/07/13.

Bonta, J., and Gendreau. P. (1990) Re-examining the Cruel and Unusual Punishment of Prison Life. *Law and Human Behavior* 14(4), pp.347–372.

Boyle, J. (1977) *A Sense of Freedom*. London: Canongate /Pan Books.

Burnett, R. (1992) *The Dynamics of Recidivism*. Oxford: University of Oxford Centre for Criminological Research.

Burnett, R., and Maruna, S. (2004) So Prison Works Does It?: The Criminal Careers of 130 Men Released From Prison Under Home Secretary Michael Howard. *Howard Journal of Criminal Justice* 43(4), pp.405–419.

Clemmer, D. (1958) *The Prison Community*. New York, NY: Rinehart.

Clemmer, D. (1970) Prisonization, in Johnston, N., Savitz, L., and Wolfgang, M.E. (eds.) *The Sociology of Punishment and Correction*. New York: Wiley.

Cohen, M.L. (2009) Choral Singing and Prison Inmates: Influences of Performing in a Prison Choir. *Journal of Correctional Education* 60(1), pp.52–65.

Cohen, S., and Taylor, L. (1972) *Psychological Survival*. Harmondsworth: Penguin.

Collins, H. (1997) *Autobiography of a Murderer*. London: Macmillan.

Condry, R. (2012) Prisoners and Their Families, in Crewe, B., and Bennett, J. (eds.) *The Prisoner*. Routledge, pp.67–78.

Cornwell, D. (2009) *The Penal Crisis and the Clapham Omnibus: Questions and Answers in Restorative Justice*. Hampshire: Waterside Press.

Cox, A., and Gelsthorpe, L. (2008) *Beats & Bars. Music in Prisons: An Evaluation*. Cambridge: University of Cambridge.

Crawley, E., and Sparks, R. (2006) Is There Life After Imprisonment? How Elderly Men Talk About Imprisonment and Release. *Criminology and Criminal Justice* 6(1), pp.63–82.

Crewe, B. (2009) *The Prisoner Society: Power, Adaptation and Social Life in an English Prison*. Oxford: Oxford University Press, Clarendon Studies in Criminology.

Crewe, B. (2012) Prison Culture and the Prisoner Society, in Crewe, B., and Bennett, J. (eds.) *The Prisoner*. New York, NY: Routledge, pp.27–39.

Crewe, B., and Bennett, J. (eds.) (2012) *The Prisoner*. New York, NY: Routledge.

Currie, C. (1989) *Art In Prison: An Evaluation of a New Zealand Prison Programme*. Wellington: Institute of Criminology, University of Wellington.

Dean, C., and Field, J. (2003) *Building Lives Through an Artistic Community*, IFECS A Conference 2003, Australasian Corrections Education Association Inc. http://www.acea.org.au/Content/2003%20papers/Paper%20Dean_Field.pdf, accessed 09/07/13.

Djurichkovic, A. (2011) *Arts in Prisons*. Report for Arts Access Australia, Sydney: University of Technology, Sydney. http://www.artsaccessaustralia.org/resources/research-and-reports/136-art-in-prisons, accessed 09/07/13.

Donati, P. (2011) *Relational Sociology: A New Paradigm for the Social Sciences*. Abingdon: Routledge.

Edgar, K., and Martin, C. (2002) *Conflicts and Violence in Prison*. Egham, Surrey: ESRC Violence Research Programme. http://www.esrc.ac.uk/my-esrc/grants/L133251042/outputs/Read/a8f0a518-9265-4a8f-afbc-1a8cbcf86544, accessed 04/04/15.

Edgar, K., O'Donnell, I., and Martin, C. (2003) *Prison Violence: The Dynamics of Conflict, Fear and Power*. Cullompton: Willan.

Elliot, A.J. (1999) Approach and Avoidance Motivation and Achievement Goals. *Educational Psychologist* 34(3), pp.169–189.

Erikson, E.H. (1950) *Childhood and Society*. New York, NY: Norton.

Flanagan, O.J. (1981) Psychology, Progress, and the Problem of Reflexivity: A Study in the Epistemological Foundations of Psychology. *Journal of the History of the Behavioral Sciences* 17(3), pp.375–386.

Gendreau, P., Goggin, C., and Cullen, F. (1999) *The Effects of Prison Sentences on Recidivism, A Report to the Corrections Research and Development and Aboriginal Policy Branch, Solicitor General of Canada*. Ottawa: Public Works & Government Services Canada.

Goddard, G. (2005) *Fair! An Evaluation of a 'Music in Prisons' and National Youth Theatre Collaboration and HMP YOI, Bullwood Hall*. London: Irene Taylor Trust.

Goffman, E. (1961) *Asylums: Essays on the Social Situation of Mental Patients and Other Inmates*. New York, NY: Anchor Books.

Goffman, E. (1963) *Stigma: Notes on the Management of Spoiled Identity*. Harmondsworth: Prentice-Hall.

Grounds, A.T., and Jamieson, R. (2003) No Sense of an Ending: Researching the Experience of Imprisonment and Release Among Republican Ex-prisoners. *Theoretical Criminology* 7(3), pp.347–362.

Gussak, D. (2004) Art Therapy With Prison Inmates: A Pilot Study. *Arts in Psychotherapy* 31(4), pp.245–259.

Gussak, D. (2007) The Effectiveness of Art Therapy in Reducing Depression in Prison Populations. *International Journal of Offender Therapy and Comparative Criminology* 5(4), pp.444–460.

Gussak, D. (2009) The Effects of Art Therapy on Male and Female Inmates: Advancing the Research Base. *Arts in Psychotherapy* 36(1), pp.5–12.

Ham, J.N. (1980) Aged and Infirm Male Prison Inmates. *Aging*, pp.24–31.

Haney, C. (2003) Mental Health Issues in Long-Term Solitary and 'Supermax' Confinement. *Crime and Delinquency* 49(1), pp.124–156.

Harrington, M., and Spohn, C. (2007) Do Race, Age, and Sex Matter in Sentencing Decisions? Use of the Total Incarceration Variable in a Non-guideline Jurisdiction. *Journal of Research in Crime and Delinquency* 44(1), pp.36–63.

Heenan, D. (2006) Art as Therapy: An Effective Way of Promoting Positive Mental Health? *Disability & Society* 21(2), pp.179–191.

Home Office. (1990) *Crime, Justice and Protecting the Public*. London: HMSO.

James, E. (2003) *A Life Inside: A Prisoner's Notebook*. London: Atlantic.
Jeglic, E.L., Vaudernoff, H.A., and Doriovick, P.J. (2005) The Function of Self-Harm in a Forensic Population. *International Journal of Offender Therapy and Cognitive Criminology* 49(2), pp.131–142.
Jewkes, Y. (2005) Prisoners and the Press. *Criminal Justice Matters* 59(1), pp.26–27.
Jewkes, Y. (2012) Identity and Adaptation in Prison, in Crewe, B., and Bennett, J. (eds.) *The Prisoner*, Cullompton: Willan, pp.40–52.
Johnson, L.M. (2008) A Place for Art in Prison: ARDT as a Tool for Rehabilitation and Management. *Southwest Journal of Criminal Justice* 5(2), pp.100–120.
Larner, J., and Tefferteller, R. (1964) *The Addict in the Street*. New York, NY: Grove Press.
Liebling, A. (1999) Doing Research in Prison: Breaking the Silence? *Theoretical Criminology* 3(2), pp.147–173.
Liebling, A. (2004) *Prisons and Their Moral Performance: A Study of Values, Quality, and Prison Life*. Oxford: Oxford University Press.
Liebling, A. (2012, 29 May) Can Human Beings Flourish in Prison? PPT Lecture, London. http://www.insidetime.org/resources/Publications/Can-Humans-Flourish-in-Prison_PPT_Liebling_Lecture-29May12.pdf, accessed 04/03/13.
Liebling, A., and Maruna, S. (2005) *The Effects of Imprisonment*. Cullompton: Willan.
Maruna, S., and Toch, H. (2005) The Impact of Incarceration on the Desistance Process, in Travis, J., and Visher, C. (eds.) *Prisoner Reentry and Public Safety in America*. New York, NY: Cambridge University Press, pp.139–178.
Mathiesen, T. (1966) The Sociology of Prisons: Problems for Future Research. *British Journal of Sociology* 17(4), pp.360–379.
McGuire, J. (ed.) (1995) *What Works: Reducing Offending*. Chichester: Wiley.
McNeill, F., Anderson, K., Colvin, S, Overy, K., Sparks, R., and Tett, L. (2011) Kunst projecten en What Works, een stimulans voor desistance? *Justitiele Verkenningen* 37(5), pp.80–101.
Menning, N. (2010) Singing With Conviction: New Zealand Prisons and Maori Populations. *International Journal of Community Music* 3(1), pp.111–120.
Pearson, G. (1987) *The New Heroin Users*. Oxford: Blackwell.
Sapsford, R.J. (1978) Life-Sentence Prisoners: Psychological Changes During Sentence. *British Journal of Criminology* 18(2), pp.128–145.
Sennett, R. (2003) *Respect: The Formation of Character in a World of Inequality*. London: Allan Lane.
Silber, L. (2005) Bars Behind Bars: The Impact of a Women's Prison Choir on Social Harmony. *Music Education Research* 7(2), pp.251–271.
Sim, J. (1994) Tougher Than the Rest: Men in Prison, in Newburn, T., and Stanko, E. (eds.) *Men, Masculinities and Crime: Just Boys Doing Business*. London: Routledge, pp.100–117.
Smith, R., Grimshaw, R., Romeo, R., and Knapp, M. (2007) *Poverty and Disadvantage Among Prisoners' Families*. Centre for Crime and Justice Studies and Joseph Rowntree Foundation.
Soyer, M. (2014) The Imagination of Desistance: A Juxtaposition of the Construction of Incarceration as a Turning Point and the Reality of Recidivism. *British Journal of Criminology* 54, pp.91–108.
Sykes, G.M. (1958) *Society of Captives: A Study of a Maximum Security Prison*. Princeton, NJ: Princeton University Press.
Toch, H. (1975) *Men in Crisis: Human Breakdowns in Prison*. Chicago, IL: Aldine.
Toch, H. (1992) *Violent Men: An Inquiry Into the Psychology of Violence*. Washington, DC: American Psychological Association.

Wacquant, L. (2000) The New 'Peculiar Institution': On the Prison as Surrogate Ghetto. *Theoretical Criminology* 4(3), pp.377–389.

Wahidin, A. (2006) Time and the Prison Experience. *Sociological Research Online* 11(1). http://socresonline.org.uk/11/1/wahidin.html, accessed 04/03/13.

Zamble, E., and Porporino, F. (1988) *Coping, Behaviour and Adaptation in Prison Inmates.* New York, NY: Springer.

11 The dynamics of desistance[1,2]

This book has elaborated how desistance is accomplished (or not) through the life stories of 6 men comprising part of a co-offending peer group, whose lives had shared beginnings but divergent outcomes. In so doing, Chapter 4 and the individual stories comprising Chapters 5–10 reveal the dynamics of offending and desistance as they occurred within and between individuals-in-relation while situating their lived experiences within their shared historical, structural and cultural contexts. Donati's relational sociology (2011) was the conceptual lens through which the roles of different social relations in variously constraining or enabling change were investigated and, thus, through which individual and relational contributions to desistance were analysed.

The conceptual schema applied in this study (see Figure 11.1) is an adaptation of the morphogenetic framework as theorised by Archer, to illustrate the conceptual schema progressed by Donati (2011) (see Chapter 3). In so doing, the analysis has demonstrated how social relations (different from conditioning structures) are configured in the T2–T3 phase (see Figure 11.3 below) to observe what happens in interactions with significant others. They have constraints and enablements from outside, as well as their own internal network dynamics, which are distinct from what happens inside individuals (individual contributions) (see Figure 11.2 below) as they autonomously evaluate their situation, take decisions and so on (analysed through Archer's internal conversation). The elaborated structure, or outcomes, (T4 in Figure 11.1) thus emerge as products of both the individual's application of their personal reflexivity (individual contributions) and of the interactive dynamics of their relational network(s) (relational contributions). This is because, as the preceding chapters have illustrated, social relations have their own powers and qualities in contributing to the final outcome.

Drawing on Donati's (2011) relational sociology in general and his theory of relational reflexivity in particular, and therefore taking the social relation, rather than the individual or the structural, as the primary unit of analysis, the individual stories have illuminated how desistance is co-produced between individuals-in-relation. Each story foregrounds a conceptualisation of a reflexive individual whose ultimate concerns emerge from, are immersed in, respond to and shape their relational worlds. In revealing these relational processes, the individual stories have illustrated the centrality of the relational to the individual and thus to

The dynamics of desistance 213

Structural Conditioning [conditioning structures]
―――――――――――――――――――――
T 1

        Interactions in Networks [black box: individual and relational contributions]
        ――――――――――――――――――――――――
        T 2   T 3

            Structural Reproduction (morphostasis) (i.e persistence)
            ――――――――――――――――――――― **Outcomes**
                                    T 4
            Structural Elaboration (morphogenesis) (i.e desistance)

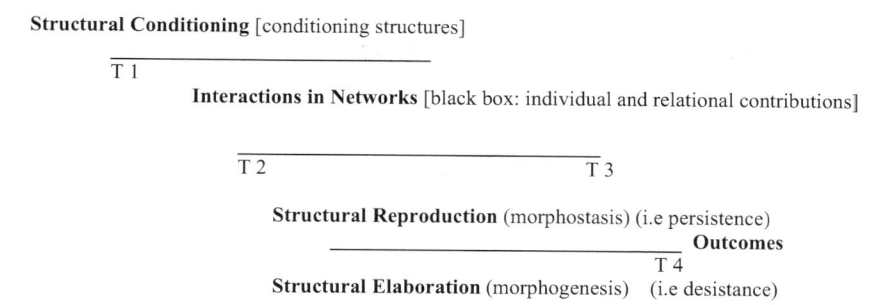

Figure 11.1 Overview of investigative framework

Structural Conditioning [conditioning structures]   **ME**
―――――――――――――――――――――
T 1

       Social Interaction [personal reflexivity: individual contributions] **I**
       ――――――――――――――――――――――
       T 2   T 3

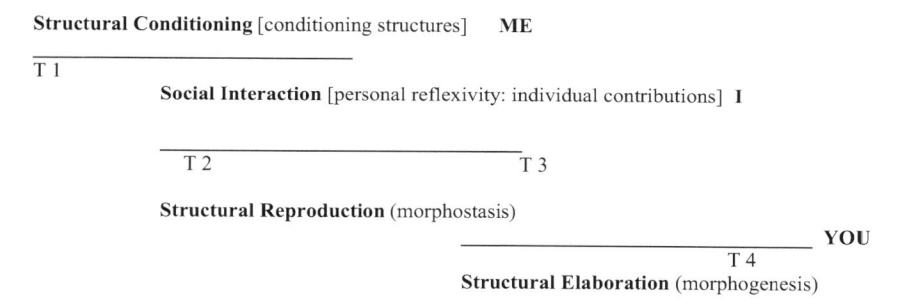

          Structural Reproduction (morphostasis)
               ――――――――――――――――――――― **YOU**
                                     T 4
             Structural Elaboration (morphogenesis)

Figure 11.2 The morphogenetic sequence applied to the internal conversation (individual contributions)

    Structural Conditioning [conditioning structures]   **I**
    ――――――――――――――――――――――
    T 1
           Interactions in Networks [relational contributions]
           ――――――――――――――――――――― **Me- We**
           T 2   T 3

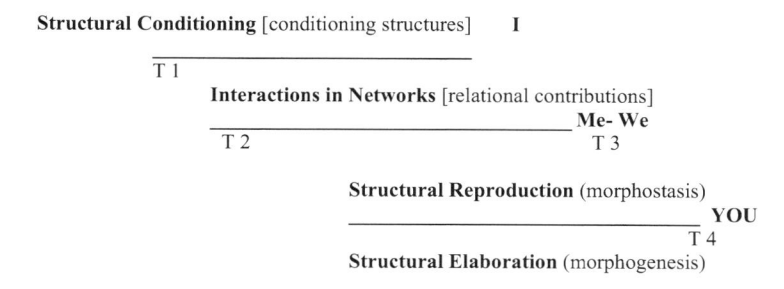

                Structural Reproduction (morphostasis)
                  ――――――――――――――――――――― **YOU**
                                           T 4
                Structural Elaboration (morphogenesis)

Figure 11.3 The morphogenetic sequence applied to social relations (relational contributions)

processes of change in a broad sense, and to desistance from crime in particular. Taken together, what the individual stories have revealed is an understanding of desistance as a complex, individualised, reflexive and relational process. This chapter represents the final substantive chapter of these eight data chapters and examines the dynamics of desistance as they emerge across these stories.

214 *The dynamics of desistance*

This chapter commences with a brief collective biographical overview and then proceeds to explore the recurrent elements across individuals' narratives of change elaborated under the superordinate themes '*Roles, religiosity, reflexivity, relationality and desistance*' and '*The meanings and outcomes of work*' through the lens of the conceptual framework deployed throughout this book.

Brief collective biographical overview

While noting Andy's persistence in offending, there is nothing remarkable about the age-graded trajectories of these individuals' offending careers. However, as the preceding chapters have illuminated, there are significant points of convergence and divergence across these men's pathways out of crime, following the fragmentation of the Del.

The fragmentation of the Del and its consequences influenced the dynamics of each person's offending behaviour and their relational networks. Seth, Jed and Jay relocated to London, and, alongside others who comprised one side of the warring Del, formed a 'revised group'. Of these three, only Seth relocated with the intention of desisting. Seth saw the move, his pending fatherhood and participation in employment as an opportunity to consolidate the process of change he had already begun in prison. For Jay, his participation in employment, enabled by the mutual support and exchange of resources among the revised group, diminished the desirability of participation in acquisitive crime, and his use of Amphetamine reduced his participation in violent crime. However, his recreational drug use progressively led to his participation in drug dealing and poly-drug misuse which he ultimately ceased following his conversion to Christianity, to which he attributes his desistance from crime. Jed similarly had no intention to desist following his relocation to London but, like Jay, the economic outcomes of his participation in employment diminished the desirability of involvement in acquisitive crime while enabling the maintenance of a lifestyle that included participation in alcohol-related violence. Jed desisted for a period of 14 years after he met his partner Rachel, although following his return to Coaston and his inability to acquire employment, he temporarily reverted to offending.

Table 11.1 Overview of offending trajectories

	Born / age	Offence type	No. of self-reported convictions	Age at onset[3]	Age at desistance[4]	Length of offending career: years
Andy	1961 / 48	Acquisitive	19	13	N/A	35
Seth	1965 / 43	Acquisitive & Violent	50	9	22 (1987)	13
Harry	1961 / 47	Acquisitive & Violent	3 pages	13	33 (1994)	20
Jed	1961 / 48	Acquisitive & Violent	80	14	30 (1991)	16
Jay	1963 / 46	Acquisitive & Violent	20	13	29 (1992)	16
Evan	1965 / 43	Acquisitive	100	14	29 (1994)	15

Following the feud, Andy associated with the Nixons in prison (the opposing 'side' of the Del) and continued to do so following his release and his return to Coaston. This resulted in a violent reprisal by the Websters, and from this juncture, Andy had no further contact with either faction although, like Evan, he continued to engage in acquisitive crime alone and has spent a total of 32 years in prison. Unlike the others, Harry and Evan prudentially avoided positioning themselves with either side of the warring Del. They both remained in Coaston and both continued to engage in offending behaviour enabled by their participation in alternative relational networks. For Harry, his involvement with 'the football crowd', with whom his brother associated, influenced his diversification into football-related violent offending. With his deepening connection to his partner Millie, however, he eventually relinquished housebreaking but it was not until he became a father that he ultimately desisted. After a brief period of abstaining from acquisitive crime following his release from prison, Evan, echoing Jay's story, diversified from acquisitive crime into drug dealing, reflecting his involvement in drug use with an alternative friendship group. Like Jay, he desisted from offending following his conversion to Christianity.

Despite differences in their responses to the fragmentation of the Del, broad commonalities across their individual pathways emerged relating to the role of extant and new social networks, intimate relationships, families of formation and employment in variously triggering, enabling or constraining desistance. However, what the individual analyses particularly revealed were distinct differences in *how* these social relations variously enabled or constrained desistance. Taking the social relation as a central unit of analysis has facilitated an exploration of the shifting configurations, meanings and influences of these social relations both over time and in interaction with other social relations. This has yielded interesting differences as to how, when and why these social relations variously enabled or constrained an individual's process of change, which can be broadly attributable to important differences in the nature, form and meaning of these different social relations, and in individual responses to them, refracted through the lens of their individual and relational concerns. It is, however, a summation of the recurrent elements of the change process, manifesting across these individuals' stories, which this chapter is concerned to reveal.

Roles, religiosity, reflexivity, relationality and desistance

The role of extant and new social networks in supporting desistance

In elaborating the role that extant and new social relationships play in variously constraining or enabling desistance, Chapter 4 and the individual stories comprising Chapters 5–10 illustrated that the outcomes cannot be reduced to the (interpersonal) effects of one person on another. Rather it is the application of the reflexivity of an individual or of individuals-in-relation, brought to bear on social relations through the lens of their individual or relational concerns, that is critical in contributing to the outcomes. Thus the impact of friends and friendship groups, intimate relations, families of formation and employment (discussed in turn) on individual behaviour is attributable to the bonds maintained *between* people; bonds that constitute their reciprocal orientations towards each other and the chains of meaning that these particular types of social relations entail for individuals, who bring their own reflexivity to bear in a manner consistent with their ultimate concerns (Donati, 2011). The chains of meanings that characterise a given social relation are 'the complicated tissue of relations between culture, personality, social norms' and lived experiences (Donati, 2011 p.130).

Conditioning structures enabling change: friendship groups (T1 Figure 11.1)

This sub-section offers an illustrative overview of the way conditioning structures (T1) shape the situations of actions for individuals and their friendship groups, and the ways in which these individuals and collectivities in turn influence and shape their conditioning structures (T4–T4).

The conditioning influence of the structural/cultural context (T1–T2 in Figure 11.1) shapes the social environment and, as part of that, people's situations of action such that some courses of action are enabled and others constrained (Archer, 2007; Donati, 2011). The properties of the structural/cultural context include the results of past actions, the accessibility of roles and resources and the prevalence of internalised beliefs (Archer, 1995, 2010), as well as the sets of relations in which people find themselves (Donati, 2011). The conditioning structures can also, then, be understood as the sets of relational rules prescribing how one should behave in a certain way towards others, according to the norms that the context prescribes, which the individual must follow reflexively, or the constraints which can be negotiated step by step in a relational way (Donati, 2011, personal communication). What is normatively expected of a person form the constraints and enablements in their conditioning structures, but these are different in different contexts and social spheres – for example, among the 'revised group', 'the Christians' and 'the football crowd' – and they may be more or less constraining or enabling, more or less explicit or implicit, requiring more or less reflexivity.

Notwithstanding the divergent responses among 'the revised group' to the shift in conditioning structures that their collective relocation to London engendered (see Jed's, Seth's and Jay's stories), they shared a desire to extricate themselves from the 'relational bads' (Donati, 2011) (of betrayal, mistrust, and interpersonal violence) emerging from the feud, as well as a desire to access the employment opportunities afforded by the construction boom in London. Employment in a new environment heralded economic and social changes to the 'revised group's' conditioning structures that enabled change (however differently manifest) (T1 in Figure 11.1). The recognition and pursuit of these opportunities can be construed as an outcome of the exercise of reflexivity and as an expression of their individual and collective agency (T2–T3). Critically, re-establishing a revised and collaborative relational network in a new location facilitated the re-emergence of the relational goods of social trust, solidarity, and social connectedness; goods that had been threatened by the feud and from which other goods including new knowledge, skills, employment and economic resources were derived as secondary emergent effects (Donati, 2006). These secondary effects in turn necessarily shaped the collective conditioning structures of the revised group (T1 in the next morphogenetic cycle).

While the divide within the group triggered an individual and collective reflexive re-evaluation of their relationships with each other and their associated and shared practices, some of the group members' (such as Adam and Seth) individual relational concerns with their intimate partners (T1) (discussed further below) also impacted the internal network dynamics within the group. Personal relationships exerted a distinct change promotive influence on the behaviour of *some* of those in the revised group[5] and their lifestyles. However, the acquisition of new relationships and associated social roles and practices exerted a significant influence not only on individual behaviour but on the interactive dynamics of the revised group. This operated in conjunction with an increasing disillusionment with their previous lifestyles and the threat continued offending potentially posed to these new roles and relationships, to their shifting identities and to employment opportunities. The priorities and concerns of individuals shifted away from the group and towards their families of formation. Associated changes in their behaviour then exerted a constraint on the behaviour of others, who found they had less support from their desisting peers for engagement in offending behaviour. This reflected a change in the relational rules in this revised relational context, to which they responded by reflecting on their position and modifying their behaviour, motivated by a desire to support each other. Their individual and relational contributions (T2–T3 in Figure 11.1) to the outcomes (T4) are discussed further below. Critically, individuals' capacities to access and thus realise and sustain these opportunities emerged from the *mutual and reciprocal* exchange of support and resources among the revised group, as an outcome of their *collaborative* efforts, of shifts in their *interactive* dynamics and in the diversified *relational* contexts the move facilitated, both within and beyond the group. Individuals responded differently to these changes in the group through the lens of their own individual and relational concerns. I have suggested that individual responses to these changes in their conditioning structures illustrate that the outcomes cannot be explained in terms of external forces exerting an exogenous effect; rather they reflect individuals' varying receptivity and response to these changes, reflexively mediated through the lens of their individual and relational concerns (discussed further in the following sub-sections).

The shifts in Harry's conditioning structures as a consequence of the fragmentation of the Del (T1 in Figure 11.1) and his association with an alternative 'subculture' ('the football crowd' (atT4–T1) enabled him to continue offending. Collectively, the interactive dynamics and shared projects and practices he moved into (T2–T3) heralded a diversification in the context in which his violent offending behaviour occurred. Identification to and with this new group necessarily required an acceptance and adoption of the norms and rules of associational belonging (Hogg and Hardie, 1991) characteristic of the membership of this group (T1). These norms or rules included attendance at each football game and an explicit and unwavering support of the club which was often expressed through violent conflicts with members of the opposing club. The changes in Harry's conditioning structures manifest in his extrication from the Del and his association with a new group thus enabled changes in his personal and social identity, and moral status, in the transition from offender to football fan or 'hooligan'. However, whilst representing a measurable break from his former lifestyle, not least in terms of shifts in the frequency and context of, and thus justifications and motivations for, his offending (the nature of which was also altered as an outcome of his relationship with Millie), there is evidence of some continuity in terms of his immersion in an alternative subculture which afforded him a source of status, recognition, masculinity, community and belonging in which anti-social and violent behaviours were variously tolerated and expected. Football and the associated 'fan' culture and social life structured Harry's social relationships, lifestyle and identity for eight years after the fragmentation of the Del.

Following the fragmentation of the Del, both Jay and Evan (independently of each other) participated in recreational drug use. Ultimately, their addiction (and the lifestyle it engendered) created the conditions which, differently, shaped and influenced their offending behaviour, lifestyles and subjective well-being, as the pursuit of drugs manifested as their ultimate concern. Independently, their addiction and association with similarly situated others structured their situations of action (T1 in the next phase of the morphogenetic cycle) and generated new constraints and enablements. As an outcome of their increasing desperation that the deleterious consequences that their addiction produced for their physical and mental well-being, relational contexts and lifestyles (at T4–T1), both Jay and Evan became progressively receptive to their friends' faith-based interventions and testimonies of change. Their internalisation of the teachings of Pentecostal Christianity, influenced by their interactions with friends from the Del who had converted (T2–T3), ultimately shaped their identities, behaviours and lifestyle (T4), and, in turn, the sets of relations in which they were involved (at T1 in the next phase of the morphogenetic cycle).

Religion traditionally encapsulates particular beliefs, values, attitudes and practices that, in conjunction with the relational ties formed through religious institutions, create a new world, and thus shapes the conditioning structures, for the convert to inhabit (Rambo, 1993) (T1 in the next phase of the morphogenetic cycle). As both Jay's and Evan's stories illustrated, in the process of being 'born again' it is not only the individual's sense of morality that is reconfigured, but his sense of what it means to be a man (van Klinken, 2012) which, together, shaped their identities, behaviours and lifestyles and created the conditions in which a new way of living was realisable and a new experience of the self was brought into being.

Critically (and as implied in the foregoing analysis) conditioning structures can only exert constraints and enablements *in relation to* something for someone – so the extent to which they constrain and enable is dependent on how the individual receives and responds to them, which itself cannot be disconnected from the way in which significant others receive and respond to them, and thus which influences their interactions. The following sub-section offers an overview of what this process of individual reflexivity entails before situating it in the relational context in which it arises.

Individual/personal reflexivity and the change process: friendship groups T2–T3 (Figures 11.1 and 11.2)

Archer (2003) specifies that personal reflexivity is the mediating force between conditioning structures and agency; further, this process of reflexive deliberation is the means through which people identify and order the ultimate concerns which they commit themselves to. Archer argues that reflexivity performs this mediating role 'by virtue of the fact that we deliberate about ourselves in relation to the social situations we confront, certainly fallibly, certainly incompletely' (Archer, 2007 p.42). The process of reflexivity is conceptualised by Archer as an 'internal conversation'; she argues that it is this dialogue about ourselves in relation to our social worlds that makes active agents, people who can exercise some governance in, or exercise control over, their lives as opposed to passive agents to whom things simply happen. The activation of the causal powers of the conditioning structures depends on the individual's ultimate concerns and in turn the projects and practices (broadly, the means through which people intend to realise their ultimate concerns) that they commit themselves to. In turn, people can be said to actively mediate their own social and cultural conditioning in that 'reflexive deliberations have causal powers, that is intrinsic ones which enable us to monitor and modify ourselves, and extrinsic ones which allow us to mediate and modify our societies' (Archer, 2003 p.46).

Figure 11.2 illustrates Archer's morphogenetic sequence applied to the internal conversation. Archer disaggregates the self into the temporal concepts of 'Me', 'I' and 'You'. Generally, 'Me' refers to the pre-existing self; 'I' refers to the present self; 'You' refers to the future self. The conditioning 'Me' phase, and the emerging results of previous reflexive deliberations fed through previous interactions, condition an individual's actions at T1. The 'I' phase (at T2–T3) evokes an internal conversation, conditioned by the pre-existing self, the 'Me', which defines a future direction, and in so doing shapes and influences the 'You' of the future (T4). It is through these means that we decide on courses of actions by deliberating about ourselves, our current concerns and social contexts, and by envisioning and pursuing projects that reflect and define who we are, that enable us to realise our ultimate concerns in circumstances that are, to some extent, pre-defined. This internal conversation temporarily concludes when the different parts of the self arrive at a consensus about the projected course of action that best reflects the individual's 'constellations of concerns', (Archer, 2007 p.42) but which is also realisable within the constraints of the individual's social circumstances. Archer suggests that the internal conversation can be conceptualized as a three-part schema, namely discernment, deliberation and dedication (see Chapter 3). This internal conversation 'takes place' in the middle stage (T2–T3) of each morphogenetic cycle (Archer, 2000 p.231).

As elaborated across the individual stories, individual responses to the changes in their conditioning structures that the feud heralded illustrate that the outcomes cannot be explained in terms of external forces exerting an exogenous effect; rather these outcomes reflect individuals' varying receptivity and responses to these changes reflexively mediated through the lens of their individual and relational concerns. Upon their relocation to London, neither Jed nor Jay had the intention of desisting. However, their reflexive response to the changes in their conditioning structures engendered by the move, participation in employment and association with the revised group (T1 in Figure 11.2), triggered a reflexive process in which they reviewed the possible alternative lifestyle choices available to them (discernment), in contrast to their 'current' lifestyle (T2–T3). Both relocation to a new environment and participation in employment diminished the desirability of acquisitive crime in the early stages of change as an outcome of their review (deliberation) of the perceived costs, benefits and implications of participation in work and the attendant lifestyle changes (contra offending) this necessitated in a new environment and a revised relational context. At this stage, Jay and Jed both 'dedicated' themselves to these changes in their projects (courses of action) and practices (ways of being in the world) (Archer, 2007). Whilst this did not in itself manifest in desistance, it did result in the relinquishment of acquisitive crime and contributed to their decision to modify their behaviours and lifestyles (T4).

Not all 'internal conversations' necessarily result in morphogenesis (or change). Evan's frequent imprisonment during his mid-twenties (T1 in Figure 11.2) triggered a period of reflexivity in which he compared and measured his own progress and behaviour against his friends' desistance from crime and normative developmental transitions (T2–T3). However, this did not provide the impetus or motivation to initiate change; his addiction had led to a diminished sense of agency and self-efficacy such that Evan felt powerless to influence his conditioning structures and exercise control over his behaviour[6] (T4). Reflecting Archer's (2010, 2012) concept of fractured reflexivity, his internal conversation reinforced to him that positive change was unlikely. In this context, then, the internal conversation does not lead to a purposeful course of action and only intensifies personal distress leading (albeit temporarily) to passivity among agents who feel unable to effect change in their conditioning structures, producing morphostasis (T4–T1) and a continuation of existing projects and practices.

Implicit in these examples of the exercise of reflexivity are individuals' comparative positioning of themselves against their primary reference groups. This would suggest, as indeed Donati (2011) argues, that Archer's (2000, 2003) formulation of the 'internal conversation' needs to be expanded by connecting it to the properties and powers of people's social networks, and recognising that these networks may operate with a different kind of reflexivity. Donati theorises that personal reflexivity refers to that internal conversation the individual has within him/herself, and which is 'a relational operation on the part of an individual mind to an 'Other' who can be internal (the ego as an Other)' (Donati, 2011 p.195) in the case of personal reflexivity or 'external (alter)' (Donati, 2011 p.195) in reference to another person or persons, denoting a more socially expanded form of reflexivity, which has an 'interactive character' (Donati, 2011 p.193) but which also takes the social context into consideration (see Figure 11.3). He argues that social networks can be a context wherein personal reflexivity takes place, but that social relations can themselves have their own reflexivity of a different form to personal reflexivity which he terms relational reflexivity (discussed further below).

The process of reflexivity, through which projects and practices are decided on, realised and sustained, is relational insofar as it is shaped by the relational networks in which it emerges (Donati, 2011). This set of relations affect what can and does fulfil an individual and so the individual brings his/her personal reflexivity to bear with regard to his/her participation in this relational context. To illustrate, in response to the shifting conditioning structures influenced by 'between-individual' changes such as the fragmentation of the Del, the increasing interpersonal violence and the development of a new intimate relationship with Lesley (T1 in Figure 11.2), Seth began evaluating his current lifestyle through the lens of his similarly shifting ultimate concerns for a different life (discernment phase). During his subsequent imprisonment, he conducted an evaluative review of the perceived costs, benefits and implications of pursuing individual self-change, which included relinquishing past associates in prison, against the interpersonal conflicts and pressures that this would generate (deliberation phase). Evidently, this comparative evaluation is not as solipsistic in focus as Archer's exposition implies; the decision to distance himself was the outcome of his personal reflexivity applied not solely to himself but to his relationships. In turn, Seth's experience of altruistic work through the '*Training for Freedom*' programme (see Chapter 5) reinforced his commitment to change (dedication phase) through his association with a group of community volunteers (T2–T3). In particular, his relationships and interactions with his co-workers and his experience of helping others were significant in communicating an alternative experience of self, and in turn, the possibility that another way of being was realisable. This change process that began in prison was consolidated following his relocation to London (T4–T1).

As Archer observes, people's ultimate concerns need not always be honourable; the projects may be illegal and the practices dishonest and, further, can be an outcome of fractured processes of reflexivity, as in Andy's case, in which the individual feels buffeted by circumstance and bound to a life of criminal activity. Reflecting on his subordinate position in the prisoner community (T1 in Figure 11.2), Andy drew on his repository of personal experiences in the Del and, emulating established patterns of interaction with them, Andy decided to ingratiate himself with dominant prisoners (T2–T3) for whom he smuggled and sold drugs, thereby ensuring a level of personal protection (T4) which, ultimately, created further constraints in his conditioning structures (T4–T1) (see Andy's story).

In this vein, then, social networks can be a context in which reflexivity can take place in triggering, through 'the looking glass self' (Cooley, 1902/1922), a reflexive, evaluative process. However, this process of reflexivity is of a more socially expanded form than Archer's concept of personal reflexivity would admit insofar as it is applied not just to oneself, but to one's relationships as a context in which reflexivity takes place. For Harry, the initial impetus to initiate deliberate changes to his lifestyle through participation in work emerged as an outcome of his individual reflexivity triggered by his comparative positioning of himself against his friends comprising 'the football crowd' all of whom were in employment (T1 in Figure 11.2). His desire to fit in with what they apprehended as 'normal' as he perceived it thus informed this reflexive process (T2–T3) and his motivation to pursue and subsequently personify this new social role as 'worker' (T4).

Similarly, Evan's association and interactions with Jay and Peter prior to his conversion had imbued Christianity with plausibility as 'a hook for change' (Giordano, Cernkovich and Rudolph, 2002 p.992) through his observation of the effects of their transformation following their conversions to Christianity. Indeed, as similarly observed in Jay's and Seth's stories, the recognition of change in a credible person is particularly influential where a given individual can identify with the change agent(s) and internalize the benefits of responding to this influence (Kelman, 1958) in the hope of achieving similar outcomes. Jay and Peter's continuing compassion, support and recognition of him as someone of worth at the height of his addiction (T1 in Figure 11.2) had the effect of triggering a process of personal reflexivity through an appraisal of *their* behaviour and how different they and their lives had become (T2–T3), which created in him an increasing openness to their faith-based interventions and which prompted, in part, his own conversion (T4).

Relational reflexivity and the change process: friendship groups T2–T3 (Figures 11.1 and 11.3)

What emerges from the life stories of these men is that individual and collective action is guided not only by individual concerns but by the good of the relationships which matter to them. In this context, compromises by individuals-in-relation are deliberated over and decided upon in order to sustain these relations and maintain the emergent relational goods. This is what Donati (2011) refers to as relational reflexivity. The reciprocal adjustments or modifications to their behaviours and related compromises made by individuals-in-relation are the outcome of relational reflexivity which is motivated by a mutual concern to maintain the social relation, in this case of friendship, and the emergent, co-indivisible relational goods. It is precisely because of the relation, the bond between them and the emergent relational goods of trust, of care and of concern for example, that such relations are able to influence the subjects participating in the relation, since it exceeds their individual and combined contribution to it. It is concerned with elaborating what Donati refers to as a new awareness of 'we', a new way of being in relation as a relational good for each person participating in the relation (Donati, 2011). This is distinct, then, from reflecting on one's own position in a network or comparing one's self to others within one's primary reference group.

The social relation is conceptualised, following Donati, as those bonds maintained between people that constitute their reciprocal orientations towards each other; it is the 'reality in between', that which exists *between* people, and which '"constitute" their reciprocal orientations and actions as distinct from all that characterizes single actors' (Donati, 2011 p.60). The impact of a given social relation on individuals' behaviour is attributable to the bonds maintained *between* people that constitute their reciprocal orientations towards each other, the emergent effects of their interactive dynamics, as well as the chains of meanings that a given type of social relation, as opposed to another, entails for individuals, who bring their own personal reflexivity to bear in a manner consistent with their ultimate concerns (Donati, 2011). It should be noted that this is distinct from the idea of '*social relations as a context*' (i.e. as the cultural and structural connections in a context under investigation) and *social relations as interaction* (as the emergent effects in/of an interactive dynamic)' (Donati, 2011 p.89). Social relations as interaction can be further understood as a) a context in which personal reflexivity is brought to bear, as discussed above and/or b) the manner in which social relations are configured by those participating in the relation as an outcome of the application of their relational reflexivity.

Concerned to support his friends to start over, Adam encouraged 'the revised group' to relocate and trained them in steel-fixing (see Chapter 4). Adam's concern for his friends can be construed as evidence of his application of his personal reflexivity, not simply to himself or to his individual social mobility, but to his relationships as a way of exercising his leadership in a different way (i.e. in a context which produced relational goods). Moreover, in 'Seth's story', for example it was observed that the desisting friends among the revised group benefited from the reciprocal support and reinforcement of their efforts to change that their mutual recognition of each other's efforts implied. Seth, for example, described how Adam acted as a type of mentor, using his own experiences to advise him on the possibilities and pitfalls ahead. In particular, as previously observed, the shifting priorities and concerns of some of the revised group (including Adam and Seth) away from the group and towards their families of formation and associated shifts in their behaviour similarly exerted a constraint on the behaviour of others, who found they had less support from their desisting peers for engagement in offending behaviour, reflecting a shift in the relational rules and expectations in this revised relational context. Individuals' modifications of their interactive dynamics, as an outcome of their reflexivity applied to this revised relational context, were thus underpinned by their shared concern with elaborating a new way of being-in-relation as a means of maintaining their shared relational goods.

In echoes of Seth's receptivity to the influence of his elder brother Adam, Jay was particularly receptive to Peter's testimony of conversion, as in turn Evan was to Jay and Peter, due to the existing reciprocal bond between them. Peter's concern for Jay (and in turn Peter and Jay's concern for Evan) can be construed as evidence of Peter's application of his personal reflexivity, not simply to himself, but to this relationship. Informed by their faith, these friends' concern for and means of relating to their friend in trouble were further underpinned by the relational ethic of subsidiarity which is a way to supply the means or a way to move resources to support the other without making him or her passive or dependent but in such a way that it allows and assists the other to do what is required in accordance with his or her ultimate concerns. Subsidiarity cannot work without solidarity (sharing a common or mutual responsibility through reciprocity which implies interdependence) (Donati, 2009). These principles consign mutual responsibilities on each person for supporting change and in taking responsibility for personal change (see Jay's and Evan's stories).

It is through these reciprocal relations that those participating in them find a shared intrinsic commitment to 'their communal experiential basis as beneficiaries of worth [in reference to the relational goods produced] unobtainable in any other way' (Archer, 2000 p.10). In terms of friendships, those which were most causally influential were characterised by fraternity, which denotes a particular type of friendship based on mutuality and reciprocity (Pahl, 2000) (elaborated in Chapter 4). Reciprocity can be conceptualised as the expression of fraternity, and this forms a strong social bond, particularly where the means or manner of relating express solidarity and subsidiarity, however informed. Reciprocity can therefore be conceptualised as mutual helping performed in a certain way (Donati, 2009), i.e. given in the context of solidarity – one of common responsibility. Where once these relationships and reciprocities contributed to their collective involvement in offending (see Chapter 4), these particular friends also supported each other, albeit to differing degrees and with different effects and at different stages, to pursue constructive changes in their lifestyles and relationships.

This section has summarised the elements of the change process for individuals in the context of their interactions with their extant and new social networks. As previously noted, this differentiation between social relations is for analytic purposes; as the individual stories revealed, there is considerable interaction between the different social relations in which a given individual participates. This section, however, illustrated the role of conditioning structures in variously constraining and enabling change, to which individuals apply their personal reflexivity (which is the mediating force between conditioning structures and individual or collective action) which, in turn, shapes the conditioning structures at the next phases of the morphogenetic cycle. In particular, this section further demonstrated that the application of individual reflexivity needs to be positioned in the relational context within which it arises, and, critically, that social relations can operate with their own, distinct, kind of reflexivity, which Donati (2011) terms relational reflexivity. In so doing, this section concluded by revealing that it is the nature and intensity of the bond between individuals-in-relation, and the manner of their relating, that is of further significance in understanding the relational contributions to the outcomes.

The role of intimate relationships and families of formation in supporting desistance

This section illustrates the recurrent elements of the change process pertaining to the role of intimate relationships and families of formation in supporting desistance, theorized through the conceptual schema deployed in this study and elaborated above.

Conditioning structures enabling change: intimate relations and families of formation (T1: Figure 11.1)

As previously noted, intimate relations have constraints and enablements from outside which influence the nature and form the social relation takes, but they also have 'pre-established assumptions that do not depend on them and implies things which go beyond their individuality' (Donati, 2011 p.66). Nevertheless, the form and shape that the relation takes is not pre-determined but differs between individuals-in-relation depending on how they personify and interiorise the relation; ergo neither is the form and shape the relation takes permanently fixed. Thus social relations are:

> that reference – symbolic and intentional – which connects social subjects as it actualises or generates a connection between them expressive of their reciprocal actions which consist in the influence *that the terms of the relation have on one another* and on the effect of the reciprocity emerging between them.
> (Donati, 2011 p.88, emphasis added)

This symbolic reference, the terms of the relation, denote those 'chains of meanings' brought to that 'type' of relationship rather than another (to a family for example rather than those that exist between members of a church). What emerged across the individual stories was the centrality of the men's internalised configuration of hegemonic 'traditional' working class masculinity (Connell, 2002), later refracted through the lens of Pentecostal Christianity by Jay and Evan, in influencing their expectations of their marital relationship and their associated gender roles, and thus the shape and form of this social relation.

To illustrate, the contingent interaction between Jed's role of provider and his participation in employment meant that changes to his conditioning structures (T1 in Figure 11.1), notably as an outcome of the loss of his employment on his return to Scotland, threatened his sense of masculine identity, particularly when Rachel assumed the role of economic provider. Jed responded to the accumulating strain and pressure he experienced by reverting to crime (T4 in Figure 11.1) as an outcome of his reflexive evaluation on the different means through which he might maintain this role (T2–T3 in Figures 11.1, 11.2) which ultimately contributed to the demise of his marriage (T4). In this vein, economic and cultural dynamics influence both the nature and form the social relation takes and, in turn, the interactive dynamics between individuals in relation. Indeed, the conditional interaction between the social relation of family and the social relation of employment in shaping the meaning and outcomes of work (discussed below) emerged as a recurrent element across the individual stories. The interaction between these social relations and their combined influence on individuals' personal social identities, as mediated through the lens of individuals' priorities, goals and relational concerns, directly or indirectly influenced their potential to enable or constrain processes of change, at different stages in a given individual's life.

In similar vein, the meaning and experience of fatherhood exists through specific socio-cultural processes, and thus are influenced by a given individual's conditioning structures (T1 in Figure 11.1), which shape the situations of actions for individuals on which their personal reflexivity is brought to bear (T2–T3 in Figures 11.1, 11.2). For both Seth and Harry, the meaning of fatherhood was further influenced by their own experiences of being parented (T1 in Figure 11.1). These meanings manifested differently in their desires to be involved in and provide for their families, further reflecting their wider, internalised cultural and class values and beliefs regarding their roles as partner and parent. These values and beliefs influenced their appropriation of the 'traditional' nature and form of the social relation of family and the associated sets of relational rules that shaped their interactive dynamics (Donati, 2011).

Moreover, changes in individual's conditioning structures (primarily in the form of employment, but also in relation to the wider sets of relations in which they participated) (see for example Jed's, Seth's and Harry's stories) variously enabled their personification and realisation of this social role, or, alternatively, constrained it (see for example Evan's story). Indeed, the experience (and influence) of fatherhood is often mediated through shifts in peer relationships, intimate relationships and employment which interact to open up new possibilities (Moloney et al., 2009) (T1 in Figure 11.1). These enabling elements for Seth, for example, included investment in a significant intimate relationship, participation in employment, a fresh start in a new environment, and the support of a revised peer group network with similarly established relational attachments.

Individual/personal reflexivity and the change process: intimate relations and families of formation T2–T3 (Figures 11.1 and 11.2)

In Chapter 2, it was observed that life-course transitions such as marriage or parenthood are often thought to alter the socio-structural context (or conditioning structures) of an individual's life, rendering offending incompatible with the acquired lifestyle and roles that the individual occupies. Alternatively, the individual is cast as perhaps yielding to a new set of routines that inhibit offending behaviour (see for example Farrington and West, 1995; Hirschi, 1969; Laub and Sampson, 1993, 2001, 2003). However, such explanations fail to illuminate *how* conditioning structures shape decisions by ignoring how the individual perceives and responds to such influences, and vice versa (Vaughan, 2007).

In Evan's story, it was revealed that his period of primary desistance (aged 22) was enabled by his participation in temporary employment, motivated by his desire to avoid further imprisonment, which enabled his abstinence from acquisitive crime (T1 in Figure 11.2). However, in this period, his relationship with Monica emerged as his ultimate concern; one which further diminished the desirability of offending behaviour, and its consequences (T2–T3). Moreover, spending time at work and with Monica had a significant impact on his formerly routine social activities and the social spaces he occupied, which further enabled his abstinence from crime (T4). While, then, these changes to his conditioning structures had the effect of enabling his abstinence from offending, it was Evan's reflexive re-prioritisation of his individual and relational concerns which motivated his pursuit of a different lifestyle, underpinned by his desire to maintain the relational goods emerging from his relationship with Monica, to which they were mutually oriented (T2–T3). As elaborated more fully in his individual story, Evan's initial abstinence from offending at this stage, then, was contingent on the maintenance of this relationship, which had triggered a re-prioritisation of his ultimate concerns and which, in turn, underpinned the ensuing changes he initiated in his projects and practices (T4). These changes were not sustained following their temporary separation (T1) which itself had an enduring effect on their interactive dynamics and on the nature of the bond between. For Evan, this diminished the salience of the relationship in the context of his shifting constellation of concerns (T2–T3).

The 'normative orientation' of the spouse is also considered to exert a positive influence on individual behaviour (Giordano, Cernkovich and Holland, 2003 p.306). However, attachment to a pro-social partner does not explain *why* someone becomes more amenable to change at one time rather than another, particularly where, as in Harry's case, attitudinal changes do not automatically translate into a re-orientation of values (see also Seth's story). Like Seth, despite having in Millie a 'pro-social' partner, Harry's relationship was neither causative of nor conditional on his desistance. As elaborated in his individual story, however, Harry had engaged in an internal conversation (personal reflexivity) which acknowledged, but was not significantly altered by, being in a new role position in relation to Millie (T2–T3 in Figure 11.2). While he continued to engage in football-related violence, his concern for Millie and his desire to maintain their relationship meant that he ceased house-breaking to limit the shame and stigma this might cause her (T4). It was not until he became a father, however, that he engaged in a more socially expanded form of reflexivity (discussed below).

In echoes of the relationship between Monica and Evan, Jay's reflexive orientation towards the maintenance of his relationship with Harriet emerged as Jay's ultimate concern, which led to a diminution of the desirability of the offending behaviour in this relational context, to which he responded by initiating adjustments in his behaviours, in accordance with his shifting priorities (T2–T3 in Figure 11.2). Unlike Millie, however, Harriet engaged in offending behaviour, which some control theorists might identify as a causal explanation for Jay's continued offending despite his aspirations to desist. As previously observed, however, the process of reflexivity, through which projects and practices are decided on, realised and sustained, is relational insofar as it is shaped by the relational context in which it emerges. To recapitulate, the impact of a given social relation, in this case, intimate relationships, on individuals' behaviours are attributable to the bonds maintained *between* people that constitute their reciprocal orientations towards each other, the emergent effects of their interactive dynamics, (T2–T3) *and* the chains of meanings that these particular types of social relation entail for individuals (T1), who bring their own personal reflexivity to bear in a manner consistent with their ultimate concerns (Donati, 2011). As with Seth, Jed and Harry, Jay's internalised configuration of hegemonic 'traditional' working class masculinity (Connell, 2002) influenced his expectations of the marital relationship and their associated gender roles (T1). However, Jay's reflexive orientation towards this relationship, and, thus, openness to change, was in anticipation of the realisation of an ideal type relationship which would bring about a sense of normalcy. While Harriet's participation in offending is not irrelevant, critically the ideal type relationship to which Jay initially oriented himself never materialised. When his efforts and expectations were frustrated, he drew on the repository of his personal experiences of his father's violence towards his mother as a means of exercising his control and asserting his masculinity. The asymmetry of their attachments influenced the nature of their interactive dynamics (T2–T3) which progressively emerged as reflexively oriented towards actions which generated the emergent relational bads (Donati, 2011) of jealousy, betrayal, conflict and violence (T4), and ultimately heralded the demise of their relationship, and Jay's reunion with the revised group in London (T4–T1).

Relational reflexivity and the change process: intimate relations and families of formation T2–T3 (Figures 11.1 and 11.3)

As previously observed, neither Seth's nor Harry's intimate relationships were conditional on or causative of desistance (see also Jay's and Evan's stories). As their individual stories illustrated, it was the reciprocal and collaborative adjustments made by both parties to maintain the relationship, oriented to the sustenance of the emergent relational goods which they mutually valued. This in turn generates a more socially expanded form of reflexivity (relational reflexivity) as people make adjustments in their own behaviours towards each other motivated by a concern to maintain the social relation, in this case of intimate relationships, and the emergent relational goods. Those intimate relations that exerted the most influence were those in which the relation was characterised by mutuality and affective concern, to which each party oriented themselves to the other in such a way that enabled both to realise their individual and relational concerns (see also Jed's, Jay's and Evan's stories with regard to their later relationships). In this vein, the manner of their relating (subsidiarity) in the context of solidarity is also significant in understanding the relational contributions to the outcomes.

Harry was the only individual whose role and identity as a father occupied a central place in his narrative of change. For Seth, for example, his experience of becoming and being a father, in the context of his changing conditioning structures, reinforced his established commitment to desist but unlike Harry, desistance was not directly attributable to becoming a father (see also Jed). For Harry, fatherhood (T1 in Figure 11.3) provided the impetus to initiate and sustain changes in his practices (T4) as an outcome of his concern surrounding the potential impact that offending and its outcomes would have on this social relation (T2–T3 in Figure 11.3). At this point, Harry's reflexive evaluation of his lifestyle against his shifting sense of what mattered to him, informed by his own values and beliefs surrounding fatherhood, reflected a reorientation of his relational concerns, which required a shift in his practices if it was to be realised. Desistance (T4 in Figure 11.3) was one shift in practice emerging from Harry's perception of the impact his offending would have on this social relation, underpinned by a desire to maintain a constructive paternal image, which was critical to his self-concept. Here, then, it is the social relation of the family that is being invoked as both a constraint upon offending and an enablement for a new way of living. Importantly, the social relation of the family here is not reducible to the individuals involved, as some existing explanations of desistance would suppose; rather, it refers to that which emerges from the reciprocal orientation of those in the family. Thus, it is changes in the social relation and how *it* becomes more reflexive that underpinned this process of change for Harry.

This section has summarised the elements of the change process for individuals in the context of their involvement in intimate relationships and their families of formation. In so doing, it has illustrated the role of conditioning structures – such as the influence of shared, internalised configurations of hegemonic 'traditional' working class masculinity – in shaping expectations of their marital relationship and associated gender roles. It has also revealed the significance of the conditional, contingent and mutually influential interaction of assumption of these social roles and identities with participation in employment; and the constraints and enablements in the form of economic and cultural processes – all of which influenced the shape and form of the social relation of the family. Moreover, the analysis has revealed the roles of intimate relationships and families of formation in triggering individuals' reflexive evaluation of their ultimate concerns – resulting, variously, in a diminution of the desirability of offending, suspension of offending, or in consolidating and sustaining commitments to desist. In particular, as with the social relation of friendships, both the manner of relating and the reciprocal and mutual orientation of individuals-in-relation towards the maintenance of the emergent relational goods emerged as significant in understanding the relational contributions to the change process.

The meanings and outcomes of work

The desistance promotive meanings and outcomes of work

Across the individual stories it was revealed that the relationship between employment and desistance resides in the way in which the meanings and outcomes of either the nature of the work and/or participation in employment influence an individual's personal and social identity and interact with a person's priorities, goals and relational concerns at various stages in a given individual's life.

As observed in Jay's and Jed's stories, following their separate relocation to London, it was the initial economic outcomes of participation in employment (T1 of Figure 11.1) that were significant in contributing to their abstinence from acquisitive crime (T4). Employment represented an alternative, licit and less risky means of acquiring economic capital, and, as discussed, this provoked their reflexive deliberation on the pros and cons of involvement in acquisitive crime, through the lens of the alternative opportunities and lifestyles that a frequent and substantial income offered (see similarly Evan's initial experience of employment) (T2–T3 Figure 11.1 and 11.2). Moreover, as noted in both Jed's and Seth's stories, working together as a team (T1 Figure 11.1 and 11.3) became a definitive feature of the lifestyles among 'the revised group' which reinforced a sense of common purpose and which enabled the internalisation of identities, both as individuals and as a collective, in which participation in work occupied a central place (Rhodes, 2008) (T2–T3 Figure 11.1 and 11.3). In the early stages, working together in steel-fixing represented an important means of re-establishing a sense of identification with and belonging among the revised group, which, in view of their shifting priorities, practices and relational dynamics, further exerted a constraining effect on individuals' offending behaviour (T4 Figure 11.1 and 11.3).

Over time, however, the meanings and outcomes of participation in work were imbued with further significance when Jed's, Seth's and Harry's children were born, enabling their roles of 'good provider' and, in turn, their personification of identities as men, fathers and partners. Indeed, as Owens states, 'employment is part of the idea of what is acceptable' (Owens, 2009 p.50), akin to Giordano et al.'s notion of the 'respectability package' (2002 p.1013), which refers to the interdependence of and interaction between employment and investment in significant intimate relations and/or parenthood. Employment and family roles form the basis of 'a general 'law-abiding adult citizen' identity construct' (Uggen, Manza and Behrens, 2004 p.263).

While employment did not motivate or trigger desistance for Seth, Harry, Jed, Evan or Jay, it assisted all of them to sustain it in the context of broader enabling shifts in their conditioning structures (which includes the sets of relations in which they participated), which, in turn, endowed their participation in work with meaning. Social relationships play a constitutive part of a responsible and legitimate identity and employment represents an important means through which these aspects of one's identity might be realised, performed and recognised (Rhodes, 2008). For Seth, Jed and Harry, in particular, the role of breadwinner or provider was, to varying degrees, a dominant component of each of their adult masculine (and, in that, desisting) identities; in this vein, fatherhood connects the world of work to the world of family (Hauari and Hollingworth, 2009; Robinson and Hockey, 2011). Indeed, Laub and Sampson (2001 p.51) argue that desistance emerges as an outcome of the interactions between the social relations of marriage and/or family and employment insofar as they 're-order short-term situational inducements to crime and, over time, re-direct long-term commitments to conformity'. However, while it might be argued that the availability of roles and the accompanying 'scripts' (Rumgay, 2004), behaviours and practices attributed to the role might become habituated, people do not march through life mechanically animating fixed role structures. The personification or interiorisation of a role, which is neither pre-determined nor fixed, is accomplished by an individual reflecting on their situation through the lens of their ultimate concerns and the range of actions available to them (Archer, 2003; Donati, 2011).

Returning to Figure 11.3, 'Me' refers to the self as primary agent; this is the identity attributed to him/her by others, specifically the networks of individuals or primary contacts with whom s/he associates. 'We' refers to the individual as a corporate agent and his/her relationships to and with the associational belongings of which s/he is a part – such as a specific workplace, family, or community of believers (T2–T3). When s/he assumes a social role (or assumes certain tasks in society) s/he becomes an actor ('You') inasmuch as s/he interiorises or personifies a role i.e. as a worker, or parent or partner (T4). Donati (2011) clarifies that, in all these relational spheres, one's ultimate concerns are progressively defined in relation to how the 'I' (the self) (at T1 in Figure 3.5) defines his/her choices when s/he acts as a 'You' (T4) and must respond both to the needs and requirements of his/her relational contexts and to the aspirations of his/her 'I', when s/he considers whether s/he is satisfied or not with the 'Me' that has been attributed to him/her by others, and when s/he meets and compares the meaning of his/her belonging (the 'We'/Us to which he belongs) against that of other membership groups (T2–T3). It is in performing or personifying a role, in carrying out the tasks associated with that role, in acting as a 'You', that the self ('I') asks itself if it is gaining satisfaction from its activities, choices, lifestyle or not. Ultimate concerns are the answers given to the existential questions that people ask of themselves when they attempt to make sense of who they are and the world around them and when they consider their level of satisfaction with their way of life. In this vein, Donati proposes that every way of being a self (as I, Me, We, You) is a dialogue (an internal conversation) with his/her own 'I', his/her personal identity. Social identity is formed from the dialogue between the 'I' and the other relational spheres.

To illustrate, while Harry's participation in employment certainly constrained his participation in social activities within which his offending occurred, it was the meanings and outcomes of participation in employment refracted through the lens of his individual and relational concerns which were significant in enabling his desistance. Initially, Harry's desire to fit in with the football crowd motivated his pursuit of employment (T2–T3 in Figure 11.3). His initial experience of participation in work, and the sense of personal progression it engendered, provided Harry with a sense of self-respect, self-worth and self-esteem, and the formal recognition of his efforts and capacities through promotion communicated to him that his efforts were acknowledged, recognised and respected (T4–T1). Taking responsibility and being invested with responsibility is, as observed in 'Seth's story', a means of social recognition and is the result of being trusted, which can engender a sense of responsibility on the part of the person feeling trusted. 'Social recognition . . . expresses the capacity and need that . . . people have for longer-term *reciprocal* relations of trust and responsibility in the wider society' (Barry, 2006 p.136, italics in original), which can positively influence an individual's self-concept (T1 in Figure 11.3). Critically, the meaning of and impetus to sustain employment for Harry was further altered by the birth of his son (his relationship of ultimate concern) (T2–T3) shortly after starting work, and fulfilling his role as a 'good provider' by making a financial contribution to the family reinforced Harry's commitment to maintaining his employment over time, even though he derived little satisfaction from the nature of his employment (T4–T1). Conversely, Jed's separation from Rachel and the children, and thus the loss of this social role and identity, rendered his subsequent participation in work meaningless. The economic outcomes that had, in his late twenties, been a motivation to sustain employment no longer satisfied him (T4–T1); given his dissatisfaction with the nature of the employment (T2–T3), participation in employment represented nothing more than engagement in a purposeless and cyclical routine that generated money that he didn't know what to do with. This suggests that an individual's priorities and relational concerns (configured in T2–T3), influenced by the pre-existing self (T1), have a significant bearing on the meanings and outcomes of work (T4–T1)

Both Evan's and Jay's faith is expressed through the nature of their work, which, since their respective conversions, has been oriented to supporting individuals and communities in need. Both men conceptualise their work as an expression of their faith, in terms of a life lived in service to others, informed by the Christian relational ethics of subsidiarity and solidarity referred to previously. For Jay and Evan, it is the meaning and outcomes of the work that are of enduring significance in consolidating their new, 'born-again' identity and thus their subjective well-being (T4–T1 in Figure 11.3). While their faith imbued the nature of this work with meaning, participating in this work thus contributed to and enabled the realization of their religious identities (T2–T3). Their participation in these works, then, can be construed as an outcome of both their conversion and of desistance; both of which have shaped their generative commitments.

Constraints and limitations

Employment is not static in nature but denotes a vast array of 'different working conditions, skill requirements, values and rewards' (Owens, 2009 p.58) and, thus, divergences in experiences of participation in work, itself a social relation, all of which have a bearing on the potential influence and impact of employment on a given individual. As illustrated in the foregoing analysis, even within the same job, the perception and value of this job will vary in accordance with an individual's priorities, concerns and experience.

A significant constraint emerging for both Seth and Jed, albeit manifesting differently, related to the hard drinking, hardworking culture of the steel-fixing industry. As observed in 'Seth's story', the pub performs an important social function as the primary social space for men in the construction industry, who are working away from their families and hometowns, living in crowded, often insubstantial, accommodation in unfamiliar geographical locations (Tilki, 2006). For Seth, while enabling the maintenance of social relations within his working environment, which was critical in terms of accessing further work, the hard-drinking, hard-working culture ultimately interfered with his capacity to sustain direct family involvement and heralded his return to alcohol use, which in turn placed a strain on his marriage. Similarly, following the conclusion of his relationship with Rachel, Jed's co-residence and association with similarly situated men in the construction industry contributed to a prolonged period of chaotic alcohol use, that ultimately threatened his health, and which, necessarily, constrained his capacity to continue working.

As observed in Chapter 4, association with a friendship or peer group, however formed, encourages collective participation in, or an amplification of, behaviours that individuals might not normally undertake alone, motivated both by fear of losing the respect of their friends (or colleagues), as measured against the extent to which individuals behaved in accordance with the norms of the group and by their need to belong. The need for relatedness reflects the human need to mutually and reciprocally relate to other people and 'involves feeling connected (or feeling that one belongs in a social milieu)' (Vallerand, 1997 p.300). This was particularly acute for Jed against the backdrop of the dissolution of his relationships with Rachel, their children and their mutual friends.

While Harry considers his past, in particular his limited education and employment experience and criminal record, to exert constraints on his social mobility, Jay utilises his prior experiences of offending to inform his approach to his current role in social care. Nevertheless, he considers that the professional nature of his current occupation places a constraint on the use of self-disclosure in his work with young people, which would seem to suggest that a professional (rather than a religious) identity is harder to reconcile with a previously spoiled identity (Goffman, 1963). Anticipating the judgements and negative stereotypes that people with convictions are often subjected to, Jay considers that others' perceptions of his past may diminish his professional standing and authority, which he suspects would unnecessarily obstruct or distract from the contributions he can make to their outcomes.

In similar vein, despite the recognition of his transformation that Evan experienced through his association with a community of believers, and despite the recognition of change he experienced from people in the community, the enduring proximity of a previously 'spoiled identity' (Goffman, 1963) embedded in this sense of place, in Coaston, and in the memories of the community, constrained his sense of personal progression. While, on the one hand, he was recognised as a reformed individual, he perceived that the recognition he received reflected the distance he had travelled from his past self, which, on the other hand, remained the dominant identity through which lens the positive social recognition he received was refracted. Moving to a new location enabled him to be recognised as the person he had become, as an Evangelist and not just as the reformed version of the person he had been (see similarly Jed's story).

The constraints and limitations on the constructive outcomes of employment variously cohere around the degree to which the nature of, or experience of participating in, employment creates an environment of and resource for social recognition. For Jay and Evan, their consciousness and internalisation of negative social discourses surrounding offenders and their perceptions of stigma located in their working environments, in its broadest sense, implied a form of misrecognition of who they had become. For Jed and Seth, their desire for recognition, to fit in and belong within a given social milieu, generated constraints in other areas of their lives. While the social relation of employment can enable or support desistance, the relational space and social places of work can manifest as sites of recognition and misrecognition that are more or less enabling or constraining. While, then, individuals' self-relations are, to greater or lesser degrees, dependent on the ways that others see them and treat them (Laitinen, 2003), simultaneously, the credibility or legitimacy of the person conveying positive regard or social recognition, or conversely attributing stigma, is also relevant to the potency of the attribution (Ikaheimo and Laitinen, 2011; Shih, 2004). In each case, the emergent constraints related to the desire for recognition by their primary reference group,[7] which for Jed and Seth were their workmates and for Evan and Jay were the individuals and communities on whose behalf they worked.

Conclusion

What this analysis has revealed is that desistance is variously enabled or constrained by the interaction of the social relations of friendship, intimate relations, families of formation and employment as mediated through the lens of an individual's personal priorities, values, aspirations and relational concerns. It is these concerns that imbue these particular transitional opportunities, events and experiences with significance. Their potential to enable or constrain processes of change at various stages in an individual's life is, thus, mediated through an individual's more or less reflexive response to the constraints and enablements inhering in their conditioning structures. Such an analysis thus marks a departure from current explanations for desistance that fail to illuminate *how* social structures shape decisions, ignoring how the individual-in-relation perceives and responds to such influences. But it also extends agentic and cognitive explanations by moving beyond their explanations of the onset of desistance and by offering an elaboration of how social relations sustain or hinder desistance over time.

As discussed in Chapter 2, quantitative research tends to focus on the degree to which intimate relationships or parenthood, for example, are causative of or conditional on desistance, in terms of the sequencing of relational investments and desistance. In contrast, qualitative analyses tend to focus on revealing the relative contribution of the identified change agent to the outcomes, be it through the role of the partner, for example, as change agent (as in social control theories), or the role of the individual as change agent (as in more agentic or cognitive theories of desistance). Applying Donati's theory of relational reflexivity allows for a more nuanced analysis. However, what this chapter also illustrated was that the outcomes of these processes are not static but are influenced by changes in conditioning structures, which can, depending on the individual's response to these changes, engender constraints and limitations. What this in turn confirms, then, is that desistance can be a complex, contingent, individualised, reflexive and relational process.

Notes

1 Parts of this chapter draw from Donati, P. (2011) *Relational Sociology: A New Paradigm for the Social Sciences*. Abingdon: Routledge. Reproduced with permission from Routledge.

Parts of this chapter were previously published in Weaver, B., and McNeill, F. (2015) Lifelines: Desistance, Social Relations and Reciprocity. *Criminal Justice and Behavior* 42(1), pp.95–107. Reproduced with permission from Sage.

2 The term 'dynamic' refers to a) the distinct elements of the change process and b) the processes through which desistance is enabled. It recognises thus the influence and interaction between the elements that contribute to desistance as well as the activity and change that occurs within and between those elements over time.
3 Age at onset refers to onset of an established pattern of offending.
4 Age at desistance refers to the age at which an individual considers they desisted. It is noteworthy that both Seth and Jed offended again at a later date, although, as discussed later in this chapter, they regard this as conceptually different from their earlier offending.
5 The contributions of different social relations are separated out for analytic purposes but, as preceding chapters have illustrated, there is considerable interaction between the various social relations which necessarily influences outcomes.
6 Arguably, imprisonment often exerts similar effects (see Andy's story).
7 Relatedly, Harry's primary reference group was the family and he chose not to disclose his offending past to his son.

References

Archer, M. (1995) *Realist Social Theory: The Morphogenetic Approach*. Cambridge: Cambridge University Press.
Archer, M. (2000) *Being Human: The Problem of Agency*. Cambridge: Cambridge University Press.
Archer, M. (2003) *Structure, Agency and the Internal Conversation*. Cambridge: Cambridge University Press.
Archer, M. (2007) *Making Our Way Through the World: Human Reflexivity and Social Mobility*. Cambridge: Cambridge University Press.
Archer, M. (2010) Routine, Reflexivity and Realism. *Sociological Theory* 28(3), pp.272–303.
Archer, M. (2012) *The Reflexive Imperative in Late Modernity*. Cambridge: Cambridge University Press.
Barry, M. (2006) *Youth Offending in Transition: The Search for Social Recognition*. Abingdon: Routledge.
Cooley, C.H. (1922) *Human Nature and the Social Order*. New York, NY: Scribner. (Original work published 1902.)
Connell, R.W. (2002) *The Men and the Boys*. Cambridge: Polity Press.
Donati, P. (2006) L'Analisi Relazionale: Regole, Quadro Metodologico, Esempi [The analysis of relational rules, methodological framework examples], in Donati, P. (ed.), *Sociologia. Una Introduzione Allo Studi Della Societe* [*Sociology. An introduction to the study of society*]. Cedam, Italy: Padova, pp.195–251.
Donati, P. (2009) What Does 'Subsidiarity' Mean? The Relational Perspective. *Journal of Markets and Morality* 12(2), pp.211–243.
Donati, P. (2011) *Relational Sociology: A New Paradigm for the Social Sciences*. Abingdon: Routledge.
Farrington, D.P., and West, D.J. (1995) The Effects of Marriage, Separation, and Children on Offending by Adult Males, in Blau, Z.S., and Hagan, J. (eds.) *Current Perspectives on Aging and the Life Cycle: Vol. 4. Delinquency and Disrepute in the Life Course: Contextual and Dynamic Analyses*. Greenwich, CT: JAI Press, pp.249–281.
Giordano, P.C., Cernkovich, S.A., and Holland, D.D. (2003) Changes in Friendship Relations Over the Life Course: Implications for Desistance From Crime. *Criminology* 41(2), pp.293–328.

Giordano, P.C., Cernkovich, S.A., and Rudolph, J.L. (2002) Gender, Crime and Desistance: Toward a Theory of Cognitive Transformation. *American Journal of Sociology* 107, pp.990–1064.
Goffman, E. (1963) *Stigma: Notes on the Management of Spoiled Identity*. Harmondsworth: Prentice-Hall.
Hauari, H., and Hollingworth, K. (2009) *Understanding Fathering: Masculinity, Diversity and Change*. York: Joseph Rowntree Foundation. Available at: http://www.jrf.org.uk/sites/files/jrf/understanding-fathering-diversity-full.pdf, accessed 09/02/11.
Hirschi, T. (1969) *Causes of Delinquency*. Berkeley: University of California Press.
Hogg, M., and Hardie, E. (1991) Social Attraction, Personal Attraction, and Self-Categorization: A Field Study. *Personality and Social Psychology Bulletin* 17(2), pp.175–180.
Ikaheimo, H., and Laitinen, A. (2011) Recognition and Social Ontology – An Introduction, in Ikaheimo, H., and Laitinen, A. (eds.) *Recognition and Social Ontology*. Leiden, Netherlands: Brill, pp.1–24.
Kelman, H.C. (1958) Compliance, Identification and Internalization: Three Processes of Attitude Change. *Conflict Resolution* 2(1), pp.51–60.
Laitinen, A. (2003, 12 November) Social Equality, Recognition and Preconditions of Good Life. *Social Inequality Today: Macquarie University*.
Laub, J.H., and Sampson, R.J. (1993) Turning Points in the Life Course: Why Change Matters to the Study of Crime. *Criminology* 31(3), pp.301–325.
Laub, J.H., and Sampson, R.J. (2001) Understanding Desistance from Crime, in Tonry, M.H., and Morris, N. (eds.) *Crime and Justice: An Annual Review of Research*, Vol. 26. Chicago, IL: University of Chicago Press, pp.1–78.
Laub, J.H., and Sampson, R.J. (2003) *Shared Beginnings, Divergent Lives*. Cambridge, MA: Harvard University Press.
Moloney, M., MacKenzie, K., Hunt, G., and Joe-Laidler, K. (2009) The Path and Promise of Fatherhood for Gang Members. *British Journal of Criminology* 49(3), pp.305–325.
Owens, B. (2009) Training and Employment in an Economic Downturn: Lessons for Desistance Studies. *Irish Probation Journal* 6, pp.49–65.
Pahl, R. (2000) *On Friendship*. Cambridge: Polity Press.
Rambo, L.R. (1993) *Understanding Religious Conversion*. New Haven, CT: Yale University Press.
Rhodes, J. (2008) Ex-offenders' Social Ties and the Routes Into Employment. *Internet Journal of Criminology* 1, pp.1–20.
Robinson, V., and Hockey, J. (2011) *Masculinities in Transition*. London: Palgrave Macmillan.
Rumgay, J. (2004) Scripts for Safer Survival: Pathways Out of Female Crime. *Howard Journal of Criminal Justice* 43(4), pp.405–419.
Shih, M. (2004) Positive Stigma: Examining Resilience and Empowerment in Overcoming Stigma. *Annals of the American Academy of Political and Social Science* 591(1), pp.175–185.
Tilki, M. (2006) The Social Contexts of Drinking Among Irish Men in London: Evidence From a Qualitative Study. *Drugs, Education, Prevention and Policy* 13(3), pp.247–261.
Uggen, C., Manza, J., and Behrens, A. (2004) Less than the Average Citizen: Stigma, Role Transition and the Civic Reintegration of Convicted Felons, in Maruna, S., and Immarigeon, R. (eds.) *After Crime and Punishment: Pathways to Offender Reintegration*. Cullompton: Willan, pp.258–290.

Vallerand, R.J. (1997) Toward a Hierarchical Model of Intrinsic and Extrinsic Motivation, in Zanna, M.P. (ed.) *Advances in Experimental Social Psychology*, Vol. 29. San Diego, CA: Academic Press, pp.271–360.

Van Klinken, A. (2012) Men in the Remaking: Conversion Narratives and Born-Again Masculinity in Zambia. *Journal of Religion in Africa* 42(3), pp.215–239.

Vaughan, B. (2007) The Internal Narrative of Desistance. *British Journal of Criminology* 47(30), pp.390–404.

Weaver, B., and McNeill, F. (2015) Lifelines: Desistance, Social Relations and Reciprocity. *Criminal Justice and Behavior* 42(1), pp.95–107.

12 Conclusion[1]

Introduction

This chapter draws together the preceding chapters. Chapter 2 comprised a review of the research literature to provide the academic context to the study prior to elaborating the conceptual or analytic framework underpinning the study in Chapter 3. The data analysis was presented in eight data chapters. Chapter 4 and the individual stories comprising Chapters 5–10 revealed the dynamics of offending and desistance as they occurred within and between individuals-in-relation while situating their lived experiences within their shared historical, structural and cultural contexts. In particular, Chapter 4 presented a group-level analysis of their shared lives as a co-offending peer group while the individual stories charted individuals' lives following the fragmentation of the Del in Chapters 5–10. Chapter 11 presented a group-level thematic analysis of the recurrent elements of the change process, manifesting across these individuals' stories, to identify the structural, individual and relational contributions to the desistance process.

This book set out to reveal the role of a co-offending peer group in shaping and influencing offending and desistance. In taking social relations as a central unit of analysis, rather than solely the individual agent and/or social structure, this book has explored the relative contributions of individual actions, social relations and social systems to the process of desistance. The aim of this has been to gain a greater understanding of the dynamics of offending and desistance as it occurs between co-offending peers and, as part of that, to reveal the role of social relations more broadly in accounting for desistance over time. In what follows, then, this chapter provides a summation of the analysis examining the dynamics of desistance through the lens of a co-offending peer group and the role of social relations in accounting for desistance over time to elaborate how a relational perspective can generate new insights into the dynamics of offending and desistance. The chapter concludes with a discussion of the implications for policy, practice and research.

Desistance through the lens of a peer group

In elaborating the means through which the group acted as a resource for enabling and supporting each other's process of change, this study showed how, for different individuals, these relations triggered reflexive evaluation of their priorities, behaviours and lifestyles. In so doing, the analysis revealed both what triggers reflexivity and what reflexivity entails as well as how these processes contribute to identity formation. It was observed that one's social networks can be a context that triggers this evaluative review through a process of comparing and measuring one's *self* against that of one's associates, refracted through the lens of 'the looking glass self' (Cooley, 1902/1922). In other words, people's perceptions of how they think other people see *them* can give impetus to or motivate the initiation of behavioural or lifestyle changes. It was similarly identified that individuals' observation of change in significant others also had the effect of triggering this process of personal reflexivity through an appraisal of *their* behaviour and how different they and their lives had become which motivated individuals to make changes in their own behaviours and/or lifestyles. The observation of change in their friends – with whom they had a fraternal relationship and shared experiences – enhanced their receptivity to their influence in the hope that similar outcomes could be achieved by them. Moreover, that key people from within their existing or original friendship group (Adam, Jay and Peter for example) had *become* positive influences is what imbued their influence with credibility and which, in turn, generated hope in others (Seth, Jay and Evan for example) that they too could realise related outcomes.

It was also observed that, as an outcome of a more relational mode of reflexivity, their commitment to the maintenance of these significant relationships motivated these individuals-in-relation to make reciprocal adjustments or modifications to their behaviours as a collective so as to respect and support each other's shifting lifestyle choices. Where once these relationships and reciprocities contributed to their collective involvement in offending, later these particular friends also supported each other, albeit to differing degrees and with different effects and at different stages, to pursue constructive changes in their lifestyles and relationships. This adds a new perspective to the literature discussing the role of peers in relation to onset and persistence (see for example Farrington, 1992; Haynie, 2001, 2002; Warr, 1993, 2002) and desistance (see for example Calverley, 2013; Giordano, Cernkovich and Holland, 2003; Graham and Bowling, 1995; Massoglia and Uggen, 2010; Uggen and Kruttschnitt, 1998); a literature which tends to polarise peers into 'anti-social' pressures or 'pro-social' influences, with each category representing different people or groups. As I observed in Chapter 2, discussion principally surrounds the would-be-desister's decisive (Paternoster and Bushway, 2009) or developmental (Giordano et al., 2003) disassociation from 'negative' influences and either re-connection with pro-social former associates or development of new pro-social relationships (see for example Giordano et al., 2003; Knight and West, 1975). These studies are, however, usually refracted through the lens of the individual desister (see for example Warr, 1998; Cromwell, Olson and D'Aunn, 1991) or more infrequently from the standpoint of the individual situated in a structural network of relations in a given context (see for example Haynie, 2001). The findings of this study therefore give impetus for alternative methodological approaches to conducting future research in this area (discussed below).

In particular, what the life stories of these men revealed was the centrality of the relational to the individual and thus to processes of persistence in and desistance from offending. Association with a peer group (whether the Del, The Revised Group, or with colleagues or fellow religious believers) encourages collective participation in, or an amplification of, behaviours that individuals might not normally undertake alone, motivated, for example, by fear of losing the respect of their friends or colleagues, as measured against the extent to which individuals behaved in accordance with the relational rules and norms of the group and by their need to belong. Belonging was a theme that emerged through the men's narratives of the days of the Del but the desire to belong, to fit in, to be accepted within different relational spheres emerged as a dominant theme throughout the men's life stories. The desire for belonging and recognition is not peculiar to the men who once comprised the Del. However, what this seems to suggest is a conceptualisation of the individual as a reflexive being whose individual and relational concerns emerge from, are immersed in, respond to and shape their relational worlds. The implications of this for how we understand and respond to people are discussed further below.

Individuals' identities are, in this sense, shaped by the sets of relationships in which they participate and the associated social roles they personify and interiorise (whether as a member of the Del, as a father, as a worker or as a Christian). But this shaping of identity depends on the extent to which the individual recognises or imputes credibility and legitimacy to the person(s) conveying positive regard or social recognition, or conversely attributing stigma. Credibility and legitimacy influence people's receptivity to influence and, in that, affect the potency of others' judgements of the individual (Ikaheimo and Laitinen, 2011; Shih, 2004). In 'the Del', for example, Harry and Andy were unconcerned by the views of others outside their primary reference group, at least partly because of the potency of the influence of their peers and the importance they attributed to the perceptions their peers had of them, which were more significant to their self-concepts than the 'reflected appraisals' of the 'generalised other' (Cooley, 1902/1922). However, following the fragmentation of the Del, shifting relational contexts triggered a reflexive evaluation, through which process individuals began to question, or at least consider anew, how they were perceived through 'the looking glass self' (Cooley, 1902/1922) to which they variously responded by making adjustments to their behaviours. For example, Jed and Jay modified their behaviours in alignment with the relational expectations of the revised group.

The relationship between personal and social identity is, then, as Donati (2011) observes, a dialectical one which can be influenced by the reactions of and recognition (or mis-recognition) conveyed by others, particularly those whose perceptions are of personal significance to the individual. While Harry, Jed and Jay in certain relational spheres elected not to disclose their pasts, Evan ultimately relocated to London and (in the context of his religious conversion) was more open about his history. While his transformation was recognised among the community of believers with whom he associated in Coaston, the enduring proximity of a 'spoiled identity' (Goffman, 1963), embedded in the memories of the community in which he had previously offended, constrained his sense of personal progression. While on the one hand he was recognised as a reformed person, he perceived that the recognition he received reflected the distance he had traveled from his past self, which, on the other hand, somehow remained the dominant identity attributed to him. Remaining in the same location thus ultimately constrained the social recognition of the person he had become, rather than of the reformed version of the person he had been. In this sense, social relations can be sites of recognition or misrecognition.

Identities are thus tried, tested, performed and negotiated in different relational spheres which are more or less constraining or enabling to the extent that these (changing) identities (whether as a worker, father, provider, husband or as a man) are realised and recognised by those participating in the relation. In similar vein, people's behaviour is necessarily shaped by the relational networks, or sets of social relations, in which they participate. But, critically, behaviour is also an outcome of the individual's reflexive evaluation of the meaning that these relations (and conformity to the relational rules that inhere in these different relational spheres) have for them, as reflected through the lens of their individual and relational concerns. In this way, shifting social relations can motivate individuals to behave in a way that they might not otherwise have done.

What the analysis of these men's life stories revealed, then, is that desistance is variously enabled or constrained by the interaction of the social relations of friendship, intimate relations, families of formation, faith communities and employment as reflexively mediated through the lens of a given individual's personal priorities, values, aspirations and relational concerns at a given stage in an individual's life. Ultimately, desistance emerged for these men as a means to realizing and maintaining their individual and relational concerns with which continued offending became (sometimes incrementally) incompatible. What this study in particular has revealed is that desistance occurs primarily within and through social relations and the reciprocal informal exchanges that take place between family and friends and the social relations that manifest through work and (for some) faith. Desistance, in this sense, occurs in the context of shifting engagements with, commitments to and reflexivity about different facets of civil society. The implications of this are discussed further below.

The significance of social relations

Social relations play a constitutive part of one's identity. Employment, for example, represents an important means through which aspects of a given individual's identity might be realised, performed and, in turn, recognised, either by enabling or reinforcing the role of provider, for example, or in enabling the expression of one's masculine or religious identity. The constraints on and of the desistance promotive or reinforcing effects of a given social relation cohere around the degree to which the nature of, or experience of participating in, the social relation creates an environment of and resource for social recognition. How social relations are configured by individuals-in-relation is influenced by the context and form of the social relation, the normative expectations of the relation, the interactive dynamics between those in relation (themselves informed by internalised cultural, class or religious beliefs and values for example) and the interaction with and influence of other social relations within which the individual participates. Taking the social relation as a central unit of analysis thus facilitated an exploration of the shifting configurations, meanings and influences of the various social relations, of friendship, intimate relationship, families of formation and employment, over time – and in interaction with each other. The analysis of the individual stories (see Chapters 5–10) illustrated interesting differences as to how, when and why these social relations variously enabled or constrained processes of desistance, which can be attributable to important differences in the nature, form and meaning of these different social relations, and in individuals' responses to them, refracted through the lens of their individual and relational concerns.

This study has also revealed that while social relations have their own capacity to influence, enable or constrain processes of change, it cannot be said that one social relation rather than another exerts particular desistance promotive effects. Rather, as this study has revealed, it is the meanings and significance of the social relation to individuals-in-relation, and the emergent effects of their interaction, which can be influenced by their interface with other social relations, which are critical to understanding the outcomes (elaborated further below). It was, for example, Seth's constellation of relational concerns that triggered his initial reflexive re-evaluation of what was important to him, in the shadow of the feud. Relatedly, following his release from a subsequent prison sentence, it was the interaction of becoming and being a family man in the context of his intimate relationship with Rachel which provided him with an alternative circle of belonging and source of social connectedness, which was enabled and reinforced by shifts in the relational dynamics of the revised group and involvement in stable employment. In this vein, it is also the manner of relating and, in turn, the emergent effects of the reality in-between those individuals-in-relation, which is central to understanding how social relations operate and, as part of that, influence change.

It is also misleading to suggest that social relations are causative of or conditional on behavioural change. Social relations can only exert influence where the individual is receptive because of their individual and relational concerns and their desire to maintain the relationship so as to maintain emergent relational goods that cannot be produced outside the relation (Donati, 2011). The nature, form and meaning of the social relation and its emergent effects are dynamic, and the related reflexive processes and subsequent outcomes are not static but are influenced by changes in conditioning structures, which can engender new constraints and enablements. Individuals' reflexive responses to these new constraints and enablements can motivate a realignment or reprioritisation or reorientation of their ultimate concerns, and in turn a shift in their projects and practices, which subsequently influences their conditioning structures. What emerges from this study then, is a conceptualization of the desistance process as a complex, contingent, individualised, reflexive and inherently relational process. The dynamics of desistance (and offending) thus have to be understood in the individual,

Conclusion 243

relational and structural contexts within which these behaviours are embedded and sustained (or otherwise). The individual, relational and structural contributions to the desistance process as they occur within and between individuals were elaborated fully in Chapters 5–11. What follows is a brief summation of the key elements of the change process with regard to the individual, relational and structural contributions to it.

The conditioning influence of the structural or cultural context works through shaping the situations of actions for individuals and individuals-in-relation, be it intimate relationships, family or friendship, or religious or work-related groups. Situations of actions are conditioned in multiple ways – from the accessibility of resources (for example the availability of employment), to the prevalence of beliefs (for example surrounding masculinities and gender roles), to the sets of relations in which people find themselves – such that some courses of action would be impeded and others enabled (Archer, 2007a; Donati, 2011). In this way, conditioning structures can also be understood as involving the sets of relational rules prescribing how one should conduct oneself in a certain way towards others, and which will be different in different contexts, as well as being more or less explicit and more or less constraining and enabling (for example between the Del and the Revised Group). Critically conditioning structures can only exert constraint and enablement in relation to something for someone or some people. The extent to which they constrain or enable is dependent on how the individual receives and responds to them (discussed below) which, this study has revealed, cannot be disconnected from the way in which others receive and respond to them, in turn influencing their interactive dynamics.

The individual contributions are broadly conceptualised as the decisions and actions of an individual as an outcome of the application of their personal reflexivity, which Archer (2007a and b) illustrates through reference to an internal conversation. It is through this process that people decide on courses of action by ruminating on themselves, their concerns and social situations, imagining and pursuing projects and practices that define who they are and enable them to realise their ultimate concerns within the constraints and enablements of their conditioning structures. In this vein, reflexivity incorporates notions of transcendence through which we can imagine ourselves and our relations differently from what we/they are and thus capable of actualizing things as yet unrealised (Donati, 2011). The process of reflexivity occurs across three phases of discernment, deliberation and dedication, as individuals engage the temporal concepts of the self in a dialogue (the pre-existing self or 'Me'; the present self – one's 'I'; and the 'You' of the future). In this context, this reflexive process can lead to behavioural modifications which may include, for example, relinquishing one crime type or desistance (morphogenesis) or persistence (morphostasis).

However, as elaborated both in Chapter 11 and above, social networks are a context within which personal reflexivity takes place and this has specific implications for how we understand the relational contributions to the outcomes or, put differently, the role of social relations in processes of change. Indeed, what emerged from this study was the frequency with which the exercise of reflexivity was triggered by individuals' comparative positioning of themselves against their primary reference groups. Thus as Donati (2011) recognised, Archer's (2000, 2003, 2007a) formulation of the 'internal conversation' needs to be expanded to connect it to the properties and influences of the social relations and networks of relations in which people participate. Social relations can thus be conceptualised as a) a context in which personal reflexivity is brought to bear, as discussed above, and/or b) the manner in which social relations are configured by those participating in the relation as an outcome of the application of their relational reflexivity (Donati 2011). This was particularly evident in the orientations and practices of 'the revised group' and 'the Christians' as well as within some intimate relations and families of formation (see Harry's, Jed's and Seth's stories). So, it is changes in the social relation and how *it* becomes more reflexive that underpins processes of change over time. This study has therefore illustrated how different social relations operate with their own reflexivity of a different kind, which Donati terms 'relational reflexivity'. In short, relational reflexivity is concerned with elaborating a new awareness of 'we', a new way of being in relation as a relational good for each person participating in the relation. It is through these means that the social relation has its own powers to influence the subjects participating in it.

It is the relation between people, their reciprocal orientation to the maintenance of that relation, that makes them reflexive in a relational, instead of merely in a personal way. As elaborated in Chapter 3, this notion of reciprocity is central to Donati's conceptualisation of social relations. In terms of friendships, those which were most causally influential were characterised by fraternity, which denotes a particular type of friendship based on mutuality and reciprocity (Pahl, 2000) (elaborated in Chapter 4). Reciprocity can be conceptualised as the expression of fraternity which forms a strong social bond, particularly where the means or manner of relating express solidarity and subsidiarity, however informed. It has previously been stated that subsidiarity and solidarity are two ways of relating to others in such a way as to acknowledge the human dignity of the other. Reciprocity can therefore be conceptualised as mutual helping performed in a certain way (Donati, 2009), i.e. help given in the context of solidarity and of common responsibility. Subsidiarity is the means or the ways in which this help is offered such that it enables the other to do what must be done to realise his ultimate concerns (this was evident particularly among the 'revised group' and 'the Christians'). Those intimate relations that exerted the most influence were those in which the relation was characterised by mutuality and affective concern, to which each party oriented themselves to the other in such a way that enabled both parties to realise their individual and relational concerns (see also Jed's, Jay's and Evan's stories with regard to their later relationships). In this vein, the manner of their relating (subsidiarity) in the context of solidarity is also significant in understanding the relational contributions to the outcomes.

It is also worth reiterating that it is through these processes that individuals and individuals-in-relation and/or groups can influence their conditioning structures. The elaborated structure or outcomes are the products of an individual's application of their personal reflexivity (individual contributions) and of the interactive dynamics of their relational networks, which can include the interaction between social relations and the influence of (certain configurations of) social relations, which have their own properties and powers to feed back on, and thus influence, their behaviours of individuals-in-relation (relational contributions).

Such an analysis thus marks a departure from current explanations for desistance that fail to illuminate how social structures shape decisions, ignoring how the individual-in-relation perceives and responds to such influences. But it also extends agentic and cognitive explanations by moving beyond their explanations of the onset of desistance and by offering an elaboration of how social relations sustain or hinder desistance over time. Donati's relational sociology thus provides a new conceptual framework for understanding the desistance process that gives proper recognition to the individual actions, social relations and social systems and the inner characteristics and influences which are peculiar to them. To conclude, this study has revealed the role of friendship groups, intimate relationships and families of formation, faith communities and employment in, differently, triggering individuals' reflexive evaluation of their ultimate concerns – resulting, variously, in a diminution of the desirability of offending, suspension of offending, or in consolidating and sustaining commitments to desist. In particular, both the manner of relating and the reciprocal and mutual orientation of individuals-in-relation towards the maintenance of the emergent relational goods emerged as significant in understanding the relational contributions to the change process.

Implications of findings

Ultimately, what the foregoing analysis reveals is that desistance occurs primarily within and through the fourth sector of civil society – the informal sector, where informal exchanges take place between family and friends and the social relations that manifest through work and, for some, faith. This would suggest that we need to take the role of civil society seriously in considering how the other sectors[2] might support desistance, not least in terms of the manner of relating. If desistance is to be enabled and supported by sectors outside the fourth sector, then it can be inferred from this analysis that focussing on means and processes that are (re)integrative and inclusive might be a useful starting point for considering how penal policy and practices within and across the other sectors might work to support desistance.

As previously observed (in Chapter 3), Donati's relational paradigm provides an account of social integration (and therefore of the nature of civil society) based upon people's reciprocal orientation to relational goods (at all levels). Penal policies and practices have become so focused on what Archer (2011) refers to as market exchange relations and political command relations that the contributions of the kinds of social relations that inhere in civil society have been at best marginalised and at worst ignored. Yet, as Archer (2011) argues, the former are simply procedural transactions which operate with an instrumental or systems rationality which has the effect of fragmenting and disrupting human relations. They do not generate the relational good that is characteristic of a friendship, for example, such as trust. Rather, Archer argues, these rationalities – proceeding by command (in the form of increasing bureaucratic regulation) and commodification – generate relational 'evils' or bads which fragment and disrupt human relations (2011).

Donati (2011) instead advocates a politics of 'fraternity' (in the form of collective action, cooperation and mutual aid) in the pursuit of the collective or common good in society. He suggests that subsidiarity and solidarity are key concepts of the common good; they are, ideally, mutually reinforcing and necessary to realising the common good. Donati (2009) argues that commitment to the common good and mutual respect for the human dignity of each person is the hallmark of a resilient civil society and that to violate human dignity is to undermine, if not fracture, the likelihood of realising the common good. Donati (2009) reasons thus that while the state has a responsibility to deliver security and justice, these tasks must be accomplished in such a way that is subsidiary to civil society.

Donati (2009) further clarifies that the common good is not synonymous with justice. Rather, he reasons, justice is a means to reach the common good. A person who commits a crime has to be punished because he has violated not only the norms of society (Duff, 2001) but also the shared responsibility (solidarity) to uphold or pursue the common good. If, however, punishment has a merely punitive or vengeful aim, or if it is simply incapacitative and exclusionary, it is likely to have the effect of fracturing relations and severing natural norms of reciprocity (on which see Andy's story). Rather, it should seek

> ... to re-establish the circuit of reciprocity. If an act of solidarity toward those who commit a crime is not subsidiary to them (in order to have them reenter the circuits of social reciprocity), it would not be a right action.
> (Donati, 2009 p.227)

This would suggest that to restore or reinforce reciprocities in pursuit of the common good, justice must be realised through means that are restorative or reintegrative and that allow people to fulfil their reciprocal obligations. This seems to require some recognition of mutual responsibility in supporting change, consistent with concepts of 'earned redemption' (Bazemore, 1998 p.768). This form of mutual responsibility is forward looking, and asks not ' "why did you do it?" but rather "what is to be done?"' (Maruna, 2006b).

If, then 'the common good emerges as an outcome of collective, social action which is underpinned by "reciprocal solidarity and subsidiarity"' (Donati, 2009 p.228), this in turn then has implications for relations between state and civil society in seeking to support desistance. Doing so requires some reconsideration as to how we might reconfigure relations between the different sectors of society so as to 'support, enhance and work with the organically occurring community processes of reconciliation and earned redemption' (Maruna, 2006a p.16).

Policy implications

As this study has demonstrated, the change process extends beyond the operations and interventions of the penal system to what individual and informal support systems and networks contribute. The implication is that both practice and policy might become oriented to promoting supportive, reflexive relational networks premised on reciprocity, or mutual helping and obligations to support each person to realise his or her ultimate concerns. This would therefore seem to require that both policy and practice become oriented to supporting and generating

> [networks of] relationships to produce changes in both context and in behaviour through the modification of existing relations; . . . [which] activate the natural potential of social networks and make use of innovative forms . . . of relationality.
>
> (Donati, 2011 p.95)

In this global era of fiscal constraint, related social policies emerging from concepts of personalisation, co-production and *The Big Society* have ostensible potential to support the implementation of relevant initiatives in this regard. Personalisation appears with striking frequency in government publications on public service policy across the UK (Ferguson, 2007; see also Cabinet Office, 2009; Scottish Government, 2008, 2009) although it is generally associated with the *Third Way* social policy reform agenda of the New Labour Government. Personalisation is essentially focused on devolving control of service provision to the service user, harnessing their strengths and predilections in the context of their extant networks and capacities to inform the design and delivery of services (Weaver, 2011). Personalisation 'enables the individual alone, or in groups, to find the right solutions for them and to participate in the delivery of a service. From being a recipient of services, citizens can become actively involved in selecting and shaping the services they receive' (Scottish Government, 2009 p.10). However, in practice, personalisation approaches remain essentially individualistic and, whilst speaking to individual and network strengths, do so within the parameters of statutory constraint and current service provision and resources. If we are our relational concerns, then a truly personalised approach to working with people with convictions requires policy and practice to attend to the relational contexts in which people's ultimate concerns emerge and through which relevant supports can be developed and protected. This implies the need for changes to the organization of current services and the products they produce.

Within and beyond services, policies might become more oriented to supporting community reintegration by generating initiatives that promote active citizenship (Edgar, Jacobson and Biggar, 2011) and generativity (Maruna, 2001). Such an approach might include the building of and interaction with social and community networks to enable change and the mobilization of their resources in the development, delivery and innovation of penal practice which might further enhance their credibility and legitimacy with those they aim to support (Weaver 2011, 2013). The related policy emphasis on how ex/offenders, volunteers, families and community groups might become involved in justice services (Ministry of Justice, 2008a, 2008b, 2009, 2010) is, at least in principle, consistent with concepts of co-production and civil society.

Co-production is a term for such collaborative efforts, reflecting, in this context, the interdependent relationship between professional service providers, service users, and communities as co-producers in enabling change (Pestoff, 2012). However, co-production as both a term and a concept is beleaguered by different definitions, by disagreement about how it should be interpreted and operationalised, and by a limited empirical evidence base. Bovaird and Loeffler (2013 p.4) define co-production as 'the public sector harnessing the assets and resources of users and communities to achieve better outcomes'. While this is somewhat operationally vague, and while it does not specify the contributions of the third sector, it retains an emphasis on reciprocity; it incorporates recognition of the relationships that exist between the various co-producers or stakeholders; it focuses on outcomes and not just services; and it encompasses an active role for both service users and for communities. The essence of co-production is collaboration and the reciprocal contribution of each party's resources to producing mutually agreed outcomes. Realizing this, however, means not only relinquishing monopolies of power and professional or service-defined expertise but the generation of reciprocal relationships underpinned by mutual responsibilities. To facilitate participation, co-production requires organizational flexibility and policy support for the regeneration of community development and engagement approaches so that policies and practices are not constrained by the more narrow objectives and capacities of services alone. This is broadly compatible with the emerging *Justice Reinvestment* model which refers to the redistribution of public money spent on penal measures to 'local community based initiatives designed to tackle the underlying problems which give rise to criminal behaviour' (Allen, 2007 p.5). Justice Reinvestment's emphasis on decentralisation and the devolution of power and decision-making from national to local government bodies further resonates with the rhetoric of the *Big Society* thesis (Cabinet Office, 2010) and the *Rehabilitation Revolution* (MOJ, 2010), at least where they share an emphasis on mixed sector service provision premised on models of social enterprise, mutuals and co-operatives.

The increasing policy emphasis in the UK on localised practices, building community assets, capacity, reciprocity and social capital, and on partnerships – between the statutory, private and third sectors, communities, service users and families – and the growing recognition of their mutual roles in supporting change could be construed as an opportunity for the pursuit of a more reciprocal and collaborative approach to justice that statutory services cannot achieve alone. However, underpinning the Big Society and the *Rehabilitation Revolution*, and the subsequent *Transforming Rehabilitation* agenda (MOJ, 2013) lies an unmistakable economic rationale manifest in the withdrawal of traditional state services, increasing privatisation and market competition. Unlike the Justice Reinvestment model, the *Rehabilitation Revolution* and the *Transforming Rehabilitation* agenda are not accompanied by a *redistribution* of economic resources from prisons to communities, but by the *withdrawal* of funding across services.

Relatedly, the simultaneous emphasis on 'payment by results' in England presents particular challenges to community and voluntary organisations. Though these organisations are central to Justice Reinvestment, the Rehabilitation Revolution, the *Transforming Rehabilitation* agendas and to the realization of co-productive arrangements, they are inadequately resourced and are unlikely to withstand the financial risk of managing a payment-by-results contract. In consequence, this policy turn is more likely to represent the further privatisation and commodification of justice (McCulloch and McNeill, 2007). In similar vein, the emphasis on competition risks undermining more cooperative partnerships that already exist between statutory and voluntary sectors, and the narrow focus on reducing re-offending in the short term is likely to constrain the development of innovations that might promote the less easily measured objectives of social justice and integration. Not only is recidivism an inaccurate measure of change but if desistance is characterised by lapse and relapse, then the effects of interventions may be longer term and more subtle than immediately discernible. How performance will be measured is one question, but it is one that focuses primarily on the activities and interventions of services, which is only one dynamic in the wider process of change.

Given the centrality of employment to the men's narrative of reforms, progressing beyond an economic definition of work seems apt in an era of increasing unemployment, albeit no panacea. Nonetheless, volunteering, 'to the extent that [it] produces a public good . . . benefits nonparticipants and participants alike' (Uggen and Janikula, 1999 p.356) and has been positively associated with desistance in that it establishes notions of reciprocity and mutuality, promotes generativity and, through social recognition, acknowledges citizenship. As this study suggests, volunteering and civic engagement may also be a route to accessing new social networks, and generating social capital. As with Justice Reinvestment, however, further consideration needs to be given as to how initiatives promoting active citizenship might be adequately resourced and supported by wider social policies. Currently, participation in voluntary work can impact on benefit entitlement, and unemployed people are consistently pressured to relinquish these activities to enter the formal employment market (Seyfang, 2006). This seems to conflict with the *Big Society*'s emphasis on relinquishing power and promoting choice and volunteerism within local communities and appears mindless of the realities of increasing cuts and unemployment that exert a disproportionately negative impact on already disadvantaged populations and communities.

Indeed, it can be argued that current UK penal policy has made little progress in enabling opportunities for people with convictions to access employment opportunities, despite a succession of policy initiatives including, but not limited to, '*Reducing Re-Offending National Action Plan*' (Home Office, 2004), '*Reducing Re-offending through Skills and Employment*' (HM Government 2005), '*Reducing Re-offending through Skills and Employment: Next Steps*' (HM Government, 2006), and '*Breaking the Cycle: Effective Punishment, Rehabilitation and Sentencing of Offenders*' (Ministry of Justice, 2010). Indeed, the latter proposed the introduction of 'working prisons' which are intended to provide work for prisoners; another policy strand focused on making prisoners on release eligible for direct entry onto the Work Programme (DWP, 2011). While, then, current penal policy ostensibly recognises the significance of employment in the resettlement process, this emphasis on labour, surrounded by rhetoric of tough and rigorous

250 *Conclusion*

punishments, seeks to instil discipline in and a work ethos among the prison population. While at the point of release, former prisoners in receipt of Job Seekers Allowance are mandated to engage in Work Programmes, the emphasis is on supply side programmes and on supporting the acquisition of skills and experiences, rather than substantially supporting participation in employment. One alternative mechanism is proposed below in the form of through-the-prison-gate social cooperative structures of employment.

Practice implications

As Chapter 2 illustrated, while there is some consensus that supporting desistance requires practitioners to attend to individuals' personal concerns and an increased level of involvement in families and communities, there is limited discussion on how these shifts in probation practice might be realised or how justice services, however broadly defined, might reconfigure their relationship to and with individuals, families and communities (although see Maruna and LeBel, 2010; Weaver, 2013). Indeed, Chapter 2 illuminated that much of the research on desistance has not been directly concerned with or focused on the role of criminal justice interventions or practices at all, albeit with notable exceptions. This study does not mark a departure from the norm in this regard. However, it has been suggested that understanding how and why people desist can inform professional practice (see for example McNeill, 2003, 2006), which, as Porporino (2010) suggests, means listening carefully to the kinds of supports that individuals (and, it could be added, families and communities) need in order to relate to each other in such a way as to enable and support naturally occurring processes of desistance. Furthermore, and again with notable exceptions (i.e. Farrall et al., 2010; Barry, 2013) our collective preoccupation with how change happens has also led us to neglect what happens after change occurs, and it is hoped that this is one area in which this book represents a departure. While much of the desistance research casts new light on the dynamics of the change process and some on the means through which change might be supported, even desistance focused discourses of practice have focused on what either the desister does or on what professionals do; what has been missing heretofore is an appreciation and elaboration of the non-professional relational contexts of offending and desistance and how these contexts are suffused with concerns linked to the character and obligations of reciprocity in social groups. This underlines the need to attend to these relational contexts and to consider how these contexts might also shape and influence approaches to practice and, as part of that, inform the development of the kinds of assets and reflexive relational networks that can support not just desistance but social integration.

If, then, as this study suggests, desistance is about more than simply reducing re-offending, this would suggest that supporting desistance requires going beyond a sole focus on the individual, as if their offending behaviour occurred freely and in isolation, to address the social opportunities and obstacles that either help or hinder desistance (see for example Barry, 2006; Farrall, 2002). This means recognising the individual in the context of their relationships with families and communities (or lack thereof). In turn, this requires the building both of professional relationships and of social and community networks to enable change. Recognizing individuals and families and other informal networks of support as assets, involved in mutual support and delivery of penal practices, may assist in re-establishing and building 'circuits of social reciprocity' (Donati, 2009 p.227). In this reformulation of relationships between the various sectors of society, the third and fourth sectors have a critical role to play.

As this study suggests, this means creating the kinds of practices, premised on the principles and practices of subsidiarity and solidarity, that can generate, support and sustain the kinds of relational goods and reflexive relational networks that reside at the heart of the desistance process. This might require promoting under-utilised peer, familial and community support resources in the process of supervision as much as utilising the resources that reside within networks, families and communities beyond supervision, in facilitating social reintegration. However, as this study has demonstrated, being tied into social relations does not in itself produce desistance. Suggestions that social capital might support desistance through increased social mobility through connection to various network structures are not only too limited in their recognition of agency and reflexivity, they also fail to acknowledge why and how being connected into such networks exerts an influence on the individual. If we understand social capital as 'an instantiated informal norm that promotes co-operation between individuals' (Fukuyama, 2001 p.7) then we need to understand social capital as a property and a quality of social relationships. As a relational good, social capital is neither an asset possessed by the individual, nor a collective property of a social structure, but a configuration of those social networks which are shared by people who will not be able to produce such goods outside their reciprocal relations (Donati, 2007). The implication is that policies and practices focus less on the structural outcomes derived from participation in a given network and more on the connections between people and on fostering the reflexivity of the individual who is being connected by the good of the relationship.

Recognizing then that the process of desistance, and the people who support it, extend beyond penal practices and practitioners, the focus here is on *how* practitioners might begin to reconfigure their relationships with and to individuals, families, groups and communities in order to co-produce desistance. This may include supporting and enabling peer-productive practices (Pestoff, 2012) such as peer mentoring, self-help, activism and mutual aid and their vital contribution in collaboratively co-producing desistance promoting community justice services (see for example Maruna and LeBel, 2009; Weaver, 2011; Weaver and McCulloch, 2012).

Taking a whole person approach and focusing on people's quality of life, not just their offences, suggests a role for practitioners in advocating on behalf of individuals, and in forging partnerships with people's families, where appropriate, and other organizations such as local authorities, voluntary organisations, user led organisations (Weaver, 2011), social enterprises and mutual cooperatives (Weaver and Nicholson, 2012), all of whom have a role to play in co-producing desistance.[3] Practice should therefore 'focus on people as interdependent citizens embedded in a wide network of support including formal public services, as well as a host of less formal interactions and relationships' (Needham, 2009 p.27). This means that practitioners also have a role in supporting the development or maintenance of a person's positive social relationships, with friends and families, as well as engaging them as part of the change process.

Current approaches to group work in probation practice across the UK typically bring a collection of individuals together on the basis of various demographic criteria to participate in correctional programmes underpinned by cognitive behavioural psychology to address 'criminogenic needs'. Building on the dynamics of the change process elaborated in this study, a desistance focused and co-productive approach to working with groups may have more of an appreciative, rather than correctional, focus and should be strengths-based and collaborative; should create the kinds of environments for and resources of social recognition; should promote and enable the exercise of both personal and relational reflexivity; should be oriented to generating and enhancing social capital, and thereby should support the development of new supportive social networks. Mutual aid based groups have the potential to perform all these functions. While mutual aid manifests in a range of peer-to-peer activity, mutual aid groups can also function collaboratively with practitioners in the public and voluntary sectors to co-produce services (Burns and Taylor, 1998). In groups, mutual aid is premised on the reciprocal exchange of help; the group member is both provider and recipient of help for the purpose of co-producing mutual/collective and individual goals. In this sense, mutual aid is both a process and an outcome (Steinberg, 2014). Mutual aid groups are widely established in the community – not least in the recovery from addictions movement (for example, Alcoholics Anonymous or Narcotics Anonymous) and recovery in a mental health context – but practitioners could also support the co-design and co-implementation of mutual aid based group work practices (Steinberg, 2014).

The development of multi-stakeholder social cooperative structures of employment may represent both a means of building community capacity, and thus co-producing community based desistance-supporting resources, and a means of enabling access to employment. In general terms, co-ownership by practitioners, service users, and, as appropriate, community members or groups is the defining characteristic of social cooperatives and mutual public services (Weaver and Nicholson, 2012). They enable members to create their own employment and provide support to each other through their membership of the social co-operative. The role of the professional in these structures is to facilitate the promotion, development, and success of each social co-operative rather than simply providing either expert assistance or rehabilitative services to individual members. Mutual or social co-operatives can offer vital social supports, contribute to the development of a more pro-social identity, increase levels of self-esteem and self-efficacy and provide a sense of purpose for both individuals and communities. Through the negotiation of mutual rights and responsibilities, mutual and social co-operatives can also promote active citizenship and generate wider and more sustainable social capital (Weaver and Nicholson, 2012).

Social cooperatives provide a structure through which to deliver these collaborative multi-sectorial approaches to supporting change, based on the values of self-responsibility, mutual-aid, democracy, equality and solidarity (Majee and Hoyt, 2010) and can circumnavigate some of the systemic obstacles to employment, such as criminal records and employer discrimination (McEvoy, 2008) that offenders routinely encounter. As part of a cooperative, people with convictions and professionals can thus, potentially, 'co-produce' the social supports and associated relational or public goods (Donati, 2011, 2014) that can assist social integration and desistance. They have the potential to support integration, citizenship and reciprocal relationships (Majee and Hoyt, 2010, 2011), the very factors that are suppressed by the repetitive routine and minimally stimulating environment of prison and its aftermath (Armstrong and Weaver, 2013). However, not only are social cooperatives a rarity in the justice system in the UK, but their potential has never been explored. Indeed, social co-operatives, comprising an equal partnership of professionals, ex/offenders and community members, arguably pose particular conceptual and practical challenges in a penal context that has traditionally been the sole domain of professional actors and where service provision is framed by legal statute, risk and compulsion, but perhaps it is time to face up to these challenges rather than circumnavigating them.

Limitations of the study and implications for future research

As previously recognised, one of the limitations of this research is the small sample size, comprising six white males, on which this study was based and, in that, the discrete geographical area from which the participants were drawn. This study does not claim statistical generalisability of the findings to other populations in other places and times. Nonetheless, I suspect that analytical generalisability is possible; although structural and cultural contexts of individual actions and relational interactions will vary, the need to attend to the relational in understanding and supporting desistance seems likely to be universal. Future research could test out the extent to which this research is indeed analytically generalisable though further in-depth research with other groups, or individuals who have limited, or no, social networks, or whose offending occurs in isolation. How different cultural and social environments and gender dynamics might play out requires further investigation. While such studies are not likely to refute the significance of social relations, they could usefully elaborate how they differ for people in different conditioning structures. Future research, then, could usefully focus on studying a number of naturally forming groups from within the same or across different geographical locations. This would enable an investigation as to whether the findings of this research can be identified within and across populations of people who once co-offended and have since desisted across a range of cultural contexts. This could be progressed by either a retrospective qualitative research design or by a prospective longitudinal research design. In so doing, this would enable a broader analysis of the dynamics of offending and desistance within and across naturally forming groups.

As suggested earlier, a limitation of this study was that it focused solely on analysing the life stories of a naturally forming group. A more thorough analysis of the role of social relations in the change process would suggest the inclusion of a broader base of participants, including, for example, parents, partners and new social network members, to understand their experiences of desistance processes and how to support them. In so doing, it would further understandings of the relational contributions to the change process. This could be progressed through either a qualitative or a mixed method study, which may be either retrospective or prospective in focus.

Conclusion

This study set out to explore the relationships between structure, agency, reflexivity, identity and the desistance process to inform how a paradigm shift in penal practice, based on the implications of understandings of the desistance process, might be realised. Following a review of the literature it was identified that while there was some consensus that social relations were a central element of the change process, no desistance studies had adequately analysed how dynamics within a naturally forming group might constrain or enable desistance or, in that, the impact that a co-offending peer group can exert on criminal careers – both empirically and theoretically. The analysis of the life stories of the men who formed part of 'the Del' makes something of an original methodological contribution to the literature both in studying a co-offending peer group and in, albeit retrospectively, capturing the processes of involvement in the group, onset and maintenance of offending, extrication from the group and desistance. In turn this has generated new empirical insights and theoretical conceptualizations of the role of a co-offending peer group in onset, persistence and desistance; of the role of social relations in the process of change; and of the dynamics of the desistance process. Moreover this study has reconceptualised the relationships between structure, agency, reflexivity and identity and the desistance process by revealing what reflexivity entails, elaborating different forms of reflexivity and by reconceptualising the role of individuals, social relations and structures in the desistance process. In so doing, the findings and implications of this study have generated new insights as to how a relational perspective might inform penal policy and practice.

Notes

1 Parts of this chapter draw from Donati, P. (2011a) *Relational Sociology: A New Paradigm for the Social Sciences*. Abingdon: Routledge. Reproduced with permission from Routledge.

Parts of this chapter were previously published in Weaver, B. (2012) The Relational Context of Desistance: Some Implications and Opportunities for Social Policy. *Social Policy and Administration* 46(4), pp.395–412. Reproduced with permission from Wiley.

Parts of this chapter were previously published in Weaver. B. (2013) Co-producing Desistance: Who Works to Support Desistance? in Durnescu, I., and McNeill, F.,

Understanding Penal Practices. Abingdon: Routledge, pp.193–205. Reproduced with permission from Routledge.
2 The first sector generally refers to the state, the second sector to the market economy, and the third sector to organised groups within civil society including charities, NGOs, self-help groups, social enterprises and various networks.
3 For an elaboration of approaches to working with individuals, families, groups and communities, see Weaver (2013).

References

Allen, R. (2007) From Restorative Prisons to Justice Reinvestment, in Allen, R., and Stern, V. (eds.), *Justice Reinvestment: A New Approach to Crime and Justice*. London: International Centre for Prison Studies, King's College London, pp.5–8.
Archer, M. (2000) *Being Human: The Problem of Agency*. Cambridge: Cambridge University Press.
Archer, M. (2003) *Structure, Agency and the Internal Conversation*. Cambridge: Cambridge University Press.
Archer, M. (2007) *Making Our Way Through the World: Human Reflexivity and Social Mobility*. Cambridge: Cambridge University Press.
Archer, M. (2011) 'The Logic of the Gift: Can It Find a Place Within Normal Economic Activity?' http://www.secondspring.co.uk/uploads/articles_19_953760526.pcf, accessed 28/8/12.
Armstrong, S., and Weaver, B. (2013) Persistent Punishment: User Views of Short Prison Sentences. *Howard Journal of Criminal Justice* 52(3), pp.285–305.
Barry, M. (2006) *Youth Offending in Transition: The Search for Social Recognition*. Abingdon: Routledge.
Barry, M (2013) Desistance by Design: Reflections on Criminal Justice Theory, Policy and Practice. *European Journal of Probation* 5(2), pp.47–65.
Bazemore, G. (1998) Restorative Justice and Earned Redemption. *American Behavioral Scientist* 41(6), pp.768–813.
Bovaird, T., and Loeffler, E. (2013) The Role of Co-production for Better Health and Wellbeing, in Loeffler, E., Power, G., Bovaird, T., and Hine-Hughes, F. (eds.) *Co-production of Health and Wellbeing in Scotland*. Governance International, pp.20–27.
Burns, D., and Taylor, M. (1998) *Mutual Aid and Self-Help: Coping Strategies for Excluded Communities*. Bristol: Policy Press.
Cabinet Office. (2009) *Working Together: Public Services on Your Side*. London: HM Government.
Cabinet Office. (2010) *Building the Big Society*. London: HM Government.
Calverley, A. (2013) *Cultures of Desistance: Rehabilitation, Reintegration and Ethnic Minorities*. Abingdon: Routledge.
Cooley, C.H. (1922) *Human Nature and the Social Order*. New York, NY: Scribner. (Original work published 1902.)
Cromwell. P.F., Olson. J.N., and D'Aunn, W.A. (1991) *Breaking and Entering: An Ethnographic Analysis of Burglary*. Newbury Park, CA: Sage.
Donati, P. (2007) L'approccio relazionale al capital sociale. *Sociologia e politiche sociali* 10(1), pp.9–39.
Donati, P. (2009) What Does 'Subsidiarity' Mean? The Relational Perspective. *Journal of Markets and Morality* 12(2), pp.211–243.
Donati, P. (2011) *Relational Sociology: A New Paradigm for the Social Sciences*. Abingdon: Routledge.

Donati, P. (2014) Morphogenic Society and the Structure of Social Relations, in Archer, M.S. (ed.) *Late Modernity: Trajectories Towards Morphogenic Society*. Lausanne, Switzerland: Springer, pp.143–172.

Duff, A. (2001) *Punishment, Communication and Community*. Oxford: Oxford University Press.

DWP (2011) *Access to the Work Programme for Prison Leavers From 'Day One': Equality Impact Assessment*. https://www.gov.uk/government/uploads/system/uploads/attachment_data/file/220255/eia-work-programme-for-prison-leavers.pdf, accessed 07/12/14.

Edgar, K., Jacobson, J. and Biggar, K. (2011) *Time Well Spent*. London: Prison Reform Trust.

Farrall, S. (2002) *Rethinking What Works With Offenders: Probation, Social Context and Desistance From Crime*. Cullompton: Willan.

Farrall, S., Bottoms, A.E., and Shapland, J. (2010) Social Structures and Desistance From Crime. *European Journal of Criminology* 7(6), pp.546–570.

Farrington, D.P. (1992) Criminal Career Research in the United Kingdom. *British Journal of Criminology* 32(4), pp.521–536.

Ferguson, I. (2007) Increasing User Choice or Privatizing Risk: The Antinomies of Personalization. *British Journal of Social Work* 37(3), pp.387–403.

Fukuyama, F. (2001) Social Capital, Civil Society and Development. *Third World Quarterly* 22(1), pp.7–20.

Giordano, P.C., Cernkovich, S.A., and Holland, D.D. (2003) Changes in Friendship Relations Over the Life Course: Implications for Desistance From Crime. *Criminology* 41(2), pp.293–328.

Goffman, E. (1963) *Stigma: Notes on the Management of Spoiled Identity*. Harmondsworth: Prentice-Hall.

Graham, J., and Bowling, B. (1995) *Young People and Crime*. Home Office Research Study No. 145. London: HMSO.

Haynie, D.L. (2001) Delinquent Peers Revisited: Does Network Structure Matter? *American Journal of Sociology* 106(4), pp.1013–1057.

Haynie, D.L. (2002) Friendship Networks and Delinquency: The Relative Nature of Peer Delinquency. *Journal of Quantitative Criminology* 18(2), pp.99–134.

Home Office (2004) *Reducing Reoffending National Action Plan*. London: Author. www.homeoffice.gov.uk/docs3/5505reoffending.pdf, accessed 05/12/14.

HM Government (2005) *Reducing Re-offending Through Skills and Employment*. London: HMSO. https://www.gov.uk/government/uploads/system/uploads/attachment_data/file/272207/6702.pdf, accessed 05/12/14.

HM Government (2006) *Reducing Re-offending Through Skills and Employment: Next Steps*. London: HMSO. http://dera.ioe.ac.uk/7665/1/reducing_re-offending_through_skills_and_employment_next_steps.pdf, accessed 05/12/14.

Ikaheimo, H., and Laitinen, A. (2011) Recognition and Social Ontology – An Introduction, in Ikaheimo, H., and Laitinen, A. (eds.) *Recognition and Social Ontology*. Leiden, Netherlands: Brill, pp.1–24.

Knight, B.J., and West, D.J. (1975) Temporary and Continuing Delinquency. *British Journal of Criminology* 15(1), pp.43–50.

Majee, W., and Hoyt, A. (2010) Are Worker-Owned Cooperatives the Brewing Pots for Social Capital? *Community Development* 41(4), pp.417–430.

Majee, W., and Hoyt, A. (2011) Cooperatives and Community Development: A Perspective on the Use of Cooperatives in Development. *Journal of Community Practice* 19(1), pp.48–61.

Maruna, S. (2001) *Making Good: How Ex-convicts Reform and Rebuild their Lives*. Washington, DC: American Psychological Association Books.

Maruna, S. (2006a) Who Owns Resettlement? Towards Restorative Reintegration. *British Journal of Community Justice* 4(2), pp.23–33.

Maruna, S. (2006b) Redemption: RIP? Re-reading Tookie's Self-Narrative. Presentation available at: http://www.docstoc.com/docs/37135608/Slide-1---Shadd-Maruna, accessed 08/05/13.

Maruna, S., and LeBel, T. (2009) Strengths-Based Approaches to Reentry: Extra Mileage Toward Reintegration and Destigmatization. *Japanese Journal of Sociological Criminology* 34, pp.58–80.

Maruna, S., and LeBel, T. (2010) The Desistance Paradigm in Correctional Practice: From Programs to Lives, in McNeill, F., Raynor, P., and Trotter, C. (eds.) *Offender Supervision: New Directions in Theory and Practice*. Cullomptom: Willan, pp.65–89.

Massoglia, M., and Uggen, C. (2010) Settling Down and Aging Out: Toward an Interactionist Theory of Desistance and the Transition to Adulthood. *American Journal of Sociology* 116(2), pp.543–582.

McCulloch, T., and McNeill, F. (2007) Consumer Society, Commodification and Offender Management. *Criminology and Criminal Justice* 7(3), pp.223–242.

McEvoy, K. (2008) *Enhancing Employability in Prison and Beyond: A Literature Review*. Belfast: Queens University.

McNeill, F. (2003) Desistance-Focussed Probation Practice, in Chui, W.H., and Nellis, M. (eds.) *Moving Probation Forward: Evidence, Arguments and Practice*. Harlow: Pearson Longman, pp.146–162.

McNeill, F. (2006) A Desistance Paradigm for Offender Management. *Criminology and Criminal Justice* 6(1), pp.37–60.

Ministry of Justice (2008a) *Third Sector Strategy: Improving Policies and Securing Better Public Services Through Effective Partnerships, 2008–2011*. London: HMSO.

Ministry of Justice (2008b) *Working With the Third Sector to Reduce Re-offending: Securing Effective Partnerships 2008–2011*. London: HMSO.

Ministry of Justice (2009) *Engaging Communities in Criminal Justice*. London: HMSO.

Ministry of Justice (2010) *Breaking the Cycle: Effective Punishment, Rehabilitation and Sentencing of Offenders*. London: HMSO.

Ministry of Justice (2013) *Transforming Rehabilitation: A Strategy for Reform*. London: HMSO.

Needham, C. (2009) *Co-production: An Emerging Evidence Base for Adult Social Care Transformation*. SCIE Research Briefing, No. 31.

Pahl, R. (2000) *On Friendship*. Cambridge: Polity Press.

Paternoster, R., and Bushway, S. (2009) Desistance and the 'Feared Self': Toward an Identity Theory of Criminal Desistance. *Journal of Law and Criminology* 99(4), pp.1103–1156.

Pestoff, V. (2012) Innovations in Public Services: Co-Production and New Public Governance in Europe, in Botero, A., Paterson, A., and Saad-Sulonen, J. (eds.) *Towards Peer Production in Public Services: Cases From Finland*. Aalto University publication series Crossover 15/2012. Helsinki, Finland. http://p2pfoundation.net/Co-Production_and_New_Public_Governance_in_Europe, accessed 07/04/13.

Porporino, F. (2010) Bringing Sense and Sensitivity to Corrections: From Programmes to 'Fix' Offenders to Services to Support Desistance, in Brayford, J., Cowe, F., and Deering, J. (eds.) *What Else Works? Creative Practice With Offenders*. Cullompton: Willan, pp.61–86.

Shih, M. (2004) Positive Stigma: Examining Resilience and Empowerment in Overcoming Stigma. *The Annals of the American Academy of Political and Social Science* 591(1), pp.175–185.

Scottish Government (2008) *Personalisation: A Shared Understanding*, Changing Lives Service Development Group. Edinburgh: Author.

Scottish Government (2009) *Personalisation: A Shared Understanding; Commission for Personalisation; a Personalized Commissioning Approach to Support and Care Services*, Changing Lives Development Group. Edinburgh: Author.

Seyfang, G. (2006) Harnessing the Potential of the Social Economy? Time Banks and UK Public Policy. *International Journal of Sociology and Social Policy* 26(9), pp.430–443.

Steinberg, D.M. (2014) *A Mutual-Aid Model for Social Work With Groups*. Abingdon: Routledge.

Uggen, C., and Janikula, J. (1999) Volunteerism and Arrest in the Transition to Adulthood. *Social Forces* 78(1), pp.331–362.

Uggen, C., and Kruttschnitt, C. (1998) Crime in the Breaking: Gender Differences in Desistance. *Law and Society Review* 32(2), pp.339–366.

Warr, M. (1993) Parents, Peers and Delinquency. *Social Forces* 72(1), pp.247–264.

Warr, M. (1998) Life-Course Transitions and Desistance from Crime. *Criminology* 36(2), pp.183–216.

Warr, M. (2002) *Companions in Crime: The Social Aspects of Criminal Conduct*. Cambridge: Cambridge University Press.

Weaver, B. (2011) Co-producing Community Justice: The Transformative Potential of Personalisation for Penal Sanctions. *British Journal of Social Work* 41(6), pp.1038–1057.

Weaver, B. (2012) The Relational Context of Desistance: Some Implications and Opportunities for Social Policy. *Social Policy and Administration* 46(4), pp.395–412.

Weaver, B. (2013) Co-producing Desistance: Who Works to Support Desistance? in Durnescu, I., and McNeill, F. (eds.) *Understanding Penal Practices*. Abingdon: Routledge, pp.193–205.

Weaver, B., and McCulloch, T. (2012) Co-producing Criminal Justice: A Review of the Evidence. SCCJR Research Report No. 05/2012.

Weaver, B., and Nicholson, D. (2012) Co-producing Change: Resettlement as a Mutual Enterprise. *Prison Service Journal* 204, pp.9–16.

Annex[1]
Research methods

This annex outlines the purpose of the research and offers a portrait of the participants on whom the research was based. A review of the methods through which the research was operationalised ensues, followed by a synopsis of the research design, sampling, transcription and analytical processes. The chapter concludes with an acknowledgement of the methodological limitations of the study.

Research purpose and participants

The principal objective of this study was to re-examine the relationships between structure, agency, identity and reflexivity in the desistance process, emerging from the life-stories of a naturally forming group of people who grew up and offended together. This investigation was intended to produce a multi-layered analysis of the dynamics of offending and desistance by using narrative approaches to elicit the life stories of six men, who comprised part of a co-offending peer group or gang (called 'the Del') during their childhood, adolescence and early adulthood. The participants were all in their forties and whilst their origins are both shared and comparable (i.e. socially, geographically, culturally) their lives have resulted in divergent outcomes. One of the central research objectives was to look for commonalities as well as differences across their life stories to gain a deeper understanding of the ways in which the group, as a social relation, shapes and affects criminal behaviour and desistance, and how individual, relational, cultural and structural contexts influence onset, persistence and desistance, and, thus, precursors, processes and consequences. This narrative tradition is not only well recognised across the social sciences but has some precedence within criminological research in general and also in what has come to be known as the 'desistance literature' in particular (see, for example, Farrall and Bowling, 1999; Gadd and Farrall, 2004; Giordano, Cernkovich and Rudolph, 2002; Maruna, 2001; Sampson and Laub, 1993).

A brief résumé of the life-story method in criminology and desistance

Although the life (hi)story/(auto)biographical method were placed centre stage in early criminological studies of 'deviance', from the Chicago School, this research method has largely existed on the fringes of criminological research (Goodey, 2000; Maguire, 2000; Maruna and Matravers, 2007). More recently, the voice of the offender – or at least data from offenders – has been integral to the emergence of 'desistance studies', less so in the strand of it that derives from 'criminal careers research' (heavily influenced by rational choice theory), more so in the strand influenced by narrative theory, which requires detailed attention to offenders' life experiences (see Chapter 2). Maruna's (1997, 2001) work, in particular, refocused attention not only on narrative-as-data, but also on the significance of a narrative restructuring of one's own self-understanding as a key element in processes of personal change. More commonly, however, offenders' words have been fragmented, lifted out of context, trimmed to support particular criminological theories or policy initiatives (including those based on rational choice theory) in ways that undermine the idea of taking 'offender perspectives' seriously, of understanding or respecting the person who lives the life and speaks the words.

The relative neglect of properly rounded 'ex/offender' perspectives, (rather than as just data subjects) in the desistance literature is surprising if only because narrative, life (hi)story or (auto)biographical method has had an honoured, albeit marginal place in criminology, particularly in the US (Bennett, 1981), with whole books being based around one person's account of their involvement in crime (see for example *The Jack Roller* by Clifford Shaw (1930); *The Professional Thief* by Edwin Sutherland (1937); and Klockar's (1974) *The Professional Fence*), some of which were studies of desistance *avant la lettre*. Despite the belated discovery of auto/biographical method by British sociologists of deviance in the 1970s, the more widely read accounts of the lives of those who offended by Tony Parker (Soothill, 1999) and some influential prisoner autobiographies (Boyle, 1977; McVicar, 1974), such literature has since became more marginal in criminology (Goodey,2000; Maguire, 2000; Maruna and Matravers, 2007, although see Devlin and Turney, 2000; Hobbs, 1995; Nellis, 2002). This mostly reflects its perceived lack of fit with the conventions of scientific method, the belief that because individual subjective accounts (or single case studies) lack validity, reliability and generalisability they have nothing of comparable worth to recommend them to scholars and policy-makers (Goodey, 2000; Maruna and Matravers, 2007; Stake, 1978). However, the institutional dismissal of this literature may reflect something altogether different, and although there is a long tradition of 'prisoner autobiographies' contributing to debate on penal reform (Nellis, 2012), Garland (1992 p.419) is right to suggest that offenders' voices have also been subordinated in the 'criminological monologue', not so much for what they lack methodologically, but because of their potential threat to expert (or even common-sense) discourses:

> ... if only they were allowed to speak [ex/offenders] might challenge some of the certainties with which we divide the world into normal and abnormal, right and wrong.

Yet, as Maruna (1999) suggests, we need to obtain a coherent story of the individual if we are to understand changes in behaviour, such as desistance. To understand the individual and his/her behaviour, one is required to develop an understanding of the world from the perspective of the individual, and to locate that perspective in the wider context of his/her biography, as it is created within a specific community and culture, and temporal, historic context. It is this reflexive perception of self that, in part, shapes future choices and thus behaviour (see Chapter 3). This requires methodological, empirical and theoretical attention to people's life stories, their narratives of themselves, within which their identity is constructed and reconstructed. Indeed, as Vaughan (2007 p.390) states: 'desistance can only be grasped through an understanding of the agent's ultimate concerns – the commitments that matter most and dictate the means by which he or she lives', for it is the *meaning* that choices or opportunities to desist hold for the individual which underlie their reasons for action in any direction.

Research design

Areas of exploration

To obtain such a holistic understanding of the individual, this research examined the cultural, class and familial contexts of participants as these pertained to their individual biographies. In addition, individuals' perceptions of turning points and significant life events, key social relations such as extant and new social networks, intimate relationships and families of formation and employment, and parenthood were explored. The research interview was designed to elicit their life stories, focusing on factors related to offending behaviour and where applicable, their persistence in or desistance from these behaviours. The areas of interest in relation to participants' offending behaviour were broadly experiential, and sought to reveal the participants' subjective perceptions and understandings of what the various stages of onset, persistence and desistance, or otherwise, meant to the individuals. By collecting the life stories of these men who formed part of a co-offending peer group, the research was designed to reveal the different pathways traversed by each individual given their relatively shared beginnings and explore their different and often interconnected trajectories through life.

Interview design

Data were gathered in 2009 through the conduct of life-story interviews with six adult males in their forties, who knew each other during early childhood, adolescence and early adulthood; who came from comparable socio-economic backgrounds, who resided in the same small geographical location in the west of Scotland, with equivalent access to education or employment opportunities, with shared class and cultural origins, all of whom have had a history of persistent offending, commencing in late childhood/early adolescence. The life-story interview involved participants in between two and four interviews, which lasted an average of 307 minutes (or 5.1 hours) in total with the shortest lasting for three hours, and the longest lasting for eight hours. Interviews took place in participants' private homes with the exception of one participant who, through necessity, was interviewed in a private room in prison.

The interview schedule incorporated elements of the research instruments developed by McAdam at the Foley Center for the Study of Lives,[2] Northwestern University, and in particular, 'The Life Story Interview'; 'Personal Faith, Politics and Life Story'; and 'Guided Autobiography'. The structure of the interview enabled participants to narrate their life stories in relation to relevant themes. The interview schedule was divided into three parts. The first part contained thematic enquiry surrounding the context of participants' lives – including familial and social relationships, environment, education, life stages, significant events and images of the self. The second part was designed to elicit a detailed account of each individual's criminal career through onset, maintenance to desistance. The third part was designed to gauge personal ideologies and perceptions of their futures. Using such broad themes avoided restricting participants by imposing an order or prescribed route through them; rather the interview was designed to allow the participants' own narrative trajectory to emerge. The interview schedule also contained a range of 'prompt' type questions which the researcher asked where it was deemed relevant and where they were not covered by the participant's initial responses. Interviews were recorded (with permission), fully transcribed and coded into emergent and superordinate themes using the 'Interpretive Phenomenological Analysis' method (Smith, Flowers and Larkin, 2009).

The sample

The form of sampling deployed in this study might be conceptualised as a form of snowball sampling, insofar as I had prior contact with a member of the sample population who identified other members of the sample population (Francis, 2000). Snowball sampling is an effective approach to accessing difficult to locate populations, although the extent to which it is representative is questionable, as broad comparisons to the wider population are difficult, nor is the basis for selection by individuals ordinarily transparent. However, the six individuals in this research were selected precisely because they were part of a 'natural' peer group, and as such have not been selected from a wider pool or category of possible respondents. It is their group experience, as well as their individual experience, that I was keen to research. As such, it might also be construed as a 'self-selected' sample, which is also an acceptable and ethical way of sampling, although, again, there are problems with this method in respect of typicality, representativeness and bias (Francis, 2000; Jupp, Davies and Francis, 2000). The inclusion/exclusion criteria were simply that the participants were known to the initial contact and comprised members of the group. Participants occupy a shared age range and the naturally occurring central characteristics of the group include shared geographical origins and collective involvement in persistent offending behaviour. There were no criteria or screening procedures beyond this.

'Adam',[3] who was once part of the group, negotiated access to the participants who are all white adult males between the ages of 40 and 50 years old, who have either engaged or continue to engage in persistent offending behaviour. The participants were provided with my contact details so that arrangements could be made for a preliminary meeting with me prior to interview to ensure informed consent. However, without exception, the participants chose to pass on their contact details to Adam; I then contacted them and the same process of arranging a preliminary meeting ensued. Importantly, this process gave the researcher and the participants an initial chance to meet, and it provided an opportunity to build rapport in advance of the initial interview, and it allowed for time for cooling off and reflection prior to first interview. The intention behind this was not only to enhance processes of informed consent but to assist the process of narrative and recollection.

There remains the perennial criticism made of qualitative research, but particularly of single case studies, that the individual case is not typical and that therefore one cannot generalise from the findings. Equally, collating six case studies could have the same criticism levied at it. The simplest response to this is that large-scale quantitative methodologies can be used to test how frequently any particular phenomenon occurs but they are limited in their capacity to answer questions surrounding agency, meaning, subjective truth and the internal complexities of the human self and transformative processes with which this research was concerned. Nonetheless, as the level of data analysis occurs at the level of the individual or individuals-in-relation, this places firm boundaries around the generalisability of conclusions that might be drawn from the data beyond this level (Jupp, 1989).

'External validity' can, however, extend the problem of generalisability to other units of analysis at the same level, i.e. to other individuals beyond those contained in the study. This is possible insofar as the individuals interviewed were broadly typical and representative of other groups of people who offend (Jupp, 1989). Indeed, this sample could broadly be classified as 'Street Criminals', a category employed by Maguire (2000 p.122) to denote those offenders that make up the bulk of offences recorded annually in criminal statistics – the perpetrators of so-called 'volume crime' (ibid): the thefts, burglaries, assaults, vehicle crime and acts of vandalism. The suggestion put forward here is that, as street criminals, broad inferences can be made to other individuals, which is borne out by the data (in Chapters 4–10) and the demographic profiles collated and delineated therein. It may be countered that larger samples using less in-depth methods might enable generalisability although it might also be argued that this is due to the absence of sufficient information that might contradict the generalisations made. While it might be more persuasive to argue for generalisability from large-scale studies, it does not follow that this is the route to the desired quality.

Nonetheless, as this study examines the life-stories of a small group of men in a specific social and cultural context, and in a particular historical period, I make no claims as to the statistical generalisability of the findings to other populations in other places and times. Notwithstanding this, I would contend that analytical generalisability is possible; although structural and cultural contexts of individual actions and relational interactions will vary, the need to attend to the relational in understanding and supporting desistance seems likely to be universal.

Transcribing data

Each interview was transcribed in accordance with the guidelines proposed by Smith et al. (2009), proponents of Interpretive Phenomenological Analysis (IPA), the analytic method deployed throughout this study. The researcher transcribed a verbatim account of each audio-recorded interview. Unlike other narrative analytical approaches (Riessman, 1993) or conversation analysis, IPA transcription does not require the researcher to record length of pauses or non-verbal utterances (Smith et al., 2009). However, in accordance with IPA the researcher produced a semantic record of the interviews, that is, of each word spoken by both the researcher and the participants.

Analytical considerations

Retrospective studies can be influenced by participants' failure to recall events or the correct ordering of events. Life stories can be vulnerable to deliberate distortions as narrators attempt to imbue their actions with a rationality which they did not have at the time, or non-deliberate distortions due to subconscious suppressions of painful memories, for example, or subjective interpretations of events and experiences that may not be echoed by other protagonists involved at the time. Where narratives are gathered retrospectively one cannot ignore questions surrounding memory, or autobiographical memory, about transformations over time in individuals' narratives and the accompanying self-reflexive understandings of self and perceptions of significant events that a retrospective gaze imputes into a narrative (Rubin, 1995). Indeed, with prospective studies one is less likely to be confronted by such biases, since one has a record of what was said earlier on the same topic. Habermas and Bluck (cited by McAdams, 2006 p.105) propose that autobiographical memories are shaped by an individual's current goals, which influence how autobiographical information is absorbed and organised in the first place. Thus, like the life story, autobiographical memory is contoured by the person's current goals and anticipations of the future; the life story itself, however, consists of a more enclosed set of temporally and thematically organised scenes and scripts that together constitute identity. It is contended here that the content of these narratives presented important analytic considerations as to *why* participants recollect or narrativise as they do, reflecting their interpretations of themselves, the messages they have internalised, their hopes, motivations and goals, and as such this in itself was significant in understanding processes of change over time. Moreover, as the participants comprised a naturally forming group, the cross analysis facilitated the verification, where appropriate, of recollection and sequencing of events. However, as the data analysis chapters reveal, how people experienced and responded to shared events and occurrences differed, and this was of significant theoretical interest in itself.

Analysis

The data were analysed using Interpretive Phenomenological Analysis (IPA) (Smith et al., 2009). IPA was selected as a method of analysis precisely because it facilitates a finely grained data analysis, oriented to a detailed exploration as to how participants make sense of their personal and social world. The analytic focus is on the meanings that particular experiences and events hold for participants. The approach is phenomenological in that it involves detailed examination of the participant's life-world in its own terms; it enables the exploration of personal experience and is concerned with an individual's personal perception as opposed to an attempt to produce an objective statement of the object or event itself. It is also interpretive in its recognition of the researcher's engagement in a double hermeneutic in trying to make sense of how participants make sense of their worlds (Smith et al., 2009). IPA is also idiographic in that it is particularly suitable for small sample sizes which enable the researcher to analyse and reveal the experiences of each participant.

The data were analysed using the procedures outlined by Smith et al. (2009). The aim was to create a comprehensive account of themes which have significance within the original texts. IPA delineates a flexible framework to facilitate an iterative and inductive cycle of analysis (Smith et al., 2009). Each transcript was read several times while listening to the original audio recording to ensure that meaning, conveyed through intonation, was not lost. At this stage, I noted initial perceptions in the left hand margin. This was a time-consuming process conducted through a line-by-line analysis of the transcript to examine semantic content and language use on an exploratory level. What emerged from this was an extremely comprehensive set of comments on the data. Following Smith et al. (2009), using different coloured pens on a hard copy of the transcript, I then categorised these perceptions into descriptive, linguistic and conceptual observations. Descriptive comments focused on describing the content of what the participant said, noting key words and phrases used by each participant. Linguistic comments focused on the way that the participant used language, which reflects the ways in which the content and meaning were presented; for example, the use of metaphors and repetition. Conceptual comments operated on a more interpretive and theoretical level.

The next stage of my analysis consisted of analysing and mapping the interrelationships, connections and patterns between these initial notes which informed the generation of 'emergent themes' which were noted in the right hand margin (Smith et al., 2009 p.91). Essentially, emergent themes are what Smith et al. (2009 p.92) describe as 'a concise and pithy statement of what was important in the various comments attached to a piece of transcript'. Building up the emergent themes from the initial notes, created from a close analysis of the transcript, meant that the emergent themes were characterised both by the participants' words and my conceptual interpretation.

The next stage in the process of analysis involved making connections between emergent themes and organising them into clusters of related themes. To achieve this, I typed all the emergent themes from each case in chronological order into a list. By studying the list and moving themes around, I was able to form groups of related themes. The relationship between these themes was captured by the development or identification of a superordinate theme. This process was repeated across each case prior to pursuing a cross-case analysis to identify convergences and divergences within and across emergent and superordinate themes.

While themes were generated inductively, rather than from a pre-existing theoretical position, during the analysis of the individual cases, the frequency with which each individual drew on their relationships with significant people in their lives prompted a theoretical analysis during the process of cross-case analysis. This remains consistent with the hermeneutic phenomenological underpinnings of IPA, in that what emerged was a dynamic relationship between the comparison of individual life-stories and Donati's (2011) relational sociology, the latter providing a theoretical framework through which to refract the 'second-order analysis' (Smith et al., 2009 p.166), but the analysis and the specific content were driven by the life-stories themselves in the 'first-order analysis' (ibid p.166) and in this sense were inductive in IPA style. The process of analysis yielded four superordinate themes: *The Relational Context of Offending*; *Experience of Punishment* (Seth and Andy only); *Roles/Religiosity, Reflexivity, Relationality and Desistance*; *The Meanings and Outcomes of Work*.

Conclusion

This annex has located the methodological approach underpinning this study in its criminological and methodological context and delineated the process through which the study was conducted.[4] The study engaged in an exploratory and qualitative study of six men comprising part of a co-offending peer group, the Del, who once offended together but whose lives have, to varying degrees, since diverged. The main aim of this research was to develop a nuanced and in-depth analysis of the dynamics of offending and desistance and, thus, the individual and relational contributions to the outcomes. This was realised, methodologically, through the depth and length of the successive interviews conducted with each participant, which generated a vast amount of data and which enabled the researcher to assess and analyse internal narrative coherency and the close, detailed, multi-layered analysis of individual transcripts, followed by a process of cross-case analysis.

While it may be suggested that a larger sample might have enabled wider generalisations to be drawn, the focus was on what occurs within and between people in relation who comprised a naturally forming group. As previously proposed, the generalisability of this study may not reside in the sample but in both the methodology and the analysis. To facilitate a larger scale enquiry, a co-offending peer group and a larger number of that group willing to participate in the research would need to be identified. Alternatively, a number of co-offending peer groups from within the same or across different geographical locations willing to participate in the research would have facilitated a broader analysis of the dynamics of offending and desistance within and across naturally forming groups. Indeed, this may be an area for further research. That said, as suggested earlier, the level of detailed analysis included in this study is better suited to small-scale samples, which may have been forfeited, due to scale, scope and reasons of expedience in a larger study.

A more thorough analysis of the role of social relations in the change process would suggest the inclusion of a broader base of participants, including, for example, parents, partners and new social network members, to understand their experiences and develop a more robust analysis of the relational contributions to the change process. However, the significance of the relational context within and through which identities are formed and lives are played out emerged from the data analysis of this study. Whilst then this is a limitation of the methodological approach of the study, it is simultaneously an implication for new directions in desistance research. Notwithstanding this, studying a co-offending peer group and taking the social relation as a central unit of analysis gives this study a methodological and theoretical distinctiveness, and, as this book illustrates, extends current knowledge of the dynamics of offending and desistance.

Notes

1 Parts of this chapter were previously published in Weaver, B. (2012) The Relational Context of Desistance: Some Implications and Opportunities for Social Policy. *Social Policy and Administration* 46(4). pp.395–412. Reproduced with permission from Wiley.
  Parts of this chapter were previously published in Weaver, B. and McNeill, F. (2015) Lifelines: Desistance, Social Relations and Reciprocity. *Criminal Justice and Behavior* 42(1), pp.95–107. Reproduced with permission from Sage.
  Parts of this chapter were previously published in Weaver, A. and Weaver, B., (2013) Autobiography, Empirical Research and Critical Theory in Desistance: A View From the Inside Out. *Probation Journal* 60(3), pp.259–277.
2 http://www.sesp.northwestern.edu/foley/instruments/interview/
3 It should be noted that Adam did not participate in this study as a participant.
4 A fuller account of the methodological and ethical considerations underpinning the conduct of the research is available on request.

References

Bennett, J. (1981) *Oral History and Delinquency: The Rhetoric of Criminology*. Chicago, IL: University of Chicago Press.
Boyle, J. (1977) *A Sense of Freedom*. London: Canongate/Pan Books.
Devlin, A., and Turney, B. (2000) *Going Straight: After Crime and Punishment*. Winchester: Waterside Press.
Donati, P. (2011) *Relational Sociology: A New Paradigm for the Social Sciences*. Abingdon: Routledge.
Farrall, S., and Bowling, B. (1999) Structuration, Human Development and Desistance From Crime. *British Journal of Criminology* 39(2), pp.253–268.
Francis, P. (2000) Getting Criminological Research Started, in Jupp, V., Davies, P., and Francis, P. (eds.) *Doing Criminological Research*. London: Sage, pp.29–58.
Gadd, D., and Farrall, S. (2004) Criminal Careers, Desistance and Subjectivity: Interpreting Men's Narratives of Change. *Theoretical Criminology* 8(2), pp.123–156.
Garland, D. (1992) Criminological Knowledge and Its Relation to Power: Foucault's Genealogy and Criminology Today. *British Journal of Criminology* 32(4), pp.403–422.
Goodey, J. (2000) Biographical Lessons for Criminology. *Theoretical Criminology* 4(4), pp.473–498.
Giordano, P.C., Cernkovich, S.A., and Rudolph, J.L. (2002) Gender, Crime and Desistance: Toward a Theory of Cognitive Transformation. *American Journal of Sociology* 107, pp. 990–1064.
Hobbs, D. (1995) *Bad Business*. Oxford: Oxford University Press.
Jupp, V. (1989) *Methods of Criminological Research*. London: Routledge.

Jupp, V., Davies, P., and Francis, P. (eds.) (2000) *Doing Criminological Research*. London: Sage.
Klockar, C.B. (1974) *The Professional Fence*. London: Tavistock.
Maguire, M. (2000) Researching Street Criminals, in King, R.D., and Wincup, E. (eds.) *Doing Research on Crime and Justice*. Oxford: Oxford University Press, pp.121–152.
Maruna, S. (1997) Going Straight: Desistance From Crime and Life Narratives of Reform, in Lieblich, A., and Josselson, R. (eds.) *The Narrative Study of Lives*, Vol. 5. Thousand Oaks, CA: Sage, pp.59–93.
Maruna, S. (1999) *Desistance and Development: the Psychosocial Process of 'Going Straight'*. The British Criminology Conferences: Selected Proceedings. Vol. 2. Papers from the British Criminology Conference, Queens University, Belfast, 15–19 July 1997.
Maruna, S. (2001) *Making Good: How Ex-convicts Reform and Rebuild their Lives*. Washington, DC: American Psychological Association Books.
Maruna, S., and Matravers, A. (2007) $N = 1$: Criminology and the Person. *Theoretical Criminology* 11(4), pp.427–442.
McAdams, D.P. (2006) *The Redemptive Self: Stories Americans Live By*. Oxford: Oxford University Press.
McVicar, J. (1974) *McVicar by Himself*. London: Arrow.
Nellis, M. (2002) Prose and Cons: Offender Auto / Biographies, Penal Reform and Probation Training. *Howard Journal of Criminal Justice* 41(5), pp.434–468.
Nellis, M. (2012) Prose and Cons: Autobiographical Writing by British Prisoners, in Cheliotis, L. (ed.) *The Arts of Imprisonment: Control, Resistance and Empowerment*. Farnham: Ashgate.
Riessman, C.K. (1993) *Narrative Analysis*. Qualitative Research Methods Series, No. 30. Newbury Park, CA: Sage.
Rubin, D.C. (1995) *Remembering Our Past: Studies in Autobiographical Memory*. Cambridge: Cambridge University Press.
Sampson, R.J., and Laub, J.H. (1993) *Crime in the Making: Pathways and Turning Points Through Life*. Cambridge, MA: Harvard University Press.
Shaw, C.R. (1930) *The Jack Roller*. Chicago, IL: University of Chicago Press.
Smith, J.A., Flowers, P., and Larkin, M. (2009) *Interpretative Phenomenological Analysis: Theory, Method and Research*. London: Sage.
Soothill, K. (1999) *Criminal Conversations: An Anthology of the Work of Tony Parker*. London: Routledge.
Stake, R.E. (1978) The Case Study Method in Social Inquiry. *Educational Researcher* 7(2), pp.5–8.
Sutherland, E.H. (1937) *The Professional Thief by a Professional Thief*. Chicago, IL: University of Chicago Press.
Vaughan, B. (2007) The Internal Narrative of Desistance. *British Journal of Criminology* 47(3), pp.390–404.
Weaver, A., and Weaver, B. (2013) Autobiography, Empirical Research and Critical Theory in Desistance: A View From the Inside Out. *Probation Journal* 60(3), pp.259–277.
Weaver, B., (2012) The Relational Context of Desistance: Some Implications and Opportunities for Social Policy. *Social Policy and Administration* 46(4), pp.395–412.
Weaver, B., and McNeill, F. (2015) Lifelines: Desistance, Social Relations and Reciprocity. *Criminal Justice and Behavior* 42(1), pp.95–107.

Index

Note: Page numbers with *f* indicate figures; those with *t* indicate tables.

age, employment impact on criminality and 19
age-crime curve 10, 12
age-crime relationship 10–11
aggregate data *vs.* individual-level data 11
Andy, desistance process of: analysis conclusions 206–7; art and 200–1; avoidance goals of 205; biographical overview 196–7; drug use and 198–9; effects of prison and 201–4; institutionalisation concept and 202–3; morphogenetic sequence 207*f*; offending trajectories of 214*t*; prisoner community experience and 197–201; prison release and 204–6; victimisation endured by 200
anti-social pressures, peers and 112
Archer, M. 48–54, 57, 58, 61, 106, 149, 151, 182, 212, 219, 220, 243, 244, 245–6
associations, oscillations in 76
attachment, control theory and 14
avoider-veterans 205

Barry, M. 3, 10, 30
Behrens, A. 26
being hooked, concept of 82
belief, control theory and 14
Bennett, J. 197
Bersani, B. 16, 18
Big Society thesis 248, 249
Blumstein, A. 11
Bottoms, A. E. 10, 23, 24–5, 27, 31, 105, 182
Bovaird, T. 248
Bowling, B. 23

Breaking the Cycle: Effective Punishment, Rehabilitation and Sentencing of Offenders (Ministry of Justice) 249
bridging social capital 118
Burnett, R. 205
Bushway, S. 9, 12–13, 25, 55, 158, 167, 183

Calverley, A. 20–1
Capabilities Approach 31
career criminals 22–3
Cernkovich, S.A. 53, 112, 134–5
chains of meanings 136, 225
change in criminality 9
civic reintegration 26
Cloward, R. 74
commitment, control theory and 14
condemnation script 182
conditioning structures and friendship groups 216–19
co-offending, dynamics of 66–99; becoming and belonging 71–5; context/conditioning structures overview 68–71, 68*f*; fragmentation 93–4; group embeddedness 75–83; identities 85–8; individual, relational self and 89–93; introduction to 66–7; lives/reputations/restrictions, imprisoning 83–5; reformation, fragmentation to 94–7; relational context 71–94; sample overview 67–8
co-production 248
Corrigan, P. 86
Côté, J. 26
craft love 201
Craig, C. 75

270 *Index*

Crewe, B. 197, 198, 199, 203
critical realism, relational sociology and 47–63; Archer and 48–54; conceptual schema for 59–63; Donati and 54–8; internal conversation and, deconstructing 51–4; introduction to 47–9; morphogenetic approach to 49–51; relational reflexivity and 58–9
Critical Realist Morphogenetic Approach (Archer) 3
Cromwell, P. F. 18–19
crystallization of discontent 13
Curran, K. 166
Cusson, M. 15

D'Aunn, W. A. 18–19
dedication phase of reflexivity 108, 151
the Del (gang) 2; alcohol role in offending 81; becoming/belonging 71–5; context/conditioning structures 68–71; criminal career phases of 2; fragmentation of 93–4; identity/identification of 83–8; individual and relational self 89–93; introduction to 66–7; member overview 67–8; member study findings 97–9; nature/dynamics of 75–83; offending profiles of 80–1; as protective structure 83; reformation, fragmentation to 94–7; relational context of offending 71–94; reputation and, maintaining 83–5; sexual abuse and 72; stigma and, resistance to 87–8; territorialism and 77; violence in home and 71–2
deliberation phase of reflexivity 107, 149
desistance: analysis conclusions (*see* desistance analysis conclusions); components of 9; criminological interest in 1; definitions of 8–9; dynamics of (*see* dynamics of desistance); empirical/theoretical context of 1–2; friendship groups and 2; process of 1–2; rationale for study of 2–3; research (*see* desistance research); supporting, through supervision 28–32; as temporary non-offending 9; theories of (*see* theories of desistance)
desistance analysis conclusions: findings, implications of 245–6; future research 253–4; overview of 238; peer group view 238–41; policy implications 246–50; practice implications 250–3; social relations, significance of 241–5; study limitations 253–4

desistance paradigm, of probation practice 7, 8*t*
desistance research 7–34; analysis 264–6; analytical considerations 264; data, transcribing of 264; definitions 8–9; exploration areas 261; findings for 32–4; interview design 261–2; introduction to 7–8; life-story method used in 259–61; methods 259–67; purpose and participants 259; sampling methods used 262–3; support through supervision 28–32; theories (*see* theories of desistance)
desisters 23
Deuchar, R. 77
diachronic self-control 27
differential association, social learning theories and 13–14
discernment phase of reflexivity 106; triggering events for 149
discontent, crystallization of 13
Donati, P. 48–9, 54–63, 92, 93, 95, 115, 135, 142, 165–6, 186, 212, 220, 224, 231, 240, 244, 245, 246; *see also* relational sociology (Donati)
drift notion, attachment and 14
dynamics of desistance 212–34; analysis conclusions 234; collective biographical overview 214–15; conditioning structures and friendship groups 216–19; extant and new social networks role in 215–16; families of formation role in 224–9; individual/personal reflexivity, change process and 219–22; intimate relationships role in 224–9; overview of 212–14; relational reflexivity, change process and 222–4; work constraints and limitations to 232–4; work meanings and outcomes of 229–32

embeddedness 89
Emirbayer, M. 25
employment: desistance and 18–20; Evan and 191–2, 232–4; as facilitator of marriage and family formation 19–20; factors of 19; Harry and 141, 232–4; Jay and 175, 232–4; Jed and 156–8, 232–4; Seth and 121–3, 232–4
established gangs 73
Evan, desistance process of: analysis conclusions 192–3; biographical overview 180–1; Christianity and

183–6; drug addiction and 182–3; extant and new social networks role in 181–7; families of formation role in 187–9; intimate relationships role in 187–9; life stages and 181; morphogenetic sequence 193*f*; offending trajectories of 214*t*; Prison Fellowship and 190–1; relationships and 181–2, 187–9; work constraints and limitations to 191–2; work meanings and outcomes of 190–1
external identification 85

families of formation, desistance and 113–17; Evan and 187–9, 224–9; Harry and 134–8, 224–9; Jay and 170–3, 224–9; Jed and 150–4, 224–9; Seth and 113–17, 224–9
Farrall, S. 9, 19, 23, 26, 27, 28, 30–1
Flynn, N. 27
Foote, N. 88
friendship groups, desistance and 2

generative activities 23
Giddens, A. 23
Gillespie, V. B. 166
Giordano, P. C. 21, 24, 53, 112, 114, 115, 119, 134–5, 148–9, 154
Glueck, E. 11
Glueck, S. 11
Goffman, E. 28
Gottfredson, M. 11
Great Debate, in criminology 11

Habermas, J. 57
Hagan, J. 89
Hall, P. M. 88
Haney, C. 203
Harry, desistance process of: analysis conclusions 141–3; biographical overview 131–2; extant familial/new social networks role in 132–4; families of formation role in 134–8; football fathering and 137; intimate relationships role in 134–8; life stages of 132; morphogenetic sequence 142*f*; offending trajectories of 214*t*; social identification of 132–13; work constraints and limitations to 141; work meanings and outcomes of 138–41
Healy, D. 25
Herrnstein, R. J. 11
Hirschi, T. 11, 14

Holland, D. D. 112, 134–5
Holligan, C. 77
homo economicus 47
homo relatus 47
homo sociologicus 47
hope concept, desistance research and 120–1
Howard, M. 205
Humphrey, S. E. 119

'I' concept of self 51, 52*f*, 61
identification, process of 88
identity theory of criminal desistance 12–13
Immarigeon, R. 32–3
individual and agentic theories of desistance 10–13; described 10; rational choice theories as 12–13
individual-level data *vs.* aggregate data 11
institutionalisation 202
interactionist theories of desistance 13, 22–7; Bottoms/Shapland analysis of 24–5; civic reintegration and 26; cognitive/agentic theories and 23–4; described 10, 22; Healy analysis of 25–6; King analysis of 25; life-course perspective of 23; *Making Good* (Maruna) study 22–3
internal conversation (Archer) 49; deconstructing 51–3; dedication phase of 53; deliberation phase of 53; discernment phase of 52–3; morphogenetic sequence applied to 52*f*, 213*f*
internal identification 85
intimate relationships, desistance and 113–17; Evan and 187–9, 224–9; fatherhood and 136–7, 224–9; Harry and 134–8, 224–9; Jay and 170–3, 224–9; Jed and 150–4, 224–9; Seth and 113–17, 224–9
involvement, control theory and 14

Jay, desistance process of: analysis conclusions 175–7; biographical overview 162–3; extant and new social networks role in 163–70; families of formation role in 170–3; intimate relationships role in 170–3; life stages and 163; marriage and 162–3, 170–2; morphogenetic sequence 176*f*; offending trajectories of 214*t*; Pentecostal conversion and 165–9; work constraints

and limitations to 175; work meanings and outcomes of 173–5
Jed, desistance process of: analysis conclusions 158–9; biographical overview 146–7; extant social networks role in 147–50; families of formation role in 150–4; intimate relationships role in 150–4; life stages and 147; marriage and 151–3; morphogenetic sequence 159*f*; offending trajectories of 214*t*; work constraints and limitations to 156–8; work meanings and outcomes of 155–6
Justice Reinvestment model 248, 249

King, A. 133
King, S. 25, 31–2
Kintrea, K. 77
Klein, M. W. 76
Kruttschnitt, C. 9

Laub, J. H. 9, 14, 15, 24, 113, 230
Learning to Labour (Willis) 69
LeBel, T. 24, 32–3, 186
Leibrich, J. 28
Lemert, E. M. 9
life stages: Evan 181; Harry 132; Jay 163; Jed 147; Seth 105
Lim, C. 21
Loeffler, E. 248
Lyngstad, T. H. 16, 113

Making Good (Maruna) 22–3
Manza, J. 26
Marranci, G. 20
marriage 15–17; as causal factor in desistance 16, 113; correlations between desistance and 15–16, 113–17; employment as facilitator of 19–20; gender roles and impact of, on criminality 17; Jay and 162–3, 170–2; Jed and 151–3; as outcome of desistance 16–17, 113
Marsiglio, W. 116
Maruna, S. 3, 9, 10, 12, 19, 22–3, 26, 32–3, 137, 166, 167, 169, 182, 186
masculine identity: alcohol and 122–3; football crowd and 133–4; Pentecostal Christian males and 168–9
maturational reform theories, described 11
Matza, D. 14, 80
McAdams, D. P. 190
McCulloch, T. 32

McNeill, F. 7, 23, 33
'Me' concept of self 51, 52*f*, 61
Meisenhelder, T. 28
Mische, A. 25
Moloney, M. 18
Monsbakken, C. W. 17
Morgeson, F. P. 119
morphogenetic approach (Archer) 48–9; applied to internal conversation 52*f*; constraints of 53–4; described 49–51; phases of 49, 50*f*
Mouzelis, N. 24
Muir, G. 31
Murray, C. 76

Nagin, D. S. 15
network boundaries, porous 76
non-treatment paradigm, of probation practice 7, 8*t*

offending, relational context of 71–94; becoming and belonging 71–5; fragmentation 93–4; group embeddedness 75–83; identities 85–8; individual, relational self and 89–93; lives/reputations/restrictions, imprisoning 83–5
offending trajectories overview 214*t*
Ohlin, L. 74
Olson, J. N. 18–19
ontogenic theories 10, 12; described 11; *see also* individual and agentic theories of desistance
Owens, B. 119
Oxford Recidivism Study 24

Pahl, R. 78–9
parenthood, desistance and 17–18
Paternoster, R. 12–13, 25, 55, 158, 167, 183
peer group, desistance analysis thru 238–41
permanent cessation 9
personal disgrace 29
personal reflexivity 48, 50; defined 58
Pinsonneault, P. 15
Pleck, J. H. 116
Porporino, F. 33, 257
primary desistance 9
private remorse 29
probation practice: desistance paradigm of 7, 8*t*; McNeill and shift in 7; non-treatment paradigm of 7, 8*t*;

Index

revised paradigm of 7, 8*t*; 'what works' paradigm of 7, 8*t*
probation supervision, desistance through 28–32; Farrall study of 30–1; King study of 31–2; Leibrich study of 28–9; McCulloch study of 32; Rex study of 29–30
projects, Archer definition of 50
propensity to offend 9
pro-social influences, peers and 112
public humiliation 29
public stigma 86
Putnam, R. D. 21
Pyrooz, D.C. 89

rational choice theories of desistance 12–13
reasoning decision-makers 12
reciprocity 244
Reducing Re-Offending National Action Plan (Home Office) 249
Reducing Re-offending through Skills and Employment (HM Government) 249
Reducing Re-offending through Skills and Employment: Next Steps (HM Government) 249
reflexivity: defined 58; phases of 106–8; relational theory of 58–9, 222–4, 244
Rehabilitation Revolution 248
relational goods 56
relational sociology (Donati) 3, 212; individual contributions to 61–2; investigative framework applied to 59–61, 60*f*; morphogenetic sequence applied to 213*f*; overview of 54–8; reflexivity concept and 58–9; relational contributions to 62–3, 62*f*
rel-azione 55
religion/spirituality: desistance and 20–2; football allegiance and 133; Islamic faith and, discovery of 21; life satisfaction and 21; Muslims in prison and 20–1; *see also* Evan, desistance process of; Jay, desistance process of
research methods 259–67; analysis 264–6; analytical considerations 264; data transcription 264; exploration, areas of 261; interview design 261–2; life-story method described 259–61; purpose/ participants 259; sampling methods 262–3
revised paradigm, of probation practice 7, 8*t*

Rex, S. 29–30
Rudolph, J. L. 53
Rumgay, J. 24

Sampson, R. J. 9, 14, 15, 16, 17, 24, 113, 230
Savolainen, J. 19
Scottish Desistance Study (Barry) 30
secondary desistance 9
sectarianism 76–7
self-binding self-control 27
self-stigma 86
Sennett, R. 201
Seth, desistance process of: alcohol and 121–3; analysis conclusions 123–5; biographical overview 104–5; extant social networks role in 110–13; families of formation role in 113–17; intimate relationships role in 113–17; life stages and 105; morphogenetic sequence 124*f*; offending trajectories of 214*t*; punishment experience of 105–10; self, investment in 105–8; *Training for Freedom* programme and 108–10; work constraints and limitations to 121–3; work meanings and outcomes of 117–21
shame, desistance and 29
Shapland, J. 24–5, 31, 105, 182
Sheffield Desistance Study 31
Shover, N. 8
situational theories of desistance 27–8; described 10
Skardhamar, T. 16, 19, 113
social and structural theories of desistance 13–22; described 10; differential association 13–14; employment 18–20; marriage 15–17; parenthood 17–18; religion/spirituality 20–2; social control 14–15
social control theories, informal 14–15; aspects of 14
social identity 85–6, 132–3, 153–4
social institutions 13, 14
social networks, desistance and 110–13
social relations, significance of 241–5
sociogenic theories 10; *see also* social and structural theories of desistance
solidarity, defined 4
spirituality *see* religion/spirituality
street gangs 76
structural influences 13
structure-agency debate 22

subsidiarity, described 4
system reflectivity 59

termination, defined 9
territorialism 77
theories of desistance 9–10; individual and agentic 10–13; interactionist 22–7; situational 27–8; social and structural 13–22; *see also individual headings*
Training for Freedom programme 108–10
Transforming Rehabilitation (Ministry of Justice) 248
turning point events 24, 261; for Jay 96, 164; for Seth 105, 108, 109, 110, 117

Uggen, C. 9, 19, 26

van Klinken, A. 168–9
Vigil, J.D. 73

Warr, M. 14
Watson, A. 86
'what works' paradigm, of probation practice 7, 8*t*, 29
Whyte, W. 80
Wiles, P. 23
Willis, P. 69, 70
Wilson, J.Q. 11
Wilson, L. 166
Wimer, C. 113
work, social characteristics of 119
work meanings and outcomes, desistance: Evan and 190–1, 230–2; Harry and 138–41, 230–2; Jay and 173–5, 229–32; Jed and 155–6, 229–32; Seth and 117–21, 230, 231

'You' concept of self 51, 52*f*